Gender

Key Concepts in Critical Theory

Series Editor
Roger S. Gottlieb

Key Concepts in Critical Theory

Gender

EDITED BY CAROL C. GOULD

Humanity
Books

an imprint of Prometheus Books
59 John Glenn Drive, Amherst, New York 14228-2197

Published 1999 by Humanity Books, an imprint of Prometheus Books

03 02 01 00 99   8 7 6 5 4

Library of Congress Cataloging-in-Publication Data

Gender / edited by Carol Gould.
     p.   cm. — (Key concepts in critical theory)
    Originally published: Atlantic Highlands, NJ : Humanities Press International, Inc., 1997
    Includes bibliographical references and index.
    ISBN 1–57392–590–X
    1. Sex role. 2. Sex differences. 3. Sex harassment. 4. Feminist theory.
I. Gould, Carol C. II. Series.
HQ1075.G455   1997
305.3—dc20   305.3   96–5575
                                 Gend   CIP

Printed in the United States of America on acid-free paper

CONTENTS

PART II: GENDER, OPPRESSION, AND SEXUAL IDENTITY

PART III: FAMILY, CLASS, RACE, AND CULTURE

PART IV: GENDER, SCIENCE, AND PHILOSOPHY

PART VII: LAW AND DIFFERENCE: PRIVACY, PORNOGRAPHY,
            AND REPRODUCTIVE RIGHTS

SERIES EDITOR'S PREFACE

THE VISION OF A rational, just, and fulfilling social life, present in Western thought from the time of the Judaic prophets and Plato's *Republic*, has since the French Revolution been embodied in systematic *critical theories* whose adherents seek a fundamental political, economic, and cultural transformation of society.

These critical theories—varieties of Marxism, socialism, anarchism, feminism, gay/lesbian liberation, ecological perspectives, discourses by antiracist, anti-imperialist, and national liberation movements, and utopian/critical strains of religious communities—have a common bond that separates them from liberal and conservative thought. They are joined by the goal of sweeping social change; the rejection of existing patterns of authority, power, and privilege; and a desire to include within the realms of recognition and respect the previously marginalized and oppressed.

Yet each tradition of Critical Theory also has its distinct features: specific concerns, programs, and locations within a geometry of difference and critique. Because of their intellectual specificity and the conflicts among the different social groups they represent, these theories have often been at odds with one another, differing over basic questions concerning the ultimate cause and best response to injustice, the dynamics of social change, the optimum structure of a liberated society, the identity of the social agent who will direct the revolutionary change, and in whose interests the revolutionary change will be made.

In struggling against what is to some extent a common enemy, in overlapping and (at times) allying in the pursuit of radical social change, critical theories to a great extent share a common conceptual vocabulary. It is the purpose of this series to explore that vocabulary, revealing what is common and what is distinct, in the broad spectrum of radical perspectives.

For instance, although both Marxists and feminists may use the word "exploitation," it is not clear that they really are describing the same phenomenon. In the Marxist paradigm the concept identifies the surplus labor appropriated by the capitalist as a result of the wage-labor relation. Feminists have used the same term to refer as well to the unequal amounts of housework, emotional nurturance, and child raising performed by women in the nuclear family. We see some similarity in the notion of group inequality (capitalists/workers, husbands/wives) and of unequal exchange. But we also see critical differences: a previously "public" concept extended to the

ix

private realm; one first centered in the economy of goods now moved into the life of emotional relations. Or, for another example, when deep ecologists speak of "alienation" they may be exposing the contradictory and destructive relations of humans to nature. For socialists and anarchists, by contrast, "alienation" basically refers only to relations among human beings. Here we find a profound contrast between what is and is not included in the basic arena of politically significant relationships.

What can we learn from exploring the various ways different radical perspectives utilize the same terminology?

Most important, we see that these key concepts have histories and that the theories of which they are a part and the social movements whose spirit they embody take shape through a process of political struggle as well as of intellectual reflection. As a corollary, we can note that the creative tension and dissonance among the different uses of these concepts stem not only from the endless play of textual interpretation (the different understandings of classic texts, attempts to refute counterexamples or remove inconsistencies, rereadings of history, reactions to new theories), but also from the continual movement of social groups. Oppression, domination, resistance, passion, and hope are crystallized here. The feminist expansion of the concept of exploitation could only grow out of the women's movement. The rejection of a purely anthropocentric (human-centered, solely humanistic) interpretation of alienation is a fruit of people's resistance to civilization's lethal treatment of the biosphere.

Finally, in my own view at least, surveys of the differing applications of these key concepts of Critical Theory provide compelling reasons to see how complementary, rather than exclusive, the many radical perspectives are. Shaped by history and embodying the spirit of the radical movements that created them, these varying applications each have in them some of the truth we need in order to face the darkness of the current social world and the ominous threats to the earth.

ROGER S. GOTTLIEB

DEDICATION

To Simone de Beauvoir and the many
others who have opened a way
and
to future generations of
feminist theorists

ACKNOWLEDGMENTS

The editor wishes to acknowledge the generous help, support, and exceptional judgment provided by Marx Wartofsky at every stage in the preparation of this volume.

The editor thanks the following for permission to reprint the selections included below:

Selection from *The Second Sex* by Simone de Beauvoir, trans. H. M. Parshley, © 1952 and renewed 1980 by Alfred A. Knof, Inc. Reprinted by permission of the publisher.

Selection from Sherry B. Ortner, "Is Female to Male as Nature Is to Culture?" in *Women, Culture, and Society*, eds. Michelle Zimbalist Rosaldo and Louise Lamphere, with the permission of the publishers, Stanford University Press, © 1974 by the Board of Trustees of the Leland Stanford Junior University.

Selection from Nancy J. Chodorow, "Gender, Relation, and Difference in Psychoanalytic Perspective," © 1979 by Nancy Chodorow.

Selection from Roger Gottlieb, "Mothering and the Reproduction of Power," in *Socialist Review*, vol. 77, © 1984.

Selection from Alison M. Jaggar, "Human Biology in Feminist Theory: Sexual Equality Reconsidered," in *Beyond Domination: New Perspectives on Women and Philosophy*, ed. Carol C. Gould, Rowman and Littlefield, © 1984 by Alison M. Jaggar.

Selection from Nancy Holmstrom, "Do Women Have a Distinct Nature?" in *Philosophical Forum*, vol. 14, no. 1 (fall 1982), © 1982.

Selection from Ann Ferguson, "A Feminist Aspect Theory of the Self?" in *Science, Morality, and Feminist Theory*, Supplementary Volume 13, *Canadian Journal of Philosophy*, eds. Marsha Hanen and Kai Nielsen, University of Calgary Press, © 1987.

Selection from Victor J. Seidler, *Recreating Sexual Politics: Men, Feminism, and Politics*, Routledge, © 1991.

Selection from Judith Butler, *Gender Trouble*, Routledge, © 1990.

Selection from Marilyn Frye, *The Politics of Reality: Essays in Feminist Theory*, © 1983 by Marilyn Frye, The Crossing Press.

Selection from Sandra Lee Bartky, *Femininity and Domination*, Routledge, © 1990.

Selection from Arthur Brittan, *Masculinity and Power*, Blackwell, © 1989.

Selection from Luce Irigaray, *This Sex Which Is Not One*. Translated from the French by Catherine Porter with Carolyn Burke. © 1985 by Cornell University. Used by permission of the publisher, Cornell University Press.

Selection from Ruth Ginsberg, "Audre Lorde's (Nonessentialist) Lesbian Eros," in *Hypatia*, vol. 7, no. 4 (fall 1992), © 1992 by Ruth Ginsberg.

Selection from Linda J. Nicholson, *Gender and History*, © 1986 by Columbia University Press. Reprinted with permission of the publisher.

Selection from Elizabeth V. Spelman, *Inessential Woman: Problems of Exclusion in Feminist Thought*, Beacon Press, © 1988 by Elizabeth V. Spelman; reprinted by permission of Beacon Press.

Selection from Patricia J. Williams, *The Alchemy of Race and Rights*. Reprinted by permission of the publishers, Harvard University Press. © 1991 by the President and Fellows of Harvard College.

Selection from Patricia Hill Collins, *Black Feminist Thought*, Routledge, © 1990.

Selection from Uma Narayan, "The Project of Feminist Epistemology: Perspectives from a Nonwestern Feminist," in *Gender/Body/Knowledge*, eds. Alison M. Jaggar and Susan R. Bordo, Rutgers University Press, © 1989 by Rutgers, the State University. Reprinted by permission of Rutgers University Press.

Selection from Sandra Harding, *The Science Question in Feminism*. © 1986 by Cornell University. Used by permission of the publisher, Cornell University Press.

Evelyn Fox Keller, "The Gender/Science System: Or Is Sex to Gender as Nature Is to Science?" in *Hypatia*, vol. 2, no. 3 (fall 1987), © 1987 by Evelyn Fox Keller.

Selection from Carol C. Gould, "The Woman Question: Philosophy of Liberation and the Liberation of Philosophy," in *Philosophical Forum*, vol. 5, nos. 1–2 (fall–winter 1973–74), © 1974.

Selection from Genevieve Lloyd, *The Man of Reason: "Male" and "Female" in Western Philosophy*, University of Minnesota Press, © 1984, 1993.

Selection from Jane Flax, "Postmodernism and Gender Relations in Feminist Theory," in *Signs*, vol. 12, no. 4, (Summer, 1987), © 1987 by the University of Chicago.

Selection from Christine Pierce, "Postmodernism and Other Skepticisms," in *Feminist Ethics*, ed. Claudia Card, University Press of Kansas, © 1991.

Selection from Susan Bordo, "Feminism, Postmodernism, and Gender-Skepticism," in *Feminism/Postmodernism*, ed. Linda Nicholson, Routledge, © 1990.

Selection from Virginia Held, "Non-contractual Society: A Feminist View," in *Science, Morality, and Feminist Theory*, Supplementary Volume 13, *Canadian Journal of Philosophy*, eds. Marsha Hanen and Kai Nielson, University of Calgary Press, © 1987.

Selection from Carol Gilligan, "Moral Orientation and Moral Development," in *Women and Moral Theory*, eds. Eva F. Kittay and Diana T. Meyers, Rowman and Littlefield, © 1987.

Selection from Joan C. Tronto, "Women and Caring: What Can Feminists Learn about Morality from Caring?" in *Gender/Body/Knowledge*, eds. Alison M. Jaggar and Susan R. Bordo, Rutgers University Press, © 1989 by Rutgers, the State University. Reprinted by permission of Rutgers University Press.

Selection from Seyla Benhabib, "The Generalized and the Concrete Other," in *Praxis International*, vol. 5, no. 4 (January 1986); reprinted as *Feminism as Critique*, eds. Seyla Benhabib and Drucilla Cornell, University of Minnesota Press, © 1987.

Selection from Sara Ruddick, *Maternal Thinking*, Beacon Press, © 1989, 1995 by Sara Ruddick. Reprinted by permission of Beacon Press.

Selection from Marilyn Friedman, "The Social Self and the Partiality Debates," in *Feminist Ethics*, ed. Claudia Card, © 1991 by the University Press of Kansas. Used by permission of the publisher.

Selection from Carole Pateman, *The Sexual Contract*, with the permission of the publishers Stanford University Press. © 1988 Carole Pateman. Originating Publisher: Polity Press, Cambridge, U.K.

Selection from Carol C. Gould, "Feminism and Democratic Community Revisited," in *Democratic Community: NOMOS XXXV*, eds. John W. Chapman and Ian Shapiro, New York University Press, © 1993.

Selection from Susan Moller Okin, *Justice, Gender, and the Family*. © 1989 by BasicBooks. Reprinted by permission of BasicBooks, a division of HarperCollins Publishers, Inc.

Selection from Richard A. Wasserstrom, "On Racism and Sexism," in *Today's Moral Problems*, ed. Richard Wasserstrom, Macmillan, 1975; reprinted from *UCLA Law Review*, vol. 24, © 1977 by Richard A. Wasserstrom.

Selection from Iris Marion Young, "Impartiality and the Civic Public," in *Feminism as Critique*, eds. Seyla Benhabib and Drucilla Cornell, University of Minnesota Press, © 1987.

Selection from Nancy Fraser, "Rethinking the Public Sphere: A Contribution to the Critique of Actually Existing Democracy," in *Habermas and the Public Sphere*, ed. Craig Calhoun, MIT Press, © 1992.

Selection from Karen J. Warren, "The Power and the Promise of Ecological Feminism," in *Environmental Ethics*, vol. 12 (summer 1990), © 1990.

Hilary Charlesworth, "Human Rights as Men's Rights," in *Women's Rights, Human Rights: International Feminist Perspectives*, eds. Julie Peters and Andrea Wolper, Routledge, © 1995.

Selection from Martha Minow, *Making All the Difference: Inclusion, Exclusion, and American Law*. © 1990 by Cornell University. Used by permission of the publisher, Cornell University Press.

Selection from Deborah Rhode, "Feminist Critical Theories," in *Stanford Law Review*, vol. 42 (February 1990), © 1990 by the Board of Trustees of the Leland Stanford Junior University.

Selection from Anita L. Allen, "Women and Their Privacy: What Is at Stake?" in *Beyond Domination: New Perspectives on Women and Philosophy*, ed. Carol C. Gould, Rowman and Littlefield, © 1984.

Selection from Eva Feder Kittay, "Pornography and the Erotics of Domination," in *Beyond Domination: New Perspectives on Women and Philosophy*, ed. Carol C. Gould, Rowman and Littlefield, © 1984.

Selection from Catharine A. Mackinnon, *Only Words*, Harvard University Press, © 1995 by Catharine A. Mackinnon.

Selection from James W. Knight and Joan C. Callahan, *Preventing Birth*, University of Utah Press, © 1989.

Selection from Sara Ann Ketchum, "Selling Babies and Selling Bodies," in *Hypatia*, vol. 4, no 3 (fall 1989), © 1989 by Sara Ann Ketchum.

H. M. Malm, "Commodification or Compensation: A Reply to Ketchum," in *Hypatia*, vol. 4, no 3 (fall, 1989), © 1989 by H. M. Malm.

PREFACE

WHAT IS GENDER? HOW should we understand whatever differences there are between the "feminine" and the "masculine"? What is the distinction between sex and gender, that is, between biological or genetic features taken to differentiate males from females, and the socially constructed differences in character traits and role expectations for men and women? Recognizing that gender differences have most often been used to subordinate or oppress women, is there also a positive appropriation of the experience of women and of gender that can transform our traditional practices in ethics, politics, and the law? Though they previously had been relegated to the margins of social theory, gender issues have recently come to animate a lively and important discussion among feminist philosophers and social scientists, as well as among the public at large. This collection focuses on current approaches to these issues but also includes some of the earlier essays that have shaped the contemporary discussion. It gathers in one place many of the most important essays on gender, written from different points of view but sharing a theoretical emphasis on the social construction of gender and a normative commitment to social critique.

The concept of gender can be illuminated in an introductory way by making two distinctions, which run through the discussion in many of the articles in this volume. First, it can be distinguished from the idea of a biologically determined nature or essence that is fixed by genetic structure. This is most often identified as a difference between "gender" and "sex." Second, the idea of gender difference may be contrasted with the notion of a universal human nature or with a focus on human beings as human, where this transcends any specific differences among the individuals. In the first, an older identification of gender with sex, according to which feminine and masculine characteristics were taken to be the natural concomitant of biological differences between the sexes, has come to be replaced by the idea that gender (unlike sex) is not biologically given but is rather the result of a process of socialization that defines roles and characteristics in varying and changeable ways. There remain alternative accounts of how this process of gendering takes place and also of how it is to be evaluated and what the relation is between gender and oppression. Still another move in the reformulation of the sex/gender distinction is the more radical constructivist view that sex itself, as a biological feature, is socially constituted.

xvii

On such a view, what counts as biological difference in the first place emerges through a process of cultural or social choice.

The second distinction also develops in the context of a critique of an older and more traditional view that holds that the proper subject of both philosophical theory and of political and legal practice is the universally human, that is, human nature as such. While this universality (in its classical formulations) asserted the equality of all human beings, it tended historically to identify "human" with "male," and "humankind" with "mankind." One response to this problem has been to attempt to degender this universality so that it is not consciously or unconsciously biased against women. Another response, however, is to criticize this abstract universality itself for excluding differences from its account of the human, and to propose that gender differences need to be critically appropriated. On this view, they merit theoretical study and have new practical import. This emphasis on concrete differences raises the question of the relation between gender and such other social characteristics as race and class. It also poses a challenge to the traditional focus on impartiality, individual rights, and justice in ethics, politics, and the law, and suggests the need for taking differences seriously and drawing on the distinctive experiences of women.

The principle of organization of this collection of essays may be discerned from this preliminary sketch of the issues. It moves from more theoretical considerations concerning the concept of gender and the alternative ways of understanding it to more normative and applied contexts of its role in ethics and in political and legal practices. Part I takes up the issue of the social construction of gender, beginning with Simone de Beauvoir's classic statement of woman as the "other." Subsequent essays here present a range of perspectives on the cultural and social status of gender and its relation to biology, as well as on the processes through which such gendering takes place. The question of gendered character traits—masculine and feminine— and their relation to social role is discussed here, as is the relation of gender to the formation of the self and the constitution of sexual identity.

Part II pursues the analysis of gender in its sociocultural and psychological aspects and considers some of the specific ways in which women have been subordinated and oppressed. There is also a reflection on the varying historical forms of masculinity and their relation to male domination. This part then goes on to deal with the formation of female sexual identity in the context of oppression. The essays in Part III continue this examination of concrete manifestations of gender discrimination by focusing on the family in its historically changing forms in class societies, on relations between racism and sexism, and on the problems of gender in non-Western cultures. In these ways, the question of gender is situated more broadly in relation to other social realities.

One of the striking features of contemporary discussions of gender is the extent to which traditional theoretical and philosophical categories have been transformed by feminist thought. In Part IV, questions about the nature of scientific knowledge, of philosophical method, and of the role of reason itself are posed from feminist perspectives. There is also a critical discussion of postmodernism as a way of theorizing gender.

In Part V, as in the remaining two sections of the book, ethical/normative questions become the explicit focus for analysis. In this part, universalist moral conceptions such as justice and impartiality are contrasted with alternatives that emphasize moral concern for particular others. Here, the experience of women, especially in concrete contexts of mothering, is seen as giving rise to an ethics of care, marked by personal responsiveness or attentiveness to the needs of the other.

This general focus on difference is carried through the next section of the book, in application to the political domain. The idea of a social contract in liberal theory is critically examined in terms of its patriarchal sources in a prior "sexual contract," which defines the subordination of women in civil life. By contrast, the potential contribution of women's experience to a reformulated conception of democratic community is developed, in which considerations of both justice and care play a part. The issue of the gender-biased nature of traditional theories of justice is discussed, as is the question of the requirements of justice in the division of family responsibilities for child care and housework and also the assimilationist ideal of a fully gender-neutral society. The historic formation of the public sphere in its exclusion of women is challenged by alternative proposals for a more inclusive public domain or for one that recognizes multiple publics. The broad question of ecology is explored in an ecofeminist perspective, and the global issue of international human rights is subjected to a critique of its presently gendered character as male-dominant.

The final part of this collection takes up a range of questions concerning gender and the law. It is argued that there is a need for a new theoretical framework for law that takes serious account of difference, including that of gender and the social relations its entails. The neglect of gender, even in critical approaches to the law (e.g., in the Critical Legal Studies movement), is examined, and an alternative feminist approach is sketched. The crucial legal concept of privacy and privacy rights in their relation to women then becomes the focus of discussion, in terms of such rights as informational privacy, anonymity, and solitude. A critical analysis of pornography as a social phenomenon of gender domination and as hate literature is followed by an attack on the idea that pornography falls under the legal category of "protected speech." The last group of essays deals with moral and legal questions concerning certain reproductive rights. Elective abortion is considered in terms of the status of the fetus and the issue of the recognition of moral personhood. Paid "surrogate motherhood" arrangements are then debated in terms of whether or not they violate moral injunctions against treating babies as objects of sale or against using women's bodies as mere means.

The essays gathered here, for all their richness and multiplicity, represent only a sampling of the extraordinary literature on gender that has emerged in the last few decades. The reader is invited to supplement these studies with further reading and to contribute new ideas to the ongoing thinking on these important questions.

CAROL C. GOULD

PART I

The Social Constitution of Gender

SELECTION 1
FROM
The Second Sex

SIMONE DE BEAUVOIR

FOR A LONG TIME I have hesitated to write a book on woman. The subject is irritating, especially to women; and it is not new. Enough ink has been spilled in the quarreling over feminism, now practically over, and perhaps we should say no more about it. It is still talked about, however, for the voluminous nonsense uttered during the last century seems to have done little to illuminate the problem. After all, is there a problem? And if so, what is it? Are there women, really? Most assuredly the theory of the eternal feminine still has its adherents who will whisper in your ear: "Even in Russia women still are *women*"; and other erudite persons—sometimes the very same—say with a sigh: "Woman is losing her way, woman is lost." One wonders if women still exist, if they will always exist, whether or not it is desirable that they should, what place they occupy in this world, what their place should be. "What has become of women?" was asked recently in an ephemeral magazine.[1]

But first we must ask: What is a woman? "*Tota mulier in utero*," says one, "woman is a womb." But in speaking of certain women, connoisseurs declare that they are not women, although they are equipped with a uterus like the rest. All agree in recognizing the fact that females exist in the human species; today as always they make up about one half of humanity. And yet we are told that femininity is in danger; we are exhorted to be women, remain women, become women. It would appear, then, that every female human being is not necessarily a woman; to be so considered she must share in that mysterious and threatened reality known as femininity. Is this attribute something secreted by the ovaries? Or is it a Platonic essence, a product of the philosophic imagination? Is a rustling petticoat enough to bring it down to earth? Although some women try zealously to incarnate this essence, it is hardly patentable. It is frequently described in vague and dazzling terms that seem to have been borrowed from the vocabulary of the seers, and indeed in the times of St. Thomas it was considered an essence as certainly defined as the somniferous virtue of the poppy.

But conceptualism has lost ground. The biological and social sciences no longer admit the existence of unchangeably fixed entities that determine given characteristics, such as those ascribed to woman, the Jew, or the Negro. Science regards any characteristic as a reaction dependent in part upon a *situation*. If today femininity no longer exists, then it never existed. But does the word *woman*, then, have no specific content? This is stoutly affirmed by those who hold to the philosophy of the Enlightenment, of rationalism, of nominalism; women, to them, are merely the human beings arbitrarily designated by the word *woman*. Many American women particularly are prepared to think that there is no longer any place for woman as such; if a backward individual still takes herself for a woman, her friends advise her to be psychoanalyzed and thus get rid of this obsession. In regard to a work, *Modern Woman: The Lost Sex*, which in other respects has its irritating features, Dorothy Parker has written: "I cannot be just to books which treat of woman as woman. . . . My idea is that all of us, men as well as women, should be regarded as human beings." But nominalism is a rather inadequate doctrine, and the antifemininists have had no trouble in showing that women simply *are not* men. Surely woman is, like man, a human being; but such a declaration is abstract. The fact is that every concrete human being is always a singular, separate individual. To decline to accept such notions as the eternal feminine, the black soul, the Jewish character, is not to deny that Jews, Negroes, women exist today—this denial does not represent a liberation for those concerned, but rather a flight from reality. Some years ago a well-known woman writer refused to permit her portrait to appear in a series of photographs especially devoted to women writers; she wished to be counted among the men. But in order to gain this privilege she made use of her husband's influence! Women who assert that they are men lay claim none the less to masculine consideration and respect. . . .

If her functioning as a female is not enough to define woman, if we decline also to explain her through "the eternal feminine," and if nevertheless we admit, provisionally, that women do exist, then we must face the question: What is a woman?

To state the question is, to me, to suggest, at once, a preliminary answer. The fact that I ask it is in itself significant. A man would never get the notion of writing a book on the peculiar situation of the human male.[2] But if I wish to define myself, I must first of all say: "I am a woman"; on this truth must be based all further discussion. A man never begins by presenting himself as an individual of a certain sex; it goes without saying that he is a man. The terms *masculine* and *feminine* are used symmetrically only as a matter of form, as on legal papers. In actuality the relation of the two sexes is not quite like that of two electrical poles, for man represents both the positive and the neutral, as is indicated by the common use of *man* to designate human beings in general; whereas woman represents only the negative, defined by limiting criteria, without reciprocity. In the midst of an abstract discussion it is vexing to hear a man say: "You think thus and so because you are a woman"; but I know that my only defense is to reply: "I think thus and so because it is true," thereby removing my subjective self from the argument. It would be out of the question to reply: "And you think the contrary because you are a man," for it is understood that the fact of being a man is no peculiarity. A man is in the right in being a man; it is the woman who is in the wrong. It amounts to this: Just as for the ancients there was an absolute vertical with reference to which the oblique was defined, so there is an absolute human type, the masculine. Woman has ovaries, a uterus; these peculiarities imprison her in her subjectivity, circumscribe her within the limits of her own nature. It is often said that she thinks with her glands. Man superbly ignores the fact that his anatomy also includes glands, such as the testicles, and that they secrete hormones. He thinks of his body as a direct and normal connection with the world, which he believes he apprehends objectively, whereas he regards the body of woman as a hindrance, a prison, weighed down by everything peculiar to it. "The female is a female by virtue of a certain *lack* of qualities," said Aristotle; "we should regard the female nature as afflicted with a natural defectiveness." And St. Thomas for his part pronounced woman to be an "imperfect man," an "incidental" being. This is symbolized in Genesis where Eve is depicted as made from what Bossuet called "a supernumerary bone" of Adam.

Thus humanity is male and man defines woman not in herself but as relative to him; she is not regarded as an autonomous being. Michelet writes: "Woman, the relative being. . . ." And Benda is most positive in his *Rapport d'Uriel*: "The body of man makes sense in itself quite apart from that of woman, whereas the latter seems wanting in significance by itself. . . . Man can think of himself without woman. She cannot think of herself without man." And she is simply what man decrees; thus she is called "the sex," by which is meant that she appears essentially to the male as a sexual being. For him she is sex—absolute sex, no less. She is defined and differentiated with reference to man and not he with reference to her; she is the incidental, the inessential as opposed to the essential. He is the Subject, he is the Absolute—she is the Other.[3]

The category of the *Other* is as primordial as consciousness itself. In the most primitive societies, in the most ancient mythologies, one finds the expression of a duality—that of the Self and the Other. This duality was not originally attached to the division of the sexes; it was not dependent upon any empirical facts. It is revealed in such works as that of Granet on

Chinese thought and those of Dumézil on the East Indies and Rome. The feminine element was at first no more involved in such pairs as Varuna-Mitra, Uranus-Zeus, Sun-Moon, and Day-Night than it was in the contrasts between Good and Evil, lucky and unlucky auspices, right and left, God and Lucifer. Otherness is a fundamental category of human thought.

Thus it is that no group ever sets itself up as the One without at once setting up the Other over against itself. If three travelers chance to occupy the same compartment, that is enough to make vaguely hostile "others" out of all the rest of the passengers on the train. In small-town eyes all persons not belonging to the village are "strangers" and suspect; to the native of a country all who inhabit other countries are "foreigners"; Jews are "different" for the anti-Semite, Negroes are "inferior" for American racists, aborigines are "natives" for colonists, proletarians are the "lower class" for the privileged.

Lévi-Strauss, at the end of a profound work on the various forms of primitive societies, reaches the following conclusion: "Passage from the state of Nature to the state of Culture is marked by man's ability to view biological relations as a series of contrasts; duality, alternation, opposition, and symmetry, whether under definite or vague forms, constitute not so much phenomena to be explained as fundamental and immediately given data of social reality."[4] These phenomena would be incomprehensible if in fact human society were simply a *Mitsein* or fellowship based on solidarity and friendliness. Things become clear, on the contrary, if, following Hegel, we find in consciousness itself a fundamental hostility toward every other consciousness; the subject can be posed only in being opposed—he sets himself up as the essential, as opposed to the other, the inessential, the object.

But the other consciousness, the other ego, sets up a reciprocal claim. The native traveling abroad is shocked to find himself in turn regarded as a "stranger" by the natives of neighboring countries. As a matter of fact, wars, festivals, trading, treaties, and contests among tribes, nations, and classes tend to deprive the concept *Other* of its absolute sense and to make manifest its relativity; willy-nilly, individuals and groups are forced to realize the reciprocity of their relations. How is it, then, that this reciprocity has not been recognized between the sexes, that one of the contrasting terms is set up as the sole essential, denying any relativity in regard to its correlative and defining the latter as pure otherness? Why is it that women do not dispute male sovereignty? No subject will readily volunteer to become the object, the inessential; it is not the Other who, in defining himself as the Other, establishes the One. The Other is posed as such by the One in defining himself as the One. But if the Other is not to regain the status of being the One, he must be submissive enough to accept this alien point of view. Whence comes this submission in the case of woman?

There are, to be sure, other cases in which a certain category has been able to dominate another completely for a time. Very often this privilege depends upon inequality of numbers—the majority imposes its rule upon the minority or persecutes it. But women are not a minority, like the American Negroes or the Jews; there are as many women as men on earth. Again, the two groups concerned have often been originally independent; they may have been formerly unaware of each other's existence, or perhaps they recognized each other's autonomy. But a historical event has resulted in the subjugation of the weaker by the stronger. The scattering of the Jews, the introduction of slavery into America, the conquests of imperialism are examples in point. In these cases the oppressed retained at least the memory of former days; they possessed in common a past, a tradition, sometimes a religion or a culture.

The parallel drawn by Bebel between women and the proletariat is valid in that neither ever formed a minority or a separate collective unit of mankind. And instead of a single historical event it is in both cases a historical development that explains their status as a class and accounts for the membership of *particular individuals* in that class. But proletarians have not always existed, whereas there have always been women. They are women in virtue of their anatomy and physiology. Throughout history they have always been subordinated to men,[5] and hence their dependency is not the result of a historical event or a social change—it was not something that *occurred*. The reason why otherness in this case seems to be an absolute is in part that it lacks the contingent or incidental nature of historical facts. A condition brought about at a certain time can be abolished at some other time, as the Negroes of Haiti and others have proved; but it might seem that a natural condition is beyond the possibility of change. In truth, however, the nature of things is no more immutably given, once for all, than is historical reality. If woman seems to be the inessential which never becomes the essential, it is because she herself fails to bring about this change. Proletarians say "We"; Negroes also. Regarding themselves as subjects, they transform the bourgeois, the whites, into "others." But women do not say "We," except at some congress of feminists or similar formal demonstration; men say "women," and women use the same word in referring to themselves. They do not authentically assume a subjective attitude. The proletarians have accomplished the revolution in Russia, the Negroes in Haiti, the Indo-Chinese are battling for it in Indo-China; but the women's effort has never been anything more than a symbolic agitation. They have gained only what men have been willing to grant; they have taken nothing, they have only received.[6]

The reason for this is that women lack concrete means for organizing themselves into a unit which can stand face to face with the correlative unit. They have no past, no history, no religion of their own; and they have no such solidarity of work and interest as that of the proletariat. They are not even promiscuously herded together in the way that creates community feeling among the American Negroes, the ghetto Jews, the workers of Saint-Denis, or the factory hands of Renault. They live dispersed among the males, attached through residence, housework, economic condition, and social standing to certain men—fathers or husbands—more firmly than they are to other women. If they belong to the bourgeoisie, they feel solidarity with men of that class, not with proletarian women; if they are white, their allegiance is to white men, not to Negro women. The proletariat can propose to massacre the ruling class, and a sufficiently fanatical Jew or Negro might dream of getting sole possession of the atomic bomb and making humanity wholly Jewish or black; but woman cannot even dream of exterminating the males. The bond that unites her to her oppressors is not comparable to any other. The division of the sexes is a biological fact, not an event in human history. Male and female stand opposed within a primordial *Mitsein*, and woman has not broken it. The couple is a fundamental unity with its two halves riveted together, and the cleavage of society along the line of sex is impossible. Here is to be found the basic trait of woman: She is the Other in a totality of which the two components are necessary to one another.

One could suppose that this reciprocity might have facilitated the liberation of woman. When Hercules sat at the feet of Omphale and helped with her spinning, his desire for her held him captive; but why did she fail to gain a lasting power? To revenge herself on Jason, Medea killed their children; and this grim legend would seem to suggest that she might have obtained a formidable influence over him through his love for his offspring. In *Lysistrata* Aristophanes gaily depicts a band of women who joined forces to gain social ends through the sexual needs of their men; but this is only a play. In the legend of the Sabine women, the latter soon abandoned their plan of remaining sterile to punish their ravishers. In truth woman has not been socially emancipated through man's need—sexual desire and the desire for offspring—which makes the male dependent for satisfaction upon the female.

Master and slave, also, are united by a reciprocal need, in this case economic, which does not liberate the slave. In the relation of master to slave the master does not make a point of the need that he has for the other; he has in his grasp the power of satisfying this need through his own action; whereas the slave, in his dependent condition, his hope and fear, is quite conscious of the need he has for his master. Even if the need is at bottom equally urgent for both, it always works in favor of the oppressor and against the oppressed. That is why the liberation of the working class, for example, has been slow.

Now, woman has always been man's dependent, if not his slave; the two sexes have never shared the world in equality. And even today woman is heavily handicapped, though her situation is beginning to change. Almost nowhere is her legal status the same as man's,[7] and frequently it is much to her disadvantage. Even when her rights are legally recognized in the abstract, long-standing custom prevents their full expression in the mores. In the economic sphere men and women can almost be said to make up two castes; other things being equal, the former hold the better jobs, get higher wages, and have more opportunity for success than their new competitors. In industry and politics men have a great many more positions and they monopolize the most important posts. In addition to all this, they enjoy a traditional prestige that the education of children tends in every way to support, for the present enshrines the past—and in the past all history has been made by men. At the present time, when women are beginning to take part in the affairs of the world, it is still a world that belongs to men—they have no doubt of it at all and women have scarcely any. To decline to be the Other, to refuse to be a party to the deal—this would be for women to renounce all the advantages conferred upon them by their alliance with the superior caste. Man-the-sovereign will provide woman-the-liege with material protection and will undertake the moral justification of her existence; thus she can evade at once both economic risk and the metaphysical risk of a liberty in which ends and aims must be contrived without assistance. Indeed, along with the ethical urge of each individual to affirm his subjective existence, there is also the temptation to forgo liberty and become a thing. This is an inauspicious road, for he who takes it—passive, lost, ruined—becomes henceforth the creature of another's will, frustrated in his transcendence and deprived of every value. But it is an easy road; on it one avoids the strain involved in undertaking an authentic existence. When man makes of woman the *Other*, he may, then, expect her to manifest deep-seated tendencies toward complicity. Thus, woman may fail to lay claim to the status of subject because she lacks definite resources, because she feels the necessary bond that ties her to man regardless of reciprocity, and because she is often very well pleased with her role as the *Other*.

But it will be asked at once: How did all this begin? It is easy to see that the duality of the sexes, like any duality, gives rise to conflict. And doubtless the winner will assume the status of absolute. But why should man have won from the start? It seems possible that women could have won the victory; or that the outcome of the conflict might never have been decided. How is it that this world has always belonged to the men and that things have begun to change only recently? Is this change a good thing? Will it bring about an equal sharing of the world between men and women?

These questions are not new, and they have often been answered. But the very fact that woman *is the Other* tends to cast suspicion upon all the justifications that men have ever been able to provide for it. These have all too evidently been dictated by men's interest. . . .

Is it enough to change laws, institutions, customs, public opinion, and the whole social context, for men and women to become truly equal? "Women will always be women," say the skeptics. Other seers prophesy that in casting off their femininity they will not succeed in changing themselves into men and they will become monsters. This would be to admit that the woman of today is a creation of nature; it must be repeated once more that in human society nothing is natural and that woman, like much else, is a product elaborated by civilization. The intervention of others in her destiny is fundamental: if this action took a different direction, it would produce a quite different result. Woman is determined not by her hormones or by mysterious instincts, but by the manner in which her body and her relation to the world are modified through the action of others than herself. The abyss that separates the adolescent boy and girl has been deliberately opened out between them since earliest childhood; later on, woman could not be other than what she *was made*, and the past was bound to shadow her for life. If we appreciate its influence, we see clearly that her destiny is not predetermined for all eternity.

We must not believe, certainly, that a change in woman's economic condition alone is enough to transform her, though this factor has been and remains the basic factor in her evolution; but until it has brought about the moral, social, cultural, and other consequences that it promises and requires, the new woman cannot appear. At this moment they have been realized nowhere, in Russia no more than in France or the United States; and this explains why the woman of today is torn between the past and the future. She appears most often as a "true woman" disguised as a man, and she feels herself as ill at ease in her flesh as in her masculine garb. She must shed her old skin and cut her own new clothes. This she could do only through a social evolution. No single educator could fashion a *female human being* today who would be the exact homologue of the *male human being*; if she is raised like a boy, the young girl feels she is an oddity and thereby she is given a new kind of sex specification. Stendhal understood this when he said: "The forest must be planted all at once." But if we imagine, on the contrary, a society in which the equality of the sexes would be concretely realized, this equality would find new expression in each individual.

If the little girl were brought up from the first with the same demands and rewards, the same severity and the same freedom, as her brothers, taking part in the same studies, the same games, promised the same future, surrounded with women and men who seemed to her undoubted equals, the meanings of the castration complex and of the Oedipus complex would be profoundly modified. Assuming on the same basis as the father the material and moral responsibility of the couple, the mother would enjoy the same lasting prestige; the child would perceive around her an androgynous world and not a masculine world. Were she emotionally more attracted to her father—which is not even sure—her love for him would be tinged with a will to emulation and not a feeling of powerlessness; she would not be oriented toward passivity. Authorized to test her powers in work and sports, competing actively with the boys, she would not find the absence of the penis—compensated by the promise of a child—enough to give rise to an inferiority complex; correlatively, the boy would not have a superiority complex if it were not instilled into him and if he looked up to women with as much respect as to men.[8] The little girl would not seek sterile compensation in narcissism and dreaming, she would not take her fate for granted; she would be interested in what she was *doing*, she would throw herself without reserve into undertakings.

I have already pointed out how much easier the transformation of puberty would be if she looked beyond it, like the boys, toward a free adult future: Menstruation horrifies her only because it is an abrupt descent into femininity. She would also take her young eroticism in much more tranquil fashion if she did not feel a frightened disgust for her destiny as a whole; coherent sexual information would do much to help her over this crisis. And thanks to coeducational schooling, the august mystery of Man would have no occasion to enter her mind: It would be eliminated by everyday familiarity and open rivalry.

Objections raised against this system always imply respect for sexual taboos; but the effort to inhibit all sex curiosity and pleasure in the child is quite useless; one succeeds only in creating repressions, obsessions, neuroses. The excessive sentimentality, homosexual fervors, and platonic crushes of adolescent girls, with all their train of silliness and frivolity, are much more injurious than a little childish sex play and a few definite sex experiences. It would be beneficial above all for the young girl not to be influenced against taking charge herself of her own existence, for then she would not seek a demigod in the male—merely a comrade, a friend, a partner. Eroticism and love would take on the nature of free transcendence and not that of resignation; she could experience them as a relation between equals. There is no intention, of course, to remove by a stroke of the pen all the difficulties that the child has to overcome in changing into an adult; the most intelligent, the most tolerant education could not relieve the child of experiencing things for herself; what could be asked is that obstacles should not be piled gratuitously in her path. Progress is already shown by the fact that "vicious" little girls are no longer cauterized with a red-hot iron. Psychoanalysis has given parents some instruction, but the conditions under which, at the present time, the sexual training and initiation of woman are accomplished are so deplorable that none of the objections advanced against the idea of a radical change could be considered valid. It is not a question of abolishing in woman the contingencies and miseries of the human condition, but of giving her the means for transcending them.

Woman is the victim of no mysterious fatality; the peculiarities that identify her as specifically a woman get their importance from the significance placed upon them. They can be surmounted, in the future, when they are regarded in new perspectives. Thus, as we have seen, through her erotic experience woman feels—and often detests—the domination of the male; but this is no reason to conclude that her ovaries condemn her to live forever on her knees. Virile aggressiveness seems like a lordly privilege only within a system that in its entirety conspires to affirm masculine sovereignty; and woman *feels* herself profoundly passive in the sexual act only because she already *thinks* of herself as such. Many modern women who lay claim to their dignity as human beings still envisage their erotic life from the standpoint of a tradition of slavery: since it seems to them humiliating to lie beneath the man, to be penetrated by him, they grow tense in frigidity. But if the reality were different, the meaning expressed symbolically in amorous gestures and postures would be different, too: A woman who pays and dominates her lover can, for example, take pride in her superb idleness and consider that she is enslaving the male who is actively exerting himself. And here and now there are many sexually well-balanced couples whose notions of victory and defeat are giving place to the idea of an exchange.

As a matter of fact, man, like woman, is flesh, therefore passive, the plaything of his hormones and of the species, the restless prey of his desires. And she, like him, in the midst of the carnal fever, is a consenting, a voluntary gift, an activity; they live out in their several fashions the strange ambiguity of existence made body. In those combats where they think they confront one another, it is really against the self that each one struggles, projecting into the partner that part of the self which is repudiated; instead of living out the ambiguities of their situation, each tries to make the other bear the abjection and tries to reserve the honor for the self. If, however, both should assume the ambiguity with a clear-sighted modesty, correlative of an authentic pride, they would see each other as equals and would live out their erotic drama in amity. The fact that we are human beings is infinitely more important than all the peculiarities that distinguish human beings from one another; it is never the given that confers superiorities: "virtue," as the ancients called it, is defined at the level of "that which depends on us." In both sexes is played out the same drama of the flesh and the spirit, of finitude and transcendence; both are gnawed away by time and laid in wait for by death; they have the same essential need for one another; and they can gain from their liberty the same glory. If they were to taste it, they would no longer be tempted to dispute fallacious privileges, and fraternity between them could then come into existence.

I shall be told that all this is utopian fancy, because woman cannot be "made over" unless society has first made her really the equal of man.

Conservatives have never failed in such circumstances to refer to that vicious circle; history, however, does not revolve. If a caste is kept in a state of inferiority, no doubt it remains inferior; but liberty can break the circle. Let the Negroes vote and they become worthy of having the vote; let woman be given responsibilities and she is able to assume them. The fact is that oppressors cannot be expected to make a move of gratuitous generosity; but at one time the revolt of the oppressed, at another time even the very evolution of the privileged caste itself, creates new situations; thus men have been led, in their own interest, to give partial emancipation to women: It remains only for women to continue their ascent, and the successes they are obtaining are an encouragement for them to do so. It seems almost certain that sooner or later they will arrive at complete economic and social equality, which will bring about an inner metamorphosis. . . .

Let us not forget that our lack of imagination always depopulates the future; for us it is only an abstraction; each one of us secretly deplores the absence there of the one who was himself. But the humanity of tomorrow will be living in its flesh and in its conscious liberty; that time will be its present and it will in turn prefer it. New relations of flesh and sentiment of which we have no conception will arise between the sexes; already, indeed, there have appeared between men and women friendships, rivalries, complicities, comradeships—chaste or sensual—which past centuries could not have conceived. To mention one point, nothing could seem to me more debatable than the opinion that dooms the new world to uniformity and hence to boredom. I fail to see that this present world is free from boredom or that liberty ever creates uniformity.

To begin with, there will always be certain differences between man and woman; her eroticism, and therefore her sexual world, have a special form of their own and therefore cannot fail to engender a sensuality, a sensitivity, of a special nature. This means that her relations to her own body, to that of the male, to the child, will never be identical with those the male bears to his own body, to that of the female, and to the child; those who make much of "equality in difference" could not with good grace refuse to grant me the possible existence of differences in equality. Then again, it is institutions that create uniformity. Young and pretty, the slaves of the harem are always the same in the sultan's embrace; Christianity gave eroticism its savor of sin and legend when it endowed the human female with a soul; if society restores her sovereign individuality to woman, it will not thereby destroy the power of love's embrace to move the heart.

It is nonsense to assert that revelry, vice, ecstasy, passion, would become impossible if man and woman were equal in concrete matters; the contradictions that put the flesh in opposition to the spirit, the instant to time, the swoon of immanence to the challenge of transcendence, the absolute of pleasure to the nothingness of forgetting, will never be resolved; in sexuality will always be materialized the tension, the anguish, the joy, the frustration, and the triumph of existence. To emancipate woman is to refuse to confine her to the relations she bears to man, not to deny them to her; let her have her independent existence and she will continue none the less to exist for him *also*: Mutually recognizing each other as subject, each will yet remain for the other an *other*. The reciprocity of their relations will not do away with the miracles—desire, possession, love, dream, adventure—worked by the division of human beings into two separate categories; and the words that move us—giving, conquering, uniting—will not lose their meaning. On the contrary, when we abolish the slavery of half of humanity, together with the whole system of hypocrisy that it implies, then the "division" of humanity will reveal its genuine significance and the human couple will find its true form. "The direct, natural, necessary relation of human creatures is the *relation of man to woman*," Marx has said.[9] "The nature of this relation determines to what point man himself is to be considered as a *generic being*, as mankind; the relation of man to woman is the most natural relation of human being to human being. By it is shown, therefore, to what point the *natural* behavior of man has become *human* or to what point the *human* being has become his *natural* being, to what point his *human nature* has become his *nature*."

The case could not be better stated. It is for man to establish the reign of liberty in the midst of the world of the given. To gain the supreme victory, it is necessary, for one thing, that by and through their natural differentiation men and women unequivocally affirm their brotherhood.

Notes

1. *Franchise*, dead today.
2. The Kinsey Report [Alfred C. Kinsey and others, *Sexual Behavior in the Human Male* (W. B. Saunders Co., 1948)] is no exception, for it is limited to describing the sexual characteristics of American men, which is quite a different matter.
3. E. Lévinas expresses this idea most explicitly in his essay *Temps et l'Autre*. "Is there not a case in which otherness, alterity [*altérité*], unquestionably marks the nature of a being, as its essence, an instance of otherness not consisting purely and simply in the opposition of two species of the same genus? I think that the feminine represents the contrary in its absolute sense, this contrariness being in no wise affected by any relation between it and its correlative and thus remaining absolutely other. Sex is not a certain specific difference . . . no more is the sexual difference a mere contradiction. . . . Nor does this difference lie in the duality of two complementary terms, for two complementary terms imply a pre-existing whole. . . . Otherness reaches its full flowering in the feminine, a term of the same rank as consciousness but of opposite meaning."

I suppose that Lévinas does not forget that woman, too, is aware of her own consciousness, or ego. But it is striking that he deliberately takes a man's point of view, disregarding the reciprocity of subject and object. When he writes that woman is mystery, he implies that she is mystery for man. Thus his description, which is intended to be objective, is in fact an assertion of masculine privilege.

4. See C. Lévi-Strauss, *Les Structures élémentaires de la parenté*. My thanks are due to C. Lévi-Strauss for his kindness in furnishing me with the proofs of his work. [...]

5. With rare exceptions, perhaps, like certain matriarchal rulers, queens, and the like.—TR.

6. See part 2, ch. 8 [of *The Second Sex*].

7. At the moment an "equal rights" amendment to the Constitution of the United States is before Congress.—TR.

8. I knew a little boy of eight who lived with his mother, aunt, and grandmother, all independent and active women, and his weak old half-crippled grandfather. He had a crushing inferiority complex in regard to the feminine sex, although he made efforts to combat it. At school he scorned comrades and teachers because they were miserable males.

9. *Philosophical Works*, vol. 4 (Marx's italics).

FROM

Is Female to Male as Nature Is to Culture?

SHERRY B. ORTNER

MUCH OF THE CREATIVITY of anthropology derives from the tension between two sets of demands: that we explain human universals, and that we explain cultural particulars. By this canon, woman provides us with one of the more challenging problems to be dealt with. The secondary status of woman in society is one of the true universals, a pan-cultural fact. Yet within that universal fact, the specific cultural conceptions and symbolizations of woman are extraordinarily diverse and even mutually contradictory. Further, the actual treatment of women and their relative power and contribution vary enormously from culture to culture, and over different periods in the history of particular cultural traditions. Both of these points—the universal fact and the cultural variation—constitute problems to be explained.

My interest in the problem is of course more than academic: I wish to see genuine change come about, the emergence of a social and cultural order in which as much of the range of human potential is open to women as is open to men. The universality of female subordination, the fact that it exists within every type of social and economic arrangement and in societies of every degree of complexity, indicates to me that we are up against something very profound, very stubborn, something we cannot rout out simply by rearranging a few tasks and roles in the social system, or even by reordering the whole economic structure. In this paper I try to expose the underlying logic of cultural thinking that assumes the inferiority of women; I try to show the highly persuasive nature of the logic, for if it were not so persuasive, people would not keep subscribing to it. But I also try to show the social and cultural sources of that logic, to indicate wherein lies the potential for change. . . .

NATURE AND CULTURE[1]

How are we to explain the universal devaluation of women? We could of course rest the case on biological determinism. There is something genetically inherent in the male of the species, so the biological determinists would argue, that makes them the naturally dominant sex; that "something" is lacking in females, and as a result women are not only naturally subordinate but in general quite satisfied with their position, since it affords them protection and the opportunity to maximize maternal pleasures, which to them are the most satisfying experiences of life. Without going into a detailed refutation of this position, I think it fair to say that it has failed to be established to the satisfaction of almost anyone in academic anthropology. This is to say, not that biological facts are irrelevant, or that men and women are not different, but that these facts and differences only take on significance of superior/inferior within the framework of culturally defined value systems.

If we are unwilling to rest the case on genetic determinism, it seems to me that we have only one way to proceed. We must attempt to interpret female subordination in light of other universals, factors built into the structure of the most generalized situation in which all human beings, in whatever culture, find themselves. For example, every human being has a physical body and a sense of nonphysical mind, is part of a society of other individuals and an inheritor of a cultural tradition, and must engage in some relationship, however mediated, with "nature," or the nonhuman realm, in order to survive. Every human being is born (to a mother) and ultimately dies, all are assumed to have an interest in personal survival, and society/culture has its own interest in (or at least momentum toward) continuity and survival, which transcends the lives and deaths of particular individuals. And so forth. It is in the realm of such universals of the human condition that we must seek an explanation for the universal fact of female devaluation.

I translate the problem, in other words, into the following simple question. What could there be in the generalized structure and conditions of existence, common to every culture, that would lead every culture to place a lower value upon women? Specifically, my thesis is that woman is being identified with—or, if you will, seems to be a symbol of—something that every culture devalues, something that every culture defines as being of a lower order of existence than itself. Now it seems that there is only one thing that would fit that description, and that is "nature" in the most generalized sense. Every culture, or, generically, "culture," is engaged in the process of generating and sustaining systems of meaningful forms (symbols, artifacts, etc.) by means of which humanity transcends the givens of natural existence, bends them to its purposes, controls them in its interest. We may thus broadly equate culture with the notion of human consciousness, or with the products of human consciousness (i.e., systems of thought and technology), by means of which humanity attempts to assert control over nature. . . .

The formulation I would like to defend and elaborate on in the following section, then, is that women are seen "merely" as being *closer* to nature than men. That is, culture (still equated relatively unambiguously with men) recognizes that women are active participants in its special processes, but at the same time sees them as being more rooted in, or having more direct affinity with, nature.

WHY IS WOMAN SEEN AS CLOSER TO NATURE?

It all begins of course with the body and the natural procreative functions specific to women alone. We can sort out for discussion three levels at which this absolute physiological fact has significance: (1) woman's *body and its functions*, more involved more of the time with "species life," seem to place her closer to nature, in contrast to man's physiology, which frees him more completely to take up the projects of culture; (2) woman's body and its functions place her in *social roles* that in turn are considered to be at a lower order of the cultural process than man's; and (3) woman's traditional social roles, imposed because of her body and its functions, in turn give her a different *psychic structure*, which, like her physiological nature and her social roles, is seen as being closer to nature. I shall discuss each of these points in turn, showing first how in each instance certain factors strongly tend to align woman with nature, then indicating other factors that demonstrate her full alignment with culture, the combined factors thus placing her in a problematic intermediate position. . . .

1. *Woman's physiology seen as closer to nature.* This part of my argument has been anticipated, with subtlety, cogency, and a great deal of hard data, by de Beauvoir (1953). De Beauvoir reviews the physiological structure, development, and functions of the human female and concludes that "the female, to a greater extent than the male, is the prey of the species" (60). She points out that many major areas and processes of the woman's body serve no apparent function for the health and stability of the individual; on the contrary, as they perform their specific organic functions, they are often sources of discomfort, pain, and danger. The breasts are irrelevant to personal health; they may be excised at any time of a woman's life. "Many of the ovarian secretions function for the benefit of the egg, promoting its maturation and adapting the uterus to its requirements; in respect to the organism as a whole, they make for disequilibrium rather than for regulation—the woman is adapted to the needs of the egg rather than to her own requirements" (24). Menstruation is often uncomfortable, sometimes painful; it frequently has negative emotional correlates and in any case involves bothersome tasks

of cleansing and waste disposal; and—a point that de Beauvoir does not mention—in many cultures it interrupts a woman's routine, putting her in a stigmatized state involving various restrictions on her activities and social contacts. In pregnancy many of the woman's vitamin and mineral resources are channeled into nourishing the fetus, depleting her own strength and energies. And finally, childbirth itself is painful and dangerous (24–27 *passim*). In sum, de Beauvoir concludes that the female "is more enslaved to the species than the male, her animality is more manifest" (239). . . .

Thus if male is, as I am suggesting, everywhere (unconsciously) associated with culture and female seems closer to nature, the rationale for these associations is not very difficult to grasp, merely from considering the implications of the physiological contrast between male and female. At the same time, however, woman cannot be consigned fully to the category of nature, for it is perfectly obvious that she is a full-fledged human being endowed with human consciousness just as a man is; she is half of the human race, without whose cooperation the whole enterprise would collapse. She may seem more in the possession of nature than man, but having consciousness, she thinks and speaks; she generates, communicates, and manipulates symbols, categories, and values. She participates in human dialogues not only with other women but also with men. As Lévi-Strauss says, "Woman could never become just a sign and nothing more, since even in a man's world she is still a person, and since insofar as she is defined as a sign she must [still] be recognized as a generator of signs" (1969a, 496).

Indeed, the fact of woman's full human consciousness, her full involvement in and commitment to culture's project of transcendence over nature, may ironically explain another of the great puzzles of "the woman problem"—woman's nearly universal unquestioning acceptance of her own devaluation. For it would seem that, as a conscious human and member of culture, she has followed out the logic of culture's arguments and has reached culture's conclusions along with the men. As de Beauvoir puts it (59):

> For she, too, is an existent, she feels the urge to surpass, and her project is not mere repetition but transcendence towards a different future—in her heart of hearts she finds confirmation of the masculine pretensions. She joins the men in the festivals that celebrate the successes and victories of the males. Her misfortune is to have been biologically destined for the repetition of Life, when even in her own view Life does not carry within itself its reasons for being, reasons that are more important than life itself.

In other words, woman's consciousness—her membership, as it were, in culture—is evidenced in part by the very fact that she accepts her own devaluation and takes culture's point of view.

I have tried here to show one part of the logic of that view, the part that grows directly from the physiological differences between men and women. Because of woman's greater bodily involvement with the natural functions surrounding reproduction, she is seen as more a part of nature than man is. Yet in part because of her consciousness and participation in human social dialogue, she is recognized as a participant in culture. Thus she appears as something intermediate between culture and nature, lower on the scale of transcendence than man.

2. *Woman's social role seen as closer to nature.* Woman's physiological functions, I have just argued, may tend in themselves to motivate[2] a view of woman as closer to nature, a view she herself, as an observer of herself and the world, would tend to agree with. Woman creates naturally from within her own being, whereas man is free to, or forced to, create artificially, that is, through cultural means, and in such a way as to sustain culture. In addition, I now wish to show how woman's physiological functions have tended universally to limit her social movement, and to confine her universally to certain social contexts which *in turn* are seen as closer to nature. That is, not only her bodily processes but the social situation in which her bodily processes locate her may carry this significance. And insofar as she is permanently associated (in the eyes of culture) with these social milieux, they add weight (perhaps the decisive part of the burden) to the view of woman as closer to nature. I refer here of course to woman's confinement to the domestic family context, a confinement motivated, no doubt, by her lactation processes.

Woman's body, like that of all female mammals, generates milk during and after pregnancy for the feeding of the newborn baby. The baby cannot survive without breast milk or some similar formula at this stage of life. Since the mother's body goes through its lactation processes in direct relation to a pregnancy with a particular child, the relationship of nursing between mother and child is seen as a natural bond, other feeding arrangements being seen in most cases as unnatural and makeshift. Mothers and their children, according to cultural reasoning, belong together. Further, children beyond infancy are not strong enough to engage in major work, yet are mobile and unruly and not capable of understanding various dangers; they thus require supervision and constant care. Mother is the obvious person for this task, as an extension of her natural nursing bond with the children, or because she has a new infant and is already involved with child-oriented activities. Her own activities are thus circumscribed by the limitations and low levels of her children's strengths and skills.[3] She is confined to the domestic family group; "woman's place is in the home."

Woman's association with the domestic circle would contribute to the view of her as closer to nature in several ways. In the first place, the sheer fact of constant association with children plays a role in the issue; one can easily see how infants and children might themselves be considered part of nature. Infants are barely human and utterly unsocialized; like animals they are unable to walk upright, they excrete without control, they do not speak. Even slightly older children are clearly not yet fully under the sway of culture. They do not yet understand social duties, responsibilities, and morals; their vocabulary and their range of learned skills are small. One finds implicit recognition of an association between children and nature in many cultural practices. For example, most cultures have initiation rites for adolescents (primarily for boys; I shall return to this point below), the point of which is to move the child ritually from a less than fully human state into full participation in society and culture; many cultures do not hold funeral rites for children who die at early ages, explicitly because they are not yet fully social beings. Thus children are likely to be categorized with nature, and woman's close association with children may compound her potential for being seen as closer to nature herself. It is ironic that the rationale for boys' initiation rites in many cultures is that the boys must be purged of the defilement accrued from being around mother and other women so much of the time, when in fact much of the woman's defilement may derive from her being around children so much of the time. . . .

Now, since women are associated with, and indeed are more or less confined to, the domestic context, they are identified with this lower order of social/ cultural organization. What are the implications of this for the way they are viewed? First, if the specifically biological (reproductive) function of the family is stressed, as in Lévi-Strauss's formulation, then the family (and hence woman) is identified with nature pure and simple, as opposed to culture. But this is obviously too simple; the point seems more adequately formulated as follows: The family (and hence woman) represents lower-level, socially fragmenting, particularistic sorts of concerns, as opposed to interfamilial relations representing higher-level, integrative, universalistic sorts of concerns. Since men lack a "natural" basis (nursing, generalized to child care) for a familial orientation, their sphere of activity is defined at the level of interfamilial relations. And hence, so the cultural reasoning seems to go, men are the "natural" proprietors of religion, ritual, politics, and other realms of cultural thought and action in which universalistic statements of spiritual and social synthesis are made. Thus men are identified not only with culture, in the sense of all human creativity, as opposed to nature; they are identified in particular with culture in the old-fashioned sense of the finer and higher aspects of human thought—art, religion, law, etc. . . .

In short, we see once again some sources of woman's appearing more intermediate than man with respect to the nature/culture dichotomy. Her "natural" association with the domestic context (motivated by her natural lactation functions) tends to compound her potential for being viewed as closer to nature, because of the animal-like nature of children, and because of the infrasocial connotation of the domestic group as against the rest of society. Yet at the same time her socializing and cooking functions within the domestic context show her to be a powerful agent of the cultural process, constantly transforming raw natural resources into cultural products. Belonging to culture, yet appearing to have stronger and more direct connections with nature, she is once again seen as situated between the two realms.

3. *Woman's psyche seen as closer to nature.* The suggestion that woman has not only a different body and a different social locus from man but also a different psychic structure is most controversial. I will argue that she probably *does* have a different psychic structure, but I will draw heavily on Chodorow to establish first that her psychic structure need not be assumed to be innate; it can be accounted for, as Chodorow convincingly shows, by the facts of the probably universal female socialization experience.[4] Nonetheless, if we grant the empirical near universality of a "feminine psyche" with certain specific characteristics, these characteristics would add weight to the cultural view of woman as closer to nature. . . .

THE IMPLICATIONS OF INTERMEDIACY

My primary purpose in this paper has been to attempt to explain the universal secondary status of women. Intellectually and personally, I felt strongly challenged by this problem; I felt compelled to deal with it before undertaking an analysis of woman's position in any particular society. Local variables of economy, ecology, history, political and social structure, values, and worldview—these could explain variations within this universal, but they could not explain the universal itself. And if we were not to accept the ideology of biological determinism, then explanation, it seemed to me, could only proceed by reference to other universals of the human cultural situation. Thus the general outlines of the approach—although not of course the particular solution offered—were determined by the problem itself, and not by any predilection on my part for global abstract structural analysis.

I argued that the universal devaluation of women could be explained by postulating that women are seen as closer to nature than men, men being seen as more unequivocally occupying the high ground of culture. The culture/nature distinction is itself a product of culture, culture being minimally defined as the transcendence, by means of systems of thought and technology, of the natural givens of existence. This of course is an analytic definition, but I argued that at some level every culture incorporates this notion in one form or other, if only through the performance of ritual as an assertion of the human ability to manipulate those givens. In any case, the core of the paper was concerned with showing why women might tend to be assumed, over and over, in the most diverse sorts of worldviews and in cultures of every degree of complexity, to be closer to nature than men. Woman's physiology, more involved more of the time with "species of life"; woman's association with the structurally subordinate domestic context, charged with the crucial function of transforming animal-like infants into cultured beings; "woman's psyche," appropriately molded to mothering functions by her own socialization and tending toward greater personalism and less mediated modes of relating—all these factors make woman appear to be rooted more directly and deeply in nature. At the same time, however, her "membership" and fully necessary participation in culture are recognized by culture and cannot be denied. Thus she is seen to occupy an intermediate position between culture and nature. . . .

CONCLUSIONS

Ultimately, it must be stressed again that the whole scheme is a construct of culture rather than a fact of nature. Woman is not "in reality" any closer to (or further from) nature than man—both have consciousness, both are mortal. But there are certainly reasons why she appears that way, which is what I have tried to show in this paper. The result is a (sadly) efficient feedback system: Various aspects of woman's situation (physical, social, psychological) contribute to her being seen as closer to nature, while the view of her as closer to nature is in turn embodied in institutional forms that reproduce her situation. The implications for social change are similarly circular: A different cultural view can only grow out of a different social actuality; a different social actuality can only grow out of a different cultural view.

It is clear, then, that the situation must be attacked from both sides. Efforts directed solely at changing the social institutions—through setting quotas on hiring, for example, or through passing equal-pay-for-equal-work laws—cannot have far-reaching effects if cultural language and imagery continue to purvey a relatively devalued view of women. But at the same time efforts directed solely at changing cultural assumptions—through male and female consciousness-raising groups, for example, or through revision of educational materials and mass-media imagery—cannot be successful unless the institutional base of the society is changed to support and reinforce the changed cultural view. Ultimately, both men and women can and must be equally involved in projects of creativity and transcendence. Only then will women be seen as aligned with culture, in culture's ongoing dialectic with nature.

Notes

1. With all due respect to Lévi-Strauss (1969a, b, and *passim*).
2. Semantic theory uses the concept of motivation of meaning, which encompasses various ways in which a meaning may be assigned to a symbol because of certain objective properties of that symbol, rather than by arbitrary association. In a sense, this entire paper is an inquiry into the motivation of the meaning of woman as a symbol, asking why woman may be unconsciously assigned the significance of being closer to nature. For a concise statement on the various types of motivation of meaning, see Ullman (1963).
3. A situation that often serves to make her more childlike herself.
4. See Chodorow, 1974.

References

Simone de Beauvoir. 1953. *The Second Sex.* New York: Alfred A. Knopf, Inc.

Ullman, Stephen. 1963. "Semantic Universals." In *Universals of Language.* Ed. Joseph H. Greenberg. Cambridge: MIT Press.

Claude Lévi-Strauss. 1969a. *The Elementary Structures of Kinship.* Ed. R. Needham. Boston: Beacon Press.

———. *The Raw and the Cooked.* 1969b. New York: Harper and Row.

Nancy Chodorow. 1974. "Family Structure and Feminine Personality." In *Women, Culture, and Society.* Ed. Michelle Zimbalist Rosaldo and Louise Lamphere. Stanford, Calif.: Stanford University Press.

SELECTION 3
FROM
Gender, Relation, and Difference in Psychoanalytic Perspective

NANCY J. CHODOROW

> I would go so far as to say that even before slavery or class domination existed, men built an approach to women that would serve one day to introduce differences among us all.
> — Claude Lévi-Strauss

IN BOTH THE NINETEENTH- and twentieth-century women's movements, many feminists have argued that the degendering of society, so that gender and sex no longer determined social existence, would eliminate male dominance.[1] This view assumes that gender-differentiating characteristics are acquired. An alternate sexual politics and analysis of sexual inequality has tended toward an essentialist position, posing male-female difference as innate. Not the degendering of society, but its appropriation by women, with women's virtues, is seen as the solution to male dominance. These virtues are uniquely feminine, and usually thought to emerge from women's biology, which is then seen as intrinsically connected to or entailing a particular psyche, a particular social role (such as mothering), a particular body image (more diffuse, holistic, nonphallocentric), or a particular sexuality (not centered on a particular organ; at times, lesbianism). In this view, women are intrinsically better than men and their virtues are not available to men. Proponents of the degendering model have sometimes also held that "female" virtues or qualities—nurturance, for instance—should be spread throughout society and replace aggression and competitiveness; but these virtues are nevertheless seen as acquired, a product of women's development or social location, and acquirable by men, given appropriate development, experience, and social reorganization. (Others who argue for degendering have at times held that women need to acquire certain "male" characteristics and modes of action—autonomy, independence, asssertiveness—again, assuming that such characteristics are acquired.)

This essay evaluates the essentialist view of difference and examines the contribution that psychoanalytic theory can make to understanding the question of sex or gender difference. It asks whether gender is best understood by focusing on differences between men and women and on the uniqueness of each and whether gender difference should be a central organizing concept for feminism. The concept of difference to which I refer here is abstract and irreducible.[2] It assumes the existence of an essence of gender, so that differences between men and women are seen to establish and define each gender as a unique and absolute category.

I will not discuss differences among women. I think we have something else in mind when we speak of differences in this connection. Differences among women—of class, race, sexual preference, nationality, and ethnicity, between mothers and nonmothers—are all significant for feminist theory and practice, but these remain concrete differences, analyzable in terms of specific categories and modes of understanding. We can see how they are socially situated and how they grow from particular social relations and organization; how they may contain physiological elements (race and sexual preference, for example) yet only gain a specific meaning in particular historical contexts and social formations.

I suggest that gender difference is not absolute, abstract, or irreducible; it does not involve an essence of gender. Gender differences, and the experience of difference, like differences among women, are socially and psychologically created and situated. In addition, I want to suggest a relational notion of difference. Difference and gender difference do not exist as things in themselves; they are created relationally, that is, in relationship. We cannot understand difference apart from this relational construction.

The issues I consider here are relevant both to feminist theory and to particular strands of feminist politics. In contrast to the beginning of the contemporary women's movement, there is now a widespread view that gender differences are essential, that women are fundamentally different from men, and that these differences must be recognized, theorized, and maintained. This finds some political counterpart in notions that women's special nature guarantees the emergence of a good society after the feminist revolution and legitimates female dominance, if not an exclusively female society. My conclusions lead me to reject those currents of contemporary feminism that would found a politics on essentialist conceptions of the feminine.

There is also a preoccupation among some women with psychological separateness and autonomy, with individuality as a necessary women's goal.

This preoccupation grows out of many women's feelings of not having distinct autonomy as separate selves, in comparison, say, to men. This finds some political counterpart in equal rights arguments, ultimately based on notions of women exclusively as individuals rather than as part of a collectivity or social group. I suggest that we need to situate such a goal in an understanding of psychological development and to indicate the relationship between our culture's individualism and gender differentiation.

Psychoanalysis clarifies for us many of the issues involved in questions of difference by providing a developmental history of the emergence of separateness, differentiation, and the perception of difference in early childhood. Thus it provides a particularly useful arena in which to see the relational and situated construction of difference, and of gender difference. Moreover, psychoanalysis gives an account of these issues from a general psychological perspective, as well as with specific relation to the question of gender. In this context, I will discuss two aspects of the general subject of separateness, differentiation, and perceptions of difference and their emergence. First, I will consider how separation-individuation occurs relationally in the first "me"–"not-me" division, in the development of the "I," or self. I will suggest that we have to understand this separation-individuation in relation to other aspects of development, that it has particular implications for women, and that differentiation is not synonymous with difference or separateness. Second, I will talk about the ways that difference and gender difference are created distinctly, in different relational contexts, for girls and boys, and, hence, for women and men. The argument here advances a reading of psychoanalysis that stresses the relational ego. It contrasts with certain prevalent (Lacan-influenced) feminist readings of psychoanalysis, in particular with the views advanced by French theorists of difference like Luce Irigaray and with the Freudian orthodoxy of Juliet Mitchell.

I do not deal in this essay with the male and female body. We clearly live an embodied life; we live with those genital and reproductive organs and capacities, those hormones and chromosomes, that locate us physiologically as male or female. But, as psychoanalysis has shown us, there is nothing self-evident about this biology. How anyone experiences, fantasizes about, or internally represents her or his embodiment grows from experience, learning, and self-definition in the family and in the culture. Such self-definitions may be shaped by completely nonbiological considerations, which may also shape perceptions of anatomical "sex differences" and the psychological development of these differences into forms of sexual object choice, mode, or aim; into femininity or masculinity; into activity or passivity; into one's choice of the organ of erotic pleasure; and so forth. We cannot know what people would make of their bodies in a nongender or nonsexually organized world, what kind of sexual structuration or gender identities would develop.

We do know that the cultural, social, and psychological significance of bio-logical sex differences, gender difference, and different sexualities is not obvious. There might be a multiplicity of sexual organizations, identities, and prac-tices, and perhaps even of genders themselves. Bodies would be bodies (we do not want to deny people their bodily experience). But particular bodily attributes would not necessarily be so determining of who we are, what we do, how we are perceived, and who are our sexual partners.

DIFFERENTIATION

Psychoanalysis talks of the process of "differentiation" or "separation-individuation."[3] A child of either gender is born originally with what is called a "narcissistic relation to reality": cognitively and libidinally it expe-riences itself as merged and continuous with the world in general, and with its mother or caretaker in particular. Differentiation, or separation-individuation, means coming to perceive a demarcation between the self and the object world, coming to perceive the subject/self as distinct, or separate from, the object/other. An essential early task of infantile develop-ment, it involves the development of ego boundaries (a sense of personal psychological division from the rest of the world) and of a body ego (a sense of the permanence of one's physical separateness and the predictable boundedness of one's own body, of a distinction between inside and outside).

This differentiation requires physiological maturation (for instance, the ability to perceive object constancy), but such maturation is not enough. Differentiation happens *in relation to* the mother, or to the child's primary caretaker. It develops through experiences of the mother's departure and return, and through frustration, which emphasizes the child's separateness and the fact that it doesn't control all its own experiences and gratifications. Some of these experiences and gratifications come from within, some from without. If it were not for these frustrations, these disruptions of the expe-rience of primary oneness, total holding, and gratification, the child would not need to begin to perceive the other, the "outer world," as separate, rather than as an extension of itself. Developing separateness thus involves, in particular, perceiving the mother or primary caretaker as separate and "not-me," where once these were an undifferentiated symbiotic unity.

Separateness, then, is not simply given from birth, nor does it emerge from the individual alone. Rather, separateness is defined relationally; differ-entiation occurs in relationship: "*I*" am "*not-you.*" Moreover, "*you,*" or the other, is also distinguished. The child learns to see the particularity of the mother or primary caretaker in contrast to the rest of the world. Thus, as the self is differentiated from the object world, the object world is itself differentiated into its component parts.

Now, from a psychoanalytic perspective, learning to distinguish me and not-me is necessary for a person to grow into a functioning human being. It is also inevitable, since experiences of departure, of discontinuity in handling, feeding, where one sleeps, how one is picked up and by whom, of less than total relational and physical gratification, are unavoidable. But for our understanding of "difference" in this connection, the concept of differentiation and the processes that characterize it need elaboration.

First, in most psychoanalytic formulations, and in prevalent understandings of development, the mother, or the outside world, is depicted simply as the other, not-me, one who does or does not fulfill an expectation. This perception arises originally from the infant's cognitive inability to differentiate self and world; the infant does not distinguish between its desires for love and satisfaction and those of its primary love-object and object of identification. The self here is the infant or growing child, and psychoanalytic accounts take the viewpoint of this child.

However, adequate separation, or differentiation, involves not merely perceiving the separateness, or otherness, of the other. It involves perceiving the person's subjectivity and selfhood as well. Differentiation, separation, and disruption of the narcissistic relation to reality are developed through learning that the mother is a separate being with separate interests and activities that do not always coincide with just what the infant wants at the time. They involve the ability to experience and perceive the object/other (the mother) in aspects apart from its sole relation to the ability to gratify the infant's/subject's needs and wants; they involve seeing the object as separate from the self and from the self's needs.[4] The infant must change here from a "relationship to a subjectively conceived object to a relationship to an object objectively perceived."[5]

In infantile development this change requires cognitive sophistication, the growing ability to integrate various images and experiences of the mother that comes with the development of ego capacities. But these capacities are not enough. The ability to perceive the other as a self, finally, requires an emotional shift and a form of emotional growth. The adult self not only experiences the other as distinct and separate. It also does not experience the other solely in terms of its own needs for gratification and its own desires.

This interpretation implies that true differentiation, true separateness, cannot be simply a perception and experience of self-other, of presence-absence. It must precisely involve two selves, two presences, two subjects. Recognizing the other as a subject is possible only to the extent that one is not dominated by felt need and one's own exclusive subjectivity. Such recognition permits appreciation and perception of many aspects of the other person, of her or his existence apart from the child's/the self's. Thus, how we understand differentiation—only from the viewpoint of the infant as a self, or from the viewpoint of two interacting selves—has consequences for what we think of as a mature self. If the mature self grows only out of the infant as a self, the other need never be accorded her or his own selfhood.

The view that adequate separation-individuation, or differentiation, involves not simply perceiving the otherness of the other, but her or his selfhood/ subjectivity as well, has important consequences, not only for an understanding of the development of selfhood, but also for perceptions of women. Hence, it seems to me absolutely essential to a feminist appropriation of psychoanalytic conceptions of differentiation. Since women, as mothers, are the primary caretakers of infants, if the child (or the psychoanalytic account) only takes the viewpoint of the infant as a (developing) self, then the mother will be perceived (or depicted) only as an object. But, from a feminist perspective, perceiving the particularity of the mother must involve according the mother her own selfhood. This is a necessary part of the developmental process, though it is also often resisted and experienced only conflictually and partially. Throughout life, perceptions of the mother fluctuate between perceiving her particularity and selfhood and perceiving her as a narcissistic extension, a not-separate other whose sole reason for existence is to gratify one's own wants and needs.

Few accounts recognize the import of this particular stance toward the mother. Alice Balint's marvelous protofeminist account is the best I know of the infantile origins of adult perceptions of mother as object:

> Most men (and women)—even when otherwise quite normal and capable of an "adult," altruistic form of love which acknowledges the interests of the partner—retain towards their own mothers this naive egoistic attitude throughout their lives. For all of us it remains self-evident that the interests of mother and child are identical, and it is the generally acknowledged measure of the goodness or badness of the mother how far she really feels this identity of interests.[6]

Now, these perceptions, as a product of infantile development, are somewhat inevitable as long as women have nearly exclusive maternal responsibilities, and they are one major reason why I advocate equal parenting as a necessary basis of sexual equality. But I think that, even within the ongoing context of women's mothering, as women we can and must liberate ourselves from such perceptions in our personal emotional lives as much as possible, and certainly in our theorizing and politics.[7]

A second elaboration of psychoanalytic accounts of differentiation concerns the affective or emotional distinction between differentiation or separation-individuation, and *difference*. Difference and differentiation are, of course, related to and feed into one another; it is in some sense true that cognitive or linguistic distinction, or division, must imply difference. However, it is possible to be separate, to be differentiated, without caring about or emphasizing difference, without turning the cognitive fact into an emotional, moral, or political one. In fact, assimilating difference to differentiation is defensive and reactive, a reaction to not feeling separate enough. Such assimilation involves arbitrary boundary creation and an assertion of hyperseparateness to reinforce a lack of security in a person's sense of self as a separate person. But one can be separate from and similar to someone at the same time. For example, one can recognize another's subjectivity and humanity as one recognizes one's own, seeing the commonality of both as active subjects. Or a woman can recognize her similarity, commonality, even continuity, with her mother, because she has developed enough of an unproblematic sense of separate self. At the same time, the other side of being able to experience separateness and commonality, of recognizing the other's subjectivity, is the ability to recognize differences with a small *d*, differences that are produced and situated historically—for instance, the kinds of meaningful differences among women that I mentioned earlier.

The distinction between differentiation/separateness and difference relates to a third consideration, even more significant to our assessment of difference and gender difference. Following Mahler, much psychoanalytic theory has centered its account of early infant development on separation-individuation, on the creation of the separate self, on the "me"–"not-me" distinction. Yet there are other ways of looking at the development of self, other important and fundamental aspects to the self: "me"–"not-me" is not all there is to "me." Separation, the "me"–"not-me" division, looms larger, both in our psychological life and theoretically, to the extent that these other aspects of the self are not developed either in individual lives or in theoretical accounts.

Object-relations theory shows that in the development of self the primary task is not the development of ego boundaries and a body ego.[8] Along with the earliest development of its sense of separateness, the infant constructs an internal set of unconscious, affectively loaded representations of others in relation to its self, and an internal sense of self in relationship emerges. Images of felt good and bad aspects of the mother or primary caretaker, caretaking experiences, and the mothering relationship become part of the self, of a relational ego structure, through unconscious mental processes that appropriate and incorporate these images. With maturation, these early images and fragments of perceived experience become put together into a self. As externality and internality are established, therefore, what comes to be internal includes what originally were aspects of the other and the relation to the other. (Similarly, what is experienced as external may include what was originally part of the developing self's experience.) Externality and internality, then, do not follow easily observable physiological boundaries but are constituted by psychological and emotional processes as well.

These unconscious early internalizations that affect and constitute the internal quality of selfhood may remain more or less fragmented, or they may develop a quality of wholeness. A sense of continuity of experience and the opportunity to integrate a complex of (at least somewhat) complementary and consistent images enables the "I" to emerge as a continuous being with an identity. This more internal sense of self, or of "I," is not dependent on separateness or difference from an other. A "true self," or "central self," emerges through the experience of continuity that the mother or caretaker helps to provide, by protecting the infant from having continually to react to and ward off environmental intrusions and from being continually in need.

The integration of a "true self" that feels alive and whole involves a particular set of internalized feelings about others in relation to the self. These include developing a sense that one is able to affect others and one's environment (a sense that one has not been inhibited by overanticipation of all one's needs), a sense that one has been accorded one's own feelings and a spontaneity about these feelings (a sense that one's feelings or needs have not been projected onto one), and a sense that there is a fit between one's feelings and needs and those of the mother or caretaker. These feelings all give the self a sense of agency and authenticity.

These sense of agency, then, is fostered by caretakers who do not project experiences or feelings onto the child and who do not let the environment impinge indiscriminately. It is evoked by empathic caretakers who understand and validate the infant as a self in its own right, and the infant's experience as real. Thus, the sense of agency, which is one basis of the inner sense of continuity and wholeness, grows out of the nature of the parent-infant relationship.

Another important aspect of internalized feelings about others in relation to the self concerns a certain wholeness that develops through an internal sense of relationship with another.[9] The "thereness" of the primary parenting person grows into an internal sense of the presence of another who is caring and affirming. The self comes into being here first through feeling confidently alone in the presence of its mother, and then through this presence's becoming internalized. Part of its self becomes a good internal mother. This suggests that the central core of self is, internally, a relational ego, a sense of self-in-good-relationship. The presence or absence of others, their sameness or difference, does not then become an issue touching the infant's very existence. A "capacity to be alone," a relational rather than a reactive autonomy, develops because of a sense of the ongoing presence of another.

These several senses of agency, of a true self that does not develop reactively, of a relational self or ego core, and of an internal continuity of being, are fundamental to an unproblematic sense of self, and provide the basis of both autonomy and spontaneity. The strength, or wholeness, of the self, in this view, does not depend only or even centrally on its degree of separateness, although the extent of confident distinctness certainly affects and is part of the sense of self. The more secure the central self, or ego core, the less one has to define one's self through separateness from others. Separateness becomes, then, a more rigid, defensive, rather fragile, secondary criterion of the strength of the self and of the "success" of individuation.

This view suggests that no one has a separateness consisting only of "me"–"not-me" distinctions. Part of myself is always that which I have taken in: we are all to some degree incorporations and extensions of others. Separateness from the mother, defining oneself as apart from her (and from other women), is not the only or final goal for women's ego strength and autonomy, even if many women must also attain some sense of reliable separateness. In the process of differentiation, leading to a genuine autonomy, people maintain contact with those with whom they had their earliest relationships: Indeed this contact is part of who we are. "I am" is not definition through negation, is not "who I am not." Developing a sense of confident separateness must be a part of all children's development. But once this confident separateness is established, one's relational self can become more central to one's life. Differentiation is not distinctness and separateness, but a particular way of being connected to others. This connection to others, based on early incorporations, in turn enables us to feel that empathy and confidence that are basic to the recognition of the other as a self.

What does all this have to do with male-female difference and male dominance? Before turning to the question of gender difference, I want to reiterate what we as feminists learn from the general inquiry into "differentiation." First, we learn that we can only think of differentiation and the emergence of the self relationally. Differentiation occurs, and separation emerges, in relationship; they are not givens. Second, we learn that to single out separation as the core of a notion of self and of the process of differentiation may well be inadequate; it is certainly not the only way to discuss the emergence of self or what constitutes a strong self. Differentiation includes the internalization of aspects of the primary caretaker and of the caretaking relationship.

·Finally, we learn that essential, important attitudes toward mothers and expectations of mothers—attitudes and expectations that enter into experiences of women more generally—emerge in the earliest differentiation of self. These attitudes and expectations arise during the emergence of separateness. Given that differentiation and separation are developmentally problematic, and given that women are primary caretakers, the mother, who is woman, becomes and remains for children of both genders the other, or object. She is not accorded autonomy or selfness on her side. Such attitudes arise also from the gender-specific character of the early, emotionally charged self and object images that affect the development of self and the sense of autonomy and spontaneity. They are internalizations of feelings about the self in relation to the mother, who is then often experienced as either overwhelming or overdenying. These attitudes are often unconscious and always have a basis in unconscious, emotionally charged feelings and conflicts. A precipitate of the early relationship to the mother and of an unconscious sense of self, they may be more fundamental and determining of psychic life than more conscious and explicit attitudes to "sex differences" or "gender differences" themselves.

This inquiry suggests a psychoanalytic grounding for goals of emotional psychic life other than autonomy and separateness. It suggests, instead, an individuality that emphasizes our connectedness with, rather than our separation from, one another. Feelings of inadequate separateness, the fear of merger, are indeed issues for women, because of the ongoing sense of oneness and primary identification with our mothers (and children). A transformed organization of parenting would help women to resolve these issues. However, autonomy, spontaneity, and a sense of agency need not be based on self-other distinctions, on the individual as individual. They can be based on the fundamental interconnectedness, not synonymous with merger, that grows out of our earliest unconscious developmental experience, and that enables the creation of a nonreactive separateness.[10]

Gender Differences in the Creation of Difference

I turn now to the question of gender differences. We are not born with perceptions of gender differences; these emerge developmentally. In the traditional psychoanalytic view, however, when sexual difference is first seen it has self-evident value. A girl perceives her lack of a penis, knows instantly that she wants one, and subsequently defines herself and her mother as lacking, inadequate, castrated; a boy instantly knows having a penis is better, and fears the loss of his own.[11] This traditional account violates a fundamental rule of psychoanalytic interpretation. When the analyst finds trauma, shock, strong fears, or conflict, it is a signal to look for the roots of such feelings.[12] Because of his inability to focus on the pre-Oedipal years and the relationship of mother to child, Freud could not follow his own rule here.

Clinical and theoretical writings since Freud suggest another interpretation of the emergence of perceptions of gender difference. This view re-

but through collective social and political action.

This tends to contrast and oppose "individual change" to "social and political change" in a way that can distort the reality of the experience. It conforms with political assumptions which are dismissive of individual change, growth, and development. Within the women's movement, reworking the relationship between the "personal" and the "political," the "individual" and the "collective," has grown out of a deep respect for the value and integrity of each person's experience. There is a different vision of freedom, equality, and democracy within the idea that each woman has had an equally valid experience and has a voice to express it.

This is different from the prevailing liberal conceptions of respect for individual experience, which necessitates a certain distance from others. The ways in which each individual's experience is *validated* within a consciousness-raising group gave me, for instance, a way of recognizing how much of my individual experience as a man was formed in the relationships with my parents, school, and, later, at work. I recognized how much I *shared* with others, as men, and how much I had been limited and made to suffer through the expectations the society had of who I should be. I had learned constantly to squeeze myself into the prevailing images of men, feeling that there must be something wrong with me if I felt at odds with this process. A sense of solidarity was created through this sharing, which was at once both uniquely individual and intensely social, as we learned to explore our individual shapes rather than coerce each other to conform to values and relationships that were not of our own making. We refused to collude, even if this put us in a challenging relationship to what was traditionally expected of us, as men.

In fact, one of the things I learned was how my understanding gets limited through this false opposition between the "individual" and the "social." Not only did this leave me isolated, but also powerless to know what I wanted to change in how I relate to others to live a fuller life myself. I did not want to continue making the kind of sacrifices of my emotions, sexuality, and feelings which the society implicitly demanded as the price of growing up to be an independent and self-sufficient man who supposedly has no needs of his own. I was regaining power over my understanding in challenging this prevailing sociological distinction between the "individual" and the "social," recognizing how much I came to be who I am through the context of relationships of power and authority, often mystified as love and caring.

Within the men's group, I learned, for instance, about some of the sources of my fear of authority. I had tried to pretend that this fear did not exist and that if I was strong-willed enough these feelings would go away. I learned about some of the deeper sources of this fear and in so doing learned something valuable about how people can change. I learned more of what I can expect of myself and of the processes of coming to terms and facing my experience rather than rejecting and denying any feelings that did not seem to fit, so that I can live up to a particular ideal of masculinity. I learned something of what people have to go through in order to change. This learning is crucial if we are to talk realistically about larger social and political changes that deeply affect people's everyday lives.

As a man, I very much felt that I *should* be able to do anything, if I only put my mind to it. More than that, I felt that I should be able to do it well. I *should* be able to cope with meetings every night and I should not get tired or exhausted. I did not want to admit my "weakness," so I felt that I should be able to do a job, and organize politically, and have equal relationships with people. I put enormous demands upon myself, though I did not recognize this at all. All these things were "important" to do. I felt I should be able to do them all. This aspect of my masculine upbringing was extended within a leftist political culture which left me suspicious of specialization as a source of hierarchy and false authority, feeling that I had to be able to do everything from printing to plumbing. I was left feeling that I should be developing all these abilities and skills *all* the time. I made ludicrous demands upon myself, yet I always felt that I was not "doing enough." I had no sense of my own limits or boundaries.

Often these connections have to be emotionally explored within the context of consciousness-raising before we can assert them theoretically. In this crucial sense, reason does not operate independently of our emotions, and an Enlightenment rationalism which would pull them apart into separate spheres makes it hard to illuminate the mode of learning in either consciousness-raising or therapy. My own sense of authority might be connected with not having a strong sense of who I felt myself to be, so that I tend to be adaptive, what others expect me to be. This, in turn, at a deeper level, probably relates to not having had a father to relate to in critical years when I needed to learn "how to be a man."

In less acute forms, a sense of the absent father is experienced by many children as they grow up, as men are often unavailable, either being tied up at work or else being emotionally inaccessible.[2] But it also relates to a schooling within which "doing well" meant doing what was expected of you and conforming to rules that were externally set. In this way, the rules of the school exist as a microcosm of the rules of the larger society which dictate their own notion of "normality." As men, we have often built strong "egos" around individual achievement and success, but, paradoxically, we can be left with a relatively weak sense of "identity." It is hard to generalize, but, at some level, we are taught to *do*, not to *be*. So we often develop a weakened sense of what we want and need individually. If anything, we often tend to be scared of pleasure, of getting what we need from others in our relationships. At some level, this can leave us feeling resentful, because we have never learned how to ask for what we need.

Rather, as men, we are brought up to be "independent" and "self-sufficient," which means that we should not really want anything from others. Of course, these patterns vary enormously between different masculinities, but particular aspects also resonate across, so it is not enough simply to describe different masculinities. So for a particular style of adaptive masculinity, we tend to do what others expect of us, thinking that others should not grumble or complain since we are doing what they want. This makes us feel easier with a leftist theory that does not touch us too personally and that is ready to externalize all our feelings and thoughts. This does not help us grow or develop individually, but we do not really learn to care about this. Other things are more important, and we have to be ready to "get on with them."

As I learn to value my own experience, I am more open to learning from others. I am aware of different masculinities and of the different ways that they have dealt with authority at home and at school. Some of us challenge this authority directly. Others of us feel easier avoiding it, pretending that it is not there. Some of us feel very insecure if it is not there, though we complain about it a lot. Often these patterns reproduce themselves within political groups. I also grasped the different ways we have been forced to limit and compromise our "individuality," in order to be what others expected of us. These are different ways we have sacrificed our personal power and limited ourselves.

I often fear that if I let people know what I am "really like," then they would see what a nasty, resentful, and revengeful person I am. This is part of a Protestant inheritance. Sometimes we do not want to take the risk of showing more of ourselves. We do not want to be hurt again. So we "present ourselves" in a way that is acceptable to others, creating some kind of "inner space" within which "I can truly be myself." We take this disjunction between "inner" and "outer" so much for granted that we do not expect to be able to express our inner selves, or recognize that this could be a path of development. In different ways, we have learned not to expect much from life. We have learned to protect ourselves so that we keep what is precious to us hidden, often even to ourselves. It is difficult to escape the notion, as men, that others would put us down and prove themselves at our expense if our guard were down and we gave them half a chance. But we can also lose a sense of what we are struggling for and how we want and need to change. . . .

MEN, SELF-DENIAL, AND MORALISM

Often, as men, we have been brought up to be very hard on ourselves. As I have shown, we redefine the nature of happiness, so that we relate to happiness as if it is some kind of "reward" for reaching goals that we have set for ourselves. As Freud knew, we have little sense of the sacrifices in terms of our sexuality and emotional lives that the culture has forced us to make. The culture has moved us out of touch with our feelings and emotions so that we have difficulty connecting with what we are feeling and experiencing. We tend to locate ourselves through our rationality and intellectual understanding, keeping ourselves, as men, emotionally distant and uninvolved.

Often this means that we are really "living in our heads," unable to respond directly and emotionally, even when we want to. We are not magically different once the bedroom door closes. We discover ourselves trapped in our intellectuality, especially as middle-class men, brought up to identify our "selves" so closely with our rationality. For so long, we have been brought up within a capitalist moral culture that reproduces a secularized form of Protestantism, despises weakness and dependency, and identifies with "independence" and "self-sufficiency," that we become scared of acknowledging our needs for others. Some part of us is afraid that our emotional needs are so overwhelming that, if they were given even modified expression, they would simply crush any relationship we are in. This is scary. We prefer to be slightly aloof and distant, making sure that we can rationally defend our emotions before we can allow ourselves to acknowledge them, even though this makes it difficult for our relationships to deepen.

As men, we have been very deeply socialized into a capitalist culture of self-denial and individual ambition, from a very early age. We are competing from the very beginning in the womb. There are all kinds of dreams and expectations laid upon us about who we should be, or who we should become. We continually have to prove ourselves, for masculinity is something that cannot be taken for granted. Within a Protestant ethic, we learn that our natures are "rotten" or "bad," so that we continually have to prove that we are "other" than our natures dictate. We have to cope with incessant parental voices, that have become part of our unconscious, saying, "I always knew that you would end up as a nothing"; "I always knew that you were a worthless good-for-nothing"; "I always knew that you weren't as good as your brother." Whatever we do, we seem plagued by a feeling of worthlessness. We think that we are not good enough and, beneath the surface, it seems difficult to sustain our self-esteem.

At one level, this seems different from the strong and self-confident male able to cope with every situation. It is the other side of the coin that is constantly pushing us on, making us feel that we are never doing enough and that whatever we achieve could somehow be better done by others. The idea that "if it isn't excellent, then it isn't worth doing" operates as another way of poisoning our creativity and expression. We are continually scared of the judgments of others, and sometimes we put ourselves down as a preemptive move before they have a chance.

Sometimes we compete hard, closing off ourselves and our sensitivity so we can handle the situation and make ourselves invulnerable. At others, we refuse to compete and we are constantly putting others down and hiding our resentments of them. We are plagued by often unacknowledged jealousies, by the fear that others are better than us. Often our personal identities are brittle, as they are not built upon very firm foundations. If we remain aware of the underside of our experience, often we do not want to share it because this will reflect back upon the images of ourselves we are seeking to sustain in public. If we wish to share more, often we only feel easy enough with a couple of pints inside of us.

Self-denial goes along with a strong strain of masochism in the formation of male identity within a secularized Protestant moral culture. We constantly punish ourselves for not being good enough, not doing enough. With the early feminist challenges to sexual relationships, it was easy as men to punish ourselves for not even feeling enough, or feeling the wrong things. We found it difficult to deal with our feelings of jealousy and possessiveness and competitiveness, believing we should not be having these feelings at all. This did its own damage. In its own way, this just turned the screw even tighter. One way out was to feel even less. This did more damage to our experience. . . .

Notes

1. A useful historical account of the development of the gay movement is provided by Jeffrey Weeks's *Coming Out: Homosexual Politics in Britain*. See also his *Sex, Politics, and Society: The Regulation of Sexuality since 1800*. For accounts that focus more explicitly upon a lesbian experience, see Lillian Faderman, *Surpassing the Love of Men*; E. M. Ettorre, *Lesbians, Women, and Society*; D. G. Wolfe, *The Lesbian Community*.

2. For some different reflections on the implications of the absent father for the growth and development of children, see Alexander Mitscherlich, *Society Without the Father* (New York: Harcourt, Brace, 1963), Max Horkheimer, "Authority and the Family," in his *Critical Theory—Selected Essays* (New York: Continuum Publishing Co., 1972) and Victor J. Seidler's "Fathering, Authority and Masculinity," in *Male Order—Unwrapping Masculinity*, ed. K. Chapman and J. Rutherford (London: Lawrence & Wishart, 1988). For more Jungian inspired reflections, see *The Father*, ed. Andrew Samuel (London: Free Association, 1985).

SELECTION 9
FROM
Gender Trouble

JUDITH BUTLER

THE COMPULSORY ORDER OF SEX/GENDER/DESIRE

ALTHOUGH THE UNPROBLEMATIC UNITY of "women" is often invoked to construct a solidarity of identity, a split is introduced in the feminist subject by the distinction between sex and gender. Originally intended to dispute the biology-is-destiny formulation, the distinction between sex and gender serves the argument that whatever biological intractability sex appears to have, gender is culturally constructed: hence, gender is neither the causal result of sex nor as seemingly fixed as sex. The unity of the subject is thus already potentially contested by the distinction that permits of gender as a multiple interpretation of sex.[1]

If gender is the cultural meanings that the sexed body assumes, then a gender cannot be said to follow from a sex in any one way. Taken to its logical limit, the sex/gender distinction suggests a radical discontinuity between sexed bodies and culturally constructed genders. Assuming for the moment the stability of binary sex, it does not follow that the construction of "men" will accrue exclusively to the bodies of males or that "women" will interpret only female bodies. Further, even if the sexes appear to be unproblematically binary in their morphology and constitution (which will become a question), there is no reason to assume that genders ought also to remain as two.[2] The presumption of a binary gender system implicitly retains the belief in a mimetic relation of gender to sex whereby gender mirrors sex or is otherwise restricted by it. When the constructed status of gender is theorized as radically independent of sex, gender itself becomes a free-floating artifice, with the consequence that *man* and *masculine* might just as easily signify a female body as a male one, and *woman* and *feminine* a male body as easily as a female one.

This radical splitting of the gendered subject poses yet another set of problems. Can we refer to a "given" sex or a "given" gender without first inquiring into how sex and/or gender is given, through what means? And what is "sex" anyway? Is is natural, anatomical, chromosomal, or hormonal, and how is a feminist critic to assess the scientific discourses which purport to establish such "facts" for us?[3] Does sex have a history?[4] Does each sex have a different history, or histories? Is there a history of how the duality of sex was established, a genealogy that might expose the binary options as a variable construction? Are the ostensibly natural facts of sex discursively produced by various scientific discourses in the service of other political and social interests? If the immutable character of sex is contested, perhaps this construct called "sex" is as culturally constructed as gender; indeed, perhaps it was always already gender, with the consequence that the distinction between sex and gender turns out to be no distinction at all.[5]

It would make no sense, then, to define gender as the cultural interpretation of sex, if sex itself is a gendered category. Gender ought not to be conceived merely as the cultural inscription of meaning on a pregiven sex (a juridical conception); gender must also designate the very apparatus of production whereby the sexes themselves are established. As a result, gender is not to culture as sex is to nature; gender is also the discursive/cultural means by which "sexed nature" or "a natural sex" is produced and established as "prediscursive," prior to culture, a politically neutral surface *on which* culture acts. . . . At this juncture it is already clear that one way the internal stability and binary frame for sex is effectively secured is by casting the duality of sex in a prediscursive domain. This production of sex *as* the prediscursive ought to be understood as the effect of the apparatus of cultural construction designated by *gender*. How, then, does gender need to be reformulated to encompass the power relations that produce the effect of a prediscursive sex and so conceal that very operation of discursive production?

GENDER: THE CIRCULAR RUINS OF CONTEMPORARY DEBATE

Is there "a" gender which persons are said *to have*, or is it an essential attribute that a person is said *to be*, as implied in the question "What gender are you?"? When feminist theorists claim that gender is the cultural interpretation of sex or that gender is culturally constructed, what is the manner or mechanism of this construction? If gender is constructed, could it be constructed differently, or does its constructedness imply some form of social determinism, foreclosing the possibility of agency and transformation? Does "construction" suggest that certain laws generate gender differences along universal axes of sexual difference? How and where does the construction of gender take place? What sense can we make of a construction that cannot assume a human constructor prior to that construction? On some accounts, the notion that gender is constructed suggests a certain determinism of gender meanings inscribed on anatomically differentiated bodies, where those bodies are understood as passive recipients of an inexorable cultural law. When the relevant "culture" that "constructs" gender is understood in terms of such a law or set of laws, then it seems that gender is as determined and fixed as it was under the biology-is-destiny formulation. In such a case, not biology, but culture, becomes destiny.

On the other hand, Simone de Beauvoir suggests in *The Second Sex* that "one is not born a woman, but, rather, becomes one."[6] For Beauvoir, gender is "constructed," but implied in her formulation is an agent, a *cogito*, who somehow takes on or appropriates that gender and could, in principle, take on some other gender. Is gender as variable and volitional as Beauvoir's account seems to suggest? Can "construction" in such a case be reduced to a form of choice? Beauvoir is clear that one "becomes" a woman, but always under a cultural compulsion to become one. And clearly, the compulsion does not come from "sex." There is nothing in her account that guarantees that the "one" who becomes a woman is necessarily female. If "the body is a situation,"[7] as she claims, there is no recourse to a body that has not always already been interpreted by cultural meanings; hence, sex could not qualify as a prediscursive anatomical facticity. Indeed, sex, by definition, will be shown to have been gender all along.[8]

The controversy over the meaning of *construction* appears to founder on the conventional philosophical polarity between free will and determinism. As a consequence, one might reasonably suspect that some common linguistic restriction on thought both forms and limits the terms of the debate. Within those terms, "the body" appears as a passive medium on which cultural meanings are inscribed or as the instrument through which an appropriative and interpretive will determines a cultural meaning for itself. In either case, the body is figured as a mere *instrument* or *medium* for which a set of cultural meanings are only externally related. But "the body" it itself a construction, as are the myriad "bodies" that constitute the domain of gendered subjects. Bodies cannot be said to have a signifiable existence prior to the mark of their gender; the question then emerges: To what extent does the body *come into being* in and through the mark(s) of gender? How do we reconceive the body no longer as a passive medium or instrument awaiting the enlivening capacity of a distinctly immaterial will?[9]

Whether gender or sex is fixed or free is a function of a discourse which, it will be suggested, seeks to set certain limits to analysis or to safeguard certain tenets of humanism as presuppositional to any analysis of gender. The locus of intractability, whether in "sex" or "gender" or in the very meaning of "construction," provides a clue to what cultural possibilities can

and cannot become mobilized through any further analysis. The limits of
the discursive analysis of gender presuppose and preempt the possibilities of
imaginable and realizable gender configurations within culture. This is not
to say that any and all gendered possibilities are open, but that the boundaries
of analysis suggest the limits of a discursively conditioned experience. These
limits are always set within the terms of a hegemonic cultural discourse
predicated on binary structures that appear as the language of universal
rationality. Constraint is thus built into what that language constitutes as
the imaginable domain of gender. . . .

The contemporary feminist debates over essentialism raise the question
of the universality of female identity and masculinist oppression in other
ways. Universalistic claims are based on a common or shared epistemological
standpoint, understood as the articulated consciousness or shared structures
of oppression or in the ostensibly transcultural structures of femininity,
maternity, sexuality, and/or *écriture feminine*. The opening discussion in this
chapter argued that this globalizing gesture has spawned a number of criticisms
from women who claim that the category of "women" is normative and
exclusionary and is invoked with the unmarked dimensions of class and
racial privilege intact. In other words, the insistence upon the coherence
and unity of the category of women has effectively refused the multiplicity
of cultural, social, and political intersections in which the concrete array of
"women" are constructed.

Some efforts have been made to formulate coalitional politics which do
not assume in advance what the content of "women" will be. They propose
instead a set of dialogic encounters by which variously positioned women
articulate separate identities within the framework of an emergent coalition.
Clearly, the value of coalitional politics is not to be underestimated, but
the very form of coalition, of an emerging and unpredictable assemblage of
positions, cannot be figured in advance. Despite the clearly democratizing
impulse that motivates coalition building, the coalitional theorist can
inadvertently reinsert herself as sovereign of the process by trying to assert
an ideal form for coalitional structures *in advance*, one that will effectively
guarantee unity as the outcome. Related efforts to determine what is and is
not the true shape of a dialogue, what constitutes a subject-position, and,
most important, when "unity" has been reached, can impede the self-shaping
and self-limiting dynamics of coalition.

The insistence in advance on coalitional "unity" as a goal assumes that
solidarity, whatever its price, is a prerequisite for political action. But what
sort of politics demands that kind of advance purchase on unity? Perhaps a
coalition needs to acknowledge its contradictions and take action with those
contradictions intact. Perhaps also part of what dialogic understanding entails
is the acceptance of divergence, breakage, splinter, and fragmentation as

part of the often tortuous process of democratization. The very notion of "dialogue" is culturally specific and historically bound, and while one speaker may feel secure that a conversation is happening, another may be sure it is not. The power relations that condition and limit dialogic possibilities need first to be interrogated. Otherwise, the model of dialogue risks relapsing into a liberal model that assumes that speaking agents occupy equal positions of power and speak with the same presuppositions about what constitutes "agreement" and "unity" and, indeed, that those are the goals to be sought. It would be wrong to assume in advance that there is a category of "women" that simply needs to be filled in with various components of race, class, age, ethnicity, and sexuality in order to become complete. The assumption of its essential incompleteness permits that category to serve as a permanently available site of contested meanings. The definitional incompleteness of the category might then serve as a normative ideal relieved of coercive force.

Is "unity" necessary for effective political action? Is the premature insistence on the goal of unity precisely the cause of an ever more bitter fragmentation among the ranks? Certain forms of acknowledged fragmentation might faciliate coalitional action precisely because the "unity" of the category of women is neither presupposed nor desired. Does "unity" set up an exclusionary norm of solidarity at the level of identity that rules out the possibility of a set of actions which disrupt the very borders of identity concepts, or which seek to accomplish precisely that disruption as an explicit political aim? Without the presupposition or goal of "unity," which is, in either case, always instituted at a conceptual level, provisional unities might emerge in the context of concrete actions that have purposes other than that articulation of identity. Without the compulsory expectation that feminist actions must be instituted from some stable, unified, and agreed-upon identity, those actions might well get a quicker start and seem more congenial to a number of "women" for whom the meaning of the category is permanently moot.

This antifoundationalist approach to coalitional politics assumes neither that "identity" is a premise nor that the shape or meaning of a coalitional assemblage can be known prior to its achievement. Because the articulation of an identity within available cultural terms instates a definition that forecloses in advance the emergence of new identity concepts in and through politically engaged actions, the foundationalist tactic cannot take the transformation or expansion of existing identity concepts as a normative goal. Moreover, when agreed-upon identities or agreed-upon dialogic structures, through which already established identities are communicated, no longer constitute the theme or subject of politics, then identities can come into being and dissolve depending on the concrete practices that constitute them. Certain political practices institute identities on a contingent basis in order to accomplish whatever aims are in view. Coalitional politics requires neither an expanded category of "women" nor an internally multiplicitous self that offers its complexity at once.

Gender is a complexity whose totality is permanently deferred, never fully what it is at any given juncture in time. An open coalition, then, will affirm identities that are alternately instituted and relinquished according to the purposes at hand; it will be an open assemblage that permits of multiple convergences and divergences without obedience to a normative telos of definitional closure.

IDENTITY, SEX, AND THE METAPHYSICS OF SUBSTANCE

What can be meant by "identity," then, and what grounds the presumption that identifies are self-identical, persisting through time as the same, unified and internally coherent? More important, how do these assumptions inform the discourses on "gender identity"? It would be wrong to think that the discussion of "identity" ought to proceed prior to a discussion of gender identity for the simple reason that "persons" only become intelligible through becoming gendered in conformity with recognizable standards of gender intelligibility. Sociological discussions have conventionally sought to understand the notion of the person in terms of an agency that claims ontological priority to the various roles and functions through which it assumes social visibility and meaning. Within philosophical discourse itself, the notion of "the person" has received analytic elaboration on the assumption that whatever social context the person is "in" remains somehow externally related to the definitional structure of personhood, be that consciousness, the capacity for language, or moral deliberation. Although that literature is not examined here, one premise of such inquiries is the focus of critical exploration and inversion. Whereas the question of what constitutes "personal identity" within philosophical accounts almost always centers on the question of what internal feature of the person establishes the continuity or self-identity of the person through time, the question here will be: To what extent do *regulatory practices* of gender formation and division constitute identity, the internal coherence of the subject, indeed, the self-identical status of the person? To what extent is "identity" a normative ideal rather than a descriptive feature of experience? And how do the regulatory practices that govern gender also govern culturally intelligible notions of identity? In other words, the "coherence" and "continuity" of "the person" are not logical or analytic features of personhood, but, rather, socially instituted and maintained norms of intelligibility. Inasmuch as "identity" is assured through the stabilizing concepts of sex, gender, and sexuality, the very notion of "the person" is called into question by the cultural emergence of those "incoherent" or "discontinuous" gendered beings who appear to be persons but who fail to conform to the gendered norms of cultural intelligibility by which persons are defined.

"Intelligible" genders are those which in some sense institute and maintain relations of coherence and continuity among sex, gender, sexual practice, and desire. In other words, the specters of discontinuity and incoherence, themselves thinkable only in relation to existing norms of continuity and coherence, are constantly prohibited and produced by the very laws that seek to establish causal or expressive lines of connection among biological sex, culturally constituted genders, and the "expression" or "effect" of both in the manifestation of sexual desire through sexual practice.

The notion that there might be a "truth" of sex, as Foucault ironically terms it, is produced precisely through the regulatory practices that generate coherent identities through the matrix of coherent gender norms. The heterosexualization of desire requires and institutes the production of discrete and asymmetrical oppositions between "feminine" and "masculine," where these are understood as expressive attributes of "male" and "female." The cultural matrix through which gender identity has become intelligible requires that certain kinds of "identities" cannot "exist"—that is, those in which gender does not follow from sex and those in which the practices of desire do not "follow" from either sex or gender. "Follow" in this context is a political relation of entailment instituted by the cultural laws that establish and regulate the shape and meaning of sexuality. Indeed, precisely because certain kinds of "gender identities" fail to conform to those norms of cultural intelligibility, they appear only as developmental failures or logical impossibilities from within that domain. Their persistence and proliferation, however, provide critical opportunities to expose the limits and regulatory aims of that domain of intelligibility and, hence, to open up within the very terms of that matrix of intelligibility rival and subversive matrices of gender disorder. . . .

If there is no recourse to a "person," a "sex," or a "sexuality" that escapes the matrix of power and discursive relations that effectively produce and regulate the intelligibility of those concepts for us, what constitutes the possibility of effective inversion, subversion, or displacement within the terms of a constructed identity? What possibilities exist *by virtue of* the constructed character of sex and gender? . . . If the regulatory fictions of sex and gender are themselves multiply contested sites of meaning, then the very multiplicity of their construction holds out the possibility of a disruption of their univocal posturing.

Clearly this project does not propose to lay out within traditional philosophical terms an *ontology* of gender whereby the meaning of *being* a woman or a man is elucidated within the terms of phenomenology. The presumption here is that the "being" of gender is *an effect*, an object of a genealogical investigation that maps out the political parameters of its construction in the mode of ontology. To claim that gender is constructed is not to assert its illusoriness or artificiality, where those terms are understood to reside within a binary that counterposes the "real" and the "authentic" as oppositional. As a genealogy of gender ontology, this inquiry seeks to understand the discursive production of the plausibility of that binary relation and to suggest that certain cultural configurations of gender take the place of "the real" and consolidate and augment their hegemony through that felicitous self-naturalization.

If there is something right in Beauvoir's claim that one is not born, but rather *becomes* a woman, it follows that *woman* itself is a term in process, a becoming, a constructing that cannot rightfully be said to originate or to end. As an ongoing discursive practice, it is open to intervention and resignification. Even when gender seems to congeal into the most reified forms, the "congealing" is itself an insistent and insidious practice, sustained and regulated by various social means. It is, for Beauvoir, never possible finally to become a woman, as if there were a *telos* that governs the process of acculturation and construction. Gender is the repeated stylization of the body, a set of repeated acts within a highly rigid regulatory frame that congeal over time to produce the appearance of substance, of a natural sort of being. A political genealogy of gender ontologies, if it is successful, will deconstruct the substantive appearance of gender into its constitutive acts and locate and account for those acts within the compulsory frames set by the various forces that police the social appearance of gender. To expose the contingent acts that create the appearance of a naturalistic necessity, a move which has been a part of cultural critique at least since Marx, is a task that now takes on the added burden of showing how the very notion of the subject, intelligible only through its appearance as gendered, admits of possibilities that have been forcibly foreclosed by the various reifications of gender that have constituted its contingent ontologies. . . .

Notes

1. For a discussion of the sex/gender distinction in structuralist anthropology and feminist appropriations and criticisms of that formulation, see ch. 2, sec. 1, "Structuralism's Critical Exchange."
2. For an interesting study of the *berdache* and multiple-gender arrangements in Native American cultures, see Walter L. Williams, *The Spirit and the Flesh: Sexual Diversity in American Indian Culture* (Boston: Beacon Press, 1988). See also Sherry B. Ortner and Harriet Whitehead, eds., *Sexual Meanings: The Cultural Construction of Sexuality* (New York: Cambridge University Press, 1981). For a politically sensitive and provocative analysis of the *berdache*, transsexuals, and the contingency of gender dichotomies, see Suzanne J. Kessler and Wendy McKenna, *Gender: An Ethnomethodological Approach* (Chicago: University of Chicago Press, 1978).

3. A great deal of feminist research has been conducted within the fields of biology and the history of science that assess the political interests inherent in the various discriminatory procedures that establish the scientific basis for sex. See Ruth Hubbard and Marian Lowe, eds., *Genes and Gender*, vols. 1 and 2 (New York: Gordian Press, 1978, 1979); the two issues on feminism and science of *Hypatia: A Journal of Feminist Philosophy* 2, no. 3 (Fall 1987), and vol. 3, no. 1 (Spring 1988), and especially the Biology and Gender Study Group, "The Importance of Feminist Critique for Contemporary Cell Biology" in this last issue (Spring 1988); Sandra Harding, *The Science Question in Feminism* (Ithaca: Cornell University Press, 1986); Evelyn FoxKeller, *Reflections on Gender and Science* (New Haven: Yale University Press, 1984); Donna Haraway, "In the Beginning Was the Word: The Genesis of Biological Theory," *Signs: Journal of Women in Culture and Society* 6, no. 3, 1981; Donna Haraway, *Primate Visions* (New York: Routledge, 1989); Sandra Harding and Jean F. O'Barr, *Sex and Scientific Inquiry* (Chicago: University of Chicago Press, 1987); Anne Fausto-Sterling, *Myths of Gender: Biological Theories about Women and Men* (New York: Norton, 1979).

4. Clearly Foucault's *History of Sexuality* offers one way to rethink the history of "sex" within a given modern Eurocentric context. For a more detailed consideration, see Thomas Lacquer and Catherine Gallagher, eds., *The Making of the Modern Body: Sexuality and Society in the 19th Century* (Berkeley: University of California Press, 1987), originally published as an issue of *Representations*, no. 14 (Spring 1986).

5. See my "Variations on Sex and Gender: Beauvoir, Wittig, Foucault," in *Feminism as Critique*, ed. Seyla Benhabib and Drucilla Cornell (Basil Blackwell, dist. by University of Minnesota Press, 1987).

6. Simone de Beauvoir, *The Second Sex*, tr. E. M. Parshley (New York: Vintage, 1973), 301.

7. Ibid., 38.

8. See my "Sex and Gender in Beauvoir's *Second Sex*," *Yale French Studies, Simone de Beauvoir: Witness to a Century*, no. 72 (Winter 1986).

9. Note the extent to which phenomenological theories such as Sartre's, Merleau Ponty's, and Beauvoir's tend to use the term *embodiment*. Drawn as it is from theological contexts, the term tends to figure "the" body as a mode of incarnation and, hence, to preserve the external and dualistic relationship between a signifying immateriality and the materiality of the body itself.

PART II

Gender, Oppression, and Sexual Identity

SELECTION 10
FROM
The Politics of Reality

MARILYN FRYE

IT IS A FUNDAMENTAL claim of feminism that women are oppressed. The word 'oppression' is a strong word. It repels and attracts. It is dangerous and dangerously fashionable and endangered. It is much misused, and sometimes not innocently.

The statement that women are oppressed is frequently met with the claim that men are oppressed too. We hear that oppressing is oppressive to those who oppress as well as to those they oppress. Some men cite as evidence of their oppression their much-advertised inability to cry. It is tough, we are told, to be masculine. When the stresses and frustrations of being a man are cited as evidence that oppressors are oppressed by their oppressing, the word 'oppression' is being stretched to meaninglessness; it is treated as though its scope includes any and all human experience of limitation or suffering, no matter the cause, degree, or consequence. Once such usage has been put over on us, then if ever we deny that any person or group is oppressed, we seem to imply that we think they never suffer and have no feelings. We are accused of insensitivity; even of bigotry. For women, such accusation is particularly intimidating, since sensitivity is one of the few virtues that has been assigned to us. If we are found insensitive, we may fear we have no redeeming traits at all and perhaps are not real women. Thus are we silenced before we begin: the name of our situation drained of meaning and our guilt mechanisms tripped.

But this is nonsense. Human beings can be miserable without being oppressed, and it is perfectly consistent to deny that a person or group is oppressed without denying that they have feelings or that they suffer.

We need to think clearly about oppression, and there is much that mitigates against this. I do not want to undertake to prove that women are oppressed (or that men are not), but I want to make clear what is being said when we say it. We need this word, this concept, and we need it to be sharp and sure.

I

The root of the word 'oppression' is the element 'press'. *The press of the crowd; pressed into military service; to press a pair of pants; printing press; press the button.* Presses are used to mold things or flatten them or reduce them in bulk, sometimes to reduce them by squeezing out the gasses or liquids in them. Something pressed is something caught between or among forces and barriers which are so related to each other that jointly they restrain, restrict, or prevent the thing's motion or mobility. Mold, Immobilize. Reduce.

The mundane experience of the oppressed provides another clue. One of the most characteristic and ubiquitous features of the world as experienced by oppressed people is the double bind—situations in which options are reduced to a very few and all of them expose one to penalty, censure, or deprivation. For example, it is often a requirement upon oppressed people that we smile and be cheerful. If we comply, we signal our docility and our acquiescence in our situation. We need not, then, be taken note of. We acquiesce in being made invisible, in our occupying no space. We participate in our own erasure. On the other hand, anything but the sunniest countenance exposes us to being perceived as mean, bitter, angry, or dangerous. This means, at the least, that we may be found "difficult" or unpleasant to work with, which is enough to cost one one's livelihood; at worst, being seen as mean, bitter, angry, or dangerous has been known to result in rape, arrest, beating, and murder. One can only choose to risk one's preferred form and rate of annihilation.

Another example: It is common in the United States that women, especially younger women, are in a bind where neither sexual activity nor sexual inactivity is all right. If she is heterosexually active, a woman is open to censure and punishment for being loose, unprincipled, or a whore. The "punishment" comes in the form of criticism, snide and embarrassing remarks, being treated as an easy lay by men, scorn from her more restrained female friends. She may have to lie and hide her behavior from her parents. She must juggle the risks of unwanted pregnancy and dangerous contraceptives. On the other hand, if she refrains from heterosexual activity, she is fairly constantly harassed by men who try to persuade her into it and pressure her to "relax" and "let her hair down"; she is threatened with labels like "frigid," "uptight," "man-hater," "bitch," and "cocktease." The same parents who would be disapproving of her sexual activity may be worried by her inactivity because it suggests she is not or will not be popular, or is not sexually normal. She may be charged with lesbianism. If a woman is raped, then if she has been heterosexually active she is subject to the presumption that she liked it (since her activity is presumed to show that she likes sex), and if she has not been heterosexually active, she is subject to the presumption that she liked it (since she is supposedly "repressed and frustrated"). Both heterosexual activity and heterosexual nonactivity are likely to be taken as proof that you wanted to be raped, and hence, of course, weren't *really* raped at all. You can't win. You are caught in a bind, caught between systematically related pressures.

Women are caught like this, too, by networks of forces and barriers that expose one to penalty, loss, or contempt whether one works outside the home or not, is on welfare or not, bears children or not, raises children or not, marries or not, stays married or not, is heterosexual, lesbian, both, or neither. Economic necessity; confinement to racial and/or sexual job ghettos; sexual harassment; sex discrimination; pressures of competing expectations and judgments about *women*, *wives*, and *mothers* (in the society at large, in racial and ethnic subcultures, and in one's own mind); dependence (full or partial) on husbands, parents, or the state; commitment to political ideas; loyalties to racial or ethnic or other "minority" groups; the demands of self-respect and responsibilities to others. Each of these factors exists in complex tension with every other, penalizing or prohibiting all of the apparently available options. And nipping at one's heels, always, is the endless pack of little things. If one dresses one way, one is subject to the assumption that one is advertising one's sexual availability; if one dresses another way, one appears to "not care about oneself" or to be "unfeminine." If one uses "strong language," one invites categorization as a whore or slut; if one does not, one invites categorization as a "lady"—one too delicately constituted to cope with robust speech or the realities to which it presumably refers.

The experience of oppressed people is that the living of one's life is confined and shaped by forces and barriers which are not accidental or occasional and hence avoidable, but are systematically related to each other in such a way as to catch one between and among them and restrict or penalize motion in any direction. It is the experience of being caged in: all avenues, in every direction, are blocked or booby-trapped.

Cages. Consider a birdcage. If you look very closely at just one wire in the cage, you cannot see the other wires. If your conception of what is before you is determined by this myopic focus, you could look at that one wire, up and down the length of it, and be unable to see why a bird would not just fly around the wire any time it wanted to go somewhere. Furthermore, even if, one day at a time, you myopically inspected each wire, you still could not see why a bird would have trouble going past the wires to get anywhere. There is no physical property of any one wire, *nothing* that the closest scrutiny could discover, that will reveal how a bird could be inhibited or harmed by it except in the most accidental way. It is only when you step back, stop looking at the wires one by one, microscopically, and take a macroscopic view of the whole cage, that you can see why the bird does not go anywhere; and then you will see it in a moment. It will require no great subtlety of mental powers. It is perfectly *obvious* that the bird is surrounded by a network of systematically related barriers, no one of which would be the least hindrance to its flight, but which, by their relations to each other, are as confining as the solid walls of a dungeon.

It is now possible to grasp one of the reasons why oppression can be hard to see and recognize: one can study the elements of an oppressive structure with great care and some goodwill without seeing the structure as a whole, and hence without seeing or being able to understand that one is looking at a cage and that there are people there who are caged, whose motion and mobility are restricted, whose lives are shaped and reduced.

The arresting of vision at a microscopic level yields such common confusion as that about the male door-opening ritual. This ritual, which is remarkably widespread across classes and races, puzzles many people, some of whom do and some of whom do not find it offensive. Look at the scene of the two people approaching a door. The male steps slightly ahead and opens the door. The male holds the door open while the female glides through. Then the male goes through. The door closes after them. "Now how," one innocently asks, "can those crazy womenslibbers say that is oppressive? The guy *removed* a barrier to the lady's smooth and unruffled progress." But each repetition of this ritual has a place in a pattern, in fact in several patterns. One has to shift the level of one's perception in order to see the whole picture.

The door-opening pretends to be a helpful service, but the helpfulness is false. This can be seen by noting that it will be done whether or not it makes any practical sense. Infirm men and men burdened with packages will open doors for able-bodied women who are free of physical burdens. Men will impose themselves awkwardly and jostle everyone in order to get to the door first. The act is not determined by convenience or grace. Furthermore, these very numerous acts of unneeded or even noisome "help" occur in counterpoint to a pattern of men not being helpful in many practical ways in which women might welcome help. What *women* experience is a world in which gallant princes charming commonly make a fuss about being helpful and providing small services when help and services are of little or no use, but in which there are rarely ingenious and adroit princes at hand when substantial assistance is really wanted either in mundane affairs or in situations of threat, assault, or terror. There is no help with the (his) laundry; no help typing a report at 4:00 A.M.; no help in mediating disputes among relatives or children. There is nothing but advice that women should stay indoors after dark, be chaperoned by a man, or when it comes down to it, "lie back and enjoy it."

The gallant gestures have no practical meaning. Their meaning is symbolic. The door-opening and similar services provided are services which really are needed by people who are for one reason or another incapacitated—unwell, burdened with parcels, etc. So the message is that women are incapable. The detachment of the acts from the concrete realities of what women need and do not need is a vehicle for the message that women's actual needs and interests are unimportant or irrelevant. Finally, these gestures imitate the behavior of servants toward masters and thus mock women, who are in most respects the servants and caretakers of men. The message of the false helpfulness of male gallantry is female dependence, the invisibility or insignificance of women, and contempt for women.

One cannot see the meanings of these rituals if one's focus is riveted upon the individual event in all its particularity, including the particularity of the individual man's present conscious intentions and motives and the individual woman's conscious perception of the event in the moment. It seems sometimes that people take a deliberately myopic view and fill their eyes with things seen microscopically in order not to see macroscopically. At any rate, whether it is deliberate or not, people can and do fail to see the oppression of women because they fail to see macroscopically and hence fail to see the various elements of the situation as systematically related in larger schemes.

As the cageness of the birdcage is a macroscopic phenomenon, the oppressiveness of the situations in which women live our various and different lives is a macroscopic phenomenon. Neither can be *seen* from a microscopic perspective. But when you look macroscopically you can see it—a network of forces and barriers which are systematically related and which conspire to the immobilization, reduction, and molding of women and the lives we live.

II

The image of the cage helps convey one aspect of the systematic nature of oppression. Another is the selection of occupants of the cages, and analysis of this aspect also helps account for the invisibility of the oppression of women.

It is as a woman (or as a Chicana/o or as a black or Asian or lesbian) that one is entrapped.

"Why can't I go to the park; you let Jimmy go!"
"Because it's not safe for girls."

"I want to be a secretary, not a seamstress; I don't
    want to learn to make dresses."

"There's no work for negroes in that line; learn a
    skill where you can earn your living."[1]

When you question why you are being blocked, why this barrier is in your path, the answer has not to do with individual talent or merit, handicap or failure; it has to do with your membership in some category understood as a "natural" or "physical" category. The "inhabitant" of the "cage" is not an individual but a group, all those of a certain category. If an individual is oppressed, it is in virtue of being a member of a group or category of people that is systematically reduced, molded, immobilized. Thus, to recognize a person as oppressed, one has to see that individual *as* belonging to a group of a certain sort.

There are many things which can encourage or inhibit perception of someone's membership in the sort of group or category in question here. In particular, it seems reasonable to suppose that if one of the devices of restriction and definition of the group is that of physical confinement or segregation, the confinement and separation would encourage recognition of the group as a group. This in turn would encourage the macroscopic focus which enables one to recognize oppression and encourages the individuals' identification and solidarity with other individuals of the group or category. But physical confinement and segregation of the group as a group is not common to all oppressive structures, and when an oppressed group is geographically and demographically dispersed the perception of it as a group is inhibited. There may be little or nothing in the situations of the individuals encouraging the macroscopic focus which would reveal the unity of the structure bearing down on all members of that group.*

A great many people, female and male and of every race and class, simply do not believe that *woman* is a category of oppressed people, and I think that this is in part because they have been fooled by the dispersal and assimilation of women throughout and into the systems of class and race which organize men. Our simply being dispersed makes it difficult for women to have knowledge of each other and hence difficult to recognize the shape of our common cage. The dispersal and assimilation of women throughout economic classes and races also divides us against each other practically and economically and thus attaches *interest* to the inability to see: for some, jealousy of their benefits, and for some, resentment of the others' advantages.

To get past this, it helps to notice that in fact women of all races and classes *are* together in a ghetto of sorts. There is a women's place, a sector, which is inhabited by women of all classes and races, and it is not defined by geographical boundaries but by function. The function is the service of men and men's interests as men define them, which includes the bearing and rearing of children. The details of the service and the working condi-

---

*Coerced assimilation is in fact one of the *policies* available to an oppressing group in its effort to reduce and/or annihilate another group. This tactic is used by the U.S. government, for instance, on the American Indians.

tions vary by race and class, for men of different races and classes have different interests, perceive their interests differently, and express their needs and demands in different rhetorics, dialects, and languages. But there are also some constants.

Whether in lower-, middle-, or upper-class home or work situations, women's service work always includes personal service (the work of maids, butlers, cooks, personal secretaries),* sexual service (including provision for his genital sexual needs and bearing his children, but also including "being nice," "being attractive for him," etc.), and ego service (encouragement, support, praise, attention). Women's service work also is characterized everywhere by the fatal combination of responsibility and powerlessness: We are held responsible and we hold ourselves responsible for good outcomes for men and children in almost every respect though we have in almost no case power adequate to that project. The details of the subjective experience of this servitude are local. They vary with economic class and race and ethnic tradition as well as the personalities of the men in question. So also are the details of the forces which coerce our tolerance of this servitude particular to the different situations in which different women live and work.

All this is not to say that women do not have, assert, and manage sometimes to satisfy our own interests, nor to deny that in some cases and in some respects women's independent interests do overlap with men's. But at every race/class level and even across race/class lines men do not serve women as women serve men. "Women's sphere" may be understood as the "service sector," taking the latter expression much more widely and deeply than is usual in discussions of the economy.

III

It seems to be the human condition that in one degree or another we all suffer frustration and limitation, all encounter unwelcome barriers, and all are damaged and hurt in various ways. Since we are a social species, almost all of our behavior and activities are structured by more than individual inclination and the conditions of the planet and its atmosphere. No human is free of social structures, nor (perhaps) would happiness consist in such freedom. Structure consists of boundaries, limits, and barriers; in a structured whole, some motions and changes are possible, and others are not. If one is looking for an excuse to dilute the word 'oppression', one can use the fact of social structure as an excuse and say that everyone is oppressed.

---

*At higher class levels women may not *do* all these kinds of work, but are generally still responsible for hiring and supervising those who do it. These services are still, in these cases, women's responsibility.

But if one would rather get clear about what oppression is and is not, one needs to sort out the sufferings, harms, and limitations and figure out which are elements of oppression and which are not.

From what I have already said here, it is clear that if one wants to determine whether a particular suffering, harm, or limitation is part of someone's being oppressed, one has to look at it *in context* in order to tell whether it is an element in an oppressive structure: One has to see if it is part of an enclosing structure of forces and barriers which tends to the immobilization and reduction of a group or category of people. One has to look at how the barrier or force fits with others and to whose benefit or detriment it works. As soon as one looks at examples, it becomes obvious that not everything which frustrates or limits a person is oppressive, and not every harm or damage is due to or contributes to oppression.

If a rich white playboy who lives off income from his investments in South African diamond mines should break a leg in a skiing accident at Aspen and wait in pain in a blizzard for hours before he is rescued, we may assume that in that period he suffers. But the suffering comes to an end; his leg is repaired by the best surgeon money can buy and he is soon recuperating in a lavish suite, sipping Chivas Regal. Nothing in this picture suggests a structure of barriers and forces. He is a member of several oppressor groups and does not suddenly become oppressed because he is injured and in pain. Even if the accident was caused by someone's malicious negligence, and hence someone can be blamed for it and morally faulted, that person still has not been an agent of oppression.

Consider also the restriction of having to drive one's vehicle on a certain side of the road. There is no doubt that this restriction is almost unbearably frustrating at times, when one's lane is not moving and the other lane is clear. There are surely times, even, when abiding by this regulation would have harmful consequences. But the restriction is obviously wholesome for most of us most of the time. The restraint is imposed for our benefit, and does benefit us; its operation tends to encourage our *continued* motion, not to immobilize us. The limits imposed by traffic regulations are limits most of us would cheerfully imposed on ourselves given that we knew others would follow them too. They are part of a structure which shapes our behavior, not to our reduction and immobilization, but rather to the protection of our continued ability to move and act as we will.

Another example: The boundaries of a racial ghetto in an American city serve to some extent to keep white people from going in, as well as to keep ghetto dwellers from going out. A particular white citizen may be frustrated or feel deprived because s/he cannot stroll around there and enjoy the "exotic" aura of a "foreign" culture, or shop for bargains in the ghetto swap shops. In fact, the existence of the ghetto, of racial segregation, does deprive the white person of knowledge and harm her/his character by nurturing unwarranted feelings of superiority. But this does not make the white person in this situation a member of an oppressed race or a person oppressed because of her/his race. One must look at the barrier. It limits the activities and the access of those on both sides of it (though to different degrees). But it is a product of the intention, planning, and action of whites for the benefit of whites, to secure and maintain privileges that are available to whites generally, as members of the dominant and privileged group. Though the existence of the barrier has some bad consequences for whites, the barrier does not exist in systematic relationship with other barriers and forces forming a structure oppressive to whites; quite the contrary. It is part of a structure which oppresses the ghetto dwellers and thereby (and by white intention) protects and furthers white interests as dominant white culture understands them. This barrier is not oppressive to whites, even though it is a barrier to whites.

Barriers have different meanings to those on opposite sides of them, even though they are barriers to both. The physical walls of a prison no more dissolve to let an outsider in than to let an insider out, but for the insider they are confining and limiting while to the outsider they may mean protection from what s/he takes to be threats posed by insiders—freedom from harm or anxiety. A set of social and economic barriers and forces separating two groups may be felt, even painfully, by members of both groups and yet may mean confinement to one and liberty and enlargement of opportunity to the other.

The service sector of the wives/mommas/assistants/girls is almost exclusively a woman-only sector; its boundaries not only enclose women but to a very great extent keep men out. Some men sometimes encounter this barrier and experience it as a restriction on their movements, their activities, their control or their choices of "life-style." Thinking they might like the simple nurturant life (which they may imagine to be quite free of stress, alienation, and hard work), and feeling deprived since it seems closed to them, they thereupon announce the discovery that they are oppressed, too, by "sex roles." But that barrier is erected and maintained by men, for the benefit of men. It consists of cultural and economic forces and pressures in a culture and economy controlled by men in which, at every economic level and in all racial and ethnic subcultures, economy, tradition—and even ideologies of liberation—work to keep at least local culture and economy in male control.*

---

*Of course this is complicated by race and class. Machismo and "black manhood" politics seem to help keep Latin or black men in control of more cash than Latin or black women control; but these politics seem to me also to ultimately help keep the larger economy in *white* male control.

The boundary that sets apart women's sphere is maintained and promoted by men generally for the benefit of men generally, and men generally do benefit from its existence, even the man who bumps into it and complains of the inconvenience. That barrier is protecting his classification and status as a male, as superior, as having a right to sexual access to a female or females. It protects a kind of citizenship which is superior to that of females of his class and race, his access to a wider range of better-paying and higher-status work, and his right to prefer unemployment to the degradation of doing lower-status or "women's" work.

If a person's life or activity is affected by some force or barrier that person encounters, one may not conclude that the person is oppressed simply because the person encounters that barrier or force; not simply because the encounter is unpleasant, frustrating, or painful to that person at that time; nor simply because the existence of the barrier or force, or the processes which maintain or apply it, serve to deprive that person of something of value. One must look at the barrier or force and answer certain questions about it. Who constructs and maintains it? Whose interests are served by its existence? Is it part of a structure which tends to confine, reduce, and immobilize some group? Is the individual a member of the confined group? Various forces, barriers, and limitations a person may encounter or live with may be part of an oppressive structure or not, and if they are, that person may be on either the oppressed or the oppressor side of it. One cannot tell which by how loudly or how little the person complains.

IV

Many of the restrictions and limitations we live with are more or less internalized and self-monitored, and are part of our adaptations to the requirements and expectations imposed by the needs and tastes and tyrannies of others. I have in mind such things as women's cramped postures and attenuated strides and men's restraint of emotional self-expression (except for anger). Who gets what out of the practice of those disciplines, and who imposes what penalties for improper relaxations of them? What are the rewards of this self-discipline?

Can men cry? Yes, in the company of women. If a man cannot cry, it is in the company of men that he cannot cry. It is men, not women, who require this restraint; and men not only require it, they reward it. The man who maintains a steely or tough or laid-back demeanor (all are forms which suggest invulnerability) marks himself as a member of the male community and is esteemed by other men. Consequently, the maintenance of that demeanor contributes to the man's self-esteem. It is felt as good, and he can feel good about himself. The way this restriction fits into the structures of men's lives is as one of the socially required behaviors which, if carried off, contribute to their acceptance and respect by significant others and to their own self-esteem. It is to their benefit to practice this discipline.

Consider, by comparison, the discipline of women's cramped physical postures and attenuated stride. This discipline can be relaxed in the company of women; it generally is at its most strenuous in the company of men.* Like men's emotional restraint, women's physical restraint is required by men. But unlike the case of men's emotional restraint, women's physical restraint is not rewarded. What do we get for it? Respect and esteem and acceptance? No. They mock us and parody our mincing steps. We look silly, incompetent, weak, and generally contemptible. Our exercise of this discipline tends to low esteem and low self-esteem. It does not benefit us. It fits in a network of behaviors through which we constantly announce to others our membership in a lower caste and our unwillingness and/or inability to defend our bodily or moral integrity. It is degrading and part of a pattern of degradation.

Acceptable behavior for both groups, men and women, involves a required restraint that seems in itself silly and perhaps damaging. But the social effect is drastically different. The woman's restraint is part of a structure oppressive to women; the man's restraint is part of a structure oppressive to women.

V

One is marked for application of oppressive pressures by one's membership in some group or category. Much of one's suffering and frustration befalls one partly or largely because one is a member of that category. In the case at hand, it is the category, *woman*. Being a woman is a major factor in my not having a better job than I do; being a woman selects me as a likely victim of sexual assault or harassment; it is my being a woman that reduces the power of my anger to a proof of my insanity. If a woman has little or no economic or political power, or achieves little of what she wants to achieve, a major causal factor in this is that she is a woman. For any woman of any race or economic class, being a woman is significantly attached to whatever disadvantages and deprivations she suffers, be they great or small.

None of this is the case with respect to a person's being a man. Simply being a man is not what stands between him and a better job; whatever

---

*Cf. *Let's Take Back Our Space: "Female" and "Male" Body Language as a Result of Patriarchal Structures*, by Marianne Wex (West Germany: Frauenliteratureverlag Hermine Fees, 1979), especially 173. This remarkable book presents literally thousands of candid photographs of women and men, in public, seated, standing and lying down. It vividly demonstrates the very systematic differences in women's and men's postures and gestures.

assaults and harassments he is subject to, being male is not what selects him for victimization; being male is not a factor which would make his anger impotent—quite the opposite. If a man has little or no material or political power, or achieves little of what he wants to achieve, his being male is no part of the explanation. Being male is something he has going *for* him, even if race or class or age or disability is going against him.

Women are oppressed, *as women*. Members of certain racial and/or economic groups and classes, both the males and the females, are oppressed *as* members of those races and/or classes. But men are not oppressed *as men*.

. . . and isn't it strange that any of us should have been confused and mystified about such a simple thing?

Note

1. This example is derived from *Daddy Was a Number Runner*, by Louise Meriwether (Englewood Cliffs, NJ: Prentice-Hall, 1970), 144.

SELECTION 11
FROM
Femininity and Domination

SANDRA LEE BARTKY

I

CONTEMPORARY PHILOSOPHERS HAVE LARGELY abandoned an older philosophical psychology which distinguished sharply between reason and emotion and which regarded feeling as no more able than imagination or desire to determine the real nature of things. By contrast, the inextricability of cognition and emotion is now widely recognized. A number of Anglo-American philosophers have argued that our emotions presuppose beliefs and can therefore be evaluated for their rationality,[1] while in a similar vein, existential philosophers have maintained that affective states have a cognitive dimension in that they may be disclosive of a subject's "Being-in-the-world." Heidegger, for example, has claimed that every human being (*Dasein*) has, a priori, necessary features of existence, among which are understanding (*Verstehen*) and state-of-mind (*Befindlichkeit*). The latter—literally, "the state in which one may be found" (from *sich befinden*, "to find oneself")—refers both to the finding *that* one is situated in a world and to the particular *how* of this situation; this "finding" can occur only insofar as *Dasein* has moods, feelings, or humors that constitute its openness or "attunement" (*Gestimmtheit*) to Being. "A mood makes manifest 'how one is and how one is faring' "; boredom, joy, and above all dread are ontologically disclosive in ways that a passionless pure beholding can never be.[2] These and other states of mind constitute a primordial disclosure of self and world whereby "we can encounter something that matters to us": Indeed, insofar as emotional attunement is held to be an a priori, necessary feature of any possible human existence, it follows that pure acts of cognition are themselves impossible and that knowing will have its own affective taste.[3]

Women are situated differently than men within the ensemble of social relations. For this reason, feminist philosophers have argued that women's ways of knowing are different than men's, that both the specific character of the world's disclosure as well as the modes of this disclosure are in some, though not in all important ways gender-specific and that the abstract, purportedly genderless epistemic subject of traditional philosophy is really a male subject in disguise.[4] Now if knowing cannot be described in ways that are gender-neutral, neither can feeling. Differences between men and women are most often described in the language of character traits or dispositions: It is often said of women, for example, that they are less assertive than men, more preoccupied with their appearance, etc. But what is not captured by the language of disposition is the affective taste of a low level of assertion or a sense of the larger emotional constellation in which a feminine preoccupation with appearance is situated.

A number of recent empirical studies have confirmed what common observation has reported all along, namely, that the feeling lives of men and women are not identical.[5] But what needs to be asked about such emotional differences is not only their relationship to typical gendered traits or dispositions but, following Heidegger, the way in which such attunements are disclosive of their subjects' "Being-in-the-world," i.e., of their character as selves and of the specific ways in which, as selves, they are inscribed within the social totality. The search for a feminist reconstruction of knowledge, then, must be augmented by a study of the most pervasive patterns of gendered emotion in their revelatory moment. Insofar as women are not just situated differently than men within the social ensemble, but are actively subordinated to them within it, this project—the identification and description of these attunements—will be at the same time a contribution to the phenomenology of oppression.

What patterns of mood or feeling, then, tend to characterize women more than men? Here are some candidates: shame; guilt; the peculiar dialectic of shame and pride in embodiment consequent upon a narcissistic assumption of the body as spectacle; the blissful loss of self in the sense of merger with another; the pervasive apprehension consequent upon physical vulnerability, especially the fear of rape or assault. Since I have no doubt that men and women have the same fundamental emotional capacities, to say that some pattern of feeling in women, say shame, is gender-related is not to claim that it is gender-specific, i.e., that men are never ashamed; it is only to claim that women are more prone to experience the emotion in question and that the feeling itself has a different meaning in relation to their total psychic situation and general social location than has a similar emotion when experienced by men. Some of the commoner forms of shame in men, for example, may be intelligible only in light of the presupposition of male power, while in women shame may well be a mark and token of powerlessness. We recognize in everyday speech the proneness of certain classes of persons to particular patterns of feeling: It is often said of ghetto blacks, for example, that they have feelings of hopelessness and that they are depressed and despairing. This is not to say that rich white people never despair or feel depressed, only that members of the "underclass" are more given to feelings of hopelessness than more privileged people and that the despair they feel is peculiarly disclosive of the realities of their lives.

In what follows, I shall examine women's shame, not the alteration of pride and shame called forth by the imperatives of feminine body display, nor the shame of women who feel that they are fat, old, or ugly. . . . The shame I want to pursue now is less specific; its boundaries are blurred; it is less available to consciousness and more likely to be denied. This shame is manifest in a pervasive sense of personal inadequacy that, like the shame of embodiment, is profoundly disempowering; both reveal the "generalized condition of dishonor" which is woman's lot in sexist society.[6] I shall maintain that women typically are more shame-prone than men, that shame is not so much a particular feeling or emotion (though it involves specific feelings and emotions) as a pervasive affective attunement to the social environment, that women's shame is more than merely an effect of subordination but, within the larger universe of patriarchal social relations, a profound mode of disclosure both of self and situation . . .

II

Shame can be characterized in a preliminary way as a species of psychic distress occasioned by a self or a state of the self apprehended as inferior, defective, or in some way diminished.[7] For the Sartre of *Being and Nothingness*, shame requires an audience: Shame is "in its primary structure shame *before somebody*": it is "shame of *oneself* before the Other."[8] "Nobody," he says, "can be vulgar all alone"![9] To be ashamed is to be in the position of "passing judgment on myself as on an object, for it is as an object that I appear to the Other."[10] Only insofar as I apprehend myself as the Other's object, i.e., through the medium of another consciousness, can I grasp my own object-character. Hence, shame before the Other is primordial: I must feel shame before some actual Other before I learn to raise an internalized Other in imagination. Furthermore, "shame is by nature recognition": Unless I recognize that I *am* as I am seen by the Other, the Other's judgment cannot cast me down.[11]

Sartre's discussion of shame is highly abbreviated: Preoccupied with the role of the Other as audience, he has little to say about the mechanisms that can forge an identification of self and Other in an experience of shame. Once an actual Other has revealed my object-character to me, I can become an object for myself; I can come to see myself as I might be seen by another, caught in the shameful act. Hence, I *can* succeed in being vulgar all alone: In such a situation, the Other before whom I am ashamed is only—myself. "A man may feel himself disgraced," says Isenberg, "by something that is unworthy in his own eyes and apart from any judgment but his own."[12]

Here is a fuller characterization of the structure of shame: Shame is the distressed apprehension of the self as inadequate or diminished: it requires if not an actual audience before whom my deficiencies are paraded, then an internalized audience with the capacity to judge me, hence internalized standards of judgment. Further, shame requires the recognition that I *am*, in some important sense, as I am seen to be. . . .

Shame, then, involves the distressed apprehension of oneself as a lesser creature. Guilt, by contrast, refers not to the subject's nature but to her actions: Typically, it is called forth by the active violation of principles which a person values and by which she feels herself bound. Deigh puts it well: "Shame is felt over shortcomings, guilt over wrongdoings."[13] Shame is called forth by the apprehension of some serious flaw in the self, guilt by the consciousness that one has committed a transgression. The widely held notion that shame is a response to external and guilt to internal sanctions is incorrect: Shame and guilt are alike in that each involves a condemnation of the self by itself for some failure to measure up; it is the measures that differ. While useful conceptual distinctions can be drawn between shame and guilt, the boundaries between them tend to blur in actual experience. . . .

III

Textbooks on the psychology of women tend to confirm the everyday observation that women are in general less assertive than men, have lower self-esteem, less overall confidence, and poorer self-concepts.[14] The terms on this list refer to traits and dispositions such as assertiveness and to beliefs: To have a poor self-concept, presumably, is to have one set of beliefs about oneself, while to have a good self-concept is to have another. Missing here is any sense of the affective taste, the emotional coloration of these traits and beliefs. Certainly, everyone understands how painful it is to have low self-esteem or too little confidence. Let us pursue this: What, precisely, is the character of this pain?

Several years ago, I taught an upper-level extension course in a suburban high school. The students were mostly high school teachers, required by their school district to earn periodic graduate credit as a condition of continuing employment. None of the students were very young: Most were in their forties and fifties. Women outnumbered men by about two to one. The women, who tended on the average to be somewhat better students than the men, displayed far less confidence in their ability to master the material. I found this surprising, since the female teachers, authorities in their own classrooms, did the same work as the male teachers, had comparable seniority, similar educational credentials, and, I assume, pay equity. The school in which both men and women taught had an excellent reputation. There is nothing unique about the classroom I am about to describe: I have observed in other classrooms what I observed there. I select this particular class as an example because male and female students were mature and well-matched professionally and because their relationships seemed to be free of the sexual tensions and courtship games that sometimes complicate the relationships of younger men and women.

Though women were in the majority, they were noticeably quieter in class discussion than the men. The men engaged freely in classroom exchanges and seemed quite confident—in view of the quality of some of their remarks, overconfident. Women who did enter discussion spoke what linguists call "women's language": Their speech was marked by hesitations and false starts; they tended to introduce their comments with self-denigrating expressions ("You may think that this is a stupid question, but . . ."); they often used a questioning intonation which in effect turned a simple declarative sentence into a request for help or for affirmation from without; they used "tag" questions which had the same effect ("Camus's theme in *The Myth of Sisyphus* is the absurdity of human existence, isn't it?") and excessive qualifiers ("Isn't it true that sometimes, maybe . . .").[15] This style of speaking, whatever its substance, communicates to listeners the speaker's lack of confidence in what she is saying, and this in turn damages her credibility.

In addition to their style of speech, I was struck by the way many female students behaved as they handed me their papers. They would offer heartfelt apologies and copious expressions of regret for the poor quality of their work—work which turned out, most of the time, to be quite good. While apologizing, a student would often press the edges of her manuscript together so as to make it literally smaller, holding the paper uncertainly somewhere in the air as if unsure whether she wanted to relinquish it at all. Typically, she would deliver the apology with head bowed, chest hollowed, and shoulders hunched slightly forward. The male students would stride over to the desk and put down their papers without comment.

Now every female student did not behave in this way all of the time. Nor is this all that the women communicated. To the casual observer, the atmosphere in the classroom was both relaxed and stimulating: Both men and women took an evident interest in the material and managed a lively exchange of ideas. But, like an organ-point that sounded faintly but persistently all term, something else was detectable too: It became clear to me that many women students were ashamed of their written work and ashamed to express their ideas in a straightforward and open manner. Indeed, it would not be unusual for a student just to say, "I'm really ashamed of this paper," while handing it to me. I have no doubt that these utterances were accurate reports of feeling. At the same time, I suspect that they were rituals of self-shaming undertaken in order to bear more easily a shaming they anticipated from me: An ordeal is often easier to endure if we can choose its time and place. These apologies served also to underscore the students' desire to do well in the course, hence, to get into my good books and, by arousing pity in me for such evident emotional distress, to soften my judgment of their work. Behind a facade of friendliness and informality, two very different dramas of relationship to the teacher were being enacted: The men regarded me as a rival or as an upstart who needed to prove herself; the women, as potentially a very punitive figure who needed to be placated and manipulated. . . .

It seems to me that the demeanor of my female students in that suburban classroom bore the characteristic marks of shame, of a shame felt directly or anticipated: In their silence, the necessity for hiding and concealment; in the tentative character of their speech and in their regular apologetics, the sense of self as defective or diminished. The fear of demeaning treatment could be seen in the cringing before an Other from whom such treatment was anticipated; shame could be read even in the physical constriction of their bodies.

Now if the primordial structure of shame is such that one is ashamed of oneself before the Other, who is the Other before whom my female students were ashamed? Since I have a kindly and permissive style and make a point of never subjecting my students to ridicule, let us assume for the sake of argument that I am not this Other. The identity of this Other, whoever it turns out to be, will be hugely overdetermined, for women in a sexist society are subjected to demeaning treatment by a variety of Others; they bring to the classroom a complex experience of subordination and an elaborate repertoire of stereotyped gestures appropriate to their station. One wonders too whether there is any relationship between women's shame—both the shame that is directly linked to embodiment and the same that is not—to the persistence of religious traditions that have historically associated female sexuality with pollution and contagion. But whatever the character of this overdetermination, it remains the case that female subjectivity is not constructed entirely elsewhere and then brought ready-made to the classroom: The classroom is also a site of its constitution. What I shall suggest in the next section is that the Other so feared by my female students is, to a surprising degree—especially in light of the overdetermination of shame to which I have just referred—a composite portrait of other and earlier classroom teachers who had, in fact, subjected them but not their male counterparts to consistent shaming behavior. It should be kept in mind in what follows that the classroom is perhaps the *most* egalitarian public space that any woman in our society will ever inhabit.

IV

The Project on the Status and Education of Women of the Association of American Colleges has produced an extraordinary report which details the many ways in which the classroom climate at all educational levels may produce a diminished sense of self in girls and women. While every instructor is by no means guilty of the kinds of demeaning treatment described in the report, such treatment is widespread and pervasive. The report itself is well documented, its claims supported by a variety of empirical studies.[16]

Females, it turns out, are less likely to be called upon directly than males; indeed, women and girls are often ignored, even when they express a willingness to speak. Teachers in grade school talk to boys wherever they are in the room, to girls only when they are nearby. Teachers tend to remember the names of male students better and to call upon them by name more often. Women are not given the same length of time as men to answer questions, suggesting that they are less able to think a problem through and come up with an answer. Nor are men and women asked the same kinds of questions: Women are often asked factual questions ("When did Camus publish *The Stranger?*") while men are asked questions that require some critical or analytical ability ("What do you see as the major thematic differences between *The Stranger* and *The Plague*"?). Some instructors may make "helpful" comments to women that imply, nevertheless, women's lesser competence ("I know that women have trouble with technical concepts but I'll try to help you out"). Instructors tend to coach men more than women, nodding and gesturing more often in response to men's comments and pushing and probing for a fuller response. This suggests that the points men make in discussion are important and that they can stretch themselves intellectually if they try. Women may well receive less praise than men for work of the same quality, for studies have shown repeatedly that work when ascribed to a man is rated higher than the same work when ascribed to a woman, whether the work in question is a scholarly paper, a short story, or a painting. There is evidence that men's success generally is viewed as deserved, women's as due to luck or to the easiness of the task.[17]

Women are interrupted more than men both by their teachers and by their fellow students. Teachers are likelier to use a tone of voice that indicates interest when talking to men but to adopt a patronizing or dismissive tone when talking to women. Teachers have been observed to make more eye contact with men than with women; they may assume a posture of attentiveness when men speak but look away or look at the clock when women speak.

Ignorant of the fact that styles of communication are gender-related, instructors may assume that women's use of "women's language" means that women have nothing to say. On the other hand, women may be viewed negatively when they display stereotypically masculine traits such as ambition, assertiveness, or a pleasure in disputation. The female student may receive direct sexual overtures in the classroom, but even if this does not happen, she is far likelier than her male counterpart to receive comments about her appearance. This may suggest to her that she is primarily a decorative being who is less serious and hence less competent than the men in her class.

Instructors may use sexist humor or demeaning sexual allusions to "spice up" a dull subject. They may disparage women or groups of women generally. Or they may use sexist language, referring to human beings in generic masculine terms or calling male students "men" but female students "girls" or "gals." The linguistic disparagement of women may be echoed in a course content from which the history, literature, accomplishments, or perspectives of women have been omitted.

Here, as elsewhere, women of color are in double jeopardy, for the demeaning treatment that is visited upon women, whatever their race, is similar in many ways to the demeaning treatment that is suffered by students of color, whatever their gender. Instructors may interpret students' behavior in the light of racial stereotypes, taking, for example, the silence of a black woman as "sullenness," of a Hispanic woman as "passivity." Black women, in particular, report that their instructors expect them to be either academically incompetent or else academically brilliant "exceptions." A black woman may be singled out, in ways that underscore her sense of not belonging, by being asked for the "black woman's point of view" on some issue rather than her own view.

College teachers have been better mentors to men than to women; they are likelier to choose men for teaching and research assistantships and to contact men when professional opportunities arise. In laboratory courses, instructors have been observed to position themselves closer to men than to women, giving men more detailed instructions on how to do an assignment. They are likelier to do the assignment for women or just allow them to fail. In such courses, men are often allowed to crowd out women at demonstrations. Classroom teachers are unlikely to recognize, hence to try to alter the dynamics of mixed-sex group discussion which are no different in the classroom than they are elsewhere:

Despite the popular notion that in everyday situations women talk more than men, studies show that in formal groups containing men and women: men talk more than women; men talk for longer periods and take more turns at speaking; men exert more control over the topic of conversation; men interrupt women much more frequently than women interrupt men and men's interruptions of women more often introduce trivial or inappropriately personal comments that bring the woman's discussion to an end or change its focus.[18]

These behaviors, considered in toto, cannot fail to diminish women, to communicate to them the insignificance and lack of seriousness of their classroom personae. When one considers the length of this catalogue of microbehaviors and senses what must be its cumulative effect, one is tempted to regard the shaming behavior visited upon women in the modern classroom as the moral equivalent of the dunce-cap of old.

The classroom, as we noted earlier, is only one of many locations wherein the female sense of self is constituted. Behaviors akin to the ones just listed are enacted in many other domains of life, in, e.g., family, church, and workplace. If, as I claimed earlier, women are more shame-prone than men, the cause is not far to seek: Women, more often than men, are made to feel shame in the major sites of social life. Moreover, it is in the act of being shamed and in the feeling ashamed that there is disclosed to women who they are and how they are faring within the domains they inhabit, though as we shall see, this disclosure is ambiguous and oblique. . . .

Notes

1. See for example, Anthony Kenny, *Action, Emotion, and the Will* (London: Routledge and Kegan Paul, 1963); J. R. S. Wilson, *Emotion and Object* (Cambridge: Cambridge University Press, 1972); R. M. Gordon, "Aboutness of Emotion," *American Philosophical Quarterly* 11, no. 1 (Jan. 1974); Robert Solomon, "The Logic of Emotion," *Nous* 11, no. 1 (1977), and *The Passions* (New York: Doubleday, 1976); Irving Thalberg, "Emotion and Thought," *American Philosophical Quarterly* 1 (1964), and *Perception, Emotion, and Action* (Oxford: Basil Blackwell, 1977); Donald Davidson, "Hume's Cognitive Theory of Pride," *Journal of Philosophy* 73, no. 19 (Nov. 1976); Gabriele Taylor, *Pride, Shame, and Guilt; Emotions of Self-Assessment* (Oxford: Oxford University Press, 1985).
2. Martin Heidegger, *Being and Time*, tr. Macquarrie and Robinson (New York: Harper and Row, 1962), 173. See sec. 29, "Being-there as State-of-Mind," 172–79.
3. Ibid., 177. Michael Stocker has been one of the few Anglo-American philosophers to explore the relationship between intellect and patterns of choice, desire, and emotion. See his "Intellectual Desire, Emotion, and Action," in Amelie Oksenberg Rorty, ed., *Explaining Emotions* (Berkeley: University of California Press, 1980).
4. See, for example, Evelyn Fox Keller, *Reflections on Gender and Science* (New Haven: Yale University Press, 1985); Sandra Harding, *The Science Question in Feminism* (Ithaca: Cornell University Press, 1986); Susan Bordo, "The Cartesian Masculinization of Thought," in Sandra Harding and Jean F. O'Barr, eds., *Sex*

and Scientific Inquiry (Chicago: University of Chicago Press, 1987); Sandra Harding and Merrill Hintikka, eds., *Discovering Reality: Feminist Perspectives on Epistemology, Metaphysics, Methodology, and Philosophy of Science* (Dordrecht: Reidel, 1983): Alison M. Jaggar, *Feminist Politics and Human Nature* (Totowa, NJ: Rowman and Allanheld, 1983), esp. ch. 11; Genevieve Lloyd, *The Man of Reason* (Minneapolis: University of Minnesota Press, 1984); Mary Belenky, Blythe Clinchy, Nancy Goldberger, and Jill Tarule, *Women's Ways of Knowing* (New York: Basic Books, 1986).

5. See, for example, Leslie R. Brody, "Gender Differences in Emotional Development: A Review of Theories and Research," in Abigail J. Stewart and M. Brenton Lykes, eds., *Gender and Personality: Current Perspectives on Theory and Research* (Durham: Duke University Press, 1985); also, Arlie Hochschild, *The Managed Heart* (Berkeley: University of California Press, 1983).

6. Husseen Abdilahi Bulhan, *Frantz Fanon and the Psychology of Oppression* (New York: Plenum Press, 1985), 122. Bulhan uses this phrase to characterize slaves and oppressed persons of color. Citing the work of psychologists Orlando Patterson and Chester Pierce, Bulhan characterizes a "generalized condition of dishonor" as a status in which one's person lacks integrity, worth, and autonomy and in which one is subject to violations of space, time, energy, mobility, bonding, and identity.

7. Susan Miller, *The Shame Experience* (Hillsdale, NJ: Analytic Press, 1985), 32.

8. Jean-Paul Sartre, *Being and Nothingness*, tr. Hazel E. Barnes (New York: Philosophical Library, 1956), 221–22.

9. Ibid., 222.

10. Ibid.

11. Ibid.

12. Arnold Isenberg, "Natural Pride and Natural Shame," in Rorty, op. cit., p. 366.

13. Deigh, op. cit., 225.

14. Some relevant studies are discussed in M. W. Matlin, *The Psychology of Women* (New York: Holt, Rinehart and Winston, 1987), 129–32.

15. For discussions of "women's language," see Robin Lakoff, *Language and Women's Place* (New York: Harper and Row, 1975); Barrie Thorne and Nancy Henley, eds., *Language and Sex: Difference and Dominance.* (Rowley, MA: Newbury House Publishers, 1975); Nancy Henley, *Body Politics: Power, Sex, and Non-Verbal Communication* (Englewood Cliffs, NJ: Prentice-Hall, 1977).

16. Roberta M. Hall, with the assistance of Bernice R. Sandler, "The Classroom Climate: A Chilly One for Women?" prepared by the Project on the Status and Education of Women of the Association of American Colleges, 1818 R St., N. W., Washington, D.C. 20009. The claims I make in this section about differences in treatment of male and female students are drawn almost entirely from empirical studies cited in the body of the report or in the notes and Selected List of Resources. See esp. 17–21.

17. An excellent review and evaluation of this research can be found in Stephanie Riger and Pat Galligan, "Women in Management: An Exploration of Compeling Paradigms," *American Psychologist* 35, no. 10 (Oct. 1980): 902–10. Also see Pauline Rose Clance, *The Imposture Phenomenon* (New York: Bantam, 1985), also Pauline Rose Clance and Suzanne Jones, "The Imposture Phenomenon in High-Achieving Women: Dynamics and Therapeutic Intervention," *Psychotherapy: Theory, Research, and Practice* 15 (1978): 241–47.

18. "Classroom Climate," 8.

SELECTION 12
FROM
Masculinity and Power

ARTHUR BRITTAN

MOST DISCUSSIONS OF MASCULINITY tend to treat it as if it is measurable. Some men have more of it, others less. Those men who appear to lack masculinity are, by definition, sick or genetically inadequate. Gay men, for example, are often regarded as men who lack a proper hormonal balance, and who consequently are not "real" men. This assumption—that we can know and describe men in terms of some discoverable dimension—is problematic because it suggests that masculinity is timeless and universal.

My aim is to examine this assumption. My position is that we cannot talk of masculinity, only masculinities. This is not to claim that masculinity is so variable that we cannot identify it as a topic. I am not in favor of a doctrinaire relativism which would make it an almost impossible object of study. It seems to me that any account of masculinity must begin with its place in the general discussion of gender. Since gender does not exist outside history and culture, this means that both masculinity and femininity are continuously subject to a process of reinterpretation. The way men are regarded in late twentieth-century England is obviously different from the way that they were regarded in the nineteenth century. Moreover, versions of masculinity may vary over a limited time scale. . . .

The fact that masculinity may appear in different guises at different times does not entitle us to draw the conclusion that we are dealing with an ephemeral quality which is sometimes present and sometimes not. In the final analysis, how men behave will depend upon the existing social relations of gender. By this I mean the way in which men and women confront each other ideologically and politically. Gender is never simply an arrangement in which the roles of men and women are decided in a contingent and haphazard way. At any given moment, gender will reflect the material interests of those who have power and those who do not. Masculinity, therefore, does not exist in isolation from femininity—it will always be an expression of the current image that men have of themselves in relation to women. And these images are often contradictory and ambivalent. . . .

MALE NATURES

It may seem peculiar, after nearly a century of counterarguments, that there is still strong support for the thesis that human nature is something that can be discovered and measured, that it is knowable. Despite the apparent success of the social sciences in accounting for socialization as a learning and social process, the idea of an original and underlying basis for human behavior remains a central aspect of much academic and everyday thinking. Moreover, this thesis has been given new life by the emergence of sophisticated biological approaches such as ethology and sociobiology. While the crude social Darwinism of the nineteenth century has long since been relegated to the academic dustbin, this is not to say that its influence is dead. On the contrary, the new evolutionists have reentered the debate about human nature with new ferocity. In the case of gender, they claim that there is no way in which it can be seen as a social construction. Gender behavior is rooted in biological imperatives which serve evolutionary purposes. Of course, they are not so naive as to deny the influence of social and cultural factors, but this does not amount to anything more than suggesting that culture is itself a particular kind of manifestation of evolutionary mechanisms.[1]

Take the example of male aggressiveness. The socialization case is that aggression is learned. It is acquired in a context in which men learn that it is both rewarding and expected to behave in an assertive way. Boys grow up in environments which encourage certain kinds of conduct, rather than others. They learn to be "men." Aggression, from this point of view, is a response to specific kinds of experience. Men will only behave aggressively if they have learned it is appropriate to do so. The implication is that a society's proper functioning depends upon the inculcation of aggressive patterns of behavior in young boys. . . .

Sociobiologists take issue with this. They argue that to talk about aggression exclusively in terms of learning is to fly in the face of evidence from the study of animal populations. While agreeing that human behavior cannot be explained only in terms of evolutionary forces, they are not too worried about this. Aggression has an evolutionary significance for primate societies—it allows dominant males to pass on their genes to suitable female partners, thus ensuring the survival of the group. What is functional for the baboon or chimpanzee is, therefore, equally functional for human males, provided one accepts the evidence that there is indeed a real continuity between primate and human behavior. . . .

It is not only men's aggression which is seen as innate. Their sexuality is given the same kind of treatment. There is supposed to be something in a man's makeup which pushes him into acts of sexual assertiveness. In its extreme form, this view imbues his sexuality with transcendental power which brooks no interference. Men are at the mercy of strong drives over which they have very little control. Such an uncompromising view has not been limited to everyday discourse, but provides the rationale for a considerable amount of academic theorizing. . . .

SEXUALITY AND VIOLENCE

The conflation of sexuality and violence is a very strong strand in the commonsense account of masculinity. It is explicit on television, in the cinema, in novels written by men, being almost a necessary convention. Best-selling novels (and not only best-selling novels) all have the required rape scene, the obligatory episode of sexual violence. But this is not simply a "cultural" matter. This view is also found in academic texts and journals, where it is given credibility by its location in an evolutionary and natural-istic framework.

As Jeffrey Weeks has noted, the discussion of the biological foundation of sexual behavior rests upon a number of dubious assumptions.[2] First, there is the assumption that "argues from analogy." That is, the tendency to con-strue animal and human behavior as directly comparable. Because there are pecking orders among chickens, then it is easy enough to transpose this order into a hierarchical human social structure. The point is that evolu-tionary biologists and other experts see animal behavior in terms of catego-ries and concepts which only have meaning in a human context. Humans have class systems, animals do not. Men rape, male baboons do not. Men fight wars, they exploit other men, they develop symbol systems, animals do not. Human sexuality and aggressiveness are not simply the expression of impulses rooted in a genetic or biological substratum—they are saturated with meaning. This is not to say that men (and women) do not have the capacity to be aggressive, but this is not the same as saying that this capac-ity is causal.

Second, there is the assumption that "on average" men behave more ag-gressively than women, and that their "sex drive" is far more demanding. Official statistics indicate that most crimes of violence are committed by men, and that rape is a male activity. If only men rape, and if statistics show that the incidence of rape is high in a given population, then the conclusion must be that rape is an expression of their "natural" desires. But, if it can be demonstrated that the incidence of rape varies both his-torically and culturally, then presumably the biological case is in difficulty.

Surely it would be absurd to claim that those societies with lower rape rates are different biologically from those with higher rates?

While statistical analysis is not necessarily supposed to draw causal conclusions, there is no doubt that it is how statistical averages are regarded by both expert and nonexpert. Accordingly, while we know that only men rape, and that rape is prevalent in a great many contemporary societies, we cannot go on to state that rape is a universal feature of male behavior in all societies at all times. Once we assent to the argument that a particular behavior is universal, we are thereby proposing that human nature is timeless and unchanging.

Third, it is relatively easy to fall back on biological explanations. They appear to be so straightforward, parsimonious, and scientific. After all, if only men rape, then why should we look for explanations outside biology? Most biological accounts of human behavior appear to be perfectly logical. In addition, they tend to be consistent with other scientific explanations in which a reductionist "levels of analysis" approach is deemed appropriate. The "levels of analysis" approach takes it as gospel that some levels are more basic than others, that they have some kind of causal priority. The implication is that it is no use looking at aggression in terms of events which occur at the cultural or social level because, by definition, these events are all reducible to a lower level, a level at which biochemistry, genes, or hormones may be operative. Ultimately, the reductionist strategy is posited on the belief that "higher" levels are always dependent on "lower," and that consequently the sciences that study the latter are more capable of explaining the former. In the final reckoning, disciplines like biochemistry take precedence over disciplines such as sociology or psychology. The problem of masculinity, therefore, is a problem in biochemistry, not learning or socialization.

Furthermore, reductionist explanations tend to emphasize the centrality of the individual. Until recently, a discipline like psychology was not really concerned with collective social behavior, except in so far as individual behavior shapes social conduct. Thus, if men behave aggressively, the consequences for society are additive, not collective. Wars are fought by men with specific dispositions, not for economic, political, or moral reasons. Of course, there are other psychologies with different kinds of theoretical and empirical interest, but their concern is mainly with the level of individual functioning. The social is inevitably a backdrop to, or a by-product of, individual perception, motivation and cognition. Even today, when multidisciplinary cooperation and integration are fashionable, the temptation is to think in terms of the individual.

To be sure, the kind of crude instinctual thinking associated with early academic psychology is now a thing of the past, but it nevertheless remains true that most psychologists are committed to the primacy of psychological over social process. In rejecting the reductionist thesis about the primacy of biology and psychology, it is, however, not my intention to substitute an alternative social and cultural determinism which treats human beings as if they are the helpless victims of overwhelming external forces. To repeat, men and women do not exist outside history, but at the same time they do not exist outside their bodies. From the moment a child is born, he or she is exposed to a world in which the facts of gender are taken at their face value. A boy's genitals are the first sign of his potential membership of the category male. Such a categorization is not simply a label—it affects the way in which he defines his difference from the category female. The raw sexual features are imbued with symbolic content, but this content becomes a fact of biology. Biology and society are never separate—they mutually constitute each other. Hence, the "true facts" of biology are never pristine and uninterpreted. They are always mediated. The "facts" of sexual difference are "facts" by virtue of the generalized belief (in Western society at least), that heterosexuality is normal and natural. The "fact" that men and women have different sexual organs is translated into a principle of social organization in which men "father" and women "mother." The "fact" that men usually are breadwinners is traced back to genetic programming. . . .

PROBLEMATIC DICHOTOMIES

In separating the biological from the social we do violence to our understanding of human reality—moreover, we are assenting to a dualism which has underpinned the theorizing and analysis of human behavior ever since Descartes's time. We assume that there is sharp division between the body and society, between desire and rationality, between the person and context, between man and woman. And because most of us have been exposed to an educational system which naturalizes sexual differences and other dualisms, we tend to accept them without too much trauma and questioning.

The position taken here is to question the very basis of this dualism. It is my contention that "masculinism" provides the underpinning for a particular way of organizing gender relationships which separates biology from culture and ensures the political domination of men and the subordination of women. I do this advisedly because I do not believe that all forms of domination can be subsumed under a common explanatory framework, that is, I reject the claim that domination must always be explained in class terms, *and* I also reject the alternative claim that gender inequality explains class differences. Nevertheless, it would be very naive to suppose that class and gender relationships exist in separate compartments. Both forms of domination are in a state of constant interaction, so that it often becomes difficult to disentangle their separate contribution to a given set of social relations. Moreover, masculinism takes on a distinctive flavor when associated with capitalism.

Certainly, what appears to be paramount in the representation of masculinity in capitalist societies is an obsession with competition and achievement. In other words, masculinism appears to lend itself very nicely to the ethos of industrialism and capitalism. But, if we reject dualism in social and political theorizing, how can we reconcile this with the argument that there are two or more kinds of domination that coexist in some uneasy alliance? How can we justify the claim that patriarchy should be given a separate status from class? Surely, if we want to understand domination, we should look for a common source for that domination?

When we argue that class cannot be reduced to patriarchy and vice versa, this is not an argument for the inevitability of each. On the contrary, both patriarchy and class only exist in history. What we have to establish is the historicity of domination, not its inevitability. Whether or not patriarchy and class are twin-born seems to me to be irrelevant—what is important is the fact that domination has a history. The key point is that both forms of domination are historically constructed. Yet, this is not to say that this construction is simultaneous. Thus, for Engels, private property was the key concept for any consideration of the historicity of domination. It is its emergence which sets in motion the division of society into those who control the means of production and those who do not. Private property is responsible for the establishment of a class system in which men own the means of production and the services of their women. Patriarchy and class, therefore, have a common origin in a mode of production which is geared to the male appropriation of an economic surplus. So, from this perspective, patriarchy does not exist independently of class, and in various Marxist texts it appears to be dependent on and reducible to class.

Alternatively, we have those views which give priority to patriarchy. Patriarchy is seen as existing long before the emergence of private property and class. The emphasis here is on the way in which the sexual division of labor was turned into a system in which men seized or appropriated the key political positions in the kinship system. Usually this process is linked to the problem of childrearing. Because women were often incapacitated by the time and energy devoted to the gestation and nurturing of children, they were construed by men as not being able to contribute to political and economic life. Such a construction (for this is what it is) is the essential element in the establishment of male domination. The male perception of a biological fact (the woman's role in childbearing) is translated into the basic principle of social organization. After a while this construction comes to be regarded as natural and inevitable—it becomes part and parcel of the way in which gender is embedded into social organization and conscious-ness—the construction, once made, is constantly reproduced. (In addition, the domination of women is seen as the model for all domination. Not only do men oppress women, they also oppress other men.)

In a nutshell, the argument for the independent existence of patriarchy is based upon the social construction of men and women into two separate, but unequal, categories. The implication here is that this construction oc-curred long before the division of society into economic classes. Hence both class and patriarchy are explained in terms of the interaction of complex social events which do away with the necessity of positing some final bio-logical or psychological cause. In either case the end result is the same— the division of society into those who have power and authority, and those who do not.

Now it is the theme of this book that masculinism naturalizes male domi-nation. Yet I have shied way from calling men a class in the sense that they all share common interests in relation to women. However, it would seem to me that under certain circumstances some men do constitute a class or, to put it more accurately, they are in a class-like situation vis-à-vis women. In this respect, I refer to the kind of evidence deriving from Christine Delphy and her associates which describes the family and the household as a terrain in which men act as a class. But male domination is not only about the appropriation of a woman's labor power, it is also about the ap-propriation of her sexuality, her body. In talking about the masculine ideol-ogy, we are therefore not only referring to the economic and political position of men, but also how they define and theorize sexuality and gender. And it is the variability of these theories and definitions that, to a large extent, constitute the historical specificity of this or that form of masculinity.

Notes

1. M. D. Sahlins, *The Use and Abuse of Biology* (London: Tavistock, 1976).
2. Jeffrey Weeks, *Sexuality* (London: Tavistock, 1986), 50–53.

SELECTION 13
FROM
This Sex Which Is Not One

LUCE IRIGARAY

FEMALE SEXUALITY HAS ALWAYS been conceptualized on the basis of masculine parameters. Thus the opposition between "masculine" clitoral activity and "feminine" vaginal passivity, an opposition which Freud—and many others—saw as stages, or alternatives, in the development of a sexually "normal" woman, seems rather too clearly required by the practice of male sexuality. For the clitoris is conceived as a little penis pleasant to masturbate so long as castration anxiety does not exist (for the boy child), and the vagina is valued for the "lodging" it offers the male organ when the forbidden hand has to find a replacement for pleasure-giving.

In these terms, woman's erogenous zones never amount to anything but a clitoris-sex that is not comparable to the noble phallic organ, or a hole-envelope that serves to sheathe and massage the penis in intercourse: a non-sex, or a masculine organ turned back upon itself, self-embracing.

About woman and her pleasure, this view of the sexual relation has nothing to say. Her lot is that of "lack," "atrophy" (of the sexual organ), and "penis envy," the penis being the only sexual organ of recognized value. Thus she attempts by every means available to appropriate that organ for herself: through her somewhat servile love of the father-husband capable of giving her one, through her desire for a child-penis, preferably a boy, through access to the cultural values still reserved by right to males alone and therefore always masculine, and so on. Woman lives her own desire only as the expectation that she may at last come to possess an equivalent of the male organ.

Yet all this appears quite foreign to her own pleasure, unless it remains within the dominant phallic economy. Thus, for example, woman's autoeroticism is very different from man's. In order to touch himself, man needs an instrument: his hand, a woman's body, language . . . And this self-caressing requires at least a minimum of activity. As for woman, she touches herself in and of herself without any need for mediation, and before there is any way to distinguish activity from passivity. Woman "touches herself" all the time, and moreover no one can forbid her to do so, for her genitals are formed of two lips in continuous contact. Thus, within herself, she is already two—but not divisible into one(s)—that caress each other.

This autoeroticism is disrupted by a violent break-in: the brutal separation of the two lips by a violating penis, an intrusion that distracts and deflects the woman from this "self-caressing" she needs if she is not to incur the disappearance of her own pleasure in sexual relations. If the vagina is to serve *also*, but *not only*, to take over for the little boy's hand in order to assure an articulation between autoeroticism and heteroeroticism in intercourse (the encounter with the totally other always signifying death), how, in the classic representation of sexuality, can the perpetuation of autoeroticism for woman be managed? Will woman not be left with the impossible alternative between a defensive virginity, fiercely turned in upon itself, and a body open to penetration that no longer knows, in this "hole" that constitutes its sex, the pleasure of its own touch? The more or less exclusive—and highly anxious—attention paid to erection in Western sexuality proves to what extent the imaginary that governs it is foreign to the feminine. For the most part, this sexuality offers nothing but imperatives dictated by male rivalry: the "strongest" being the one who has the best "hard-on," the longest, the biggest, the stiffest penis, or even the one who "pees the farthest" (as in little boys' contests). Or else one finds imperatives dictated by the enactment of sadomasochistic fantasies, these in turn governed by man's relation to his mother: the desire to force entry, to penetrate, to appropriate for himself the mystery of this womb where he has been conceived, the secret of his begetting, of his "origin." Desire/need, also to make blood flow again in order to revive a very old relationship—intrauterine, to be sure, but also prehistoric—to the maternal.

Woman, in this sexual imaginary, is only a more or less obliging prop for the enactment of man's fantasies. That she may find pleasure there in that role, by proxy, is possible, even certain. But such pleasure is above all a masochistic prostitution of her body to a desire that is not her own, and it leaves her in a familiar state of dependency upon man. Not knowing what she wants, ready for anything, even asking for more, so long as he will "take" her as his "object" when he seeks his own pleasure. Thus she will not say what she herself wants; moreover, she does not know, or no longer knows, what she wants. As Freud admits, the beginnings of the sexual life of a girl child are so "obscure," so "faded with time," that one would have to dig down very deep indeed to discover beneath the traces of this civilization, of this history, the vestiges of a more archaic civilization that might give some clue to woman's sexuality. That extremely ancient civilization would undoubtedly have a different alphabet, a different language . . . Woman's desire would not be expected to speak the same language as man's; woman's desire has doubtless been submerged by the logic that has dominated the West since the time of the Greeks.

Within this logic, the predominance of the visual, and of the discrimination and individualization of form, is particularly foreign to female eroticism. Woman takes pleasure more from touching than from looking, and her entry into a dominant scopic economy signifies, again, her consignment to passivity: She is to be the beautiful object of contemplation. While her body finds itself thus eroticized, and called to a double movement of exhibition and of chaste retreat in order to stimulate the drives of the "subject," her sexual organ represents *the horror of nothing to see*. A defect in this systematics of representation and desire. A "hole" in its scoptophilic lens. It is already evident in Greek statuary that this nothing-to-see has to be excluded, rejected, from such a scene of representation. Woman's genitals are simply absent, masked, sewn back up inside their "crack."

This organ which has nothing to show for itself also lacks a form of its own. And if woman takes pleasure precisely from this incompleteness of form which allows her organ to touch itself over and over again, indefinitely, by itself, that pleasure is denied by a civilization that privileges phallomorphism. The value granted to the only definable form excludes the one that is in play in female autoeroticism. The *one* of form, of the individual, of the (male) sexual organ, of the proper name, of the proper meaning . . . supplants, while separating and dividing, that contact of *at least two* (lips) which keeps woman in touch with herself, but without any possibility of distinguishing what is touching from what is touched.

Whence the mystery that woman represents in a culture claiming to count everything, to number everything by units, to inventory everything as individualities. *She is neither one nor two.* Rigorously speaking, she cannot be identified either as one person, or as two. She resists all adequate definition. Further, she has no "proper" name. And her sexual organ, which is not *one* organ, is counted as *none*. The negative, the underside, the reverse of the only visible and morphologically designatable organ (even if the passage from erection to detumescence does pose some problems): the penis.

But the "thickness" of that "form," the layering of its volume, its expansions and contractions and even the spacing of the moments in which it produces itself as form—all this the feminine keeps secret. Without knowing it. And if woman is asked to sustain, to revive, man's desire, the request neglects to spell out what it implies as to the value of her own desire. A desire of which she is not aware, moreover, at least not explicitly. But one whose force and continuity are capable of nurturing repeatedly and at length all the masquerades of "feminity" that are expected of her.

It is true that she still has the child, in relation to whom her appetite for touch, for contact, has free rein, unless it is already lost, alienated by the taboo against touching of a highly obsessive civilization. Otherwise her pleasure will find, in the child, compensations for and diversions from the frustrations that she too often encounters in sexual relations per se. Thus maternity fills the gaps in a repressed female sexuality. Perhaps man and woman no longer caress each other except through that mediation between them that the child—preferably a boy—represents? Man, identified with his son, rediscovers the pleasure of maternal fondling; woman touches herself again by caressing that part of her body: her baby-penis-clitoris.

What this entails for the amorous trio is well known. But the Oedipal interdiction seems to be a somewhat categorical and factitious law—although it does provide the means for perpetuating the authoritarian discourse of fathers—when it is promulgated in a culture in which sexual relations are impracticable because man's desire and woman's are strangers to each other. And in which the two desires have to try to meet through indirect means, whether the archaic one of a sense-relation to the mother's body, or the present one of active or passive extension of the law of the father. These are regressive emotional behaviors, exchanges of words too detached from the sexual arena not to constitute an exile with respect to it: "mother" and "father" dominate the interactions of the couple, but as social roles. The division of labor prevents them from making love. They produce or reproduce. Without quite knowing how to use their leisure. Such little as they have, such little indeed as they wish to have. For what are they to do with leisure? What substitute for amorous resource are they to invent? Still . . .

Perhaps it is time to return to that repressed entity, the female imaginary. So woman does not have a sex organ? She has at least two of them, but they are not identifiable as ones. Indeed, she has many more. Her sexuality, always at least double, goes even further: It is *plural*. Is this the way culture is seeking to characterize itself now? Is this the way texts write themselves/are written now? Without quite knowing what censorship they are evading? Indeed, woman's pleasure does not have to choose between clitoral activity and vaginal passivity, for example. The pleasure of the vaginal caress does not have to be substituted for that of the clitoral caress. They each contribute, irreplaceably, to woman's pleasure. Among other caresses . . . Fondling the breasts, touching the vulva, spreading the lips, stroking the posterior wall of the vagina, brushing against the mouth of the uterus, and so on. To evoke only a few of the most specifically female pleasures. Pleasures which are somewhat misunderstood in sexual difference as it is imagined—or not imagined, the other sex being only the indispensable complement to the only sex.

But *woman has sex organs more or less everywhere*. She finds pleasure almost anywhere. Even if we refrain from invoking the hystericization of her entire body, the geography of her pleasure is far more diversified, more multiple in its differences, more complex, more subtle, than is commonly imagined— in an imaginary rather too narrowly focused on sameness.

"She" is indefinitely other in herself. This is doubtless why she is said to be whimsical, incomprehensible, agitated, capricious . . . not to mention her language, in which "she" sets off in all directions leaving "him" unable to discern the coherence of any meaning. Hers are contradictory words, somewhat mad from the standpoint of reason, inaudible for whoever listens to them with ready-made grids, with a fully elaborated code in hand. For in what she says, too, at least when she dares, woman is constantly touching herself. She steps ever so slightly aside from herself with a murmur, an exclamation, a whisper, a sentence left unfinished . . . When she returns, it is to set off again from elsewhere. From another point of pleasure, or of pain. One would have to listen with another ear, as if hearing *an "other meaning" always in the process of weaving itself, of embracing itself with words, but also of getting rid of words in order not to become fixed, congealed in them.* For if "she" says something, it is not, it is already no longer, identical with what she means. What she says is never identical with anything, moreover; rather, it is contiguous. *It touches (upon).* And when it strays too far from that proximity, she breaks off and starts over at "zero": her body-sex.

It is useless, then, to trap women in the exact definition of what they mean, to make them repeat (themselves) so that it will be clear; they are already elsewhere in that discursive machinery where you expected to surprise them. They have returned within themselves. Which must not be understood in the same way as within yourself. They do not have the interiority that you have, the one you perhaps suppose they have. Within themselves means *within the intimacy of that silent, multiple, diffuse touch.* And if you ask them insistently what they are thinking about, they can only reply: Nothing. Everything.

Thus what they desire is precisely nothing, and at the same time everything. Always something more and something else besides that *one*—sexual organ, for example—that you give them, attribute to them. Their desire is often interpreted, and feared, as a sort of insatiable hunger, a voracity that will swallow you whole. Whereas it really involves a different economy more than anything else, one that upsets the linearity of a project, undermines the goal-object of a desire, diffuses the polarization toward a single pleasure, disconcerts fidelity to a single discourse . . .

Must this multiplicity of female desire and female language be understood as shards, scattered remnants of a violated sexuality? A sexuality denied? The question has no simple answer. The rejection, the exclusion of a female imaginary certainly puts woman in the position of experiencing herself only fragmentarily, in the little-structured margins of a dominant ideology, as waste, or excess, what is left of a mirror invested by the (masculine) "subject" to reflect himself, to copy himself. Moreover, the role of "femininity" is prescribed by this masculine specula(riza)tion and corresponds scarcely at all to woman's desire, which may be recovered only in secret, in hiding, with anxiety and guilt.

But if the female imaginary were to deploy itself, if it could bring itself into play otherwise than as scraps, uncollected debris, would it represent itself, even so, in the form of *one* universe? Would it even be volume instead of surface? No. Not unless it were understood, yet again, as a privileging of the maternal over the feminine. Of a phallic maternal, at that. Closed in upon the jealous possession of its valued product. Rivaling man in his esteem for productive excess. In such a race for power, woman loses the uniqueness of her pleasure. By closing herself off as volume, she renounces the pleasure that she gets from the *nonsuture of her lips:* She is undoubtedly a mother, but a virgin mother; the role was assigned to her by mythologies long ago. Granting her a certain social power to the extent that she is reduced, with her own complicity, to sexual impotence.

(Re-)discovering herself, for a woman, thus could only signify the possibility of sacrificing no one of her pleasures to another, of identifying herself with none of them in particular, *of never being simply one.* A sort of expanding universe to which no limits could be fixed and which would not be incoherence nonetheless—nor that polymorphous perversion of the child in which the erogenous zones would lie waiting to be regrouped under the primacy of the phallus.

Woman always remains several, but she is kept from dispersion because the other is already within her and is autoerotically familiar to her. Which is not to say that she appropriates the other for herself, that she reduces it to her own property. Ownership and property are doubtless quite foreign to the feminine. At least sexually. But not *nearness*. Nearness so pronounced that it makes all discrimination of identity, and thus all forms of property, impossible. Woman derives pleasure from what is *so near that she cannot have it, nor have herself.* She herself enters into a ceaseless exchange of herself with the other without any possibility of identifying either. This puts into question all prevailing economies: Their calculations are irremediably stymied by woman's pleasure, as it increases indefinitely from its passage in and through the other.

However, in order for woman to reach the place where she takes pleasure as woman, a long detour by way of the analysis of the various systems 'of oppression brought to bear upon her is assuredly necessary. And claiming to fall back on the single solution of pleasure risks making her miss the process of going back through a social practice that her enjoyment requires.

For woman is traditionally a use-value for man, an exchange value among men; in other words, a commodity. As such, she remains the guardian of material substance, whose price will be established, in terms of the standard of their work and of their need/desire, by "subjects": workers, merchants, consumers. Women are marked phallically by their fathers, husbands, procurers. And this branding determines their value in sexual commerce. Woman is never anything but the locus of a more or less competitive exchange between two men, including the competition for the possession of mother earth.

How can this object of transaction claim a right to pleasure without removing her/itself from established commerce? With respect to other merchandise in the marketplace, how could this commodity maintain a relationship other than one of aggressive jealousy? How could material substance enjoy her/itself without provoking the consumer's anxiety over the disappearance of his nurturing ground? How could that exchange—which can in no way be defined in terms "proper" to woman's desire—appear as anything but a pure mirage, mere foolishness, all too readily obscured by a more sensible discourse and by a system of apparently more tangible values?

A woman's development, however radical it may seek to be, would thus not suffice to liberate woman's desire. And to date no political theory or political practice has resolved, or sufficiently taken into consideration, this historical problem, even though Marxism has proclaimed its importance. But women do not constitute, strictly speaking, a class, and their dispersion among several classes makes their political struggle complex, their demands sometimes contradictory.

There remains, however, the condition of underdevelopment arising from women's submission by and to a culture that oppresses them, uses them, makes of them a medium of exchange, with very little profit to them. Except in the quasi monopolies of masochistic pleasure, the domestic labor force, and reproduction. The powers of slaves? Which are not negligible powers, moreover. For where pleasure is concerned, the master is not necessarily well served. Thus to reverse the relation, especially in the economy of sexuality, does not seem a desirable objective.

But if women are to preserve and expand their autoeroticism, their homo-sexuality, might not the renunciation of heterosexual pleasure correspond once again to that disconnection from power that is traditionally theirs? Would it not involve a new prison, a new cloister, built of their own ac-cord? For women to undertake tactical strikes, to keep themselves apart from men long enough to learn to defend their desire, especially through speech, to discover the love of other women while sheltered from men's imperious choices that put them in the position of rival commodities, to forge for themselves a social status that compels recognition, to earn their living in order to escape from the condition of prostitute . . . these are cer-tainly indispensable stages in the escape from their proletarization on the exchange market. But if their aim were simply to reverse the order of things, even supposing this to be possible, history would repeat itself in the long run, would revert to sameness: to phallocratism. It would leave room nei-ther for women's sexuality, nor for women's imaginary, nor for women's language to take (their) place.

SELECTION 14
FROM
Audre Lorde's (Nonessentialist) Lesbian Eros

RUTH GINSBERG

SINCE THE LATE NINETEENTH century, sexual orientation and identity have been construed against a background of essentialism. That is, a
woman is these days thought to "be" a lesbian or a nonlesbian in some
essential way. I will argue momentarily that it is this essentialism that underlies a large number of the problems internal to both lesbian and feminist
theories. But first let's review three competing essentialist claims about the
sense in which one "is" or "is not" a lesbian.

I can't help it. The first of these is the claim that lesbian identity is either
something with which one is born or something that develops at a precon-
scious level of development. This notion is often expressed by those who
claim that they have always been lesbians or who report that they knew
they were lesbians, or at least very different from heterosexual women, from
a very early age. This is also the underlying belief behind the idea that a
formerly heterosexually active or heterosexually interested woman can discover that she "really is" a lesbian, although she had not recognized it previously. It also underlies the psychotherapeutic notion that someone who
"is" gay or lesbian cannot be "changed" into someone who "is" straight
(although they might be threatened, coerced, intimidated, or argued into
changing "their behavior").

There are two reasons for taking this idea seriously. One is simply the
fact that there are a large number of lesbians who report this sort of self-
knowledge. To ignore or reject these reports of self-knowledge would be to
import into lesbian theory some of the worst of patriarchal theorizing; that
is, it would be to assert that the theorizer knew better than the "subjects"
of the theory what was true about them. A second reason for taking this
idea seriously is that there are political implications of such an idea that

some lesbians believe to be valuable. There is a long tradition in moral and liberal political theory of not judging a person for that which she cannot help. Gay rights organizations have had some degree of success in the United States since the late 1960s arguing that a person either "is" or "is not" gay or lesbian but that, whichever he or she is, it is not something over which he or she has control. This civil rights approach to gay political activism is also a strategy that has convinced a fair number of liberal nonlesbian feminists to take lesbian concerns seriously within the women's liberation movement. It is, not coincidentally, quite parallel to the civil rights approach to women's liberation itself, which has argued that one cannot help whether one is female or male, and thus that whether one is female or male should have no bearing on one's civil and political rights. Depending on a lesbian's interest in allying herself with the gay civil rights movement, the drawing of this parallel will have more or less appeal.

The most compelling reason to consider rejecting the idea is because, as Frye points out, it leaves intact the assumption that if one could help it, one surely would. That is, it ignores or invalidates the responsibility some lesbians want to claim for choosing to be lesbian.

Another reason for lesbians to be wary of it is because although this sense of homosexual identity overwhelmingly is claimed by most gay men, it is claimed by a considerably smaller percentage of lesbians. Lesbians need to remain wary about the extent to which lesbian identity is assimilated as a "female version" of gay male identity. At least to whatever extent gender identity and its formation are not analogous for women and for men, lesbian and gay sexual identity formation are equally unlikely to be analogous.

I chose it. Another common essentialist claim, articulated in both Mary Daly's and Marilyn Frye's work, for example, is that lesbian sexuality is primarily an "orientation of attention" on the part of women who do choose to see women, and—importantly—not to see men, in particular ways. One often finds the notion of "woman-identified women" associated with this conception of lesbian identity. The idea here is that "being a lesbian" is not only, or even primarily, a matter of who rubs genitals with whom, but rather that it constitutes an entirely different way of seeing the world. From this perspective, women are no longer in the background, helping hands in the drama of patriarchy. Instead, women are the primary focus of all sorts of attention, including erotic attention. Lesbians who identify themselves in this way perceived lesbianism as a consciously chosen path, one that they could have rejected but did not. Many regard it as at least partly a political decision, to choose to focus their attention on women rather than on men.

Again, a major reason for taking seriously this notion is the large number of lesbians who report that this is true of themselves. The lesbian literature is full of works by lesbians who report having chosen lesbian lives as a political act, often as an explicitly feminist political act. To claim that so many smart, politically aware lesbians might actually be mistaken about themselves seems dauntingly arrogant. Another reason for taking it seriously is that, as theory, it resonates well with feminist standpoint epistemologies.

One reason to be wary of this framework is that it raises questions about whether a lesbian who claims that she has not made this choice, but rather that she can't help who it is to whom she is attracted, "is" "really" a lesbian. The thing that would distinguish someone as "really" a lesbian, on this account, is exactly the making of the choice, which the lesbian who claims she can't help it didn't do. A second reason for wariness is that this framework creates problems about how to regard women who claim to have shifted their attention in the requisite way(s) but who do not, themselves, claim lesbian identities.

I'm no different; all women are lesbians. A third way of conceiving lesbian identity, which some see as continuous with the second, is reflected in Adrienne Rich's "lesbian continuum." Rich argues that women interact with each other in a wide variety of intimate ways, from best friend to nurse to lover. One of the examples she cites is that of women who, in their capacities as nurses, caretakers, or daughters-in-law, care for women elders, creating woman-centered spiritual, emotional, and physical intimacies within the context of those relationships. Another example is that of the nursing woman suckling a girl-child, who vicariously recalls the pleasures of suckling at her own mother's breast. All of these, Rich claims, lie on a lesbian continuum; there is at least a bit of lesbian eroticism in many relationships between women, probably experienced to some extent by all women, whether acknowledged or not. What she says all women need is to rid ourselves of the homophobia that prevents us from acknowledging our own lesbian interests when and where they do occur (Rich 1980).

An important reason to take seriously the idea of a lesbian continuum is that it addresses two vexing problems at once. First, it provides a framework for recognizing, accounting for, and perhaps even stirring the lesbian imaginations of women who have not previously encountered lesbian capacities within themselves. Second, it serves to reorient lesbian theory away from the issue of the lesbian/nonlesbian dichotomy.

Clearly, neither for Rich nor for Frye is "having sex" with other women a necessary condition of lesbian identity. Indeed, a reason to be wary of both accounts is that they both seem to desexualize lesbians; that is, lesbian identity is in danger of becoming reduced to some kind of mystical spiritualism. More than a few lesbians have noted that if heterosexual women who breastfeed girl babies get to co-opt the term "lesbian," then they want another, different, word to describe themselves as women who are sexually active with other lesbians.

There is another difficulty common to all three of the views described above, raised primarily by lesbians for whom lesbian identity constitutes a chosen worldview. Basically the difficulty is this: Any functional definition of "lesbian"—that is, any description defining "lesbian" in terms of acts rather than in terms of agents—would allow that some women who have not escaped from the phallocratic conceptual scheme might "be" lesbians, by virtue of what they "do." That is, it would definitionally accommodate the existence of androcentric, or at least nonfeminist, lesbians. Crisis points provoked by this problem show up infamously—for example, as the bitter divisions within lesbian communities about how to regard the sadomasochistic practices engaged in by some lesbians. The question here is whether any behavior engaged in between lesbians qua lesbians is, by definition, necessarily "lesbian" behavior. Some feminist lesbians want to claim that sadomasochistic behavior is patriarchal behavior, not lesbian behavior, even if it occurs between two lesbians.

At the same time, any functional definition of "lesbian" would not allow that there could be any women who have managed to escape from patriarchy's worldview who do not engage in lesbian activities. That is, it would definitionally preclude the existence of nonlesbian feminists. Some lesbians endorse this result, claiming that nonlesbian feminism is not possible, that the willingness to engage in heterosexual activities is itself evidence that the woman so willing is still enmeshed in patriarchy. They view heterosexual women who make such claims as, at best, self-deceived. However, many women who consider themselves to be both woman-centered and heterosexual, and some lesbian feminists, deny this, pointing out that worldviews cannot be defined behaviorally. That is, worldviews can be defined mentalistically only in terms of characteristics of the agent, not in terms of how she acts. Crisis points provoking this problem show up as divisions between lesbians and heterosexual women, and sometimes even as challenges from profeminist men, about what it means to "be" a feminist, or even about what it means to "be" a lesbian. Such claims often suggest that there are, or might be, ways for men or heterosexual women to act that are "newly created" or "outside of patriarchy," because attitude and not behavior is thought to be "what really counts."

ESSENTIALISM

Part of the problem here is that the underlying ontological essentialism remains unquestioned. It is only since the latter half of the nineteenth century that psychological theory has supported the idea that whole persons can "be" essentially heterosexual or homosexual, or even bisexual.[1] It is difficult for me to grasp the notion of a whole person "being" lesbian or not, especially when "lesbian" is construed in Lorde's terms rather than in terms of some other, phallocratic, conceptual scheme.

Taking seriously Lorde's distinction between the erotic and the pornographic, it begins to appear as though much of the debate whether mental states or behaviors define who is and who is not a lesbian is exactly an instance of conflating the pornographic with the erotic. She argues that "the dichotomy between the spiritual [psychic and emotional] and the political is ... false" and that this is part of the pornographing of the sexual.[2] This, she says, results from an "incomplete attention to our erotic knowledge."

> For the bridge which connects them is formed by the erotic—the sensual—those physical, emotional, and psychic expressions of what is deepest and strongest and richest within each of us, being shared: the passions of love, in its deepest meanings. (Lorde 1984, 56)

Thus, the entire debate about whether "real" lesbianism consists of genital activities or acts of attention or political acts rests on this dichotomy that Lorde wishes to deny. Sarah Hoagland also resists this dichotomy when, in explaining why she refuses to define the word "lesbian" in her book *Lesbian Ethics: Toward New Value*, she states that "to define 'lesbian' is ... to succumb to a context of heterosexualism" (Hoagland 1988). Furthermore, the idea that whole persons can be defined by their erotic or sexual connections seems to import into lesbian theory some things that feminists very much want to reject.

Some of the earlier and least controversial feminist arguments were against constructing the identities of whole women in terms of their relationships to men: daughter of, wife of, employee of. Surely a woman is more than just Joe's daughter, John's wife, Harvey's secretary, no matter how much influence these men have over her. Defining whole persons in terms of their erotic attachments or sexual arrangements is both underdescriptive and overdescriptive.

Indeed, it is probably true that persons are shaped and perceptions influenced by the erotic attachments and sexual arrangements that they engage in. But persons are underdetermined by *only* the erotic attachments and sexual arrangements they engage in. They are also shaped by the work that they do, the food that they eat, the neighborhoods they live in, the chemicals they are exposed to, the ethnic backgrounds with which they identify, and the genes they were born with. ...

Without addressing here the more general problems with essentialism (a topic widely discussed elsewhere), I would like to suggest that part of the problem lies in characterizing *persons*, rather than *acts, moments, relationships, encounters, attractions, perspectives, insights, outlooks, connections,* and *feelings,* as lesbian. If one takes "lesbian" to have Lorde's, Frye's, and Hoagland's sense of externalness to the phallocratic conceptual scheme, it is easier to imagine that there are events, interactions, and feelings that occur in that context than it is to imagine that there are whole persons whose very existence permanently "is" or "is not" in that context. One can see, implicit in their descriptions of a "lesbian context," or that which is outside of the "phallocratic conceptual scheme," or the "lens through which we scrutinize all aspects of our existence," glimpses of one of the "worlds" to which María Lugones invites us to travel when she recommends that "we learn to love each other by learning to travel to each other's 'worlds'" (Lugones 1987,4).[3]

Lugones claims that "world"-travelers become different people in different worlds. Of course, she is not saying that Pat Robertson becomes Jesse Jackson by visiting Watts, or anything equally ontologically ridiculous. Nor is she speaking of potentialities or different possible worlds; she is speaking of actual "worlds" between which individuals move, becoming different in context switch. It is "the shift from being one person to being a different person" that she calls travel. She writes:

> Those of us who are "world"-travellers have the distinct experience of being different in different "worlds" and of having the capacity to remember other "worlds" and ourselves in them. . . . So, the experience is of being a different person in different "worlds" and yet of having memory of oneself as different without quite having the sense of there being an underlying "I." (Lugones 1987, 11)

This is not quite so mystical as it might first sound; I believe it is a common, ordinary experience. Most people have the experience of "being" different persons in different contexts. For example, the mature academic who teaches, conducts research, runs a household, and makes economic and personal decisions generally quite competently may find herself "being" a different person when she visits her parents' home for two weeks. She "shifts" who she actually is in different contexts. . . .

I suggest that Lorde's conception of lesbianism is one that is ontologically a matter of positioning oneself in a lesbian "world" and allowing oneself freely to become who one is constructed as in that "world." This includes all of the physical, emotional, psychic, intellectual, and probably other dimensions of lesbian existence. But who one "freely becomes" in that context will probably vary in intensity and kind from individual to individual. Undoubtedly, there are some for whom the physical or sexual aspects of lesbian existence will seem most prominent. There are some who experience lesbian existence primarily in its intellectual or emotional aspects. There are also undoubtedly some who will choose to spend more time in this "world" than others, and some who will choose to spend less, regardless of which dimensions of it are most prominent or intense for them.

The danger of this suggestion is that I imagine it raises horror in some lesbians, who envision themselves being asked to act as perpetual tour guides to "world" traveling ontological tourists who schedule brief stops in Lesbian-Land for the sake of being able to say they've been there. This fear is not unfounded. There is something horrible about the idea of millions of lesbians opening up their beds, their bars, their hearts, their souls, their homes, their music festivals, and their conferences to heterosexual "tourists" who are passing on through, taking snapshots and sending philosophical postcards on home to their menfriends, saying "Having a wonderful time; wish you were here." This is not my suggestion at all, nor is it Lugones's recommendation. . . .

Notes

1. See Card (1987). For further reading, see also Boswell (1980) and Weeks (1977). Thanks to Claudia Card and the anonymous reviewer(s) for pointing out the relevance of these works.
2. Thanks to Susan Bernick for introducing me to the possibilities and understandings illuminated by the Use of the verb-form of "pornography": to pornograph, meaning "to make pornographic." Catherine MacKinnon used the word "pornographed" at least as far back as 1982 when, speaking about Linda Marchiano on a panel at Stanford University (April 2, 1982), she said, "The film *Deep Throat*, in which Linda was pornographed, became a chic success."
3. It is only fair to Lugones to note that she was addressing "women of color in the U.S." in making this recommendation, and since I, and possibly you, may not fit that description, my suggestion that she invites "us" to do this may be a misrepresentation of her work. But elsewhere in the paper she does offer this to white/ Anglo women in the United States as a solution to our "failure to love women across national and cultural boundaries."

References

Belenky, Mary Field, Blythe McVicker Clinchy, Nancy Rule Goldberger, and Jill Mattuck Tarule. 1986. *Women's Ways of Knowing: The Development of Sex, Voice, and Mind.* New York: Basic Books.

Boswell, John. 1980. *Christianity, Social Tolerance, and Homosexuality.* Chicago: University of Chicago Press.

Card, Claudia. 1987. *Intimacy and Responsibility: What Lesbians Do.* Madison: Institute for Legal Studies, University of Wisconson–Madison Law School.

Frye, Marilyn. 1983. *The Politics of Reality: Essays in Feminist Theory.* Trumansburg, NY: Crossing Press.

Harding, Sandra. 1991. *Whose Science? Whose Knowledge?* Ithaca: Cornell University Press.

Hoagland, Sarah. 1988. *Lesbian Ethics: Toward New Value.* Palo Alto, CA: Institute of Lesbian Studies.

Hull, Gloria, and Barbara Smith. 1982. "The Politics of Black Women's Studies." In *All the Women Are White, All the Blacks Are Men, but Some of US Are Brave*, ed. Gloria T. Hull, Patricia Bell Scott, and Barbara Smith. Old Westbury, NY: Feminist Press.

Keller, Evelyn Fox. 1985. "Love and Sex in Plato's epistemology." In *Reflections on Gender and Science*. New Haven: Yale University Press.

Lorde, Audre. 1984. "Uses of the Erotic: The Erotic as Power." In *Sister Outsider: Essays and Speeches by Audre Lorde*. Trumansburg, NY: Crossing Press.

Lugones, María. 1987. "Playfulness, "World"-Travelling, and Loving Perception." *Hypatia* 2 (2): 3–19.

————. 1990. "Hispaneando y Lesbiando: On Sarah Hoagland's Lesbian Ethics." *Hypatia* 5 (3): 138–46.

Morgan, Robin. 1990. *The Demon Lover: On the Sexuality of Terrorism*. New York: Norton.

Rich, Adrienne. 1980. "Compulsory Heterosexuality and Lesbian Existence." *Signs: Journal of Women in Culture and Society* 5 (4): 631–60.

Schott, Robin May. 1988. *Cognition and Eros: A Critique of the Kantian Paradigm*. Boston: Beacon Press.

Trask, Haunani-Kay. 1986. *Eros and Power: The Promise of Feminist Theory*. Philadelphia: University of Pennsylvania Press.

Weeks, Jeffrey. 1977. *Coming Out*. London and New York: Quartet Books.

PART III

Family, Class, Race, and Culture

SELECTION 15
FROM
Gender and History

LINDA J. NICHOLSON

THE METHODOLOGICAL POSITION I am arguing for demands of feminist theory that it become more historical and demands of historically oriented social theory that it become more feminist, that is, more concerned
with the issue of gender relations. A historically oriented social theory which
focuses on gender can provide, I believe, a new and powerful means for
understanding our past.

In this chapter I wish to show the implications of employing a historical
method for analyzing women's oppression, and the implications for social
theory of focusing on gender, by turning to the modern period, i.e., from
1500 on in Western Europe. An examination of this period reveals an important pattern: the progressive decline of kinship as a principle of organizing social life. In the first two chapters I noted the steady decline of the
family over the past two centuries as many of its functions have been taken
over by the state or have become commoditized. I now wish to suggest that
such changes are only the most recent manifestations of the declining importance of kinship which extends beyond the past two centuries to at least
the beginning of the breakdown of feudalism. A point worth emphasizing,
however, is that while the declining importance of kinship over the past
two centuries may be described as a decline in the importance of the institution of the family, this very decline in the importance of kinship in the
early modern period caused the *emergence* of the institution of the family.
In this period the decline in the importance of kinship meant the emergence of a public sphere, or state, unstructured by relations of kinship, and
the increased restriction of kinship to the sphere of domestic life. Thus, in
the early modern period, while the link between kinship and politics increasingly disappeared, the link between kinship and household organization increasingly grew. One consequence is the emergence of the modern
family which unites kinship and domesticity. A second consequence is a

growing separation of the family from the external society, as expressed in the idea of the family as the sphere of the private. Thus, it is in the early modern period that a distinction between domestic and nondomestic activities takes the form of a distinction between the private and the public.

At the start of this period, the family/private sphere is a sphere of economic production, in the context of a growing nonfamilial sphere of economic exchange. This heritage of economic production within the familial is marked even in the twentieth century by its description by many as "private" activity. With the onset of industrialization, production moves outside the home and becomes itself a nonfamilial activity. In consequence, there emerges a sphere of social life, the economy, which is viewed as distinct from both the family and the state. . . .

THE FAMILY

While many feminist theorists have been cognizant of the need to "denaturalize" the family, it is from the relatively recent work of many historians, not necessarily feminist, that much of the justification for such denaturalization can be found. That scholarship arising from the field of history substantiates certain suspicions of feminist theorists is not coincidental. The changing nature of the family and its changing relation to other spheres of society has brought into being a widespread focus on the family. Indeed, part of what has changed about the contemporary family is that it has become a very public institution, an appropriate object for analysis and discussion. Thus it is not surprising that within the relatively recent past, the discipline of history has engendered a new subfield, family history, which in turn has contributed to new ways of thinking about the family.[1]

There are a variety of ways of describing what has been new in such work. At one level it has involved a reperiodization of the family. Before the last twenty years, many believed that for most of human history people were members of what might be called "extended" families which included a number of relatives outside the immediate core.[2] It was believed that as a consequence of industrialization, the extended family gave way to the nuclear family. The new family history challenged this periodization. Particularly, it pushed the emergence of the nuclear family back from the recent past to the preindustrial or early modern period, at least in Europe and colonial America. . . .

Ariè's work *Centuries of Childhood* has become most famous for its claim that the concept of childhood has been historically specific to the modern period. More relevant to the present purposes, however, is his assertion that this has been true also of the concept of the family. Ariès argues that the concept of the family was unknown in the Middle Ages and only originated in the fifteenth and sixteenth centuries.[3] He does not take this change to imply that there was no such entity as the family, meaning the conjugal unit of parents and children, before the early modern period. Rather his argument is that the premodern family was at least very different from its progeny in regard to the silence which surrounded it:

> It would be vain to deny the existence of a family life in the Middle Ages. But the family existed in silence: it did not awaken feelings strong enough to inspire poet or artist. We must recognize the importance of this silence: not much value was placed on the family. Similarly, we must admit the significance of the iconographic blossoming which after the fifteenth and especially the sixteenth century followed this long period of obscurity: the birth and development of the concept of the family.
>
> This powerful concept was formed around the conjugal family, that of the parents and children. This concept is closely linked to that of childhood.[4]

If the family existed in silence before the early modern period, what evoked "noise" or the kind of importance which later became associated with the family was, at least for the aristocracy, the "line." The line, as Ariès notes, "extended to the ties of blood without regard to the emotions engendered by cohabitation and intimacy."[5] This description emphasizes a feature which was to importantly differentiate "family" from "line": its union of kinship and domesticity into a significant association.

The joining together of kinship and domesticity into this construction of "family" was a gradual process. Indeed, a definition of family as mother, father, and children living together did not firmly emerge as the primary definition of the family until the nineteenth century.[6] In earlier centuries the word possessed several different and distinct meanings. There is first a definition of family which has to do primarily with coresidence and includes servants as well as kin. Thus Flandrin quotes Samuel Pepys writing in 1660, "I lived in Axe yard, having my wife and servant Jane, and no more in family than us three."[7] "Family" here both in word and sense derives from the ancient Latin where "familial" includes slaves, wife, and children under one head of household. There is a second sense of family used in the seventeenth and eighteenth centuries which refers to the wider kinship network of people of a certain class. It was most frequently, though not unambiguously, used of the bourgeoisie rather than the aristocracy, members of the latter more properly being referred to as of a given "house"; it was clearly not, however, a term used of the common people.[8] There is finally a sense of "family," appearing in late seventeenth- and eighteenth-century French dictionaries and not until the nineteenth century in England, which is used more democratically and refers to close kinship. The evolution of "close kinship" to mean, however, mother, father, and children does not become definitive even in France until after the mid-eighteenth century with the conflation of the two older meanings of domesticity and kinship.[9] In short, *our* primary meaning of family, as mother, father, and children living together, is an evolutionary composite of earlier meanings: one of which had as its core domesticity, and the other, kinship. Over the course of the modern period these two components became conjoined, while eliminating on the side of domesticity, servants, and deemphasizing (though not eliminating) the more extended kinship network. This growing focus on the more nuclear kinship core was also linked with its spread to all classes. . . .

THE FAMILY AND THE STATE

If the emergence and transformation of the family has largely to do with political and economic issues understood broadly, i.e., with changing obligations of people to one another and changing relations to property, then we might expect a close interconnection between the history of the family and political and economic history. Here I would like to focus specifically on the interconnection of family and state, particularly in terms of origins. . . .

During the Middle Ages there existed a seesaw relationship between loyalty to the kin and to the state, with loyalty to the latter being in effect loyalty to the most powerful kin network of all, headed by the king.[10] In the sixteenth century in England, the state enhanced its reign, increasing its control over property, crime, and punishment. Later, it changed the nature of the loyalty it demanded. Particularistic notions of obligation and allegiance became transformed into a more universalistic moral code.[11] This transformation in the extent and nature of the relation between subjects and their king entailed that existing, more particularistic allegiances be undermined. As Stone notes, one of the tools used by the emerging state in its battle for power with such allegiances was to transfer the idea of good lordship from its association with the head of an extended kinship and clientage unit to the individual male head of household. The new state thus encouraged patriarchy within the *family*—claiming that allegiances within it were analogous to allegiances of all the king—while undermining patriarchy in its more traditional sense. Thus, as Stone concludes, the principle of patriarchy was transformed by the state from a threat to its existence into a formidable buttress to it.[12]

In short, contrary to the picture which Locke and others have given us, of the family preceding the state in time, the above analysis suggests a mutual emergence. The family as that institution which focuses on kinship ties in the conjugal, domestically centered unit arises as an understandable component of a form of society whose overarching organizational principles become now based on criteria antithetical to kinship. Moreover, also antithetical to the received picture of families creating states for reasons different from those generating families is the fact of families and states originating together and containing common features as a function of their common origins. For example, that the governmental bodies were primarily made up of men and that families/household units were perceived as headed by men, two facts crucial in understanding gender relations in the modern period, can be seen as two interrelated consequences of the origins of both the family and the state in patriarchal kinship structures. Thus families and states can be understood as institutions not inherently different in kind but with important features in common in the context of simultaneously increasing differences in function. . . .

THE FAMILY AND THE ECONOMY

The belief in the family as a quasi-natural institution and as necessarily distinct in purpose and origins from the state has, since the nineteenth century, become associated with a corollary assumption: that home and family are also necessarily distinct from the sphere of "the economy." Thus in our contemporary worldview, a description of "worker productivity" does not normally include household tasks unless these tasks are performed for a salary. This belief that activities performed outside the home and particularly outside the system of familial relations are "naturally" different in kind from those performed within the home and family is so endemic to our cultural ideology that it has sometimes been found even among the most radical critics of that ideology, such as Marxists. . . .

Here I would like to counter this belief by making a similar kind of claim as I did earlier: that the separation of the family and the economy, like the separation of the family and the state, needs to be comprehended as occurring within history. Since what we now perceive as separate spheres have common origins and interrelated histories, we should expect to find important connections between them. Thus, in preindustrial societies kinship embraces much of what we mean by the "economic." This point sometimes gets lost as a function of a prevailing contemporary convention that economic relations revolve primarily around interactions of trade or exchange. However, even as we use the term "economic," a use which reflects its history, economics is most fundamentally about the production and distribution of social resources, of which trade and exchange are only one means. Thus kinship relations, which organize the production and distribution of resources among members of social groups (as well as organizing sexuality, religion, and other human practices) are at least in part about "economics." Following from this point, gender relationships, as historically structured by kinship, have always been at least in part economic relations, a point with important implications for the relation of Marxism and feminism. Moreover, it is not only intersex relations which are economically structured through kinship rules; intergenerational relations are also so structured, as, for example, in inheritance procedures.

The above claims, on the face of it, seem obvious. They require emphasis only as a consequence of the fact that since at least the early modern period (and indeed beginning much earlier), many of the interactions around the production and distribution of resources have become structured increasingly outside the domain of kinship. Before industrialization, this meant primarily a growing sphere of trade governed by principles of exchange. The early modern family/household unit was, however, until industrialization a productive and thus "economic" unit. After industrialization this ceased to be the case. In conjunction with the growth of an "economy" outside of the household, there also developed a more limited meaning of the term "economic," so that it came primarily to refer to the production and exchange of commodities. As a result, it has become increasingly difficult to keep in sight the common origins and interconnections of the familial and the economic. As with the family and the state, these two spheres now appear to exist as worlds apart, with different and unrelated histories and concerns.

Moreover, as with the analogous view on the relation of the family and the state, this latter perspective has raised large obstacles in explicating women's history and women's lives, perhaps because it has been women who have been most strongly affected by the separation. Thus to take this separation for granted and not to focus explicitly on the how and the why of its occurrence has been to overlook a process crucial in understanding women's history. In consequence, comprehending women's history and the changing dynamics of gender has entailed throwing off this belief in necessarily separate spheres and beginning to examine the very history of the separation. . . .

Moreover, an analysis which focuses on the historical separation of the economic from the familial enables us to see both the economic nature of gender relations within the family and the gendered aspect of economic relations outside it as a consequence of the emergence of the economy out of kinship. This point runs against a liberal perspective which conceptualizes the market as an autonomous realm governed only by forces internal to itself. It also runs counter to the orthodox Marxist dictum that in the interrelation of the economic and the familial, it is always the former and never the latter which is causally prior. However, again from works such as Tilly and Scott's, among others, we can provide counterevidence to both points of view.[13] For example, Scott and Tilly note that young, unmarried women becoming primary workers in many industries in the early stages of industrialization is poorly described as capitalism invading and changing previous familial patterns. Rather they argue that this phenomenon needs to be explained at least in part in terms of preindustrial familial relations which saw women as necessary contributors to family subsistence. They describe the ways in which the conditions in the early factories replicated conditions at home, with factory owners even on occasion taking responsibility for arranging suitable marriages for their female workers.[14] They point to the persistence of the expectation that the wages of these girls would be sent to their families, noting that in some cases the factories sent the girls' wages to their parents while in other cases the girls merely sent most of it themselves.[15]

Of course, industrialization did radically affect kinship relations. Most fundamentally it entailed a general distancing of the household from the productive sphere. This accentuated the development of the idea of "separate spheres" for men and women. This idea cannot be described as mere ideology; the lives of many middle-class women did conform to the ideal. Moreover, even among the working class, where the ideal was often contradicted, the norm affected, as earlier noted, the perceptions of married women's labor.

Thus the point is not that industrialization and market forces had no effect on preindustrial values and practices; it is rather that the story is poorly understood as one where the causal arrow moves in only one direction. That, for instance, a nineteenth-century woman would become a prostitute to support the rest of her family is a story not only about the commercialization of sex but also about the persistence of familial loyalties in new contexts.[16] This methodological point becomes a political point in our own day as preindustrial values and practices of kinship and gender continue to affect market relationships in the context of a political ideology which denies that possibility. According to this ideology, with the establishment of true equality of educational opportunity, and the abolition of old prejudices about women's capabilities, the criteria of merit and effort alone determine women's participation in the economy. However, as feminists have been pointing out, the problem is not merely one of overcoming old prejudices, but rather of recognizing and coming to alter a contemporary economy long structured by values and practices of kinship and gender. Thus, for the ideology of the free marketplace to become in any way a reality for women requires a recognition of the ways in which that marketplace has been determined by aspects of human existence supposedly localized outside itself.[17]

Moreover—and now I want to take the argument to what I perceive as its most extreme conclusion—comprehending the separation of the economic from the familial as a historical phenomenon enables us to see certain very basic structural components of our economy as rooted in kinship and some of the basic categories we possess for describing it as "familial." In consequence, the connection between the familial and the economic has to be understood as more than causal, but at least in part as analytic. For example, one important category we use in describing our modern economy is the category of "private property." This concept, however, is partially a familial concept, referring to ownership by family units. Thus the increased privatization and alienability of property, usually hailed as a defining component in the rise of capitalism in the early modern period, is also analytically connected with what we mean by the rise of "family" in this period, at least for those of property. . . .

Notes

1. There are many writers who have pointed out how recent this field is. See, for example, Carl Degler, *At Odds: Women and the Family in America from the Revolution to the Present* (Oxford: Oxford University Press, 1980), v. Peter Laslett also notes it in his introduction to Peter Laslett, ed., *Household and Family in Past Time* (Cambridge: Cambridge University Press, 1972), 1. Stone similarly speaks of the rapid acceleration of work on family history in the period from the early 1940s to the 1970s and then an even more rapid growth in the 1970s in his review article on family history in the 1980s, "Past Achievements and Future Trends," *Journal of Interdisciplinary History* 22, no. 1 (Summer 1981): 51.
2. An important contributor to this idea was Frederic Le Play. See Catherine Bodard Silver, ed. and tr., *Frederic Le Play on Family, Work, and Social Change* (Chicago: University of Chicago Press, 1982).
3. Philippe Ariès, *Centuries of Childhood: A Social History of Family Life*, tr. Robert Baldick (New York: Knopf, 1962), 353.
4. Ibid., 364.
5. Ibid., 356.
6. Jean Louise Flandrin, *Families in Former Times*, Richard Southern (Cambridge: Cambridge University Press, 1979), 9.
7. Ibid., 5.
8. Ibid., 6–7.
9. Ibid., 18.
10. Lawrence Stone, *The Family, Sex and Marriage in England, 1500–1800* (New York: Harper and Row, 1979), 132–33.
11. Ibid., 133–34.
12. Ibid., 154.
13. Other examples can also be found. Mary Ryan points to the note made by colonial historians of the centrality of certain ties of kinship and marriage alliances in making possible the phenomenon of the merchant capitalist. See her article, "The Explosion of Family History," in *Reviews in American History* 10, no. 4 (Dec. 1982): 183. Even more dramatically, Barbara Harris argues that factors such as the stem family, late marriage, and high rates of celibacy, by keeping the population of the West low and raising standards of living, made possible the market conditions necessary for industrialization. Barbara J. Harris, "Recent Work on the History of the Family: A Review Article," in *Feminist Studies* 3, nos. 3–4 (Spring–Summer 1976): 165.
    Also of interest here, for underlining the possible causal efficacy of changes

in marriage rules, is Jack Goody's *The Development of the Family and Marriage in Europe* (Cambridge: Cambridge University Press, 1983). Goody points to changes in marriage rules in the centuries after Christ, promulgated by the church, whose effect was both to contribute to an emphasis on conjugality and to vastly increase the property of the church.

14. Joan W. Scott and Louise A. Tilly, "Women's Work and the Family in Nineteenth-Century Europe," *Comparative Studies in Society and History* 17, no. 1 (Jan. 1975): 53.

15. Ibid., p. 54.

16. Louise A. Tilly and Joan W. Scott, *Women, Work, and Family* (New York: Holt, Rinehart, and Winston, 1978), 117.

17. Michele Barrett and Mary McIntosh also point to the historical continuities in home and paid labor in *The Anti-Social Family* (London: Verso, 1982), 88–89.

SELECTION 16
FROM
Inessential Woman

ELISABETH V. SPELMAN

IN THE PAST THREE chapters we've explored ways in which it can be misleading to talk about gender as if it exists in isolation from other variables of human identity such as race and class. Simultaneously, we have examined ways in which gender issues are not simply parallel to but intertwined with race and class issues. For example, we have seen that we can't adequately describe Plato's proposal for a kind of "equality" between men and women without noting that he is referring to a very small group of men and women and that he thinks of females who would be philosopher-rulers as different in kind from other females. Aristotle doesn't even think of female slaves as "women," and his claims about the superiority of "men" to "women" don't apply to relations between male and female slaves. In many parts of her work, Simone de Beauvoir treats both the meaning and the consequences of being a "woman" as being dependent upon one's race, class, and nationality.

It is theoretically significant for any feminist analysis of gender and of sexism if statements that appear to be true about "men and women" clearly aren't true when we specify that we are talking about men and women of different classes or races. What Plato says about the relation between male philosopher-rulers and female philosopher-rulers doesn't apply to the relation between male philosopher-rulers and females who are part of the "masses." What Aristotle says about the natural superiority of free men to free women doesn't apply to slave men and free women. De Beauvoir cautions (and then forgets) that the kind of sexual privilege she is talking about only applies when the race and class of the men and women in question is the same.[1] If all women had the same gender—if what it meant to be a "woman" was the same for all of them no matter what their race or class or nationality—and if all women were subject to sexism in the same way, this wouldn't happen. If gender identity were isolatable from class and race identity, if sexism were isolatable from classism and racism, we could talk about rela-tions between men and women and never have to worry about whether their race or class was the same or different. We could make believe that we could get an accurate account of what Plato and Aristotle and de Beauvoir said about relations between men and women without making any refer-ence to whether the men and women in question were philosopher-rulers, guardians, artisans, or slaves, poor, black, or Jewish. If gender were isolatable from other aspects of identity, if sexism were isolatable from other forms of oppression, then what would be true about the relation between any man and woman would be true about the relation between any other man and any other woman.

Much of feminist theory has proceeded on the assumption that gender is indeed a variable of human identity independent of other variables such as race and class, that whether one is woman is unaffected by what class or race one is.[2] Feminists have also assumed that sexism is distinctly different from racism and classism, that whether and how one is subject to sexism is unaffected by whether and how one is subject to racism or classism. . . .

Once we begin to look at the social context of mothering, and hence at the social context of gender, we have to think about what it means to say that women possess the same gender. For if it is true that gender identity is not separable from other aspects of identity, then, as the examples discussed above suggest, one's sense of oneself as a "woman" is not separable from one's sense of oneself as, say, Chicana, black, or white; one is known as and knows oneself as Chicana, black woman, or white woman. Or are we in our entirety divisible into parts? Can I point to the "woman" part, then to the "white" part? Would it be desirable to be able to do so? No doubt we have linguistic habits that suggest we are so divisible: We ask and are asked "to think about ourselves as women," or "to think about our experiences as women," or "to identify with other Blacks." We say things like, "As a woman, I think that . . . , while as a Jew, I think that . . ." We say things like, "Daily, we feel the pull and tug of having to choose between which parts have served to cloak us from the knowledge of ourselves."[3] We sometimes ask ourselves where and with whom we feel most ourselves—with other women, with other lesbians, other blacks, other Hispanas, other Jews? What do such habits and grammatical possibilities tell us?

One thing they tell us is that there are a lot of different ways of sorting human beings. If we look at that variety, we of course see that sorting along one dimension cuts across another. The dimension "women" cuts across race and class and nationality; the division "race" cuts across sex and class. Any given individual will be included in any number of divisions, and no individual will be included in only one. Why there are the sortings there are depends among other things on the goals of the sorters and the point of the sorting. Is there some sorting that is more fundamental in some sense than any other? Are some principles of sorting somehow built into the nature of things, while others are more conventional and hence, it would seem, more subject to change? Can a person change any of the ways in which she is sorted? Can she disguise any of those ways? Do answers to these two questions have implications for what is more "fundamental"? These are rather metaphysical concerns—with political consequences if not political presuppositions. We can't begin to go into these questions here but we can say that the experience and meaning of being sorted out along one dimension of human identity is very much influenced by the experience and the meaning of being sorted out along another dimension. This means that even if you are sorted out along one dimension with others, your experience is nevertheless likely to be different from those others insofar as you are not sorted together along another dimension. For example, socialist feminists have shown us why accounts of living under conditions of class oppression cannot be the same for men and for women because of the invidious sorting also done along the lines of sex and gender identity.[4] By the same token, accounts of living under conditions of sexual oppression cannot be the same for women of all classes. And this, I think, tells us that while in one sense women are all of the same gender, what it means to be a "woman" depends on what else is true about oneself and the world in which one lives. All women are women, but there is no being who is only a woman. For different reasons and on different occasions, being a woman may be, both in the eyes of others and in the eyes of a woman herself, the most important fact about her. But it is not the only fact about her, and the meaning of that fact about her—to herself and to others—will depend on other facts about her. Thus it has been suggested that great differences between the lives of affluent and working-class women in Victorian England, as well as great differences between the ideologies about their lives, meant that "it was as if there were two different human species of females."[5] How many different "species" there are depends on how crucial other variables are in giving shape and meaning to women's experiences at any particular time and place. . . .

Despite my repeated insistence that gender exists and must be seen in the context of other factors of identity, it may seem as if we will never be able to say anything coherent about gender if it must be looked at in connection with race and class rather than in isolation from them. Indeed, the project of trying to see how such factors affect gender may seem methodologically unsound. The argument about its fundamental wrongheadedness would go something like this: Precisely because these other factors affect gender, in order to examine gender differences carefully we have to remove these other factors from consideration. This is the point de Beauvoir makes when she says in passing that descriptions of sexual hierarchy only apply when race and class are kept constant. If we want to understand the difference gender makes to human social and psychological development and to relations between people, we will obtain the clearest picture if we eliminate other variables that might blur the focus. In most families, the race and class of the parents is the same, and the same as that of the children. This is what makes the family an especially appropriate locus for the investigation of gender differences. Race and class typically aren't variable factors in the relationship between the father and mother, or in the relationship between mother and the children. Where they are variables, we can't be sure that it is simply gender that makes the difference in the relational stances of the boys and girls.

This reminder about the ways in which issues of race and class might influence gender issues points in two directions: On the one hand, it recognizes the important presence of race and class by saying we must make sure they are kept constant; but on the other hand, in keeping them constant, it may look as if we indeed are isolating gender from race and class. In that sense it suggests that while examination of gender differences must recognize the impact of race and class, it does so by keeping them from skewing the examination of gender.

The methodological point about the optimal conditions under which to examine gender difference seems to be an instance of a more general principle of investigation in the social (and natural) sciences: If you want to see what difference any particular difference makes to a situation, be sure to cancel out the effects of other possible differences in such a situation. For example, if we want to examine differences in the way men and women use language, presumably we won't compare how males use the Russian language with how females use the English language. If we want to examine differences in the way boys and girls are brought up, presumably we won't compare how little boys in northern India are brought up with how little girls in northern Ireland are brought up. If you want to focus on what differentiates women from men, then compare them to men of the same class or race or nationality.

But does this mean that what people share is irrelevant to what differentiates them—so irrelevant, for example, that in discussing gender differences, as long as we stick to the principle and keep race and class constant, we can describe the differences we find simply as differences between men and women?

Suppose someone undertook to describe gender differences between white men and white women of the same class in the United States. Because race is a constant, can we say that it has no significance in their relationship? The very consideration that enables us to "cancel out" race makes it necessary to reintroduce it when describing the differences. If we can only get at gender differences in this case by canceling out racial differences, that means we cannot assume that the gender differences apply when speaking about other racial groups and surely not where there are racial differences between the men and women in question. That is, our description of how sexual difference influences relations between men and women of the same race does not automatically apply to men and women of a different race nor to men of one race and women of another.

This means that simply because race and class are kept constant doesn't mean they have no effect. To talk about gender differences where race and class are constants is to talk about gender differences in the context of class and race similarity; but far from freeing us from the context of race and class, keeping them constant means they are constantly there. The same point applies when we are talking about race or class differences where gender is the same. . . .

We have, then, been asking whether the best way to acknowledge the influence of race and class differences on gender differences is to see that they are kept constant. Thus we've looked at the suggestion that the only way we can accurately describe gender is to isolate its effects from the influence of race and class. We don't need to talk about race and class, because they can't make a difference: We've ensured that, and must ensure it, in order to have a clear look at gender differences.

Our response to this line of thought has been to point out that even if the gender relations in question are those between men and women or boys and girls of the same race and class, it is inaccurate to report them simply as gender relations, since the description of them holds by hypothesis only for men and women or boys and girls of the same race and class. Moreover, we have seen a number of reasons why we can't say factor of human identity has no effect on relations between people if they share that factor. On the contrary, if it would affect their relationship were they to differ in that way, it also affects their relationship if they do not. So even if the race and class of the men and women, boys and girls, is the same, we can't assume that therefore such factors have no effect on their gender relations.

Now someone might propose that race or class could drop out in another way after reporting carefully on differences between, for example, white men and white women, black men and black women. Suppose—contrary to the examples we've discussed above—it turned out that sexism was the same between white men and white women, black men and black women. It still wouldn't follow that we needn't look at race or class or culture in order to understand male/female relationships, for our exploration tells us nothing so far about relations between men and women across race and class. And if this is different—for example, if what characterizes the relationship between white men and white women does not characterize the relationship between black men and white women, or between white men and black women—then it is misleading to talk simply of relationships between "men and women," for whether what we say is true is going to depend on which men and women we are talking about. . . .

It is a general principle of feminist inquiry to be skeptical about any account of human relations that fails to mention gender or consider the possible effects of gender differences: for in a world in which there is sexism, obscuring the workings of gender is likely to involve—whether intentionally or not—obscuring the workings of sexism. We thus ought to be skeptical about any account of gender relations that fails to mention race and class or to consider the possible effects of race and class differences on gender: for in a world in which there is racism and classicism, obscuring the workings of race and class is likely to involve—whether intentionally or not—obscuring the workings of racism and classism.

For this reason alone we may have a lot to learn from the following questions about any account of gender relations that presupposes or otherwise insists on the separability of gender, race, and class: Why does it seem possible or necessary to separate them? Whatever the motivations for doing so, does it serve the interests of some people and not others? Does methodology ever express race or class privilege—for example, do any of the methodological reasons that might be given for trying to investigate gender in isolation from race and class in fact serve certain race or class interests?

These questions are not rhetorical. For very good and very important reasons, feminists have insisted on asking how gender affects or is affected by every branch of human inquiry (even those such as the physical sciences, which seem to have no openings for such questions). And with very good reason we have been annoyed by the absence of reference to gender in inquires about race or class, racism and classism. Perhaps it seems the best response, to such a state of affairs, first to focus on gender and sexism and then to go on to think about how gender and sexism are related to race and racism, class and classism. Hence the appeal of the work of Nancy Chodorow and the variations on it by others. But however logically, methodologically, and politically sound such inquiry seems, it obscures the ways in which race and class identity may be intertwined with gender identity. Moreover, since in a racist and classist society the racial and class identity of those who are subject to racism and classism are not obscured, all it can really mask is the racial and class identity of white middle-class women. It is because white middle-class women have something at stake in not having their racial and class identity made and kept visible that we must question accepted feminist positions on gender identity.

If feminism is essentially about gender, and gender is taken to be neatly separable from race and class, then race and class don't need to be talked about except in some peripheral way. And if race and class are peripheral to women's identities as women, then racism and classism can't be of central concern to feminism. Hence the racism and classism some women face and other women help perpetuate can't find a place in feminist theory unless we keep in mind the race and class of all women (not just the race and class of those who are the victims of racism and classism). I have suggested here that one way to keep them in mind is to ask about the extent to which gender identity exists in concert with these other aspects of identity. This is quite different from saying either (1) we need to talk about race and class instead of gender or (2) we need to talk about race and class in addition to gender. Some feminists may be concerned that focus on race and class will deflect attention away from gender and from what women have in common and thus from what gives feminist inquiry its distinctive cast. This presupposes not only that we ought not spend too much time on what we don't have in common but that we have gender in common. But do we have gender identity in common? In one sense, of course, yes: All women are women. But in another sense, no: not if gender is a social construction and females become not simply women but particular kinds of women. If I am justified in thinking that what it means for me to be a woman must be exactly the same as what it means for you to be a woman (since we both are women), I needn't bother to find out anything from you or about you in order to find out what it means for you to be a woman: I can simply deduce what it means from my own case. On the other hand, if the meaning of what we apparently have in common (being women) depends in some ways on the meaning of what we don't have in common (for example, our different racial or class identities), then far from distracting us from issues of gender. In this sense it is only if we pay attention to how we differ that we come to an understanding of what we have in common.[6] . . .

Notes

1. As we saw, this didn't mean what it may suggest—that for different races and classes the sexism is always the same.
2. Notice how different this is from saying that whether one is *female* is unaffected by what race or class one is.
3. From Moraga and Anzaldúa's introduction to part 2 of *This Bridge Called My Back* (Watertown, MA: Persephone Press, 1981), 23.
4. See Alison Jaggar's *Feminist Politics and Human Nature* (Totowa, NJ: Rowman and Allanheld, 1983) for an especially useful account of socialist feminism.
5. This has been suggested by Barbara Ehrenreich and Deirdre English in *Complaints and Disorders: The Sexual Politics of Sickness* (Old Westbury, NY: Feminist Press, 1973), 11–12. See also Rosaldo, "The Use and Abuse of Anthropology."
6. Thanks to Helen Longino, Monica Jakuc, and Marilyn Schuster for helpful comments on a very early draft of this chapter.

SELECTION 17
FROM
The Alchemy of Race and Rights

PATRICIA WILLIAMS

THIS SEMESTER I HAVE been teaching a course entitled Women and Notions of Property. I have been focusing on the semantic power and property of individualistic gendered perspectives, gender in this instance having less to do with the biology of male and female than with the semiotics of power relations, of dominance and submission, of assertion and deference, of big and little; as well as on gender issues specifically based in biology, such as reproductive rights and the complicated ability of women in particular to live freely in the territory of their own bodies. An example of the stories we discuss is the following, used to illustrate the rhetoric of power relations whose examination, I tell my students, is at the heart of the course.

Walking down Fifth Avenue in New York not long ago, I came up behind a couple and their young son. The child, about four or five years old, had evidently been complaining about big dogs. The mother was saying, "But why are you afraid of big dogs?" "Because they're big," he responded with eminent good sense. "But what's the difference between a big dog and a little dog?" the father persisted. "They're *big*," said the child. "But there's really no difference," said the mother, pointing to a large slathering wolfhound with narrow eyes and the calculated amble of a gangster, and then to a beribboned Pekinese the size of a roller skate, who was flouncing along just ahead of us all, in that little fox-trotty step that keeps Pekinese from ever being taken seriously. "See?" said the father. "If you look really closely you'll see there's no difference at all. They're all just dogs."

And I thought: Talk about your iron-clad canon. Talk about a static, unyielding, totally uncompromising point of reference. These people must be lawyers. Where else do people learn so well the idiocies of High Objectivity? How else do people learn to capitulate so uncritically to a norm that refuses to allow for difference? How else do grown-ups sink so deeply into the authoritarianism of their own worldview that they can universalize their

155

relative bigness so completely that they obliterate the subject positioning of their child's relative smallness? (To say nothing of the position of the slathering wolfhound, from whose own narrow perspective I dare say the little boy must have looked exactly like a lamb chop.)

I used this story in my class because I think it illustrates a paradigm of thought by which children are taught not to see what they see; by which blacks are reassured that there is no real inequality in the world, just their own bad dreams; and by which women are taught not to experience what they experience, in deference to men's ways of knowing. The story also illustrates the possibility of a collective perspective or social positioning that would give rise to a claim for the legal interests of groups. In a historical moment when individual rights have become the basis for any remedy, too often group interests are defeated by, for example, finding the one four-year-old who has wrestled whole packs of wolfhounds fearlessly to the ground; using that individual experience to attack the validity of there ever being any generalizable four-year-old fear of wolfhounds; and then recasting the general group experience as a fragmented series of specific, isolated events rather than a pervasive social phenomenon ("You have every right to think that that wolfhound has the ability to bite off your head, but that's just your point of view").

My students, most of whom signed up expecting to experience that crisp, refreshing, clearheaded sensation that "thinking like a lawyer" purportedly endows, are confused by this and all the stories I tell them in my class on Women and Notions of Property. They are confused enough by the idea of property alone, overwhelmed by the thought of dogs and women as academic subjects, and paralyzed by the idea that property might have a gender and that gender might be a matter of words. . . .

When I was living in California I had a student, S., who was very unhappy being a man and informed me of his intention to become a woman. He said he wanted to talk to me before anyone else at the school because I was black and might be more understanding. I had never thought about transsexuality at all and found myself lost for words.[1]

After the sex-change operation, S. began to use the ladies' room. There was an enormous outcry from women students of all political persuasions, who "felt raped," in addition to the more academic assertions of some who "feared rape." In a complicated storm of homophobia, the men of the student body let it be known that they too "feared rape" and vowed to chase her out of any and all men's rooms. The oppositional forces of men and women reached a compromise: S. should use the dean's bathroom. Alas, in the dean's bathroom no resolution was to be found, for the suggestion had not been an honest one but merely an integration of the fears of each side. Then, in his turn the dean, circumspection having gotten him this far in life, expressed polite, well-modulated fears about the appearance of impropriety in having students visit his inner sanctum, and many other things most likely related to his fear of a real compromise of hierarchy.

I remember thinking how peculiar and revealing were the scripts that people shook in the face of poor S. Gender as property. Gender as privilege. Hierarchy as sexualized oppression. "I am not a homosexual," I remember S. crying out at one point in the middle of all that mess. Those words echo in me still. She was not homosexual first and foremost as to her best friend, a man with whom she was in love and for whom she had gone through the operation. She was not homosexual as to the women, whose outcry she took for fear of lesbianism. She was not homosexual as to the men, for this would have been an ultimate betrayal of her bitter, hard-won love. She was not homosexual as to the dean, as if this bit of clarity would save him from some embarrassment or reassure him that his status would not be lowered by the ambivalence of her identity.

At the vortex of this torment, S. as human being who needed to go to the bathroom was lost. Devoured by others, she carved and shaped herself to be definitionally acceptable. She aspired to a notion of women set like jewels in grammatical mountings, fragile and display-cased. She had not learned what society's tricksters and dark fringes have had to learn in order to survive: to invert, to stretch, meaning rather than oneself. She to whom words meant so much was not given the room to appropriate them. S. as "transsexual," S. as "not homosexual," thus became a mere floating signifier, a deconstructive polymorph par excellence.

In retrospect, I see clearly the connection between S.'s fate and my being black, her coming to me because I was black. S.'s experience was a sort of Jim Crow mentality applied to gender. Many men, women, blacks, and certainly anyone who identifies with the term "white" are caught up in the perpetuation and invisible privilege of this game; for "black," "female," "male," and "white" are every bit as much properties as the buses, private clubs, neighborhoods, and schools that provide the extracorporeal battlegrounds of their expression. S.'s experience, indeed, was a reminder of the extent to which property is nothing more than the mind's enhancement of the body's limitation. This is true to some extent in all cultures, I think, but particularly in ours, where possessions become the description of who we are and the reflection of our worth; and where land usually is referred to not by its use but by the name of its owner (Queens, Victoria, Washington, Pennsylvania)—as if the greater the expanse of an estate, the greater in personhood will its master become.

Another dimension of this encounter was that the property of my blackness was all about my struggle to define myself as "somebody." Into the middle of that struggle, S. was coming to me both because I was black and because others had defined her as "nobody." Initially it felt as if she were seeking in me the comfort of another nobody; I was a bit put off by the implication that my distinctive somebody-ness was being ignored—I was being used, rendered invisible through her refusal to see all of me. Very quickly, however, I realized that a literal designation of "black" in my self-definition was probably not appropriate in this situation. Though all of the above may be true, I realized that another truth existed also: A discursive property of black somebody-ness was to be part of a community of souls who had experienced being permanently invisible nobodies; "black" was a designation for those who had no place else to go; we were both nobody and somebody at the same time, if for different purposes.

This is not an easy concept. I am not saying that my blackness is unimportant or not different. In other circumstances it might be presumptuous for S. to "become black" or for me to feel obligated to stretch the definition to include her. What I am saying is that my difference was in some ways the same as hers, that simultaneously her difference was in some ways very different from mine, and that simultaneously we were in all ways the same.

Note

1. I have tried to do a fair amount of reading on the subject since then. By no means do I want to imply, in my recounting of S., any implication that this was all there was to her story or that her story explains transsexuality: there is a whole range of transsexuality beyond S. herself, as well as an S. who exists beyond my limited characterization or experience of her.

SELECTION 18
FROM
Black Feminist Thought

PATRICIA HILL COLLINS

Called Matriarch, Emasculator and Hot Momma. Sometimes Sister, Pretty Baby, Auntie, Mammy and Girl, Called Unwed Mother, Welfare Recipient and Inner City Consumer. The Black American Woman has had to admit that while nobody knew the troubles she saw, everybody, his brother and his dog, felt qualified to explain her, even to herself.
—Trudier Harris 1982, 4

RACE, CLASS, AND GENDER oppression could not continue without powerful ideological justifications for their existence. As Cheryl Gilkes contends, "Black women's assertiveness and their use of every expression of racism to launch multiple assaults against the entire fabric of inequality have been a consistent, multifaceted threat to the status quo. As punishment, Black women have been assaulted with a variety of negative images" (1983, 294). Portraying African-American women as stereotypical mammies, matriarchs, welfare recipients, and hot mommas has been essential to the political economy of domination fostering black women's oppression. Challenging these controlling images has long been a core theme in black feminist thought.

As part of a generalized ideology of domination, these controlling images of black womanhood take on special meaning because the authority to define these symbols is a major instrument of power. In order to exercise power, elite white men and their representatives must be in a position to manipulate appropriate symbols concerning black women. They may do so by exploiting already existing symbols, or they may create new ones relevant to their needs (Patterson 1982). Hazel Carby suggests that the objective of stereotypes is "not to reflect or represent a reality but to function as a disguise, or mystification, of objective social relations" (1987, 22). These controlling images are designed to make racism, sexism, and poverty appear to be natural, normal, and an inevitable part of everyday life.

Even when the political and economic conditions that originally generated controlling images disappear, such images prove remarkably tenacious because they not only keep black women oppressed but are key in maintaining interlocking systems of race, class, and gender oppression. The status of African-American women as outsiders or strangers becomes the point from which other groups define their normality. Ruth Shays, a black inner-city resident, describes how the standpoint of a subordinate group is discredited: "It will not kill people to hear the truth, but they don't like it and they would much rather hear it from one of their own than from a stranger. Now, to white people your colored person is always a stranger. Not only that, we are supposed to be dumb strangers, so we can't tell them anything!" (Gwaltney 1980, 29). As the "Others" of society who can never really belong, strangers threaten the moral and social order. But they are simultaneously essential for its survival because those individuals who stand at the margins of society clarify its boundaries. African-American women, by not belonging, emphasize the significance of belonging.

THE OBJECTIFICATION OF BLACK WOMEN AS THE OTHER

Black feminist critic Barbara Christian asserts that in America, "the enslaved African woman became the basis for the definition of our society's Other" (1985, 160). Maintaining images of black women as the Other provides ideological justification for race, gender, and class oppression.

Certain basic ideas crosscut all three systems. Claimed by black feminist theorist Bell Hooks to be "the central ideological component of all systems of domination in Western society," one such idea is either/or dichotomous thinking (1984, 29). Either/or dichotomous thinking categorizes people, things, and ideas in terms of their differences from one another (Keller 1985, 8). For example, the terms in the dichotomies black/white (Richards 1980; Irele 1983), male/female (Eisenstein 1983), reason/emotion (Hoschschild 1975; Halpin 1989), culture/nature (Asante 1987), fact/opinion (Westkott 1979; Bellah 1983), mind/body (Spelman 1982), and subject/object (Halpin 1989) gain meaning only in *relation* to their counterparts.

Another basic idea concerns the relationship between notions of differences in either/or dichotomous thinking and objectification. In either/or dichotomous thinking, difference is defined in oppositional terms. One part is not simply different from its counterpart; it is inherently opposed to its "other." Whites and blacks, males and females, thought and feeling are not complementary counterparts—they are fundamentally different entities related only through their definition as opposites. Feeling cannot be incorporated into thought or even function in conjunction with it because in either/

or dichotomous thinking, feeling retards thought, values obscure facts, and judgment clouds knowledge.

Objectification is central to this process of oppositional difference. In either/or dichotomous thinking, one element is objectified as the Other, and is viewed as an object to be manipulated and controlled. Social theorist Dona Richards (1980) suggests that Western thought requires objectification, a process she describes as the "separation of the 'knowing self' from the 'known object'" (72). Intense objectification is a "prerequisite for the despiritualization of the universe," notes Richards, "and through it the Western cosmos was made ready for every increasing materialization" (72). A Marxist assessment of the culture/nature dichotomy argues that history can be seen as one in which human beings constantly objectify the natural world in order to control and exploit it (Brittan and Maynard 1984, 198). Culture is defined as the opposite of an objectified nature that, if left alone, would destroy culture.[1] Feminist scholars point to the identification of women with nature as being central to women's subsequent objectification by men as sex objects (Eisenstein 1983). Black scholars contend that defining people of color as less human, animalistic, or more "natural" denies African and Asian people's subjectivity and supports a political economy of domination (Asante 1987).

Domination always involves attempts to objectify the subordinate group. "As subjects, people have the right to define their own reality, establish their own identities, name their history," asserts Bell Hooks (1989, 42). "As objects, one's reality is defined by others, one's identity created by others, one's history named only in ways that define one's relationship to those who are subject" (42). The treatment afforded black women domestic workers exemplifies the many forms that objectification can take. Making black women work as if they were animals or "mules uh de world" represents one form of objectification. Deference rituals such as calling black domestic workers "girls" and by their first names enable employers to treat their employees like children, as less capable human beings. Objectification can be so severe that the Other simply disappears, as was the case when Judith Rollins's employer treated her as if she were invisible by conducting a conversation while ignoring Rollins's presence in the room. But in spite of these pressures, black women have insisted on our right to define our own reality, establish our own identities, and name our history. One significant contribution of work by Judith Rollins (1985), Bonnie Thornton Dill (1980, 1988), Elizabeth Clark-Lewis (1985), and others is that they document black women's everyday resistance to this attempted objectification. . . .

African-American women occupy a position whereby the inferior half of a series of these dichotomies converge, and this placement has been central to our subordination. . . .

CONTROLLING IMAGES AND BLACK WOMEN'S OPPRESSION

"Black women emerged from slavery firmly enshrined in the consciousness of white America as 'Mammy' and the 'bad black woman,'" contends Cheryl Gilkes (1983, 294). The dominant ideology of the slave era fostered the creation of four interrelated, socially constructed controlling images of black womanhood, each reflecting the dominant group's interest in maintaining black women's subordination. Given that both black and white women were important to slavery's continuation, the prevailing ideology functioned to mask contradictions in social relations affecting all women. According to the cult of true womanhood, "true" women possessed four cardinal virtues: piety, purity, submissiveness, and domesticity. Elite white women and those of the emerging middle class were encouraged to aspire to these virtues. African-American women encountered a different set of controlling images. The sexual ideology of the period as is the case today "confirmed the differing material circumstances of these two groups of women . . . by balancing opposing definitions of womanhood and motherhood, each dependent on the other for its existence" (Carby 1987, 25).

The first controlling image applied to African-American women is that of the mammy—the faithful, obedient domestic servant. Created to justify the economic exploitation of house slaves and sustained to explain black women's long-standing restriction to domestic service, the mammy image represents the normative yardstick used to evaluate all black women's behavior. By loving, nurturing, and caring for her white children and "family" better than her own, the mammy symbolizes the dominant group's perceptions of the ideal black female relationship to elite white male power. Even though she may be well loved and may wield considerable authority in her white "family," the mammy still knows her "place" as obedient servant. She has accepted her subordination.

Black women intellectuals have aggressively deconstructed the image of African-American women as contented mammies by challenging traditional views of black women domestics (Dill 1980, 1988; Clark-Lewis 1985; Rollins 1985). Literary critic Trudier Harris's (1982) volume *From Mammies to Militants: Domestics in Black American Literature* investigates prominent differences in how black women have been portrayed by others in literature and how they portray themselves. In her work on the difficulties faced by black women leaders, Rhetaugh Dumas (1980) describes how black women executives are hampered by being treated as mammies and penalized if they do not appear warm and nurturing. But despite these works, the mammy image lives on in scholarly and popular culture. Audre Lorde's account of a shopping trip offers a powerful example of its tenacity: "I wheel my two-year-old daughter in a shopping cart through a supermarket in . . . 1967, and a little white girl riding past in her mother's cart calls out excitedly, 'Oh look, Mommy, a baby maid!'" (1984, 126).[2]

The mammy image is central to interlocking systems of race, gender, and class oppression. Since efforts to control African-American family life require perpetuating the symbolic structures of racial oppression, the mammy image is important because it aims to shape black women's behavior as mothers. As the members of African-American families who are most familiar with the skills needed for black accommodation, black women are encouraged to transmit to their own children the deference behavior many are forced to exhibit in mammy roles. By teaching black children their assigned place in white power structures, black women who internalize the mammy image potentially become effective conduits for perpetuating racial oppression. In addition, employing mammies buttresses the racial superiority of white women employers and weds them more closely to their fathers, husbands, and sons as sources of elite white male power (Rollins 1985).

The mammy image also serves a symbolic function in maintaining gender oppression. Black feminist critic Barbara Christian argues that images of black womanhood serve as a reservoir for the fears of Western culture, "a dumping ground for those female functions a basically Puritan society could not confront" (1985, 2). Juxtaposed against the image of white women promulgated through the cult of true womanhood, the mammy image as the Other symbolizes the oppositional difference of mind/body and culture/nature thought to distinguish black women from everyone else. Christian comments on the mammy's gender significance: "All the functions of mammy are magnificently physical. They involve the body as sensuous, as funky, the part of woman that white southern America was profoundly afraid of. Mammy, then, harmless in her position of slave, unable because of her all-giving nature to do harm, is needed as an image, a surrogate to contain all those fears of the physical female" (1985, 2). The mammy image buttresses the ideology of the cult of true womanhood, one in which sexuality and fertility are severed. "Good" white mothers are expected to deny their female sexuality and devote their attention to the moral development of their offspring. In contrast, the mammy image is one of an asexual woman, a surrogate mother in blackface devoted to the development of a white family.

No matter how loved they were by their white "families," black women domestic workers remained poor because they were economically exploited. The restructured post–World War II economy in which African-American women moved from service in private homes to jobs in the low-paid service sector has produced comparable economic exploitation. Removing black women's labor from African-American families and exploiting it denies black extended family units the benefits of either decent wages of black women's unpaid labor in their homes. Moreover, many white families in both the

middle class and working class are able to maintain their class position because they have long used black women as a source of cheap labor (Rollins
1985; Byerly 1986). The mammy image is designed to mask this economic
exploitation of social class (King 1973).

For reasons of economic survival, African-American women may play the
mammy role in paid work settings. But within African-American communities these same women often teach their own children something quite different.
Bonnie Thornton Dill's (1980) work on childrearing patterns among black
domestics shows that while the participants in her study showed deference
behavior at work, they discouraged their children from believing that they
should be deferent to whites and encouraged their children to avoid domestic work. Barbara Christian's analysis of the mammy in black slave narratives reveals that, "unlike the white southern image of mammy, she is cunning,
prone to poisoning her master, and not at all content with her lot" (1985, 5).

The fact that the mammy image cannot control black women's behavior
as mothers is tied to the creation of the second controlling image of black
womanhood. Though a more recent phenomenon, the image of the black
matriarch fulfills similar functions in explaining black women's placement
in interlocking systems of race, gender, and class oppression. Ironically, black
scholars such as William E. B. Du Bois (1969) and E. Franklin Frazier (1948)
described the connections among higher rates of female-headed households
in African-American communities, the importance that women assume in
black family networks, and the persistence of black poverty. However, neither scholar interpreted black women's centrality in black families as a *cause*
of African-American social class status. Both saw so-called matriarchal families
as an *outcome* of racial oppression and poverty. During the eras when Du
Bois and Frazier wrote, the oppression of African-Americans was so total
that control was maintained without the controlling image of matriarch.
But what began as a muted theme in the works of these earlier black scholars
grew into a full-blown racialized image in the 1960s, a time of significant
political and economic mobility for African-Americans. Racialization involves attaching racial meaning to a previously racially unclassified relationship, social practice, or group (Omi and Winant 1986). Prior to the
1960s, female-headed households were certainly higher in African-American
communities, but an ideology racializing female-headedness as a causal feature
of black poverty had not emerged. Moreover, "the public depiction of black
women as unfeminine, castrating matriarchs came at precisely the same moment
that the feminist movement was advancing its public critique of American
patriarchy" (Gilkes 1983, 296).

While the mammy typifies the black mother figure in white homes, the
matriarch symbolizes the mother figure in black homes. Just as the mammy
represents the "good" black mother, the matriarch symbolizes the "bad" black

mother. The modern black matriarchy thesis contends that African-American women fail to fulfill their traditional "womanly" duties (Moynihan 1965). Spending too much time away from home, these working mothers ostensibly cannot properly supervise their children and are a major contributing factor to their children's school failure. As overly aggressive, unfeminine women, black matriarchs allegedly emasculate their lovers and husbands. These men, understandably, either desert their partners or refuse to marry the mothers of their children. From an elite white male standpoint, the matriarch is essentially a failed mammy, a negative stigma applied to those African-American women who dared to violate the image of the submissive, hardworking servant. . . .

Like the mammy, the image of the matriarch is central to interlocking systems of race, gender, and class oppression. Portraying African-American women as matriarchs allows the dominant group to blame black women for the success or failure of black children. Assuming that black poverty is passed on intergenerationally via value transmission in families, an elite white male standpoint suggests that black children lack the attention and care allegedly lavished on white, middle-class children and that this deficiency seriously retards black children's achievement. Such a view diverts attention from the political and economic inequality affecting black mothers and children and suggests that anyone can rise from poverty if he or she only received good values at home. Those African-Americans who remain poor are blamed for their own victimization. Using black women's performance as mothers to explain black economic subordination links gender ideology to explanations of class subordination.

The source of the matriarch's failure is her inability to model appropriate gender behavior. In the post–World War II era, increasing numbers of white women entered the labor market, limited their fertility, and generally challenged their proscribed roles in white patriarchal institutions. The image of the black matriarch emerged at that time as a powerful symbol for both black and white women of what can go wrong if white patriarchal power is challenged. Aggressive, assertive women are penalized—they are abandoned by their men, end up impoverished, and are stigmatized as being unfeminine.

The image of the matriarch also supports racial oppression. Much social science research implicitly uses gender relations in African-American communities as one putative measure of black cultural disadvantage. For example, the Moynihan Report (1965) contends that slavery destroyed black families by creating reversed roles for men and women. Black family structures are seen as being deviant because they challenge the patriarchal assumptions underpinning the construct of the ideal "family." Moreover, the absence of black patriarchy is used as evidence for black cultural inferiority (Collins 1989). Black women's failure to conform to the cult of true womanhood can then be identified as one fundamental source of black cultural deficiency. Cheryl Gilkes posits that the emergence of the matriarchal image occurred as a counterideology to efforts by African-Americans and women who were confronting interlocking systems of race, gender, and class oppression: "The image of dangerous Black women who were also deviant castrating mothers divided the Black community at a critical period in the Black liberation struggle and created a wider gap between the worlds of Black and white women at a critical period in women's history" (1983, 297).

Taken together, images of the mammy and the matriarch place African-American women in an untenable position. For black women workers in domestic work and other occupations requiring long hours and/or substantial emotional labor, becoming the ideal mammy means precious time and energy spent away from husbands and children. But being employed when black men have difficulty finding steady work exposes African-American women to the charge that black women emasculate black men by failing to be submissive, dependent, "feminine" women. Moreover, black women's financial contributions to black family well-being have also been cited as evidence supporting the matriarchy thesis (Moynihan 1965). Many black women are the sole support of their families, and labeling these women "matriarchs" erodes their self-confidence and ability to confront oppression. In essence, African-American women who must work are labeled mammies, then are stigmatized again as matriarchs for being strong figures in their own homes.

A third, externally defined, controlling image of black womanhood—that of the welfare mother—appears tied to black women's increasing dependence on the post–World War II welfare state. Essentially an updated version of the breeder woman image created during slavery, this image provides an ideological justification for efforts to harness black women's fertility to the needs of a changing political economy.

During slavery the breeder woman image portrayed black women as more suitable for having children than white women. By claiming that black women were able to produce children as easily as animals, this objectification of black women as the Other provided justification for interference in the reproductive rights of enslaved Africans. Slaveowners wanted enslaved Africans to "breed" because every slave child born represented a valuable unit of property, another unit of labor, and, if female, the prospects for more slaves. The externally defined, controlling image of the breeder woman served to justify slaveowner intrusion into black women's decisions about fertility (King 1973; Davis 1981).

The post–World War II political economy has offered African-Americans rights not available in former historical periods (Fusfeld and Bates 1984; Wilson 1987). African-Americans have successfully acquired basic political and economic protections from a greatly expanded welfare state, particularly Social Security, Aid to Families with Dependent Children, unemployment compensation, affirmative action, voting rights, antidiscrimination legislation, and the minimum wage. In spite of sustained opposition by Republican administrations in the 1980s, these programs allow many African-Americans to reject the subsistence-level, exploitative jobs held by their parents and grandparents. Job export, deskilling, and increased use of illegal immigrants have all been used to replace the loss of cheap, docile Black labor (Braverman 1974; Gordon et al. 1982; Nash and Fernandez-Kelly 1983). The large numbers of undereducated, unemployed African-Americans, most of whom are women and children, who inhabit inner cities cannot be forced to work. From the standpoint of the dominant group, they no longer represent cheap labor but instead signify a costly threat to political and economic stability.

Controlling black women's fertility in such a political economy becomes important. The image of the welfare mother fulfills this function by labeling as unnecessary and even dangerous to the values of the country the fertility of women who are not white and middle-class. A closer look at this controlling image reveals that it shares some important features with its mammy and matriarch counterparts. Like the matriarch, the welfare mother is labeled a bad mother. But unlike the matriarch, she is not too aggressive—on the contrary, she is not aggressive enough. While the matriarch's unavailability contributed to her children's poor socialization, the welfare mother's accessibility is deemed the problem. She is portrayed as being content to sit around and collect welfare, shunning work and passing on her bad values to her offspring. The image of the welfare mother represents another failed mammy, one who is unwilling to become "de mule uh de world."

The image of the welfare mother provides ideological justifications for interlocking systems of race, gender, and class oppression. African-Americans can be racially stereotyped as being lazy by blaming black welfare mothers for failing to pass on the work ethic. Moreover, the welfare mother has no male authority figure to assist her. Typically portrayed as an unwed mother, she violates one cardinal tenet of Eurocentric masculinist thought: She is a woman alone. As a result, her treatment reinforces the dominant gender ideology positing that a woman's true worth and financial security should occur through heterosexual marriage. Finally, in the post–World War II political economy, one of every three African-American families is officially classified as poor. With such high levels of black poverty, welfare state policies supporting poor black mothers and their children have become increasingly expensive. Creating the controlling image of the welfare mother and stigmatizing her as the cause of her own poverty and that of African-American communities shifts the angle of vision away from structural sources of poverty and blames the victims themselves. The image of the welfare mother thus provides ideological justification for the dominant group's interest in limiting the fertility of black mothers who are seen as producing too many economically unproductive children (Davis 1981).

The fourth controlling image—the Jezebel, whore, or sexually aggressive woman—is central in this nexus of elite white male images of black womanhood because efforts to control black women's sexuality lie at the heart of black women's oppression. The image of Jezebel originated under slavery when black women were portrayed as being, to use Jewelle Gomez's words, "sexually aggressive wet nurses" (Clarke et al. 1983, 99). Jezebel's function was to relegate all black women to the category of sexually aggressive women, thus providing a powerful rationale for the widespread sexual assaults by white men typically reported by black slave women (Davis 1981; Hooks 1981; D. White 1985). Yet Jezebel served another function. If black slave women could be portrayed as having excessive sexual appetites, then increased fertility should be the expected outcome. By suppressing the nurturing that African-American women might give their own children, which would strengthen black family networks, and by forcing black women to work in the field or "wet nurse" white children, slaveowners effectively tied the controlling images of Jezebel and mammy to the economic exploitation inherent in the institution of slavery.

The fourth image of the sexually denigrated black woman is the foundation underlying elite white male conceptualizations of the mammy, matriarch, and welfare mother. Connecting all three is the common theme of black women's sexuality. Each image transmits clear messages about the proper links among female sexuality, fertility, and black women's roles in the political economy. For example, the mammy, the only somewhat positive figure, is a desexed individual. The mammy is typically portrayed as overweight, dark, and with characteristically African features—in brief, as an unsuitable sexual partner for white men. She is asexual and therefore is free to become a surrogate mother to the children she acquired not through her own sexuality. The mammy represents the clearest example of the split between sexuality and motherhood present in Eurocentric masculinist thought. In contrast, both the matriarch and the welfare mother are sexual beings. But their sexuality is linked to their fertility, and this link forms one fundamental reason they are negative images. The matriarch represents the sexually aggressive woman, one who emasculates black men because she will not permit them to assume roles as black patriarchs. She refuses to be passive and thus is stigmatized. Similarly, the welfare mother represents a woman of low morals and uncontrolled sexuality, factors identified as the cause of her impoverished state. In both cases black female control over sexuality and fertility is conceptualized as antithetical to elite white male interests.

Taken together, these four prevailing interpretations of black womanhood form a nexus of elite white male interpretations of black female sexuality and fertility. Moreover, by meshing smoothly with systems of race, class, and gender oppression, they provide effective ideological justifications for racial oppression, the politics of gender subordination, and the economic exploitation inherent in capitalist economies. . . .

Notes

1. Dona Richards (1980) offers an insightful analysis of the relationship between Christianity's contributions to an ideology of domination and the culture/nature dichotomy. She notes that European Christianity is predicated on a worldview that sustains the exploitation of nature: "Christian thought provides a view of man, nature, and the universe which supports not only the ascendancy of science, but of the technical order, individualism, and relentless progress. Emphasis within this world view is placed on humanity's dominance over *all* other beings, which become 'objects' in an 'objectified' universe. There is no emphasis on an awe-inspiring God or cosmos. Being 'made in God's image,' given the European ethos, translates into 'acting *as* God,' recreating the universe. Humanity is separated from nature" (69).
2. Brittan and Maynard (1984) note that ideology (1) is common sense and obvious; (2) appears natural, inevitable, and universal; (3) shapes lived experience and behavior; (4) is sedimented in people's consciousness; and (5) consists of a system of ideas embedded in the social system as a whole. This example captures all dimensions of how racism and sexism function ideologically. The status of black woman as servant is so "common sense" that even a child knows it. That the child saw a black female child as a baby maid speaks to the naturalization dimension and to the persistence of controlling images in individual consciousness and the social system overall.

References

Asante, Molefi Kéte. 1987. *The Afrocentric Idea.* Philadelphia: Temple University Press.

Bellah, Robert N. 1983. "The Ethical Aims of Social Inquiry." In *Social Science as Moral Inquiry*, ed. Norma Haan, Robert Bellah, Paul Rabinow, and William Sullivan, 360–81. New York: Columbia University Press.

Braverman, Harry. 1974. *Labor and Monopoly Capital.* New York: Monthly Review Press.

Brittan, Arthur, and Mary Maynard. 1984. *Sexism, Racism, and Oppression.* New York: Basil Blackwell.

Byerly, Victoria. 1986. *Hard Times Cotton Mills Girls.* Ithaca: Cornell University Press.

Carby, Hazel. 1987. *Reconstructing Womanhood: The Emergence of the Afro-American Woman Novelist.* New York: Oxford.

Christian, Barbara. 1985. *Black Feminist Criticism, Perspectives on Black Women Writers.* New York: Pergamon.

Clarke, Cheryl, Jewell L. Gomez, Evelyn Hammonds, Bonnie Johnson, and Linda Powell. 1983. "Conversations and Questions: Black Women on Black Women Writers." *Conditions: Nine* 3 (3): 88–137.

Clark-Lewis, Elizabeth. 1985. *"This Work Had a' End": The Transition from Live-In to Day Work.* Southern Women: The Intersection of Race, Class, and Gender. Working Paper no. 2. Memphis: Center for Research on Women, Memphis State University.

Collins, Patricia Hill. 1989. "A Comparison of Two Works on Black Family Life." *Signs* 14 (4): 875–84.

Davis, Angela Y. 1981. *Women, Race, and Class.* New York: Random House.

Dill, Bonnie Thornton. 1980. "'The Means to Put My Children Through': Child-Rearing Goals and Strategies among Black Female Domestic Servants." In *The Black Woman*, ed. La Frances Rodgers-Rose, 107–23. Beverly Hills, CA: Sage.

———. 1988. "'Making Your Job Good Yourself': Domestic Service and the Construction of Personal Dignity." In *Women and the Politics of Empowerment*, ed. Ann Bookman and Sandra Morgen, 33–52. Philadelphia: Temple University Press.

Du Bois, William E. B. 1969. *The Negro American Family.* New York: Negro Universities Press.

Dumas, Rhetaugh Graves. 1980. "Dilemmas of Black Females in Leadership." In *The Black Woman*, ed. La Frances Rodgers-Rose, 203–15. Beverly Hills, CA: Sage.

Eisenstein, Hester. 1983. *Contemporary Feminist Thought.* Boston: G. K. Hall.

Frazier, E. Franklin. 1948. *The Negro Family in the United States.* New York: Dryden Press.

Fusfield, Daniel R., and Timothy Bates. 1984. *The Political Economy of the Urban Ghetto.* Carbondale: Southern Illinois University Press.

Gilkes, Cheryl Townsend. 1983. "From Slavery to Social Welfare: Racism and the Control of Black Women." In *Class, Race, and Sex: The Dynamics of Control*, ed. Amy Swerdlow and Hanna Lessinger, 288–300. Boston: G. K. Hall.

Gordon, David M., Richard Edwards, and Michael Reich. 1982. *Segmented Work, Divided Workers.* New York: Cambridge University Press.

Gwaltney, John Langston. 1980. *Drylongso, a Self-Portrait of Black America.* New York: Vintage.

Halpin, Zuleyma Tang. 1989. "Scientific Objectivity and the Concept of 'The Other.'" *Women's Studies International Forum* 12 (3): 285–94.

Harris, Trudier. 1982. *From Mammies to Militants: Domestics in Black American Literature.* Philadelphia: Temple University Press.

Hochschild, Arlie Russell. 1975. "The Sociology of Feeling and Emotion: Selected Possibilities." In *Another Voice: Feminist Perspectives on Social Life and Social Science*, ed. Marcia Millman and Rosabeth Kanter, 280–307. Garden City, NY: Anchor.

Hooks, Bell. 1981. *Ain't I a Woman: Black Women and Feminism.* Boston: South End Press.

———. 1984. *From Margin to Center.* Boston: South End Press.

———. 1989. *Talking Back: Thinking Feminist, Thinking Black.* Boston: South End Press.

Irele, Abiola. 1983. "Introduction." In *African Philosophy, Myth and Reality*, by Paulin J. Houtondji, 7–32. Bloomington: Indiana University Press.

Keller, Evelyn Fox. 1985. *Reflections on Gender and Science.* New Haven: Yale University Press.

King, Mae. 1973. "The Politics of Sexual Stereotypes." *Black Scholar* 4 (6–7): 12–23.

Lorde, Audre. 1984. *Sister Outsider*. Trumansberg, NY: Crossing Press.

Moynihan, Daniel Patrick. 1965. *The Negro Family: The Case for National Action*. Washington, DC: GPO.

Nash, June, and Maria Patricia Fernandez-Kelly, eds. 1983. *Women, Men, and the International Division of Labor*. Albany: State University of New York.

Omi, Michael, and Howard Winant. 1986. *Racial Formation in the United States: From the 1960s to the 1980s*. New York: Routledge and Kegan Paul.

Patterson, Orlando. 1982. *Slavery and Social Death*. Cambridge: Harvard University Press.

Richards, Dona. 1980. "European Mythology: The Ideology of 'Progress.'" In *Contemporary Black Thought*, ed. Molefi Kete Asante and Abdulai Sa. Vandi, 59–79. Beverly Hills, CA: Sage.

Rollins, Judith. 1985. *Between Women: Domestics and Their Employers*. Philadelphia: Temple University Press.

Spelman, Elizabeth V. 1982. "Theories of Race and Gender: The Erasure of Black Women." *Quest* 5 (4): 36–62.

Westkott, Marcia. 1979. "Feminist Criticism of the Social Sciences." *Harvard Educational Review* 49 (4): 422–30.

White, Deborah Gray. 1985. *Ar'n't I a Woman? Female Slaves in the Plantation South*. New York: W. W. Norton.

Wilson, William Julius. 1987. *The Truly Disadvantaged: The Inner City, the Underclass, and Public Policy*. Chicago: University of Chicago Press.

SELECTION 19

FROM

The Project of Feminist Epistemology: Perspectives from a Non-Western Feminist

UMA NARAYAN

A FUNDAMENTAL THESIS OF feminist epistemology is that our location in the world as women makes it possible for us to perceive and understand different aspects of both the world and human activities in ways that challenge the male bias of existing perspectives. Feminist epistemology is a particular manifestation of the general insight that the nature of women's experiences as individuals and as social beings, our contributions to work, culture, knowledge, and our history and political interests have been systematically ignored or misrepresented by mainstream discourses in different areas. . . .

My essay will attempt to examine some dangers of approaching feminist theorizing and epistemological values in a noncontextual and nonpragmatic way, which could convert important feminist insights and theses into feminist epistemological dogmas. I will use my perspective as a non-Western, Indian feminist to examine critically the predominantly Anglo-American project of feminist epistemology and to reflect on what such a project might signify for women in non-Western cultures in general and for non-Western feminists in particular. I will suggest that different cultural contexts and political agendas may cast a very different light on both the "idols" and the "enemies" of knowledge as they have characteristically been typed in Western feminist epistemology.

In keeping with my respect for contexts, I would like to stress that I do not see non-Western feminists as a homogeneous group and that none of the concerns I express as a non-Western feminist may be pertinent to or shared by *all* non-Western feminists, although I do think they will make sense to many. . . .

NON-WESTERN FEMINIST POLITICS
AND FEMINIST EPISTEMOLOGY

Some themes of feminist epistemology may be problematic for non-Western feminists in ways that they are not problematic for Western feminists. Feminism has a much narrower base in most non-Western countries. It is primarily of significance to some urban, educated, middle-class, and hence relatively Westernized women, like myself. Although feminist groups in these countries do try to extend the scope of feminist concerns to other groups (for example, by fighting for child care, women's health issues, and equal wages issues through trade union structures), some major preoccupations of Western feminism—its critique of marriage, the family, compulsory heterosexuality—presently engage the attention of mainly small groups of middle-class feminists.

These feminists must think and function within the context of a powerful tradition that, although it systematically oppresses women, also contains within itself a discourse that confers a high value on women's place in the general scheme of things. Not only are the roles of wife and mother highly praised, but women also are seen as the cornerstones of the spiritual well-being of their husbands and children, admired for their supposedly higher moral, religious, and spiritual qualities, and so on. In cultures that have a pervasive religious component, like the Hindu culture with which I am familiar, everything seems assigned a place and value as long as it keeps to its place. Confronted with a powerful traditional discourse that values woman's place as long as she keeps to the place prescribed, it may be politically counterproductive for non-Western feminists to echo uncritically the themes of Western feminist epistemology that seek to restore the value, cognitive and otherwise, of "women's experience."

The danger is that, even if the non-Western feminist talks about the value of women's experience in terms totally different from those of the traditional discourse, the difference is likely to be drowned out by the louder and more powerful voice of the traditional discourse, which will then claim that "what those feminists say" vindicates its view that the roles and experiences it assigns to women have value and that women should stick to those roles.

I do not intend to suggest that this is not a danger for Western feminism or to imply that there is no tension for Western feminists between being critical of the experiences that their societies have provided for women and finding things to value in them nevertheless. But I am suggesting that perhaps there is less at risk for Western feminists in trying to strike this balance. I am inclined to think that in non-Western countries feminists must still stress the negative sides of the female experience within that culture and that the time for a more sympathetic evaluation is not quite ripe.

But the issue is not simple and seems even less so when another point is considered. The imperative we experience as feminists to be critical of how out culture and traditions oppress women conflicts with our desire as members of once colonized cultures to affirm the value of the same culture and traditions.

There are seldom any easy resolutions to these sorts of tensions. As an Indian feminist currently living in the United States, I often find myself torn between the desire to communicate with honesty the miseries and oppressions that I think my own culture confers on its women and the fear that this communication is going to reinforce, however unconsciously, Western prejudices about the "superiority" of Western culture. I have often felt compelled to interrupt my communication, say on the problems of the Indian system of arranged marriages, to remind my Western friends that the experiences of women under their system of "romantic love" seem no more enviable. Perhaps we should all attempt to cultivate the methodological habit of trying to understand the complexities of the oppression involved in different historical and cultural settings while eschewing, at least for now, the temptation to make comparisons across such settings, given the dangers of attempting to compare what may well be incommensurable in any neat terms.

THE NONPRIMACY OF POSITIVISM AS
A PROBLEMATIC PERSPECTIVE

As a non-Western feminist, I also have some reservations about the way in which feminist epistemology seems to have picked positivism as its main target of attack. The choice of positivism as the main target is reasonable because it has been a dominant and influential Western position and it most clearly embodies some flaws that feminist epistemology seeks to remedy.

But this focus on positivism should not blind us to the facts that it is not our only enemy and that nonpositivist frameworks are not, by virtue of that bare qualification, any more worthy of our tolerance. . . .

Western feminists too must learn not to uncritically claim any nonpositivist framework as an ally; despite commonalities, there are apt to be many differences. A temperate look at positions we espouse as allies is necessary since "the enemy of my enemy is my friend" is a principle likely to be as misleading in epistemology as it is in the domain of Realpolitik.

The critical theorists of the Frankfurt School will serve well to illustrate this point. Begun as a group of young intellectuals in the post–World War I Weimar Republic, the members were significantly influenced by Marxism, and their interests ranged from aesthetics to political theory to epistemology. Jürgen Habermas, the most eminent critical theorist today, has in his works attacked positivism and the claim of scientific theories to be value neutral or "disinterested." He has attempted to show the constitutive role played by human interests in different domains of human knowledge. He is interested, as are feminists, in the role that knowledge plays in the reproduction of social relations of domination. But, as feminist epistemology is critical of all perspectives that place a lopsided stress on reason, it must also necessarily be critical of the rationalist underpinnings of critical theory.

Such rationalist foundations are visible, for example, in Habermas's "rational reconstruction" of what he calls "an ideal speech situation," supposedly characterized by "pure intersubjectivity," that is, by the absence of any barriers to communication. That Habermas's "ideal speech situation" is a creature of reason is clear from its admitted character as a "rationally reconstructed ideal" and its symmetrical distribution of chances for all of its participants to choose and apply speech acts.

This seems to involve a stress on formal and procedural equality among speakers that ignores substantive differences imposed by class, race, or gender that may affect a speaker's knowledge of the facts or the capacity to assert herself or command the attention of others. Women in academia often can testify to the fact that, despite not being forcibly restrained from speaking in public forums, they have to overcome much conditioning in order to learn to assert themselves. They can also testify as to how, especially in male-dominated disciplines, their speech is often ignored or treated with condescension by male colleagues.

Habermas either ignores the existence of such substantive differences among speakers or else assumes they do not exist. In the latter case, if one assumes that the speakers in the ideal speech situation are not significantly different from each other, then there may not be much of significance for them to speak about. Often it is precisely our differences that make dialogue imperative. If the ideal speakers of the ideal speech situation are unmarked by differences, there may be nothing for them to surmount on their way to a "rational consensus." If there are such differences between the speakers, then Habermas provides nothing that will rule out the sorts of problems I have mentioned.

Another rationalist facet of critical theory is revealed in Habermas's assumption that justifiable agreement and genuine knowledge arise only out of "rational consensus." This seems to overlook the possibility of agreement and knowledge based on sympathy or solidarity. Sympathy or solidarity may very well promote the uncovering of truth, especially in situations when people who divulge information are rendering themselves vulnerable in the process. For instance, women are more likely to talk about experiences of sexual harassment to other women because they would expect similar experiences to have made them more sympathetic and understanding. Therefore, feminists should be cautious about assuming that they necessarily have much in common with a framework simply because it is nonpositivist. Non-Western feminists may be more alert to this error because many problems they confront arise in nonpositivist contexts.

THE POLITICAL USES OF "EPISTEMIC PRIVILEGE"

Important strands of feminist epistemology hold the view that our concrete embodiments as members of a specific class, race, and gender as well as our concrete historical situations necessarily play significant roles in our perspective on the world; moreover, no point of view is "neutral" because no one exists unembedded in the world. Knowledge is seen as gained not by solitary individuals but by socially constituted members of groups that emerge and change through history.

Feminists have also argued that groups living under various forms of oppression are more likely to have a critical perspective on their situation and that this critical view is both generated and partly constituted by critical emotional responses that subjects experience vis-à-vis their life situations. This perspective in feminist epistemology rejects the "Dumb View" of emotions and favors an intentional conception that emphasizes the cognitive aspect of emotions. It is critical of the traditional view of the emotions as wholly and always impediments to knowledge and argues that many emotions often help rather than hinder our understanding of a person or situation.

Bringing together these views on the role of the emotions in knowledge, the possibility of critical insights being generated by oppression, and the contextual nature of knowledge may suggest some answers to serious and interesting political questions. I will consider what these epistemic positions entail regarding the possibility of understanding and political cooperation between oppressed groups and sympathetic members of a dominant group—say, between white people and people of color over issues of race or between men and women over issues of gender.

These considerations are also relevant to questions of understanding and cooperation between Western and non-Western feminists. Western feminists, despite their critical understanding of their own culture, often tend to be more a part of it than they realize. If they fail to see the contexts of their theories and assume that their perspective has universal validity for all feminists, they tend to participate in the dominance that Western culture has exercised over non-Western cultures.

Our position must explain and justify our dual need to criticize members of a dominant group (say men or white people or Western feminists) for their lack of attention to or concern with problems that affect an oppressed group (say, women or people of color or non-Western feminists, respectively), as well as for our frequent hostility toward those who express interest, even sympathetic interest, in issues that concern groups of which they are not a part.

Both attitudes are often warranted. On the one hand, one cannot but be angry at those who minimize, ignore, or dismiss the pain and conflict that racism and sexism inflict on their victims. On the other hand, living in a state of siege also necessarily makes us suspicious of expressions of concern and support from those who do not live these oppressions. We are suspicious of the motives of our sympathizers or the extent of their sincerity, and we worry, often with good reason, that they may claim that their interest provides a warrant for them to speak for us, as dominant groups throughout history have spoken for the dominated.

This is all the more threatening to groups aware of how recently they have acquired the power to articulate their own points of view. Non-Western feminists are especially aware of this because they have a double struggle in trying to find their own voice: They have to learn to articulate their differences, not only from their own traditional contexts but also from Western feminism.

Politically, we face interesting questions whose answers hinge on the nature and extent of the communication that we think possible between different groups. Should we try to share our perspectives and insights with those who have not lived our oppressions and accept that they may fully come to share them? Or should we seek only the affirmation of those like ourselves, who share common features of oppression, and rule out the possibility of those who have not lived these oppressions ever acquiring a genuine understanding of them?

I argue that it would be a mistake to move from the thesis that knowledge is constructed by human subjects who are socially constituted to the conclusion that those who are differently located socially can never attain *some* understanding of our experience or *some* sympathy with our cause. In that case, we would be committed to not just a perspectival view of knowledge but a relativistic one. Relativism, as I am using it, implies that a person could have knowledge of only the sorts of things she had experienced personally and that she would be totally unable to communicate any of the contents of her knowledge to someone who did not have the same sorts of experiences. Not only does this seem clearly false and perhaps even absurd, but it is probably a good idea not to have any a priori views that would imply either that all our knowledge is always capable of being communicated to every other person or that would imply that some of our knowledge is necessarily incapable of being communicated to some class of persons.

"Nonanalytic" and "nonrational" forms of discourse, like fiction or poetry, may be better able than other forms to convey the complex life experiences of one group to members of another. One can also hope that being part of one oppressed group may enable an individual to have a more sympathetic understanding of issues relating to another kind of oppression—that, for instance, being a woman may sensitize one to issues of race and class even if one is a woman privileged in those respects.

Again, this should not be reduced to some kind of metaphysical presumption. Historical circumstances have sometimes conspired, say, to making working-class men more chauvinistic in some of their attitudes than other men. Sometimes one sort of suffering may simply harden individuals to other sorts or leave them without energy to take any interest in the problems of other groups. But we can at least try to foster such sensitivity by focusing on parallels, not identities, between different sorts of oppressions.

Our commitment to the contextual nature of knowledge does not require us to claim that those who do not inhabit these contexts can never have any knowledge of them. But this commitment does permit us to argue that it is *easier* and *more likely* for the oppressed to have critical insights into the conditions of their own oppression than it is for those who live outside these structures. Those who actually *live* the oppressions of class, race, or gender have faced the issues that such oppressions generate in a variety of different situations. The insights and emotional responses engendered by these situations are a legacy with which they confront any new issue or situation.

Those who display sympathy as outsiders often fail both to understand fully the emotional complexities of living as a member of an oppressed group and to carry what they have learned and understood about one situation to the way they perceive another. It is a commonplace that even sympathetic men will often fail to perceive subtle instances of sexist behavior or discourse.

Sympathetic individuals who are not members of an oppressed group should keep in mind the possibility of this sort of failure regarding their understanding of issues relating to an oppression they do not share. They should realize that nothing they may do, from participating in demonstrations to changing their life-styles, can make them one of the oppressed. For instance, men who share household and childrearing responsibilities with women are mistaken if they think that this act of choice, often buttressed by the gratitude and admiration of others, is anything like the woman's experience of being forcibly socialized into these tasks and of having others perceive this as her natural function in the scheme of things.

The view that we can understand much about the perspectives of those whose oppression we do not share allows us the space to criticize dominant groups for their blindness to the facts of oppression. The view that such an understanding, despite great effort and interest, is likely to be incomplete or limited, provides us with the ground for denying total parity to members of a dominant group in their ability to understand our situation.

Sympathetic members of a dominant group need not necessarily defer to our views on any particular issue because that may reduce itself to another subtle form of condescension, but at least they must keep in mind the very real difficulties and possibility of failure to fully understand our concerns. This and the very important need for dominated groups to control the means of discourse about their own situations are important reasons for taking seriously the claim that oppressed groups have an "epistemic advantage." . . .

References

Bordo, S. 1986. "The Cartesian Masculinization of Thought." *Signs* 11:439–56.

Gilligan, C. 1982. *In A Different Voice: Psychological Theory and Women's Development*. Cambridge, MA: Harvard University Press.

Harding, S. 1986. *The Science Question in Feminism*. Ithaca: Cornell University Press.

Harding, S., and M. Hintikka. 1983. *Discovering Reality: Feminist Perspectives on Epistemology, Metaphysics, Methodology, and Philosophy of Science*. Dordrecht: Reidel.

Harding, S., and J. O'Barr, eds. 1987. *Sex and Scientific Inquiry*. Chicago: University of Chicago Press.

Keller, E. F. 1985. *Reflections on Gender and Science*. New Haven: Yale University Press.

Lloyd, G. 1984. *The Man of Reason*. Minneapolis: University of Minnesota Press.

PART IV

Gender, Science, and Philosophy

SELECTION 20
FROM
The Science Question in Feminism

SANDRA HARDING

FEMINIST CRITICS FACE IMMENSE obstacles in trying to construct a theory of gender as an analytic category that is relevant to the natural sciences. These obstacles have their origins not only in familiar but inadequate notions of gender but also in certain dogmatic views about science toward which even feminists are often insufficiently critical.

OBSTACLES TO THEORIZING GENDER

In such other disciplines as history, anthropology, and literature, the need to theorize gender appeared only after the limitations of three other projects were recognized. The "woman worthies" project was concerned with restoring and adding to the canons the voices of significant women in history, novelists, poets, artists, and so forth. Their achievements were reevaluated from a nonsexist perspective. The "women's contributions" project focused on women's participation in activities that had already appeared as focuses of analysis in these disciplines—in abolition and temperance struggles, in "gathering" activities within so-called hunter cultures, in the work of significant literary circles, for instance—but were still misperceived and underdeveloped subject matters. Here, the goal of a less distorted picture of social life logically called for new accounts of these already acknowledged disciplinary subject matters. Finally, "victimology" studies documented the previously ignored or misogynistically described histories and present practices of rape, wife abuse, prostitution, incest, workplace discrimination, economic exploitation, and the like.

It was only in doing such work effectively that feminist scholars came to recognize the inadequacy of these approaches. . . . These three kinds of studies have all provided valuable insights into matters that traditional inquiry bypasses. But their limitations led feminists to see the need to formulate gender as a theoretical category, as the analytic tool through which the division of social experience along gender lines tends to give men and women different conceptions of themselves, their activities and beliefs, and the world around them.

In the natural sciences, these projects have been only marginally useful. Women have been more systematically excluded from doing serious science than from performing any other social activity except, perhaps, frontline warfare. The inevitable examples of Marie Curie and now Barbara McClintock notwithstanding, few women have been able to achieve eminence in their own day as scientists. A variety of historical, sociological, and psychological studies explain why this is so, but the fact remains that there are few woman worthies to restore to science's halls of fame. Studies of women's contributions to science have been somewhat more fruitful though still limited by the same constraints.[1] The victimology focus, which appears in all five of the feminist science critique projects, has proved valuable chiefly in exploding the myth that the science we have had actually is the "science for the people" (Galileo's phrase) imagined at the emergence of modern science.

The fact that these approaches, useful in the social sciences and humanities, have been able to find only limited targets in the natural sciences has obscured to the science critics the need for more adequate theorization of gender as an analytic category—with one important exception: In the critiques of biology, there have been great advances in providing more developed and accurate views of women's natures and activities. Here the need to theorize gender as an analytic category can be seen in identifications of a gap between the way men and women think about reproduction and reproductive technologies, in questions about whether sex difference itself is not an issue of interest more to men than to women, in suggestions that scientific method's focus on differences might be implicated in the androcentrism of such problematics, and in proposals that the concern in biology, anthropology, and psychology with interactive relationships between organisms, and between organisms and environments, may reflect a specifically feminine way of conceptualizing very abstract relationships.[2]

But biology is only one of the focuses of the feminist critiques of science. In general, the areas in which there is need for gender as an analytic category and the directions such theorizing should take still remain obscure to many feminist critics of natural science, and totally incomprehensible to most nonfeminist scientists as well as historians, sociologists, and philosophers of science. At least some of these critics do have the resources of their social science disciplines and of literary criticism with which to try to understand natural science in terms of gender categories. The methods of psychoanalysis, history, sociology, anthropology, political theory, and literary criticism have produced valuable insights; however, scientific training (and I include training in the philosophy of science) is hostile to these methods of seeking knowledge about social life, and gender theory is a theory about social life. Characteristically, neither scientists nor philosophers of science are socialized to value psychoanalysis, literary criticism, or the critical interpretive approaches to be found in history and anthropology as modes of knowledge-seeking. No wonder we have found it difficult to theorize the effects on the natural sciences of gender symbolism, gender structure, and individual gender.

In the social sciences, those areas of research most hospitable to the introduction of gender as a theoretical category are the ones with a strong *critical* interpretive tradition. (I say "critical" to distinguish this *theory* of human action and belief from the kinds of unselfconscious interpretations, rationalizations, we all routinely provide to ourselves and others in explaining our beliefs and actions.) These traditions hypothesize that "the natives" may sometimes engage in irrational actions and hold irrational beliefs that defeat the actors' conscious goals and/or unconscious interests. The causes are to be found in the contradictory social conditions, the no-win situations, within which humans must choose actions and hold beliefs. Marx and Freud provide just two examples of theorists who attempted to identify the social conditions that lead groups of individuals to patterns of irrational action and belief. The effects of their methodological proposals can be seen in the critical interpretive traditions in many areas of social science research—whether or not these traditions call themselves Marxist or Freudian or are concerned with the particular kinds of social phenomena of interest to Marx and Freud. In these inquiry traditions it is legitimate—indeed, often obligatory—to reflect on the social origins of conceptual systems and patterns of behaviour, and to include in this subject matter the conceptual systems and behaviors shaping the inquirer's own assumptions and activities. Here there is not only conceptual space but also, we might say, moral permission to reflect on gendered aspects of conceptual systems and on the gender circumstances in which beliefs are adopted. In contrast, research programs where remnants of empiricist, positivist philosophies of social science hold sway have been systematically inhospitable to gender as a theoretical category.[3] At best they have been willing to add gender as a variable to be analyzed in their subject matter—as a property of individuals and their behaviors rather than also of social structures and conceptual systems.

The physical sciences are the origin of this positivist, excessively empiricist philosophy. Their nonsocial subject matter and the paradigmatic status of their methods appear to preclude critical reflection on social influences on their conceptual systems; indeed, prevalent dogma holds that it is the virtue of modern science to make such reflection unnecessary. We are told that modern physics and chemistry eliminate the anthropomorphizing characteristic of medieval science and of the theorizing we can observe in "primitive" cultures and children—not to mention in the social sciences and humanities. The social progressiveness, the "positivism," of modern science is to be found entirely in its method. There is thought to be no need to train physicists, chemists, or biologists as critical theorists, consequently, little in their training or in the ethos of scientific endeavor encourages the development or appreciation of the critical interpretive theory and skills that have proved so fruitful in the social sciences.

However, the history, sociology, and philosophy of science are not themselves natural sciences. Their subject matters are social beliefs and practices. In the philosophy of science, the focus is on ideal beliefs and practices; in the history and sociology of science, it is on actual beliefs and practices. Whether ideal or real, social beliefs and practices are the concerns of these disciplines. Here one would have thought that critical interpretive theory and skills would be central to understanding how scientists do and should explain the regularities of nature and their underlying causal tendencies. The sociology of knowledge does take this approach, though it has been limited by its preoccupation with what we can call the "sociology of error" and the "sociology of knowers" to the exclusion of a sociology of knowledge.[4] And this tradition, too, has been stalwartly androcentric. But androcentric or not, its influence on thinking about natural science has yet to be felt within the philosophy of science or the natural sciences themselves, and is only beginning to make inroads into the traditional sociology and history of science. The philosophy, sociology, and history of the natural sciences have been dominated by empiricist philosophies hostile to theories of belief formation within which gender could be understood as a part of science's conceptual schemes, as a way of organizing the social labor of science, or as an aspect of the individual identity of scientists.

For these reasons the feminist science critics face even greater disciplinary obstacles than do feminists who seek to introduce gender as a theoretical category into the social sciences, literature, and the arts. These obstacles seem to originate in the unusual notion that science enthusiasts have of the proper way to understand the history and practices of science: This kind of social activity alone, we are told, must be understood only in terms of its enthusiasts' understanding of their own activities—in terms of the unselfconscious, uncritical interpretations "the natives" provide of their beliefs and activities. That is, scientists report their activities, and philosophers and historians of science interpret these reports so that we can "rationally" account for the growth of scientific knowledge in the very same moral, political, and epistemological terms scientists use to explain their activities to funding sources or science critics.

Social theorists will recognize this approach as a hermeneutic, intentionalist one that systematically avoids critical examination of the identifiable causal, historical influences on the growth of science which are to be found outside the intellectual, moral, and political consciousnesses of science practitioners and enthusiasts.[5] Kuhn's alternative account of the history of science has generated a veritable new industry for the social studies of science, studies that have begun to show the mystification perpetuated by such "rational reconstructions."[6] But traditional science and philosophical and popular enthusiasm for the traditional vision of science remain pugnaciously hostile to such critical causal accounts. From this perspective, my approach to science may be understood as a more thorough naturalism than science enthusiasts themselves are apparently willing to defend: I seek to identify the causal tendencies in social life that leave traces of gender projects on all aspects of the scientific enterprise. . . .

SCIENCE AS A UNIQUE METHOD OR A SET OF SENTENCES

Does the feminist case that science is gendered have to rest on showing scientific method to be sexist? Does a degendered science have to produce a new method of knowledge-seeking? Or does the feminist case have to rest on showing that the best confirmed claims the sciences have made are sexist? Does it have to show that Newton's or Einstein's laws are sexist in order to provide a plausible argument for the gendered nature of science?

The common view (or dogma) is that science's uniqueness is to be found in its method for acquiring reliable descriptions and explanations of nature's regularities and their underlying causes. Authors of science texts write about the importance of value-free observation as the test of beliefs, and especially about collecting observations through the "experimental method." We are told that it is the refined observation characteristic of experimental method that permitted Galileo's and Newton's views to win out over Ptolemy's and Aristotle's.

But exactly what is unique about this method remains obscure. For one thing, the different sciences use different methods; not a great deal is common to the methods of astronomy, particle physics, and molecular biology. For another thing, in parts of what are regarded as highly rigorous and value-free sciences—contemporary astronomy and geology, for example—controlled experiment plays an extremely small role. And controlled experiment is not a modern invention—after all, Aristotle was an experimentalist. Moreover, just try to identify the formal methodological features of knowledge-seeking that will exclude from the ranks of scientists farmers in premodern agricultural societies yet will include junior but highly trained members of biochemical research teams. When push comes to shove in the philosophy of science, we are told that induction and deduction are supposed to compete for honors as the core of scientific method.[7] But presumably, human infants as well as apes and dogs regularly use induction and deduction. These kinds of considerations lead to the suspicion that science is both more and less than any possible definition of scientific method. . . .

In light of these kinds of considerations, it is hard to see why a distinctively feminist science would have to produce a new method, at least if we mean by scientific method no more than (1) putting beliefs to the test of experimental observation, (2) relying on induction and deduction, or (3) being willing to hold all of our assumptions open to criticism. The first and second of these activities are not at all unique to modern science, and the third is not characteristic of what everyone counts as the most methodologically rigorous inquiry. What we have in this dogma is the reduction of the purportedly inherent progressiveness of science to a mythologized and obscure notion of its method (this should be—but is not always—what feminists criticize when they challenge positivism), but the distinguishing features of this scientific method cannot even be specified in a plausible way. . . .

We have been examining conceptions of scientific claims and of scientific activity that are problems both for and in feminist theory. They are problems *for* feminist theorizing because they block the possibility of feminist transformations in the way scientists, philosophers, and social theorists think about science. They are problems *in* feminist theorizing because belief in at least traces of these dogmas hides from us the inadequacies in our understanding of how science is gendered.

GENDER: INDIVIDUAL, STRUCTURAL, SYMBOLIC—AND ALWAYS ASYMMETRIC

Inadequate conceptualizations of gender are also a problem both for and in the feminist science critiques. The inadequacies within the critiques reflect in two ways the partial, and even perverse, understandings of gender that are characteristic of mainstream thinking. The first results from an excessive focus on just one or two of the forms in which gender appears in social life, obscuring the sometimes mutually supportive and sometimes oppositional but always important relationships in any given culture between the preferred expressions of gender symbolism, the way labor is divided by gender, and what counts as masculine and feminine identity and behavior. The second results from the faulty assumption that gender differences in individuals, in human activities, and in symbolic systems are morally and politically symmetrical. In addition to the use of these two inadequate concepts of gender, there are also conflicting views about what strategies can best be used to eliminate androcentrism from knowledge-seeking. Let us consider these three problems in turn.

Some of the feminist science critics do not even recognize, let alone try to account for, the relationships between symbolic gender, the division of labor by gender, and individual gender. I will describe here just two examples of this kind of undertheorized approach to gender and science. In the first example, the issue is the support two forms of gender provide the third; and in the second, an opposition between two forms of gender motivates expressions of the third.

Equity studies focus on individual gender: on how women are discriminated against within the social structure of the scientific enterprise, and on the barriers the scientific enterprise and feminine gender socialization create for women entering and remaining in science. These studies explain the low representation of women in science courses, laboratories, scientific societies, and scientific publications in terms of these factors; and they criticize the characteristics of feminine identity and behavior encouraged by our culture that work against girls' and women's achievement of the motivation or skills to enter science. The proponents of equity recommend a variety of affirmative action strategies and resocialization practices for female children in order to increase the representation of women in science.

But these critics often fail to see that the division of labor by gender in the larger society and the gender symbolism in which science participates are equally responsible for the small number of women in science and for the fact that girls usually do not want to develop the skills and behaviors considered necessary for success in science. Until both the "emotional labor" and the "intellectual and manual labor" of housework and child care are perceived as desirable human activities for all men, the "intellectual and manual labor" of science and public life will not be perceived as potentially desirable activities for all women. The equity recommendations, moreover, ask women to exchange major aspects of their gender identity for the masculine version—without prescribing a similar "degendering" process for men. Feminists who have worked on these projects have exerted themselves heroically in the face of immense hostility for over a century, and I do not mean to trivialize their truly amazonian efforts. There certainly are good political reasons why they have not mounted a campaign to get men scientists involved in child care and in transforming their own gender needs and desires. But their efforts have not achieved the results they expected. One reason is that their shallow level of social analysis fails to locate those underlying causes of discrimination against women in science that are to be found in the gendered division of labor in social life and in science's enthusiastic participation in our culture's symbol making.

In the second example, some of the "textual critiques" of science seem to imply that we could eliminate the androcentrism of science if only we would draw attention to the beliefs and behaviors commonly thought of as feminine but nevertheless characteristic of (men) scientists in history. They suggest that the growth of science has been promoted as much by intuitive thinking, by valuing relational complexes, and by nurturing attitudes toward both nature and new hypotheses as it has by formal logic and mathematics, by mechanistic views, and by the "severe testing" of hypotheses accomplished by "torturing nature." Thus they seem to say that challenging the symbolization of scientific activity as uniquely masculine could eliminate androcentrism from science.

Again, these critiques have proved valuable indeed; they have greatly advanced our understanding of how gender ideologies are used by science. But the recommendation ignores the conscious or unconscious motivations for such gender symbolizing provided by *conflicts* between divisions of labor by gender in the larger society and individual masculine identity needs. Gender totemism in science is often energized by perceived oppositions or conflicts between masculine identity needs and threatened or actual divisions of labor by gender.

The second inadequate conceptualization of gender involves the assumption that masculinity and femininity are simply partial but combinable expressions of human symbol systems, ways of dividing social labor, and individual identities and behaviors. Many feminist critics seem to say that it is possible to strip away the undesirable aspects of masculinity and femininity and thus arrive at attractive cores which, while partial, are morally and politically symmetrical. The problem for feminism, as these thinkers see it, is that science has confused the masculine with the human ideal when the human must also include the feminine. But femininity and masculinity are not so easily combined; central to the notion of masculinity is its rejection of everything that is defined by a culture as feminine and its legitimated control of whatever counts as the feminine. Masculinity requires the conception of woman as "other," as Simone de Beauvoir pointed out.[8] Femininity is constructed to absorb everything defined as not masculine, and always to acquiesce in domination by the masculine. Thus this conception of gender difference cannot explain how in our culture, as in the vast majority of others, political power and moral value are monopolized by men at the expense of women. Gender is an *asymmetrical* category of human thought, social organization, and individual identity and behavior.

Finally, we can perceive very different assessments of gender in three proposals for the appropriate goal of a feminist critique of science. One approach argues that we should try to replace the masculine voice of science's past and present with a feminine voice. We should reverse the valuation of masculine and feminine interests in and ways of knowledge-seeking, leaving science differently gendered. We should want a science *for* women.[9] The second approach calls for the creation of knowledge-seeking not in the feminine but in the feminist voice.[10] This proposal holds that the exaltation of gender—

masculine or feminine—is detrimental to a truly inclusive human science. The third approach claims that the goals of the first two are still limited by masculine metaphysical and epistemological frameworks. It urges that we try to eliminate the defensive androcentric urge to imagine a "transcendental ego" with a single voice that judges how close our knowledge claims approach the "one true story" of the way the world is. Instead, we should try to create "reciprocal selves" that are federated in solidarities—rather than united in essentialized and naturalized identities—and correspondingly "decentered" knowledge-seeking.[11] We should want a form and purpose for knowledge-seeking which, whatever their other advantages, would probably bear little resemblance to what we think of as science.

An adequate theorization of gender will always lead us to ask questions about the interactions between gender symbolism, the particular way in which social labor or activity is divided by gender, and what constitutes gendered identities and desires in any particular culture. These questions are pertinent to the culture of science in fifteenth- to seventeenth-century Europe as well as to the cultures that have supported science in later centuries. Furthermore, because of the "logical" asymmetry in the content and valuation of masculinity and femininity, it is a situation that requires explanation if we find men scientists carrying on what would appear to them to be characteristically feminine activity or holding the kinds of beliefs their culture identifies as feminine. We must ask questions about the often irrational relationship between the asymmetrical gender symbolism of activities and beliefs and the asymmetrical sexual order and forms of gendered personal identity. And we must critically examine the purposes and goals of the forms of knowledge-seeking envisioned as a result of the feminist revolution. To bring that revolution to the natural sciences requires that we deepen our understanding of the complexity of the relation between the different ways in which science is gendered, as well as that we more thoroughly abandon the dogmas of empiricism.

I have been arguing that scientific, philosophic, and popular understandings of natural science are particularly hostile to a feminist critique. This resistance may appear reasonable if one thinks of gender difference as either a "natural" elaboration of biological difference or as culturally created characteristics attributable only to individuals and their behaviors. And it will appear reasonable if one insists on an excessively empiricist understanding of "what science is."

A series of related dogmas of empiricism ground and provide justification for this hostility, securing an apparent immunity for the scientific enterprise from the kinds of critical and causal scrutiny that science recommends for all the other regularities of nature and social life. If we were to abandon these dogmas of empiricism, we could adopt the alternative view that science is a fully social activity—as social and as culturally specific as are religious, educational, economic, and family activities. We would then find valuable critical interpretive approaches to all the activities that count as scientific, as well as to those that make scientific activity possible: selecting problematics; formulating and evaluating hypotheses; designing and performing experiments; interpreting results; motivating, educating, and recruiting young people for the scientific work force; organizing that work force and the support services—in families and psychiatrists' offices, as well as in laboratories—that make it possible for some people to be scientists; selecting, funding, and developing the technologies necessary to carry out scientific inquiry and those that inquiry makes possible; assigning different social meanings and values to scientific reason and to moral, political, and emotional reason.

Feminism proposes that there are no contemporary humans who escape gendering; contrary to traditional belief, men do not. It argues that masculinity—far from being the ideal for members of our species—is at least as far from the paradigmatically admirable as it has claimed femininity to be. Feminism also asserts that gender is a fundamental category within which meaning and value are assigned to everything in the world, a way of organizing human social relations. If we regarded science as a totally social activity, we could begin to understand the myriad ways in which it, too, is structured by expressions of gender. All that stands between us and that project are inadequate theories of gender, the dogmas of empiricism, and a good deal of political struggle.

Notes

1. See, e.g., Rossiter (1982b); Walsh (1977).
2. However, these suggestions raise as many questions as they answer. For instance, does not this approach tend to universalize the feminine, and thereby reinforce problematic modernist tendencies in feminism toward a politics (and epistemology) based on identities rather than solidarities? And are not interactive models the obvious alternative to the hierarchical models of Darwinian dogma? That is, do not reasons internal to the logic of theory development suggest the fruitfulness of pursuing interactive models at this moment in the history of the biological sciences? Furthermore, does not the desire to replace hierarchical with interactive models reflect widely recognized political realities at this time in world history, rather than only feminine characteristics? We shall pursue these questions later.
3. See Stacey and Thorne (1986), who make a number of these points about sociology. Pauline Bart has also pointed out (in conversation) that in speculating about the comparative resistances that different disciplinary fields offer to feminist insights, we should not underestimate the comparative levels of personal and political threat to the leaders in these fields—primarily men—that are presented, for instance, by sociological analyses of contemporary and nearby cultures in

comparison to historical or anthropological analyses of cultures temporally or spatially distant from us. This line of reasoning would support my argument that feminist critiques of the natural sciences meet even greater hostility than critiques in other areas; scientific rationality is directly implicated in the maintenance of masculinity in our kind of culture.

4. See Bloor (1977) for criticism of the sociologies of error and knowers.
5. See Fay and Moon (1977) for discussion of the virtues and problems of intentionalist approaches to social inquiry.
6. Kuhn (1970).
7. Popper (1959, 1972); cf. Harding (1976).
8. De Beauvoir (1953).
9. This phrase is Dorothy Smith's (1977), though she may not have in mind the proposal described here.
10. See, e.g., Hartsock (1983).
11. See, e.g., the discussions in *Signs* (1981); Marks and de Courtivron (1980); Flax (1983); Haraway (1985).

References

Bloor, David. 1977. *Knowledge and Social Imagery*. London: Routledge and Kegan Paul.

De Beauvoir, Simone. 1953. *The Second Sex*, tr. H. M. Parshley. New York: Knopf.

Fay, Brian, and Donald Moon. 1977. "What Would an Adequate Philosophy of Social Science Look Like?" *Philosophy of Social Science* 7.

Flax, Jane. 1983. "Political Philosophy and the Patriarchal Unconscious: A Psychoanalytic Perspective on Epistemology and Metaphysics." In *Discovering Reality: Feminist Perspectives on Epistemology, Metaphysics, Methodology, and Philosophy of Science*, ed. S. Harding and M. Hintikka. Dordrecht: Reidel.

Haraway, Donna. 1985. "A Manifesto for Cyborgs: Science, Technology, and Socialist Feminism in the 1980s." *Socialist Review* 80.

Harding, Sandra, ed. 1976. *Can Theories Be Refuted? Essays on the Duhem-Quine Thesis*. Dordrecht: Reidel.

Hartsock, Nancy. 1983. "The Feminist Standpoint: Developing the Ground for a Specifically Feminist Historical Materialism." In *Discovering Reality: Feminist Perspectives on Epistemology, Metaphysics, Methodology, and Philosophy of Science*, ed. S. Harding and M. Hintikka. Dordrecht: Reidel.

Kuhn, Thomas S. 1970. *The Structure of Scientific Revolutions*, 2d ed. Chicago: University of Chicago Press.

Marks, Elaine, and Isabelle de Courtivron, eds. 1980. *New French Feminisms*. Amherst: University of Massachusetts Press.

Popper, Karl. 1959. *The Logic of Scientific Discovery*. New York: Basic Books.

———. 1972. *Conjectures and Refutations: The Growth of Scientific Knowledge*. 4th ed. rev. London: Routledge and Kegan Paul.

Rossiter, Margaret. 1982a. "Fair Enough?" *Isis* 72.

———. 1982b. *Women Scientists in America: Struggles and Strategies to 1940*. Baltimore: Johns Hopkins University Press.

Signs: Journal of Women in Culture and Society. 1981. Special issue on French feminism, 7, no. 1.

Smith, Dorothy. 1977. "Some Implications of a Sociology for Women." In *Woman in a Man-Made World: A Socioeconomic Handbook*, ed. N. Glazer an H. Waehrer. Chicago: Rand-McNally.

Stacey, Judith, and Barrie Thorne. 1985. "The Missing Feminist Revolution in Sociology." *Social Problems* 32.

Walsh, Mary Roth. 1977. *Doctor Wanted, No Women Need Apply: Sexual Barriers in the Medical Profession, 1835–1975*. New Haven: Yale University Press.

SELECTION 21
The Gender/Science System: or, Is Sex to Gender as Nature Is to Science?

EVELYN FOX KELLER

THE MOST CRITICAL PROBLEM facing feminist studies today is that of the meaning of gender, its relation to biological sex on the one hand, and its place with respect to other social markers of difference (e.g., race, class, ethnicity, etc.) on the other—i.e., the relation between sex, gender, and difference in general. Similarly, I would argue that the most critical problem facing science studies today is that of the meaning of science, its relation to nature, and its place with respect to other social institutions—i.e., the relation between nature, science, and interests in general. My purpose in this paper is, first, to identify some important parallels, even a structural homology, between these two questions, and second, to suggest that an exploration of this homology (including the factors responsible for its maintenance) can provide us with some useful guidelines in our attempts to address these problems.

Three different kinds of parallels between feminist studies and science studies can be identified immediately: One might be called historical, the second, epistemological, and the third, political. Historically, it is worth noting that modern feminist studies actually emerges with the recognition that women, at least, are made rather than born—i.e., with the distinction between sex and gender. In much the same way, contemporary studies of science come into being with the recognition of a distinction between science and nature—with the realization that science not only is not now, but can never be, a "mirror of nature." With the introduction of these distinctions came the growth of two new (essentially nonoverlapping) fields of study, one devoted to the analysis of the social construction of gender, and the other, of the social construction of science.

In both of these endeavors, however, scholars now find they must contend with what might best be described as a "dynamic instability"[1] in the basic categories of their respective subjects: in the one case, of gender, and the other, of science—an instability in fact unleashed by the very distinctions that had given them birth. If gender is not to be defined by sex, nor science by nature (i.e., by what *is*), how then *are* they to be defined? In the absence of an adequate answer to this question, the difficulties that both feminist and science scholars have encountered in maintaining yet containing their necessary distinctions (between sex and gender on the one hand, and between science and nature on the other) are as familiar as they have been insurmountable. It is this phenomenon that I am calling the epistemological parallel. Just as discussions of gender tend to lean toward one of two poles—either toward biological determinism, or toward infinite plasticity, a kind of generic anarchy, so too do discussions of science exhibit the same polarizing pressures—propelled either toward objectivism, or toward relativism. In one direction, both gender and science return to a premodern (and prefeminist) conception in which gender has been collapsed back onto sex, and science, back onto nature. Under the other, we are invited into a postmodernist, postfeminist (and postscientific) utopia in which gender and science run free, no longer grounded either by sex or by nature—indeed, in which both sex and nature have effectively disappeared altogether. Attempts to occupy a "middle ground"—either with respect to gender or to science—must contend not only with the conceptual difficulty of formulating such a position, but also with the peculiarly insistent pressures of a public forum urging each concept toward one pole or the other.

I invoke the label "political" for the third parallel with reference to the politics of knowledge: I believe that, finally, what is at issue in both cases is a question of status—the status, in the one case, of gender, and in the other case, of science, as theoretical categories. Is gender, as an analytical category, different from, perhaps even prior to, categories of race, class, etc.? (Or, to reverse the question, is oppression ultimately the only important variable of gender?) The parallel question is, of course: Is science substantively different from other social structures or "interest groups?"; i.e., are scientific claims to knowledge any better than other (nonscientific) claims to knowledge?

The parallels I am describing between feminist studies and social studies of science have in fact been just that, i.e., parallels; until quite recently, there has been virtually no intersection between the two disciplines, just as there has been virtually no interaction between attempts to reconceptualize gender and science—as if the two categories were independent, each having nothing to do with the other. It is only with the emergence of a modern feminist critique of science that the categories of gender and science have come to be seen as intertwined, and, accordingly, that the two subjects (feminist studies and science studies) have begun to converge. But, as I have argued elsewhere, this most recent development actually required the prior conceptualization both of gender as distinct from sex, and of science as distinct from nature. That is, the modern feminist critique of science is historically dependent on the earlier emergence of each of its parent disciplines. With such a lineage, however, it also (perhaps necessarily) inherits whatever ambiguity/unclarity/uncertainty/instability remains in each of the terms, gender and science. Indeed, it might be said that feminist studies of science has become the field in which these ambiguities are most clearly visible, and accordingly, the field that offers the best opportunity for understanding the factors that may be working against a clear and stable "middle ground" account of both concepts. I suggest also that, for this reason, an examination of the history of feminism and science can provide important insights to help point the way toward resolution of these difficulties.

To illustrate these claims, I will focus on one particular episode in the recent history of feminism and science, namely on contemporary debate over the idea of a "feminist science," and more specifically, over the question of whether or not the recently celebrated cytogeneticist, Barbara McClintock, might be regarded as an exemplar of such a "feminist science." In order to orient this debate, however, I need to preface the discussion with a few very brief remarks about the prior history of the struggles of that group most directly affected by the issues of feminism and science, namely women scientists.

Throughout this century, the principal strategy employed by women seeking entrance to the world of science has been premised on the repudiation of gender as a significant variable for scientific productivity. The reasons for this strategy are clear enough: Experience had demonstrated all too fully that any acknowledgment of gender-based difference was almost invariably employed as a justification for exclusion. Either it was used to exclude them from science, or to brand them as "not-women"—in practice, usually both at the same time. For women scientists *as scientists*, the principal point is that measures of scientific performance admitted of only a single scale, according to which, to be different was to be lesser. Under such circumstances, the hope of equity, indeed, the very concept of equity, appeared—as it still appears—to depend on the disavowal of difference. In hindsight, it is easy enough to see the problem with this strategy: If a universal standard invites the translation of difference into inequality, threatening further to collapse into duality, otherness, and exclusion, the same standard invites the translation of equality into sameness, and accordingly, guarantees the exclusion of any experience, perception, or value that is other. As a consequence, "others" are eligible for inclusion only to the extent that they can excise those differences, eradicating even the marks of that excision. Unfortunately, such operations are often only partially successful, leaving in their wake residual handicaps that detract from the ability of the survivors to be fully effective "competitors." Yet more important, they fail to provide effective protection against whatever de facto discrimination continues to prevail. What such a strategy *can* do, however, is help obscure the fact of that discrimination.

This dilemma is perhaps nowhere more poignantly illustrated than in the experiences of women scientists in the mid-twentieth century—the nadir of the history of women in American science. Having sought safety in the progressive eradication of any distinguishing characteristics that might mark their gender, by the 1950s, women scientists, qua women, had effectively disappeared from American science. Their numerical representation was no longer recorded; even, by their own choice, their tell-tale first names were withheld from publications. Unfortunately, however, this strategy failed to protect actual women from the effects of an increasingly exclusionary professional policy—it only helped obscure the effects of that policy.

The principal point here is that these women were caught on the horns of an impossible dilemma—a dilemma that was unresolvable as long as the goal of science was seen as the unequivocal mirroring of nature, and its success as admitting of only a single standard of measurement. It was only with the introduction of an alternative view of science—one admitting of a multiplicity of goals and standards—that the conditions arose for some feminists, in the late 1970s and early 1980s, to begin to argue for the inclusion of difference—in experience, perceptions, and values—as intrinsically valuable to the production of science. Very rapidly, however, the idea of difference in science gave way (in some circles) to the extremely problematic idea of a different science altogether—in particular, to the idea of a feminist science. A feminist science might mean many things to different people, but, in practice, it is almost always used to invoke the idea of a "feminine" science. As it actually happened, though, for the idea of such a feminist/feminine (or "femininist") science to really engage people's fancy, something more than simply the availability of an alternative to the traditional view of science was needed: A source of legitimation was required, and even better, an exemplar. In this need, the Nobel Prize Committee seemed fortuitously to oblige.

In 1983, that committee selected Barbara McClintock for its award in medicine and physiology for work done almost forty years earlier. With help from an enthusiastic press, they thereby turned a deviant and reclusive cytogeneticist—a woman who has made respect for difference the cornerstone of her own distinctive philosophy of science—into a new, albeit reluctant, cultural heroine. And with a small but crucial rewriting of the text, advocates of a new "femininist" science found in that moment what they needed: an exemplar who, through her "feeling for the organism," seemed to restore feminine values to science, and who (even more important), after years of struggle, had finally been validated, even vindicated, by a reluctant establishment.

Curiously enough, however, at the very same moment, this same establishment was busy welcoming McClintock back into their fold. Now it was
their turn to repudiate the differences that in the past had made her such
an anomaly. As Stephen Jay Gould informed us (*New York Review*, March
26, 1984), McClintock's "feeling for the organism" is in no way distinctive;
all good scientists (himself included) have it and use it. Other reviewers
went further. They had always appreciated her work; the claim that she
had been misunderstood, unappreciated, was simply wrong. At the very moment
that (some) feminists claimed McClintock as one of their own, as a
representative of a different science, mainstream scientists closed ranks around
her, claiming her as one of their own: There is only one science.

Because I cannot claim to have been an innocent bystander in these
developments, I need to say something about my own contribution. In writing
my book on McClintock, it seemed important to me to consciously bracket
the questions on gender and science that I had been writing about before,
and to treat the material on McClintock's life and work, and their relation
to the history of modern biology, in their own terms. It seemed unfair to
McClintock's own story to burden it with a prior moral of mine, particularly
in view of the fact that it was extremely unclear to me just what the relevance
of a feminist, or gender, critique to that story might be. McClintock herself
is not a feminist; she has throughout her life not only resisted but adamantly
repudiated all classification, and her commitment to science as a place where
"the matter of gender drops away" is staunch. If gender was to prove an
important variable in that story, particularly to an understanding of her
scientific deviance, the story itself would have to show both me and the
reader how. This stance of course left readers free to draw their own
conclusions, which indeed they did—though, perhaps predictably, usually
attributing those conclusions to me.

Partly in self-defense, and partly because it needed to be addressed, I
turned to the question of a feminist science in my subsequent book (Keller
1985)—focusing in particular on the question of the relevance of gender to
the McClintock story. On quite general grounds, I argued that if one means
by a feminist science a feminine science, the very notion is deeply problematic:
first because it ignores the fundamentally social character of the process by
which both science and scientists get named as such, and second because of
the extent to which our understanding of "feminine" and "scientific" have
been historically constructed in opposition to each other.

Other problems arise in relation to the McClintock story itself: First,
there is not only McClintock's own disavowal of all stereotypic notions of
femininity, but, in addition, there is the fact that none of the dynamics we
think of as key to feminine socialization seem to apply to her. She was
never pregnant, never parented, and, although she was a daughter, her relation

to her mother was so anomalous as to pose a challenge to conventional assumptions about mother-daughter bonding. Finally, a directly biological account of McClintock's difference won't do because she is in fact not representative of women in general—not even of women scientists; nor are her vision and practice of science absent among male scientists. What then are we to make of the fact that so much of what is distinctive about that vision and practice—its emphasis on intuition, feeling, connectedness, and relatedness—conforms so well to our most familiar stereotypes of women? And is, in fact, so rare among male scientists?

To answer this question, I argued that it was necessary to shift the focus first from sex to gender, and second, from the construction of gender to the construction of science. The question then becomes, not why McClintock relies on intuition, feeling, a sense of connectedness and relatedness in her scientific practice, but how come these resources are repudiated by stereotypic science? Put this way, the question virtually answers itself: The repudiation of these resources, I argued, derives precisely from the conventional naming of science as masculine, coupled with the equally conventional naming of these resources as feminine. The relevance of gender in the McClintock story thus shifts from its role in her personal socialization to its role in the social construction of science. For the project of reclaiming science as a gender-free endeavor—a place where "the matter of gender drops away"—I did, however, suggest one respect in which McClintock's sex may in fact have provided her with an advantage: "However atypical she is as a woman, what she is *not* is a man"—and hence is under no obligation to prove her "masculinity" (Keller 1985, 174).

In other words, I attempted to articulate the very kind of "middle ground" stance with regard to gender that I have in this paper suggested is so peculiarly difficult (for all of us) to maintain—claiming in particular that the relevance of gender to science is (a) a socially constructed relevance, but (b) *carried* by the sex of its participants (in the sense, that is, that gender-specific norms are internalized along with one's "core gender identity"). In short, I argued that gender is a fundamentally relational construct which, although not determined by sex, is never entirely independent of it. In spite of cultural variability and psychological plasticity, it means *something*—though, for many individuals, perhaps not a great deal—to identify oneself as being of one sex and not of another.

Because the responses this argument has generated provide ready evidence of the instability to which our understanding of gender is generally subject, it may be useful to review them here. Many feminists have continued to read the McClintock story as a manifesto of a "feminist science" (in the sense, i.e., of a specifically female science)—in the process, either celebrating me as its proponent, or, if they respond at all to my disclaimers, implying that I lack the courage of my convictions—sometimes even suggesting that I lack the courage of McClintock's convictions. On the other side, a number of readers (both men and women) complained that I ignored McClintock's distinctiveness in attempting to make her "an exemplar of women," or that my argument has to be wrong because of the fact that there *are* men who do think like McClintock, who do have "a feeling for the organism." Hence, they conclude, gender cannot be relevant to this story. Finally, there are those readers for whom the anxiety raised by any reference to gender whatever in the context of science is so great that they simultaneously read both "gender" and "gender-free" as "female" (see, e.g., Koblitz n.d.). For these last readers, especially, the suggestion of even a tenuous link between gender and sex for either women or men is taken as proof of their worst suspicions— i.e., that this argument constitutes a threat to the claim of women scientists to equity.

What is perhaps most notable about these readings is the extent to which they all depend, albeit in different ways, on an unwitting, almost reflexive, equation between questions about gender with questions about sex. That is, they assume that what is really at issue is not the force of gender ideology, but the force of sex. With the space between sex and gender thus eliminated, the original question of McClintock's difference automatically reduces to the exceedingly problematic (and dubious) question of whether or not men and women, by virtue of being male or female, think differently. Not surprisingly, the responses to this last question are both mixed and extremely fervent. Once read as duality, the question of difference becomes subject to only two responses: yes or no, i.e., either the embrace or the denial of duality—embrace by those who welcome it; denial by those who fear it. The entire spectrum of difference has thus been collapsed onto two poles— duality and universality.

I suggest that the conceptual collapse illustrated here—the difficulty so many of us have in thinking about difference in any other terms than either duality or universality—is rooted not in biology but in politics: not a consequence of any limitations in the way in which our brains are constructed, but rather the consequence of an implicit contest for power. I am suggesting that duality and universality are responses actually structured by, as well as employed in, a contest that is first and foremost political. As I've already implied, the Nobel Prize plays a crucial role in creating out of McClintock's science a zone of contention in the first place, inviting both feminists and mainstream scientists to claim her as one of their own. The legitimation and authority provided by the Nobel Prize endowed McClintock's scientific practice with a value worth fighting over—a value claimed by one side by the negation of difference, and by the other by its reformulation as duality. It is precisely in the context of such a competition that the question of difference itself becomes a contested zone—our conceptualization of difference molded by our perceptions (as well as the reality) of power. In other words, in this context at least, the very debate between duality and universality both presupposes and augments a prior division between an "us" and a "them," bound in conflict by a common perception of power. It refers not to a world in which we and they could be said to occupy truly separate spheres, with separate, noninteracting sources of power and authority—in such a world, there would be no debate—but, rather, to a world perceived as ordered by a single source (or axis) of power that is at least in principle commonly available; a world in which duality can be invoked (by either side) to create not so much a separation of spheres as an inside and an outside—in other words, as a strategy of exclusion. It is in just such a world that the perennially available possibility of difference becomes a matter to contest—invoked or denied according, first, to the value attached to that difference, and second, to one's position relative to the axis of power. With nothing to lose, but possibly something to gain, a difference of value can safely and perhaps usefully be claimed as a mark of duality. Standing inside the circle, however, it is more strategic to assimilate any difference that is known to be valuable, and to exclude, through the invocation of duality, those differences that promise no value.

In the particular case at hand, the power at stake is, to put it quite simply, the epistemic authority of scientists. And although I have so far been speaking as if there were only one demarcation capable of effecting exclusion, namely that between men and women, it is neither the case that all women are without scientific authority nor that all those without scientific authority are women. Another demarcation is also operative here—indeed, I would even say, primary: namely, the demarcation between science and nonscience, potentially at least as exclusionary as that between men and women. It is the threat of this second demarcation that polarizes our discussions about the nature of scientific knowledge in much the same way as the first polarizes our discussions of gender. The question of whether scientific knowledge is objective or relative is at least in part a question about the claim of scientists to absolute authority. If there is only one truth, and scientists are privy to it, (i.e., science and nature are one), then the authority of science is unassailable. But if truth is relative, if science is divorced from nature and married instead to culture (or "interests"), then the privileged status of that authority is fatally undermined. With this move, the demarcation between science and nonscience appears to have effectively dissolved. Because the notion of a feminist/feminine science engages both these demarcations simultaneously—indeed, it could be said that the very proposal of a feminist science depends on the possibility of playing one off against the other—an understanding of this debate requires that we pay attention to both sets of dynamics. Once again, an examination of the responses of women in science is especially instructive, for it is that group of individuals that is most directly positioned by these two demarcations—indeed, positioned by their intersection.

For women who have managed to obtain a foothold within the world of science, the situation is particularly fraught. Because they are "inside," they have everything to lose by a demarcation along the lines of sex that has historically only worked to exclude them. And precisely because they are rarely quite fully inside, more commonly somewhere near the edge, the threat of such exclusion looms particularly ominously. At the same time, as scientists, they have a vested interest in defending a traditional view of science— perhaps, because of the relative insecurity of their status, even more fiercely than their relatively more secure male colleagues. On two counts then, it is hardly surprising therefore that most women scientists (as well as historians and philosophers of science) vehemently resist the notion of a feminist/ feminine science: The suggestion that women, as a class, will do a different kind of science simultaneously invokes the duality of sex, and undermines (or presupposes the undermining of) our confidence in the privileged attachment of science to nature.

What *is* surprising is the extent to which so many women scientists have been able to read into McClintock's Nobel Prize the possibility of an alternative to the classical dichotomies. The McClintock story is compelling to many women working in science because it testifies for them the viability of difference within the world of science as we know it. They read the Nobel Prize not as an invitation to rebellion, but as evidence of the legitimacy of difference within the established criteria of scientific "truth"—as making room within the prevailing canon for many of the questions, methodologies, and interpretations that their more familiar version of that canon did not permit. In this, they seek a larger canon rather than a different one; a richer, perhaps even multifaceted, representation of reality, but not a separate reality. Their resistance to the reduction of difference to duality is firm, and it is, admittedly, a resistance clearly in the service of their own interests as women scientists. But it is also in the service of a larger interest, and that is the preservation of some meaning to the term "science."

Even accepting that the scientific endeavor is not as monolithic as the received view would have it, accepting that science does not and cannot "mirror" nature, the question remains, what do we mean by "science?" Does, indeed, any meaning of the term remain? If it does, that meaning must derive from the shared commitment of scientists to the pursuit of a maximally reliable (even if not faithful) representation of nature, under the equally shared assumption that, however elusive, there is only one nature. We may now realize that science is not capable of apprehending reality "as it is," as people once thought it could, but belief in the existence of separate realities (a notion in fact often associated with arguments for a "feminine science") is fundamentally antithetical to any meaning that the scientific endeavor might have. To ask women scientists to accept the notion of a different science representing a different reality (as distinct from difference in science) would be to ask them to give up their identity as scientists—in much the same way, incidentally, that traditional science has asked them to give up their identity as women. It is, finally, not so much to counterpose an alternative science as to reinforce the traditional opposition between women and science.

The celebration of difference within science seems therefore to constitute a clear advance over both the monolithic view of science that threatens to exclude diversity, and the dualistic (or relativistic) view that threatens to deny particular meaning to the category, science. At the same time, however, the attempt to avoid the problem of duality by ignoring gender altogether carries within itself a critically undermining flaw: It blocks our perception of the very important ways in which gender has been, and remains, constitutively operative in science. In particular, it ignores the fact that it is precisely in the name of gender that the very diversity we would now like to see celebrated has historically been (and continues to be) excluded. Above all, it ignores the uses of gender in maintaining a monolithic ordering of power.

Just as the engendering of culture in general has shown itself as a way of ordering the power structures of our social and political worlds, the engendering of knowledge, and of scientific knowledge in particular, has served to order the sphere of epistemic power. Knowledge *is* power—in many senses of the term. With the rise of modern science, knowledge came to be understood as a particular kind of power—namely, as the power to dominate nature. In this history, we can see the construction of gender *as* the construction of exclusion—of women, of what is labeled feminine, and simultaneously, of the alternative meanings of power that knowledge might engender. As I've argued in my book on this subject (Keller 1985), the exclusion of the feminine from science has been historically constitutive of a particular definition of science—as incontrovertibly objective, universal, impersonal—and masculine: a definition that serves simultaneously to demarcate masculine from feminine and scientists from nonscientists—even good science from bad. In the past as in the present, the sexual division of emotional and intellectual labor has provided a readily available and much relied upon tool for bolstering the particular claims that science makes to a univocal and hence absolute epistemic authority—not only in the contest between scientists and nonscientists, but equally, in contests internal to science. In turn, of course, the same authority serves to denigrate the entire excluded realm of the feminine—a realm which, as it happens, invariably includes most women.

Given the cultural uses of gender in maintaining a univocal conception of power, any gender-blind advocacy of difference (by men or women, in science or elsewhere) entails some risk. Given its particular uses to exclude those who are the cultural carriers of "femininity" from the apex of epistemic authority, women scientists incur a special risk in ignoring these uses. Once dissociated from gender (and hence from sex), the celebration of difference ironically lends itself to the same ends as the denial of difference—it can serve once again to render women themselves superfluous. The question of values, in this discourse, preempts the question of jobs. Although in many ways philosophically opposed to postmodernism, in one important respect, the response of these scientists converges on a problem that has already become evident in postmodernist literary discourse—a problem to which an increasing number of literary scholars have already begun to call attention. Put simply, the question becomes: When anyone can learn to read like a woman, what need have we for women readers? In other words, difference without gender invites another kind of degeneracy—not quite the denial of difference, but its reduction to indifference, a way of thinking about difference as potentially capable as universality of excluding actual women.[2]

Where advocates of difference within science critically depart from and effectively counter that tendency in postmodernism toward an indefinite proliferation of difference is in their reminder of the constraints imposed by the recalcitrance of nature—their reminder that, despite its ultimate unrepresentability, nature does exist. As feminists, we can offer an equally necessary counter (though necessary for different reasons) to that same proliferation by recalling the constraints imposed by the recalcitrance of sex. In truth—perhaps the one truth we actually do know—neither nature nor sex *can* be named out of existence. Both persist, beyond theory, as humbling reminders of our mortality. The question, of course, is how we can maintain this mindfulness without in the process succumbing to the forces that lend to the names we give to nature and sex the status of reality—the forces that constrain our perception and conception of both nature and sex, first, by their naming as science and gender, and second, by the particular namings of science and gender that are, at any particular time, currently normative.

Our success in maintaining awareness of the bipolar and dialectical influences of both nature and culture on the categories of gender and science may well in the end depend on the adequacy of our analysis of the nature of the forces that work against such an awareness. If these forces do in fact derive from an underlying contest for power, as the story narrated here suggests, then the most central issue at hand is the relation between gender, science and power—above all, the uses of particular constructions of gender and science in structuring our conceptual and political landscape of power. As long as power itself remains defined in the unitary terms that have prevailed, the struggles for power that ensue provide fuel, on the one hand, for the collapse between science and nature, and gender with sex, and on the other, for the repudiation of nature and/or sex. In other words, they guarantee the very instability in the concepts of gender and science that continues to plague both feminist and science studies.

Feminist analyses have suggested that it is precisely in the interpenetration of our language of gender and our language of science that the multidimensional terrains of nature, of culture, and of power have been transformed into one-dimensional contests. If so, the effective defusing of these contests would require a different kind of language, reflecting a higher dimensionality in our landscape—neither homogeneous nor divided, spacious enough to enable multiplicity to survive without degenerating into opposition. In short, we need a language that enables us to conceptually and perceptually negotiate our way between sameness and opposition, that permits the recognition of kinship in difference and of difference among kin; a language that encodes respect for difference, particularity, alterity without repudiating the underlying affinity that is the first prerequisite for knowledge. In this effort, I suggest that the mere fact of sexual difference may itself provide us with one useful reminder: It is, after all, that which simultaneously divides and binds us as a species. But surely, nature, in its mercilessly recalcitrant diversity, provides us with another.

Notes

Portions of this paper are taken from a talk given at the "Little Three" Conference, Jan. 16, 1986, Amherst, MA.

1. The term "instability" has also been employed by Sandra Harding (1986), but with a rather different charge. Where Harding finds instability productive, both politically and intellectually, I find it—again, both politically and intellectually—an obstacle to productive exchange.

2. See, e.g., the critique of Derrida and Foucault in Teresa de Lauretis, *Technologies of Gender* (Indiana University Press, 1987).

References

Harding, Sandra. 1986. "The Instability of the Analytic Categories of Feminist Theory." *Signs* 11 (4): 645–64.

Keller, Evelyn Fox. 1983. *A Feeling for the Organism: The Life and Work of Barbara McClintock.* New York: W. H. Freeman.

———. 1985. *Reflections on Gender and Science.* New Haven: Yale University Press.

Koblitz, Ann Hibner. n.d. "An Historian Looks at Gender and Science." Unpublished manuscript.

SELECTION 22
FROM

The Woman Question: Philosophy of Liberation and the Liberation of Philosophy

CAROL C. GOULD

INTRODUCTION

IS THE WOMAN QUESTION a philosophical question? Can philosophy deal with such issues as women's social role, their oppression and liberation?[1] I shall argue against a prevailing view that it cannot and try to show how a critical philosophy can do so.

The woman question is a paradigm of the sort of question which concerns a particular and limited part of society or of humanity (like questions concerning race or social class), or a particular and limited historical or social form (like capitalism or liberal democracy). In attempting to treat such questions philosophically, one is often faced with a standard methodological objection: namely, that the woman question like these others is too "special," "limited," or "partial," and therefore it is not a properly philosophical question because it does not deal with an appropriately universal subject matter.[2] Philosophy's concern, it is argued, is with the human *qua* human, or with human nature as such, rather than with such "particular" and "applied" social questions, or with such "accidental" differences as gender. An appropriate philosophical subject matter, the objection continues, is defined by a criterion of universality which abstracts from such differences. . . .

It will be seen that what is at issue is the criterion of universality itself—or rather, two opposed criteria of universality. The first I shall characterize as *abstract universality*. The alternative which I shall propose, taken from the Hegelian and Marxist dialectical tradition, is that of *concrete universality*. I hope to show that on this criterion, the woman question *is* a philosophical question, and further, that on this criterion, the task of giving a philosophical critique of the present social reality becomes a viable and necessary function of philosophy.

Feminists have taken the woman question to be a philosophical question in two very different ways. The first approach addresses the problem of universality in the following way: Since women, like men, are persons or human beings, they have all and only those rights which apply universally to humans *qua* human. The differences between men and women beyond the "real," i.e., biological, differences are interpreted as "*merely*" social, cultural, and historical. On this view, being a woman is an accidental, and neither a universal nor an essential property of being human, since one may be human and not female.[3] These feminists argue further, that to recognize a sexual polarity between men and women beyond the biological differences leaves women open to continued unequal treatment and to the continued institutionalization of these sex differences. On this view, although there are of course some philosophical issues which arise from and bear on the situation of women, women as such cannot constitute a philosophical notion or category.[4] Other feminists have argued that the sexual polarity establishes fundamental categories of human nature, and that therefore there is no common universal human nature, but only male nature and female nature. This view implies that "woman" is a fundamental philosophical notion, insofar as it establishes sex difference as essential or categorial.[5]

My position is distinct from both of these. Although I want to hold that the question of women *is* philosophical (as on the second view), this does not commit me to the claim that the differences between men and women are fundamental differences of natures. Instead, while arguing that the question of women is philosophical, I also want to claim (as on the first view), that the oppression of women as well as all significant differences between men and women are *thoroughly historical, social, and cultural*.[6] Now I can maintain these seemingly incompatible positions at the same time because I would claim that social, cultural, and historical differences can be relevant philosophical differences. Or to put it differently, that being human is essentially a social, historical, and cultural matter, and that differences which are rooted in such contexts are therefore philosophically relevant differences.

THE CRITERION OF ABSTRACT UNIVERSALITY AS A METHODOLOGICAL CRITERION FOR WHAT IS "PHILOSOPHICAL"

The objection raised at the outset claims that a properly universal subject matter cannot be constituted by "particular" or "accidental" social or historical differences. Rather, it insists on a criterion of universality which abstracts from differences in gender and therefore excludes the woman question as a philosophical one. I call this the criterion of *abstract universality* . . . and it is characteristic of Essentialism.

To summarize the methodological premises of such an Essentialist view: What is universal, and therefore the proper subject matter for philosophical inquiry, consists in what is common or the same in all members of a given class. But this cannot be merely an accidental universality, i.e., it cannot be merely contingently the case that all members of a given class share some property in common. Rather, the universal properties must also be necessary, i.e., those without which the individuals would not be members of a given class, and therefore those properties which make them the kinds of things they are.[7] Furthermore, such an essential property must be unique to the members of that class, shared by members of that class only. These conditions of universality, necessity, and uniqueness determine what the essential properties are.[8]

In order to establish such essential properties, one must abstract from all differences among members of a class, or regard these differences as *indifferent*.[9] Differences are therefore taken to be accidental, and only what is universal in the strong or nomic sense is taken to be essential.[10] As a consequence, in considering the human, all historical and social differentiation drops out and only those abstracted properties which remain invariant for all humans and in all societies count as essential. The term "abstract" here is contrasted with its opposite, "concrete," where "concrete" denotes those properties which individuate human beings or societies or which differentiate them, that is, which make them the particular individuals or societies they are. . . .

A difficulty presents itself for the Essentialist which we may call the "Hair, Mud, Dirt" difficulty, after Plato's account of it in the *Parmenides*. In Parmenides' critique of the theory of Forms, the issue arises whether there are universal forms or essences for such lowly things as hair, mud, and dirt. Socrates is unwilling to concede that there are, but cannot answer why there should not be.[11] A similar problem arises for the Essentialist when he attempts to demarcate essential from accidental properties. Specifically, one may ask (with respect to *any* essential property): "Why stop there?" Why, for example, should "human" be taken to be essential, and "male" or "female" accidental? May we not take "animal" as essential, and "human" as an accidental property (together with, say, "bovine" or "reptilian")? Most important for our purposes, why not take "male" and "female" as essential properties, since these have sometimes been taken to constitute an essential distinction of a cosmic sort (e.g., in Pythagorean dualism, or in Yin and Yang cosmology). I would hold that such an essential distinction of gender is wrong. Nonetheless, this argument suggests that the Essentialist has no methodological way to exclude such alternative demarcations of essence and accident. Moreover, he cannot argue that what is taken to be an essence is relative, or that one person's essence is another person's accident, because on his view what is essential is not a matter of choice or convention, but rather of the way things are.

The exclusion of gender as an accidental property and thus as not appropriate subject matter for philosophical discourse is therefore unfounded on the grounds of the relativity of essential properties. Since one can argue, like Parmenides, that essential properties may be established for *any* class of things and thus not only for gender, but for more "local" properties such as red-headedness, English-speaking, or being an inhabitant of New York City, the force of the Essentialist's exclusion of gender is lost. . . .

One further thing might be said in this context: If one can establish an essence for any class of things, then the Essentialist's choice of one property as essential, with respect to which certain others are accidental, does not depend on methodological considerations alone; rather, this choice must depend on other factors, if it is not a random choice. But if, as we have suggested, the Essentialist's choice depends on the uncritical acceptance of the common sense or scientific beliefs of his time as to what is essential and what accidental, then he is open to the intrusion of the uncriticized dominant beliefs or social prejudices of his own time or of his social context. What he takes to be the essential properties as well as his characterization of them may then reflect such contingent social and historical beliefs or prejudices. It is this phenomenon which I shall investigate in the following section. . . .

A CRITIQUE OF ABSTRACT UNIVERSALITY IN PRACTICE: HUMAN NATURE—UNIVERSAL OR MALE?

A practical criticism of the criterion of abstract universality is, that its use to determine essential human properties is not a value-free but a value-laden one, that it reflects the interests, needs, and prejudices of particular social groups. This is problematic for two reasons: (1) Such prejudices may introduce distortions into the very understanding of what is essential. But this is not decisive, for it could be argued that any philosophical approach is subject to the unintended intrusion of interests and needs, and that this is only what one might expect. However, (2) I shall argue further that Essentialism reflects such interests in a particularly harmful way, because it tends to mask them under the guise of universality and therefore is deceptive. I am not claiming that the criterion of abstract universality lends itself to such distortion or deception because it is somehow inherently vicious or because it is consciously conceived to mask particular interests under the guise of universality. Rather, I hope to show that it is the very abstractness of the criterion which opens it to such distortion, and this by way of its exclusion of concrete social and historical differences as accidental and therefore philosophically irrelevant.

In particular, I shall suggest that the criterion of abstract universality, in actual philosophical practice, turns out to choose those properties as essentially and universally human which the philosophers themselves have either explicitly identified as male properties, or which were associated with roles and functions in which males predominated. As a critique of abstract universality, I hope to show how allegedly transhistorical, necessary, and universal properties which are chosen to characterize human nature as such, in fact turn out upon examination to be something less than universal; in fact, they reflect the historical and social limitations and prejudices of their time, and specifically the sex bias of their social context. Thus instead of being necessary and universal, such properties are in fact contingent and particular. But if this is so, then the claim of universality itself masks this one-sidedness. However, since there is no doubt that the philosophers to be examined here were pursuing the essential in a systematically rigorous way, we may wonder why they were prone to such distortion. In the course of the discussion which follows, I shall present some hypotheses to explain this. . . .

In the cases to be examined, the connection between human nature and male nature is either explicitly made or implied, with women characterized quite differently. The case of Kant is perhaps paradigmatic here. According to Kant in the *Fundamental Principles of the Metaphysics of Morals*,

> That is practically *good*, however, which determines the will by means of the conceptions of reason . . . on principles which are valid for every rational being as such. It is distinguished from the *pleasant* as that which influences the will only by means of sensation from merely subjective causes, valid only for the sense of this or that one and not as a principle of reason which holds for every one.[12]

> Now I say: man and generally any rational being exists as an end in himself.[13]

But if we turn to Kant's *Observations on the Feeling of the Beautiful and the Sublime* (admittedly an early work), we find that women lack these humanly essential characteristics and most clearly they lack the sort of moral agency which is characteristic of human nature (*qua* rational). Thus Kant writes,

> Women will avoid the wicked not because it is unright, but only because it is ugly. . . . Nothing of duty, nothing of compulsion, nothing of obligation! . . . They do something only because it pleases them. . . . I hardly believe that the fair sex is capable of principles.[14]

Rather, "Her philosophy is not to reason, but to sense."[15] Furthermore,

> All the other merits of a woman should unite solely to enhance the character of the beautiful which is the proper reference point; . . . all education and instruction must have [this] before its eyes. . . . Deep meditation and long-sustained reflection are noble but difficult, and do not well befit a person in whom unconstrained charms should show nothing else than a beautiful nature. A woman who has a head full of Greek, like Mme. Dacier, or carries on fundamental controversies about mechanics, might as well have a beard.[16]

A similar prejudice is revealed by Fichte who, when speaking of "our race" in *The Vocation of Man*, writes:

> I must be free; for that which constitutes our true worth is not the mere mechanical act, but the free determination of free will, for the sake of duty . . .[17]

but who, when speaking of woman in *The Science of Rights*, claims that

> [she] is subjected through her own necessary wish—a wish which is the condition of her morality—to be so subjected. . . .[18]

Furthermore,

> The woman who thus surrenders her personality, and yet retains her full dignity in so doing, necessarily gives up to her lover all that she has. For, if she retained the least of her own self, she would thereby confess that it had a higher value for her than her own person; and this undoubtedly would be a lowering of that person. . . . The least consequence is, that she should renounce to him all her property and all her rights. Henceforth . . . her life has become a part of the life of her lover. (This is aptly characterized by her assuming his name.)[19]

Or, compare Rousseau in *The Social Contract*:

> To renounce one's liberty is to renounce one's quality as a man, the rights and also the duties of humanity.[20]

with the suggestion on the education of women in the *Emile*:

> They must be trained to bear the yoke from the first, so that they may not feel it, to master their own caprices and to submit themselves to the will of others.[21]

For Schopenhauer also, in his essay "On Women" (though not in *The World as Will and Representation*), it is quite clear that women lack essential human properties. He writes that woman

> is in every respect backward, lacking in reason and reflection . . . a kind of middle step between the child and the man, who is the true human

being. . . . In the last resort, women exist solely for the propagation of the race.[22]

These quotations suggest that human nature or essence, whether it be construed as freedom or reason or in some other way, is a sex-linked characteristic, since it is found only or truly in men and not women; or at the very least, that this naure is actualized only by men.[23] (Fichte's position is ambiguous because the continuous wishing to be subjected which he requires of women would seem to necessitate that they possess the human property of freedom in order to wish not to possess it.)[24] In all these cases, however, the philosophers' prejudices about women seem clearly at odds with their systematic philosophy which doesn't discriminate between the sexes. Is it the case then, that all we have here is a plain expression of the cultural prejudices of the time, in even so rational a group of philosophers? That they, like most people, are often inconsistent in their beliefs; and that they therefore simply fail to meet the very criterion of universality which they propose? Such an explanation, though commonsensical and plausible, can be shown to be too simple. Instead, let me propose another interpretation of the discrepancy.

These quotations show two things: (a) that these philosophers' views regarding universal human nature are simply contradicted by their views of concrete individuality in the case of women and that therefore their philosophical universalism is no protection against the crassest prejudices and (b) that their statements regarding women are ideological, in the sense of both reflecting and supporting the oppression of women, and that this ideological position is masked by the abstract universality which is proclaimed in their principles. . . .

Either interpretation lends support to the critique of abstract universality: (a) The first possibility suggests that because of the abstractness of the universal principle, because it has no bridge to the concrete, the conceptions of concrete individuality of the philosophers in question remain accidental and uncriticized. Thus despite its claims to normative status, the abstract universal principle lacks critical force.

However, it would appear that this sort of discrepancy between the abstract universal principle and concrete prejudices can be overcome within Essentialism, by simply insisting on greater consistency in the interpretation of the universal principle (supposing that the practitioners were cleansed of their male-dominating tendencies) and by requiring bridge laws to the concrete. While greater attention to consistency is desirable, in that it may force the Essentialist to reject those of his statements which contradict his principles, still he has no way of bringing to bear any critical reflections on the genesis or sources of his prejudice. . . .

(b) The second possibility suggests that the discrepancy between universal and female nature is an ideological distortion. . . . The form of such ideological distortion is to take (or mistake), unreflectively and therefore
uncritically, the part for the whole, the particular for the universal and
essential, or the present for the eternal. There are two sorts of distortion
possible here on ideological grounds: first, the deliberate use of ideological
distortion as an instrument for domination; second—and more significant
because more pervasive—the unconscious ideological distortions which come
from the uncritical acceptance of whatever partial view is expedient or current. Accordingly, in the instances examined here, we may distinguish ideological distortions in a strong and a weak sense. The strong sense takes
them to be instrumentalities in the subordination of women. This interpretation is suggested, e.g., in Kant's and Rousseau's recommendations for educating women or in Fichte's fervent argument that for a woman to do less
than submit and lose herself entirely (including all her property and rights)
would undoubtedly be a lowering of her person.

On the other hand, it might be more appropriate to interpret the remarks as ideological in the weaker sense—in the sense of passively reflecting the subordination of women in a male-dominated society. . . .

On this hypothesis, we might interpret Kant's view—that rationality is
the dominant and essential human characteristic and male, while beauty or
aesthetic sensibility is a subordinate characteristic and female—in the following way: At a given historical stage—namely, that of the development
of civil society and the state—the trait of rationality (and a similar argument could be made for the traits of contracting, and of freedom, and of
productive labor) became the dominant one required for social life and for
political rule and therefore it was raised to the level of *the* essential human
characteristic. On this view, by an inversion of Plato's approach, the state
is not "man writ large," but rather what is essentially human or "man" is
the state writ small. As the priorities of changing forms of society themselves change, what are taken to be "essentially human characteristics" change
with them. In the case at hand, we may hypothesize that since in historical
fact, (1) rationality played the dominant role in social life and political
rule in the transition to civil society and the political state, and (2) since
males were dominant in that social and political life of that society, therefore rationality became identified not only as the essential human trait, but
by association as a male trait. Thus it is not because male nature is rational
that men become rulers, but it is because men rule that rationality is assigned as a male trait.

What's lacking, therefore, in this alleged essential characterization of human
nature are those traits which were historically and contingently subordinate
in civil society and in the political state, and which were associated with

women, e.g., aesthetic sensitivity, intuition, caring, etc.[25] which were historically characterized by Kant for example, as nonrational (if not irrational), or as part of the life of sentiment or of the affections, by contrast to the life of reason or intellect. Therefore, though the abstract universalist does not deny that these allegedly subordinate and female traits are human, he gives them a subordinate status and doesn't see them as essential. Here, we may further hypothesize that the historically contingent fact that women played a subordinate role in social and political life therefore led to the identification of such traits as aesthetic sensitivity and intuition as feminine characteristics. Thus it is not (1) because women are intuitive and aesthetically sensitive and (2) because these traits are of secondary importance to society, that women are assigned a subordinate role, but rather (1) because women are subordinate and (2) because these traits are of secondary importance, that these traits are assigned to women as "feminine" characteristics. On this hypothesis it can be seen that the assignment of "male" and "female" characteristics as respectively dominant or subordinate, or essential and accidental, is a product of contingent priorities at a given historical stage of social and political development. . . .

However, what about cases where a consistent universalism does not assign the essential human traits to males, but simply characterizes them as human? Aren't such cases free of sex bias? An examination of some instances of this sort suggests that even here sex bias operates, insofar as the characterization of universal human nature or essence is modeled after activities performed by men in male-dominated societies. One such case is the theory of the genesis of the state in a social contract; this theory universalizes an activity—contracting—which was an activity of men only, from which women were excluded. Similarly, the universality of the Greek notion that education is for citizenship is belied by the fact that women could not be citizens, and their "education," such as it was, was not for citizenship. Furthermore, these theories made the male-dominated activity of ruling or participating in government the central consideration in political activity. Since women were excluded from participation in governance, and since such participation was taken to be the essence or nature of the human as *zoön politikon*, women were taken to be not fully human.[26]

More generally, we find that the nature and functioning of the state tends to be characterized in terms of various activities in which males for historical reasons have tended to predominate and from which women have been excluded—specifically the activities of rule, contract, the making of laws and production. For example, in Hegel's *Philosophy of Right*, the sphere of the family and of marriage is specifically excluded from the domain of right, i.e., from the public sphere of civil society and the state.[27] Further, for much of political economy, production in the narrow sense, understood in terms of the activity of men, has been taken as the model of universal human economic activity. Indeed, political economic theories often omit entirely the broader sense of production in which domestic labor might be considered productive. . . .

In the historical cases of ideological distortion which we have examined, we find the projection of a specific and historically contingent social form—male domination and the subordination of women—as a universal and unchanging one;[28] and as a result, the projection of those characteristics which have priority in such a social form as the essential and dominant features of human nature itself. The criterion of abstract universality is open to such ideological distortion precisely because it assigns historical and social difference to the realm of the accidental. As a consequence, it cannot see the historical contingency of its own time and its own society, and therefore it may uncritically adopt the dominant social relations as eternal and unchanging ones. . . .

UNIVERSALITY WITH A DIFFERENCE . . .

This failure which follows from a strictly construed Essentialism puts in question the very concept of universality at work here.[29] What is at issue, then, is this concept of universality itself. We have two choices: (1) to give up the criterion of universality altogether, and either opt for a strict nominalism, which takes only particular and concrete individuals to exist, and which sees "universals" only as names or marks to represent similarities or family resemblances among such individuals, or opt for existentialism, which in a similar way takes only unique individuals to exist, and which sees essences, universals, or natures as creations of these existing individuals. Or alternatively, (2) we can reinterpret or radically revise the concept of universality itself so that it includes differences in a systematic way. I will propose the latter course, and argue that an alternative criterion—that of concrete universality—is both philosophically more adequate and also permits a critical and philosophical approach to such questions as the woman question. . . .

What is the alternative notion of concrete universality? The concept of universality is retained but it is radically transformed. Whereas the criterion of abstract universality is concerned only with what is essentially the same and excludes accidental differences, the criterion of concrete universality is concerned also with human and social differences, and includes them not simply as accidents, but as aspects which constitute the universal or the essence itself. What is universal is differently conceived on each view: On the Essentialist view, the universal is what remains after all particular and nonnecessary differences have been removed. On the alternative view, it is the totality of all the features—both those which are shared in common, and those which are different or individuating—which constitute the universality itself. The universal is therefore identical with this totality, where this totality is constituted by the unity of all the differences.[30] The totality (or universality) is therefore an internally differentiated unity in which differences are preserved. A feature of traditional Essentialism is that the universal is abstracted or conceived apart from the individuals who exemplify it and apart from their differences, and is therefore taken in itself. On the concrete view, the universal cannot be abstracted or conceived apart from these differences, but exists only in and through them.

The most crucial difference between the two views, however, is that in the first, the differences themselves have no systematic relationship to each other or to the universal. They are literally "accidents." But it is these so-called accidents which are the characteristic feature of historical change and of actual social life. Thus concrete universality reinterprets accidental differences to be systematically related to each other; further, it takes such differences to be constitutive of the universal itself. Correlatively, the Essentialist view construes the universal as a fixed and unchanging essence, since on its definition, what is essential is what remains the same or invariant against a background of accidental changes. On the alternative view, the universal is seen not as a fixed essence, but rather as one which develops in time, and which is concretely located in history and in society. On this second view, then, universals or essences themselves emerge and change.

Concrete universality thus implies an alternative conception of the nature of history itself. As against the view that historical events are exemplifications of fixed, a priori essences, this view regards essences, as well as history itself, as constituted or created by the actions of individuals. Concrete universality conceives the present as the moment in which individuals create history through their interaction with each other and with the objective world. It sees the past as the set of interactions which provides the circumstances for present action. This action transforms these circumstances in accordance with future possibilities envisioned by these agents. This transformative activity is thus the process of history itself, which is marked by genuine novelty. This activity also constitutes essences. That is, common features of social life are generated and maintained through the actions of individuals.

On this second conception, society is understood not as a changeless set of relations among individuals who are all essentially the same at all times, but rather as a changing set of relations among individuals who are very different, in part because of these relations themselves. Whereas Essentialist political theory construes society on the model of a contract among equals, concrete universality conceives of society as a totality constituted by social differences, where these differences are acknowledged to be the essential characteristic of that society. In a class society, for example, the relation-ship between exploiters and exploited (a) is a social difference which con-stitutes the essence of that social form, (b) is a difference which is not present throughout time, but which developed historically, and (c) is a re-lationship which characterizes the individuals in terms of this difference and therefore in terms of their interactions with each other. Thus the uni-versal form or essence of a class society involves an internal differentiation (between exploiter and exploited) and a systematic interrelation between the two. Likewise, the "essence" of the family is constituted not simply by the same relation that all members of a family bear to each other, but also by the internal differences in role, function, power.

Similarly, if an Essentialist were to admit sex difference at all, he would construe male and female as fixed essences or natures; each would be de-fined independently of the other and apart from any particular historical or social context. By contrast, on the criterion of concrete universality, this difference itself would be seen as one which has emerged historically and which is constituted by the concrete forms of social interaction between men and women. Thus sexual polarity would be understood to be funda-mentally a function of historical, social, and cultural relations between men and women—including such relations as domination and subordination, the division of labor, the various historical forms of love and dependence, and social forms of relation like the family, slavery, and concubinage. Further-more, the relations between men and women would be seen as intersecting with other general relations like that of exploiter and exploited.

Thus the identity of an individual (like that of a social class or of society as a whole) cannot be established abstractly, but rather by taking into ac-count how he or she is related to others. Being a woman, therefore, is not an abstract property of some individuals, but rather a property whose defi-nition depends on the relations among women themselves and between women and men in concrete social life. Only in the ensemble or totality of these relations does either group have its "essential" character. These relations or interrelations are therefore not external relations between individuals who are already independently defined by some criterion. That is, it is not the case that men and women, as fully defined individuals with essential male and female properties, then enter into relations with each other in which these properties remain unchanged. Rather, the very properties themselves are constituted in the course of such relations. Men become men, and women became women, in the course of these interrelations. In this sense, the re-lations are "internal," or constitutive of the very properties themselves.

The criterion of concrete universality permits a different interpretation of universal norms, on the grounds of its alternative concept of universal-ity. As we have seen, the Essentialist conception of abstract universal norms was based on the exclusion of accidental differences among human beings as irrelevant for the determination of rights. These universal rights are held to pertain to human beings *qua* human, i.e., essentially. By contrast, since the concrete universal is conceived to be embodied in society and history, the concrete differences which are excluded by the criterion of abstract universality are included here. Accordingly, a concrete universal norm is formulated not simply in terms of what is the same, but in terms of relevant differences; these differences specify the conditions for applying the norm.

Indeed, if we examine the ordinary cases in which universal norms are stated, we find that the formulation of the norm often includes an explicit specification of differences. Thus in practice, the universal norm of equal justice or equal rights almost never stands alone; rather, it is followed by an exclusionary phrase such as "regardless of race, sex, creed, or country of origin," or "regardless of previous condition of servitude." Why should such additions be made if the "all" in "equal justice for all" is sufficient to assure universal application without regard to differences?

The problem is that "all" has not always meant "all" in a strictly universal sense; rather, it has been interpreted in a less than universal way. For example, the Declaration of Independence states the universal principle that "all men are created equal." Yet the Constitution originally excluded women and slaves from the fundamental equal right of suffrage. In this case, the interpretation of "all" had to be enlarged by the Fourteenth and Nineteenth Amendments. Similarly, when the Napoleonic Code specified for the first time that Jews were to have equal rights as citizens, it made clear that the prior conception of the universal rights of man and of the citizen in practice had not included Jews. This suggests that the concept "all" in, e.g., "equal justice for all" has (in its application) been a historically changing concept, and not always universal in scope. Therefore, corrections are needed in order to make the universal norm more truly universal. However, such a critical correction cannot be made simply by a repetition of the abstract norm, but rather requires a concrete specification to the effect that what has been excluded should be included.

But let us grant that such social or historical limitations can be overcome and that the abstract norm of equal justice is fully universal in scope. Would it then be adequate? Such an abstract norm will indeed be able to reveal when an injustice has been done, simply by showing that some human being has not been treated equally. We will then know *that* a violation of universality has occurred. But we will not know *why* or on what *grounds*. I would propose that it is important to know the sources of a case of injustice. Such knowledge is required if one is concerned not only with rectifying the specific case of injustice, but with eliminating the conditions which give rise to the injustice in the first place.

Thus an abstract norm of justice may permit one to deal with the effects of injustice, but not with its causes. In a case of discriminatory treatment, for example, the abstract norm can reveal that some universal human right has been violated, but it does not permit the recognition that this discrimination is on the basis of, e.g., sex or race. Since the abstract norm treats all such cases as extensionally equivalent, it cannot recognize the intensional distinctions. Thus motives or interests which lead to sex discrimination go unnoticed in the application of the norm and as a consequence, they cannot become the object of specific social critique and action.[31] By contrast, a criterion of concrete universality recognizes the specific differences which play a part in actual cases of injustice and discrimination. Such a criterion therefore enables one to focus on the causes of the injustice, and permits a criticism of the social reality in terms of the specific ways in which it falls short of the universal norms of justice and equality.

It is this capacity to be critical of present social reality which I have suggested is also required if philosophy is to be self-critical and self-correcting with regard to those prejudices and ideological distortions which flaw its very quest for universality. A criterion of concrete universality, by contrast to an abstract criterion, takes the social and historical differences of the philosopher's time and place as a clue to understanding and eliminating bias. It takes the task of philosophy to be the critical analysis of the present social reality. This concrete domain thus becomes the subject of philosophical activity proper—i.e., of criticism. But this criticism is no longer the criticism only of concepts, but also of the reality in which these concepts emerge.

It should be clear from the above that one of the central questions concerning present social reality is what I have characterized as the woman question. As I have shown in this section, it is just this sort of question which a criterion of concrete universality specifies as within the domain of philosophy. My argument has further shown that to construe the woman question as a philosophical question in this sense is to say that the conception of philosophy itself is changed. . . .

Notes

1. "The Woman Question" as it will be used in this paper denotes the range of issues which concerns women's social and economic oppression and exploitation, historically and in the present; their liberation; their roles in society, in the family; relations between the sexes; sexual equality; and the question of what constitutes women as a gender. I leave out biological characteristics as such for the reasons given in note 6 below. My use of the term "the Woman Question" differs from its historical usage within the Marxist tradition. In that tradition, the term has been used in both anthropological and social-political

discussion. It connotes a "special" question, generally subsumed under the "more universal" issue of class oppression and to be explained or elucidated in terms of it. Thus, women's liberation has typically been subsumed under the more general concern for the liberation of the working class from capitalist exploitation. "The Woman Question" therefore has the "special" status accorded to other class-subordinate questions such as "the Jewish Question," "the National Question," etc. Now although I agree that the liberation of women is closely tied to general human emancipation from exploitation, I do not hold that all forms of the oppression and exploitation of women are to be accounted for by class exploitation or what derives from it. Thus, in using the term "the Woman Question" to denote a broad range of issues, I propose to free the question from this narrow context, while retaining whatever useful connotations the term has as designating a social, historical, and economic question.

2. While it is true that most philosophers do not self-consciously go about justifying what they do on some appeal to an adequate universality of scope—they rather just do what they do, either within established norms or beyond them— the objection to treating the woman question as a philosophical question is widely met in discussion (although not explicitly in print). Even among those who do not openly raise such objections, there is often tacit consent to its inappropriateness, witnessed in part by the *fact* that the question has barely been discussed.

3. Whereas contemporary usage frequently takes "male" and "female" to refer to biological sex differences, and "man" and "woman" to refer to social and cultural sex differences, in this article I am interpreting "female" as "woman," and therefore will use the terms interchangeably. Thus, glossing the usage distinction follows from my argument, since as will be seen, I am interpreting sex difference as fundamentally social and not *fundamentally* biological in nature.

4. Alison Jagger's discussion is paradigmatic. See "On Sexual Equality," in *Ethics*, July 1974.

5. This position is implied in the writings of several radical feminists, e.g., Robin Morgan, "Introduction," *Sisterhood Is Powerful* (New York: Vintage, 1970), but it has rarely been proposed by feminist philosophers. A modified form of this position is presented by Christine Garside in "Women and Persons," in *Mother Was Not a Person*, ed. Margaret Andersen (Montreal: Content Publishing and Black Rose Books, 1972). Garside suggests that the sexual polarity is fundamental, although she regards it as the product not only of physiological factors, but also the "self-determining" identity which women have achieved through the history of their struggles and oppression. Thus Garside here appears to make sex difference a function not of nature (except in the sense of anatomical difference) but of history. However, her understanding of the difference remains abstract and ahistorical, because it is seen as determined not by the interrelations of the sexes, but rather by "self-determination," where this is understood in the existentialist sense of the creation of essence by activity. However, a question of consistency arises with respect to her work: How can sex polarity be "fundamental," if each person is uniquely self-determining? How does the self-determining, self-creating individual achieve anything but an individual nature or essence? In terms of the woman question, we might ask: Why should we suppose that an anatomically "female" person should determine herself as a woman, rather than as either a man or an androgyne? Why should she accept her heritage? The connection between Garside's claim that sex difference is fundamental, and her

claim that a woman, *qua* person, is basically self-determining, remains obscure.

6. In claiming that significant differences between men and women are thoroughly historical, social, and cultural, I am indeed denying that the difference is fundamentally or significantly biological. That there *are* biological differences between men and women is obviously true. The point is that there are infinitely many differences among individuals, any of which is logically an equal candidate for making group distinctions among humans. So for example, left- and right-handedness, hair color, the number of hairs on one's head, the religion of one's mother, and one's place of birth are all distinctions of this sort. But only some of them have been selected out for importance. Which ones have been selected is a function of the historical, social, and cultural role which has been assigned to the characteristic in question. Thus, in denying that the biological difference is an essential or fundamental difference, I am asserting that it becomes one only through its historical and cultural development, and therefore that the gender distinction between men and women is thoroughly a product of this development, and not a given fact of nature. This paper does not attempt to prove this point in a direct way, although it supports this claim indirectly. Further arguments are offered by Ruth Herschberger, *Adam's Rib* (New York: Harper and Row, 1970), and by Eva Figes, in *Patriarchal Attitudes* (New York: Fawcett Books, 1971). See also Gina Bari Kolata, "Kung Hunter-Gatherers, Feminism, Diet, and Birth Control," in *Science* 185 (Sept. 1974): 932 ff.

7. Cf. Plato, *Republic*, 1.352: ". . . a thing's function is the work that it alone can do or can do better than anything else." Here Plato, in distinguishing carving knives, chisels, and pruning knives, makes "proper function" the basis for what kind of a thing something is. Aristotle (*Nichomachean Ethics*, 1.7) similarly defines the distinctive human function to be an activity involving reason, since reason is what distinguishes humans from all other beings and therefore makes them the kind of things they are.

8. In describing a priori knowledge Kant says, "Necessity and strict universality are thus sure criteria of *a priori* knowledge and are inseparable from one another" (*Critique of Pure Reason*, B4). By "strict universality" he means not that universality derived inductively from experience, which he calls "only assumed or comparative universality," but that in which "no exception is allowed as possible." Where Kant is using the terms "necessity" and "universality" to refer to conditions which a judgment must meet if it is to be one which represents a priori knowledge, I am using these terms to denote the conditions a property must have if it is to be essential.

9. Cf. Descartes's discussion of the piece of wax in the *Meditations* ("Second Meditation"). Descartes is attempting to discover the essential property of the wax. He first lists all the "accidental" properties and then removes them, in imagination, by bringing the wax close to the fire. Taste, color, odor, shape vanish; size increases; the wax becomes liquid; it grows hot. Still, we have a clear and distinct idea that it is the "same" piece of wax through all these changes. Thus, according to Descartes, "by rejecting everything that does not belong to the wax, to see what remains, we are led to the essential properties." This reduction and exclusion of "accidental" properties is classically Essentialist.

10. Cf. Ernest Nagel, *The Structure of Science* (New York: Harcourt Brace and World, 1961), 56 ff.

11. Plato, *Parmenides*, 130 c–d.

12. Kant, *Fundamental Principles of the Metaphysic of Morals* (Indianapolis: Bobbs-Merill, 1949), 30.

13. Ibid., 45.
14. Kant, *Observations on the Feeling of the Beautiful and the Sublime*, tr. John Goldthwait (Berkeley: University of Calif., 1960), 81.
15. Ibid., 79.
16. Ibid., 76–78.
17. Fichte, *The Vocation of Man* (Indianapolis: Bobbs-Merrill, 1956), 117.
18. Fichte, *The Science of Rights* (Philadelphia: Lippincott, 1869), First Appendix, sec. 3 parts 3, 441; cf. also sec. 1, parts 2–7, 396–403.
19. Ibid., sec. 1 part 6, 401–2. Cited by E. Figes, op. cit., 124.
20. Rousseau, *The Social Contract*, book 1, ch. 4.
21. Rousseau, *Emile*, book 5. Cited by E. Figes, op.cit., 98–99.
22. Schopenhauer, "On Women," in *Selected Essays*, ed. E. B. Bax (London: George Bell, 1990), 338–46. But when talking of the hereditary nature of qualities, Schopenhauer presents a contradictory account, arguing that the faculty of reason and intelligence, and thus the capacity for reflection and deliberation are inherited from the mother, whereas the moral nature, character, and heart and will are inherited from the father (*The World as Will and Representation* [New York, Dover, 1958] 2: 517–20). See also E. Figes's discussion, op. cit., 121–23.
23. In treating these authors together, I do not mean to compare their systematic philosophies, nor to suggest that they are Essentialists in the rigorous sense discussed earlier in this paper.
24. It should be noted that Fichte himself at a few points seems to be aware of this contradiction. See *Science of Rights*. First Appendix, sec. 1 part 4, 400 and sec. 2, part 7, 418. Cf. related point in E. Figes, op. cit., 125.
25. Indeed, sensitivity to human differences, such as I argue for in this paper, has been characteristic especially of women. By contrast, what has had priority in the state and civil society—external contracting between self-interested individuals—has been characteristic especially of men.
26. Cf. Christine Garside's discussion of Aristotle's concept of woman in "Can a Woman Be Good in the Same Way as a Man?" in *Dialogue* 10 no. 3 (1971): 534–44.
27. Hegel, *Philosophy of Right*, tr. T. M. Knox (Oxford University Press, 1969), 106–22.
28. Although one would hardly include Engels in this group, there are instances, as in the example in question, where even this critic of male domination shows the limitations and influences of this ideology.
29. I do not mean to imply that these difficulties inherent in the criterion of abstract universality have gone unnoticed by philosophers, including Essentialists themselves. Essentialism has historically been aware of it as the problem of instantiation or of the principle of individuation. As I mentioned in the text, in the *Parmenides*, Plato has Parmenides question Socrates as to whether there are universal forms for such "concrete" and "particular" existences as hair, mud, and dirt.

   Leibniz introduces a critique of abstract universality in the following passage: "Never are two eggs, two leaves, or two blades of grass in a garden to be found exactly similar to each other. So perfect similarity occurs only in incomplete and abstract concepts, where matters are conceived, not in their totality but according to a certain single viewpoint, as when we consider only figures and neglect the figured matter. So geometry is right in studying similar triangles, even though two perfectly similar material triangles are never found." ("First Truths," in *Philosophical Papers and Letters*, ed. Leroy E. Loemker [Chicago: University of Chicago Press, 1956.])

Hegel proposes a radically different concept of essence and of universality as a dialectical critique of the insufficiencies of abstract universality, in the *Logic*. Finally, Marx reinterprets the problem of abstract universality as one which shows the limits of traditional philosophy, and marks its incapacity to go beyond a contemplative stance and to become critical.

30. The universal is not something apart from the differences exhibited by members of a given class; rather, it is this class with its differences included. This unity of what is the same and what is different constitutes the concrete universal. As an abstract universal, the class of humans, for example, is constituted by those individuals who share an essential property (or properties), where these individuals are identified only by virtue of this property. They are not further individuated (except by numerical difference); therefore, they are abstract individuals, one identical to the other in the only relevant respect. The universal is this abstractable essential property which is instantiated in each member of the class equally. All other properties which such individuals have are irrelevant. They are regarded as accidental properties and they determine the differences among such individuals. On such a criterion of abstract universality, therefore, such differences are philosophically dispensible. On the other hand, as a *concrete* universal, the class of human is identical with all the individuals in the class, including both the properties which they share in common and all those which individuate or differentiate each one from each other one. These individuals are therefore fully individuated concrete individuals. Their essence is not only the same abstract property which they share, but also the concrete property of being that particular class of individuals, with all the individual differences included. The distinction between essence and accident is reconstrued here: The essence is nothing apart from the totality of differences which constitute the individuals in the class. The unity of the class is therefore a unity of differences.

31. There is a further problem with abstract justice or abstract rights: namely, that its failure to take differences into account serves to mask concrete inequalities. For example, equal employment opportunities mean that all qualified applicants for a position will have an equal opportunity to apply and be considered for that position. But in the case of a profession or trade from which a particular group like women or blacks have been excluded in the past, this abstract right simply serves to preserve an existing inequality; for in fact, women and blacks will not have had the equal opportunity to qualify as applicants. In such cases, the virtue of an abstract universal norm of equality is that it disregards irrelevant differences and therefore assures in principle that they will not be taken into account. But at the same time, because it is blind to differences, it cannot recognize those existing inequalities which make its application less than equal.

SELECTION 23
FROM
The Man of Reason

GENEVIEVE LLOYD

WHAT EXACTLY DOES THE "maleness" of Reason amount to? It is clear that what we have in the history of philosophical thought is no mere succession of surface misogynist attitudes, which can now be shed, while leaving intact the deeper structures of our ideals of Reason. There is more at stake than the fact that past philosophers believed there to be flaws in female character. Many of them did indeed believe that women are less rational than men; and they have formulated their ideals of rationality with male paradigms in mind. But the maleness of Reasons goes deeper than this. Our ideas and ideals of maleness and femaleness have been formed within structures of dominance—of superiority and inferiority, "norms" and "difference," "positive" and "negative," the "essential" and the "complementary." And the male-female distinction itself has operated not as a straightforwardly descriptive principle of classification, but as an expression of values. We have seen that the equation of maleness with superiority goes back at least as far as the Pythagoreans. What is valued—whether it be odd as against even numbers, "aggressive" as against "nurturing" skills and capacities, or Reason as against emotion—has been readily identified with maleness. Within the context of this association of maleness with preferred traits, it is not just incidental to the feminine that female traits have been construed as inferior—or, more subtly, as "complementary"—to male norms of human excellence. Rationality has been conceived as transcendence of the feminine; and the "feminine" itself has been partly constituted by its occurrence within this structure.

It is a natural response to the discovery of unfair discrimination to affirm the positive value of what has been downgraded. But with the kind of bias we are confronting here the situation is complicated by the fact that femininity, as we have it, has been partly formed by relation to, and differentiation from, a male norm. We may, for example, want to insist against past

225

philosophers that the sexes are equal in possession of Reason; and that women must now be admitted to full participation in its cultural manifestations. But, as we have seen in the case of de Beauvoir's feminist appropriation of the ideal of transcendence, this approach is fraught with difficulty. Women cannot easily be accommodated into a cultural ideal which has defined itself in opposition to the feminine. To affirm women's equal possession of rational traits, and their right of access to the public spaces within which they are cultivated and manifested, is politically important. But it does not get to the heart of the conceptual complexities of gender difference. And in repudiating one kind of exclusion, de Beauvoir's mode of response can help reinforce another. For it seems implicitly to accept the downgrading of the excluded character traits traditionally associated with femininity, and to endorse the assumption that the only human excellences and virtues which deserve to be taken seriously are those exemplified in the range of activities and concerns that have been associated with maleness.

However, alternative responses are no less beset by conceptual complexities. For example, it may seem easy to affirm the value and strengths of distinctively "feminine" traits without subscribing to any covertly assumed "norm"—to have, as it were, a genuine version of Rousseau's idea that the female mind is equal, but different. But extricating concepts of femininity from the intellectual structures within which our understanding of sexual difference has been formed is more difficult than it seems. The idea that women have their own distinctive kind of intellectual or moral character has itself been partly formed within the philosophical tradition to which it may now appear to be a reaction. Unless the structural features of our concepts of gender are understood, any emphasis on a supposedly distinctive style of thought or morality is liable to be caught up in a deeper, older structure of male norms and female complementation. The affirmation of the value and importance of "the feminine" cannot of itself be expected to shake the underlying normative structures, for, ironically, it will occur in a space already prepared for it by the intellectual tradition it seeks to reject.

Thus it is an understandable reaction to the polarizations of Kantian ethics to want to stress the moral value of "feminine" concerns with the personal and particular, as against the universal and impartial; or the warmth of feeling as against the chillingly abstract character of Reason. But it is important to be aware that the "exclusion" of the feminine has not been a straightforward repudiation. Subtle accommodations have been incorporated into the social organization of sexual division—based on, or rationalized by, philosophical thought—which allow "feminine" traits and activities to be both preserved and downgraded. There has been no lack of male affirmation of the importance and attractiveness of "feminine" traits—in women— or of gallant acknowledgment of the impoverishment of male Reason. Making good the lacks in male consciousness, providing it with a necessary complementation by the "feminine," is a large part of what the suppression, and the correlative constitution, of "womankind" has been all about. An affirmation of the strengths of female "difference" which is unaware of this may be doomed to repeat some of the sadder subplots in the history of Western thought.

The content of femininity, as we have it, no less than its subordinate status, has been formed within an intellectual tradition. What has happened has been not a simple exclusion of women, but a constitution of femininity through that exclusion. It is remarkable that Hegel, the notorious exponent of the "nether world" of femininity, should have had such insight into the conceptual complexities of sexual difference. Hegel's diagnosis of "womankind," as we have seen, occurs in a wider framework, which endorses the relegation of women to the private domain. But his understanding of the complexity, and the pathos, of gender difference in some ways transcends that. He saw that life in the nether world has conditioned the modes of female consciousness; that the distinctively "feminine" is not a brute fact, but a structure largely constituted through suppression. To agree with this is not to deny that the "feminine" has its own strengths and virtues. In the current climate of critical reflection on ideals of Reason, some of the strengths of female "difference" can be seen as deriving from their very exclusion from "male" thought-style. To have been largely excluded from the dominant, and supposedly more "advanced," forms of abstract thought or moral consciousness can be seen as a source of strength when their defects and impoverishment become apparent. But such strengths must be seen in relation to structural features of gender difference. They are strengths that derive from exclusion; and the merits of such "minority consciousness" depend on avoiding asserting it as a rival norm.[1]

Attempting to identify or affirm anything distinctively "feminine" has its hazards in a context of actual inequality. If the full range of human activities—both the nurturing tasks traditionally associated with the private domain and the activities which have hitherto occupied public space—were freely available to all, the exploration of sexual difference would be less fraught with the dangers of perpetuating norms and stereotypes which have mutilated men and women alike. But the task of exposing and criticizing the maleness of ideals of Reason need not wait upon the realization of such hopes; it may indeed be an important contribution to their realization.

The denigration of the "feminine" is to feminists, understandably, the most salient aspect of the maleness of the philosophical tradition. But the issue is important for men, too. The lives of women incorporate the impoverishing restraints of Reason's transcended "nether world." But maleness, as we have inherited it, enacts, no less, the impoverishment and vulnerability of "public" Reason. Understanding the contribution of past thought to "male" and "female" consciousnesses, as we now have them, can help make available a diversity of intellectual styles and characters to men and women alike. It need not involve a denial of all difference. Contemporary consciousness, male or female, reflects past philosophical ideals as well as past differences in the social organization of the lives of men and women. Such differences do not have to be taken as norms; and understanding them can be a source of richness and diversity in a human life whose full range of possibilities and experience is freely accessible to both men and women.

Can anything be salvaged of the ideal of a Reason which knows no sex? Much of past exultation in that ideal can be seen as a self-deceiving failure to acknowledge the differences between male and female minds, produced and played out in a social context of real inequalities. But it can also be seen as embodying a hope for the future. A similar ambiguity characterizes Hegel's own famous expression of faith in Reason, summed up in his slogan that the real is the rational and the rational the real. This has, not surprisingly, been seen by many as a dubious rationalization of the status quo. But is can also be taken as the expression of an ideal—as an affirmation of faith that the irrational will not prevail. Such a faith may well appear naive; but that does not mean it is bad faith. The confident affirmation that Reason "knows no sex" may likewise be taking for reality something which, if valid at all, is so only as an ideal. Ideal equalities, here as elsewhere, can conceal actual inequalities. Notwithstanding many philosophers' hopes and aspirations to the contrary, our ideals of Reason are in fact male; and if there is a Reason genuinely common to all, it is something to be achieved in the future, not celebrated in the present. Past ideals of Reason, far from transcending sexual difference, have helped to constitute it. That ideas of maleness have developed under the guise of supposedly neutral ideals of Reason has been to the disadvantage of women and men alike.

Philosophers have defined their activity in terms of the pursuit of Reason, free of the conditioning effects of historical circumstance and social structures. But despite its professed transcendence of such contingencies, Philosophy has been deeply affected by, as well as deeply affecting, the social organization of sexual difference. The full dimensions of the maleness of Philosophy's past are only now becoming visible. Despite its aspirations to timeless truth, the History of Philosophy reflects the characteristic preoccupations and self-perceptions of the kinds of people who have at any time had access to the activity. Philosophers have at different periods been churchmen, men of letters, university professors. But there is one thing they have had in common throughout the history of the activity: They have been predominantly male; and the absence of women from the philosophical tradition has meant that the conceptualization of Reason has been done exclusively by men. It is not surprising that the results should reflect their sense of Philosophy as a male activity. There have of course been female philosophers throughout the Western tradition. But, like Philo's or Augustine's women of Reason, they have been philosophers despite, rather than because of, their femaleness; there has been no input of femaleness into the formation of ideals of Reason.

As women begin to develop a presence in Philosophy, it is only to be expected that the maleness of Philosophy's past, and with it the maleness of ideals of Reason, should begin to come into focus; and that this should be accompanied by a sense of antagonism between feminism and Philosophy. We have seen that Philosophy has powerfully contributed to the exclusion of the feminine from cultural ideals, in ways that cannot be dismissed as minor aberrations of the philosophical imagination. But it is important that the tensions between feminism and Philosophy should not be misconstrued. The exclusion of the feminine has not resulted from a conspiracy by male philosophers. We have seen that in some cases it happened despite the conscious intent of the authors. Where it does appear explicitly in the texts, it is usually incidental to their main purposes; and often it emerges only in the conjunction of the text with surrounding social structures—a configuration which often is visible only in retrospect.

Feminist unease about ideals of Reason is sometimes expressed as a repudiation of allegedly male principles of rational thought. Such formulations of the point make it all too easy for professional philosophers to dismiss as confused all talk of the maleness of Reason. As I pointed out at the beginning, contemporary philosophical preoccupation with the requirements of rational belief, the objectivity of truth and the procedures of rational argument can make it difficult for them to see the import of criticisms of broader cultural ideals associated with Reason. The claim that Reason is male need not at all involve sexual relativism about truth, or any suggestion that principles of logical thought valid for men do not hold also for female reasoners.

Philosophers can take seriously feminist dissatisfaction with the maleness of Reason without repudiating either Reason or Philosophy. Such criticisms of ideals of Reason can in fact be seen as continuous with a very old strand in the Western philosophical tradition; it has been centrally concerned with bringing to reflective awareness the deeper structures of inherited ideals of Reason. Philosophy has defined ideals of Reason through exclusions of the feminine. But it also contains within it the resources for critical reflection on those ideals and on its own aspirations. Fortunately, Philosophy is not necessarily what it has in the past proudly claimed to be—a timeless rational representation of the real, free of the conditioning effects of history.

To study the History of Philosophy can be of itself to engage in a form of cultural critique. Few today share Hegel's vision of the History of Philosophy as the steady path of Reason's progress through human history. But it does reveal a succession of ways of construing Reason which have, for better or worse, had a formative influence on cultural ideals, and which still surface in contemporary consciousness. I have tried to bring out how these views of Reason have been connected with the male-female distinction. In doing so, I have of course often highlighted points which were not salient in the philosophers' own perceptions of what they were about. Bringing the male-female distinction to the center of consideration of texts in this way may seem to misrepresent the History of Philosophy. But philosophers, when they tell the story of Philosophy's past, have always done so from the perspective of their own preoccupations, shared with their nonphilosopher contemporaries—pressing questions which were not central to the philosophers they were explicating.

To highlight the male-female distinction in relation to philosophical texts is not to distort the History of Philosophy. It does, however, involve taking seriously the temporal distance that separates us from past thinkers. Taking temporal distance seriously demands also of course that we keep firmly in view what the thinkers themselves saw as central to their projects. This exercise involves a constant tension between the need to confront past ideals with perspectives drawn from the present and, on the other hand, an equally strong demand to present fairly what the authors took themselves to be doing. A constructive resolution of the tensions between contemporary feminism and past Philosophy requires that we do justice to both demands.

Note

1. The phrase "minority consciousness" is from G. Deleuze, "Philosophie et minorité," *Critique* 369 (1978): 154–55.

SELECTION 24
FROM
Postmodernism and Gender Relations in Feminist Theory

JANE FLAX

> As the thought of the world, [philosophy] appears only when actuality is already there cut and dried after its process of formation has been completed.... When philosophy paints its grey in grey, then has a shape of life grown old. By philosophy's grey in grey it cannot be rejuvenated but only understood. The owl of Minerva spreads its wings only with the falling of the dusk.
> —G. W. F. Hegel, preface to *Philosophy of Right*

IT SEEMS INCREASINGLY PROBABLE that Western culture is in the middle of a fundamental transformation. A "shape of life" is growing old. In retrospect, this transformation may be as radical (but as gradual) as the shift from a medieval to a modern society. Accordingly, this moment in the history of the West is pervaded by profound yet little-comprehended change, uncertainty, and ambivalence. This transitional state makes certain forms of thought possible and necessary, and it excludes others. It generates problems that some philosophies seem to acknowledge and confront better than others.

I think there are currently three kinds of thinking that best present (and represent) our own time apprehended in thought: psychoanalysis, feminist theory, and postmodern philosophy. These ways of thinking reflect and are partially constituted by Enlightenment beliefs still prevalent in Western (especially American) culture. At the same time, they offer ideas and insights that are only possible because of the breakdown of Enlightenment beliefs under the cumulative pressure of historical events such as the invention of the atomic bomb, the Holocaust, and the war in Vietnam.[1]

Each of these ways of thinking takes as its object of investigation at least one facet of what has become most problematic in our transitional state: how to understand and (re)constitute the self, gender, knowledge, social relations, and culture without resorting to linear, teleological, hierarchical, holistic, or binary ways of thinking and being. My focus here will be mainly on one of these modes of thinking: feminist theory. I will consider what it could be, and I will reflect upon the goals, logics, and problematics of feminist theorizing as it has been practiced in the past fifteen years in the West. I will also place such theorizing within the social and philosophical contexts of which it is both a part and a critique. . . .

METATHEORY

Feminist theory seems to me to belong within two, more inclusive, categories with which it has special affinity: the analysis of social relations and postmodern philosophy.[2] Gender relations enter into and are constituent elements in every aspect of human experience. In turn, the experience of gender relations for any person and the structure of gender as a social category are shaped by the interactions of gender relations and other social relations such as class and race. Gender relations thus have no fixed essence; they vary both within and over time.

As a type of postmodern philosophy, feminist theory reveals and contributes to the growing uncertainty within Western intellectual circles about the appropriate grounding and methods for explaining and interpreting human experience. Contemporary feminists join other postmodern philosophers in raising important metatheoretical questions about the possible nature and status of theorizing itself. Given the increasingly fluid and confused status of Western self-understanding, it is not even clear what would constitute the basis for satisfactory answers to commonly agreed-upon questions within feminist (or other forms of social) theory.

Postmodern discourses are all deconstructive in that they seek to distance us from and make us skeptical about beliefs concerning truth, knowledge, power, the self, and language that are often taken for granted within and serve as legitimation for contemporary Western culture. . . .

Feminist theorists enter into and echo postmodernist discourses as we have begun to deconstruct notions of reason, knowledge, or the self and to reveal the effects of the gender arrangements that lay beneath their neutral and universalizing facades.[3] Some feminist theorists, for example, have begun to sense that the motto of the Enlightenment, "*sapere aude*—'have courage to use your own reason,'"[4] rests in part upon a deeply gender-rooted sense of self and self-deception. The notion that reason is divorced from "merely contingent" existence still predominates in contemporary Western thought and now appears to mask the embeddedness and dependence of the self upon social relations, as well as the partiality and historical specificity of this self's existence. What Kant's self calls its "own" reason, and the methods by which reason's contents become present or self-evident, are no freer from empirical contingency that is the so-called phenomenal self.[5]

In fact, feminists, like other postmodernists, have begun to suspect that all such transcendental claims reflect and reify the experience of a few persons—mostly white, Western males. These transhistoric claims seem plausible to us in part because they reflect important aspects of the experience of those who dominate our social world.

A FEMINIST PROBLEMATIC

This excursus into metatheory has now returned us to the opening of my paper—that the fundamental purpose of feminist theory is to analyze how we think, or do not think, or avoid thinking about gender. Obviously, then, to understand the goals of feminist theory we must consider its central subject—gender.

Here, however, we immediately plunge into a complicated and controversial morass. For among feminist theorists there is by no means consensus on such (apparently) elementary questions as: What is gender? How is it related to anatomical sexual differences? How are gender relations constituted and sustained (in one person's lifetime and, more generally, as a social experience over time)? How do gender relations relate to other sorts of social relations such as class or race? Do gender relations have a history (or many)? What causes gender relations to change over time? What are the relationships between gender relations, sexuality, and a sense of individual identity? What are the relationships between heterosexuality, homosexuality, and gender relations? Are there only two genders? What are the relationships between forms of male dominance and gender relations? Could/ would gender relations wither away in egalitarian societies? Is there anything distinctively male or female in modes of thought and social relations? If there is, are these distinctions innate or socially constituted? Are gendered distinctions socially useful or necessary? If so, what are the consequences for the feminist goal of attaining gender justice?[6]

Confronted with such a bewildering set of questions, it is easy to overlook the fact that a fundamental transformation in social theory has occurred. The single most important advance in feminist theory is that the existence of gender relations has been problematized. Gender can no longer be treated as a simple, natural fact. The assumption that gender relations are natural arose from two coinciding circumstances: the unexamined identification and confusion of (anatomical) sexual differences with gender relations, and the absence of active feminist movements. . . .

Thinking in Relations

"Gender relations" is a category meant to capture a complex set of social processes. Gender, both as an analytic category and a social process, is relational. That is, gender relations are complex and unstable processes (or temporary totalities in the language of dialectics) constituted by and through interrelated parts. These parts are interdependent, that is, each part can have no meaning or existence without the others.

Gender relations are differentiated and (so far) asymmetric divisions and attributions of human traits and capacities. Through gender relations two types of persons are created: man and woman. Man and woman are posited as exclusionary categories. One can be only one gender, never the other or both. The actual content of being a man or woman and the rigidity of the categories themselves are highly variable across cultures and time. Nevertheless, gender relations so far as we have been able to understand them have been (more or less) relations of domination. That is, gender relations have been (more) defined and (imperfectly) controlled by one of their interrelated aspects—the man.

These relations of domination and the existence of gender relations themselves have been concealed in a variety of ways, including defining women as a "question" or the "sex" or the "other"[7] and men as the universal (or at least without gender). In a wide variety of cultures and discourses, men tend to be seen as free from or as not determined by gender relations. Thus, for example, academics do not explicitly study the psychology of men or men's history. Male academics do not worry about how being men may distort their intellectual work, while women who study gender relations are considered suspect (of triviality, if not bias). Only recently have scholars begun to consider the possibility that there may be at least three histories in every culture—his, hers, and ours. *His* and *ours* are generally assumed to be equivalents, although in contemporary work there might be some recognition of the existence of that deviant—woman (e.g., women's history).[8] However, it is still rare for scholars to search for the pervasive effects of gender relations on all aspects of a culture in the way that they feel obligated to investigate the impact of relations of power or the organization of production.

To the extent that feminist discourse defines its problematic as "woman," it, too, ironically privileges the man as unproblematic or exempted from determination by gender relations. From the perspective of social relations, men and women are both prisoners of gender, although in highly differentiated but interrelated ways. That men appear to be and (in many cases) are the wardens, or at least the trustees within a social whole, should not blind us to the extent to which they, too, are governed by the rules of gender. (This is not to deny that it matters a great deal—to individual men, to the women and children sometimes connected to them and to those concerned about justice—where men as well as women are distributed within social hierarchies.)[9]

THEORIZING AND DECONSTRUCTION

The study of gender relations entails at least two levels of analysis: of gender as a thought construct or category that helps us to make sense out of particular social worlds and histories, and of gender as a social relation that enters into and partially constitutes all other social relations and activities. As a practical social relation, gender can be understood only by close examination of the meanings of "male" and "female" and the consequences being assigned to one or the other gender within concrete social practices.

Obviously, such meanings and practices will vary by culture, age, class, race, and time. We cannot presume a priori that in any particular culture there will be a single determinant or cause of gender relations, much less that we can tell beforehand what this cause (or these causes) might be. Feminist theorists have offered a variety of interesting causal explanations including the sex/gender system, the organization of production or sexual division of labor, childrearing practices, and processes of signification or language. These all provide useful hypotheses for the concrete study of gender relations in particular societies, but each explanatory scheme also seems to me to be deeply flawed, inadequate, and overly deterministic.

For example, Gayle Rubin locates the origin of gender systems in the "transformation of raw biological sex into gender."[10] However, Rubin's distinction between sex and gender rests in turn upon a series of oppositions that I find very problematic, including the opposition of "raw biological sexuality" and the social. This opposition reflects the idea predominant in the work of Freud, Lacan, and others that a person is driven by impulses and needs that are invariant and invariably asocial. This split between culture and natural sexuality may in fact be rooted in and reflect gender arrangements.

As I have argued elsewhere,[11] Freud's drive theory reflects in part an unconscious motive: to deny and repress aspects of infantile experience which are relational (e.g., the child's dependence upon and connectedness with its earliest caregiver, who is almost always a woman). Hence, in utilizing Freud's concepts, we must pay attention to what they conceal as well as reveal, especially the unacknowledged influences of anxieties about gender on his supposedly gender-neutral concepts (such as drive theory).

Socialist feminists locate the fundamental cause of gender arrangements in the organizations of production or the sexual division of labor. However, this explanatory system also incorporates the historical and philosophical flaws of Marxist analysis. As Balbus convincingly argues,[12] Marxists (including socialist feminists) uncritically apply the categories Marx derived from his description of a particular form of the production of commodities to all areas of human life at all historical periods. Socialist feminists replicate this privileging of production and the division of labor with the concomitant assumptions concerning the centrality of labor itself. Labor is still seen as the essence of history and being human. Such conceptions distort life in capitalist society and surely are not appropriate to all other cultures.[13]

An example of the problems that follow from this uncritical appropriation of Marxist concepts can be found in the attempts by socialist feminists to widen the concept of production to include most forms of human activity. These arguments avoid an essential question: Why widen the concept of production instead of dislodging it or any other singularly central concept from such authoritative power?

This question becomes more urgent when it appears that, despite the best efforts of socialist feminists, the Marxist concepts of labor and production invariably exclude or distort many kinds of activity, including those traditionally performed by women. Pregnancy and childrearing or relations between family members more generally cannot be comprehended merely as "property relations in action."[14] Sexuality cannot be understood as an exchange of physical energy, with a surplus (potentially) flowing to an exploiter.[15] Such concepts also ignore or obscure the existence and activities of other persons as well—children—for whom at least a part of their formative experiences has nothing to do with production.

However, the structure of childrearing practices also cannot serve as the root of gender relations. Among the many problems with this approach is that it cannot explain why women have the primary responsibility for childrearing; it can explain only some of the consequences of this fact. In other words, the childrearing practices taken as causal already presuppose the very social relations we are trying to understand: a gender-based division of human activities and hence the existence of socially constructed sets of gender arrangements and the (peculiar and in need of explanation) salience of gender itself.

The emphasis that (especially) French feminists place on the centrality of language (e.g., chains of signification, signs, and symbols) to the construction of gender also seems problematic.[16] A problem with thinking about (or only in terms of) texts, signs, or signification is that they tend to take on a life of their own or become the world, as the claim that nothing exists outside of a text; everything is a comment upon or a displacement of another text, as if the model human activity is literary criticism (or writing). Such an approach obscures the projection of its own activity onto the world and denies the existence of the variety of concrete social practices that enter into and are reflected in the constitution of language itself (e.g., ways of life constitute language and texts as much as language constitutes ways of life). This lack of attention to concrete social relations (including the distribution of power) results, as in Lacan's work, in the obscuring of relations of domination. Such relations (including gender arrangements) then tend to acquire an aura of inevitability and become equated with language or culture (the "law of the father") as such.

Much of French (including feminist) writing also seems to assume a radical (even ontological rather than socially constructed) disjunction between sign/mind/male/world and body/nature/female.[17] The prescription of some French feminists for the recovery (or reconstitution?) of female experience— "writing from the body"—seems incoherent given this sort of (Cartesian) disjunction. Since the body is presocial and prelinguistic, what could it say?

All of these social practices posited as explanations for gender arrangements may be more or less important, interrelated, or themselves partially constituted in and through gender relations depending upon context. As in any form of social analysis, the study of gender relations will necessarily reflect the social practices it attempts to understand. There cannot, nor should we expect there to be, a feminist equivalent to (a falsely universalizing) Marxism; indeed, the epistemologies of feminism undercut all such claims, including feminist ones.[18]

It is on the metatheoretical level that postmodern philosophies of knowledge can contribute to a more accurate self-understanding of the nature of our theorizing. We cannot simultaneously claim (1) that the mind, the self, and knowledge are socially constituted and that what we can know depends upon our social practices and contexts and (2) that feminist theory can uncover the truth of the whole once and for all. Such an absolute truth (e.g., the explanation for all gender arrangements at all times is X) would require the existence of an Archimedes point outside of the whole and beyond our embeddedness in it from which we could see (and represent) the whole. What we see and report would also have to be untransformed by the activities of perception and of reporting our vision in language. The object seen (social whole or gender arrangement) would have to be apprehended by an empty (ahistoric) mind and perfectly transcribed by/into a transparent language. The possibility of each of these conditions existing has been rendered extremely doubtful by the deconstructions of postmodern philosophers.

Furthermore, the work of Foucault (among others) should sensitize us to the interconnections between knowledge claims (especially to the claim of absolute or neutral knowledge) and power. Our own search for an Archimedes point may conceal and obscure our entanglement in an episteme in which truth claims may take only certain forms and not others.[19] Any episteme requires the suppression of discourses that threaten to differ with or undermine the authority of the dominant one. Hence, within feminist theory a search for a defining theme of the whole or a feminist viewpoint may require the suppression of the important and discomforting voices of persons with experiences unlike our own. The suppression of these voices seems to be a necessary condition for the (apparent) authority, coherence, and universality of our own.

Thus, the very search for a root or cause of gender relations (or more narrowly, male domination) may partially reflect a mode of thinking that is itself grounded in particular forms of gender (and/or other) relations in which domination is present. Perhaps reality can have "a" structure only from the falsely universalizing perspective of the dominant group. That is, only to the extent that one person or group can dominate the whole will reality appear to be governed by one set of rules or be constituted by one privileged set of social relations. Criteria of theory construction such as parsimony or simplicity may be attained only by the suppression or denial of the experiences of the other(s).

THE NATURAL BARRIER

Thus, in order for gender relations to be useful as a category of social analysis we must be as socially and self-critical as possible about the meanings usually attributed to those relations and the ways we think about them. Otherwise, we run the risk of replicating the very social relations we are attempting to understand. We have to be able to investigate both the social and philosophical barriers to our comprehension of gender relations.

One important barrier to our comprehension of gender relations has been the difficulty of understanding the relationship between *gender* and *sex*. In this context, *sex* means the anatomical differences between male and female. Historically (at least since Aristotle), these anatomical differences have been assigned to the class of natural facts or biology. In turn, biology has been equated with the pre- or nonsocial. Gender relations then become conceptualized as if they are constituted by two opposite terms or distinct types of being—man and woman. Since man and woman seem to be opposites or fundamentally distinct types of being, gender cannot be relational. If gender is as natural and as intrinsically a part of us as the genitals we are born with, it follows than it would be foolish (or even harmful) to attempt either to change gender arrangements or not to take them into account as a delimitation on human activities.

Even though a major focus of feminist theory has been to denaturalize gender, feminists as well as nonfeminists seem to have trouble thinking through the meanings we assign to and the uses we make of the concept "natural."[20] What, after all, is the natural in the context of the human world?[21] There are many aspects of our embodiedness or biology that we might see as given limits to human action which Western medicine and science do not hesitate to challenge. For example, few Westerners would refuse to be vaccinated against diseases that our bodies are naturally susceptible to, although in some cultures such actions would be seen as violating the natural order. The tendency of Western science is to disenchant the natural world.[22] More and more the natural ceases to exist as the opposite of the cultural or social. Nature becomes the object and product of human action; it loses its independent existence. Ironically, the more such disenchantment proceeds, the more humans seem to need something that remains outside our powers of transformation. Until recently, one such exempt area seemed to be anatomical differences between males and females.[23] Thus, in order to save nature (from ourselves) many people in the contemporary West equate sex/biology/nature/gender and oppose these to the cultural/social/human. Concepts of gender then become complex metaphors for ambivalences about human action in, on, and as part of the natural world.

But the use of gender as a metaphor for such ambivalences blocks further investigation of them. For the social articulation of these equations is not really in the form I stated above but, rather, sex/biology/nature/woman: cultural/social/man. In the contemporary West, women become the last refuge from not only the "heartless" world but also an increasingly mechanized and fabricated one as well.[24] What remains masked in these modes of thought is the possibility that our concepts of biology and nature are rooted in social relations; they do not merely reflect the given structure of reality itself. . . .

Notes

1. For a more extended discussion of these claims, see my forthcoming book, *Thinking Fragments: Psychoanalysis, Feminism, and Postmodernism in the Contemporary West* (Berkeley: University of California Press, forthcoming 1990).
2. Sources for and practitioners of postmodernism include Friedrich Nietzsche, *On the Genealogy of Morals* (New York: Vintage, 1969) and *Beyond Good and Evil* (New York: Vintage, 1966); Jacques Derrida, *L'écriture et la différence* (Paris: Editions du Seuil, 1967); Michel Foucault, *Language, Counter-Memory, Practice* (Ithaca: Cornell University Press, 1977); Jacques Lacan, *Speech and Language in Psychoanalysis* (Baltimore: Johns Hopkins University Press, 1968) and *The Four Fundamental Concepts of Psychoanalysis* (New York: W. W. Norton, 1973); Richard Rorty, *Philosophy and the Mirror of Nature* (Princeton: Princeton University Press, 1979); Paul Feyerabend, *Against Method* (New York: Schocken, 1975); Ludwig Wittgenstein, *On Certainty* (New York: Harper and Row, 1972) and *Philosophical Investigations* (New York: Macmillan, 1970); Julia Kristeva, "Women's Time," *Signs: Journal of Women in Culture and Society* 7, no. 11 (Autumn 1981): 13–35;

and Jean-François Lyotard, *The Postmodern Condition* (Minneapolis: University of Minnesota Press, 1984).

3. Examples of such work include Alice A. Jardine, *Gynesis: Configurations of Woman and Modernity* (Ithaca: Cornell University Press, 1985); Donna Haraway, "A Manifesto for Cyborgs: Science, Technology, and Socialist Feminism in the 1980s," *Socialist Review* 80 (1983): 65–107; Kathy E. Ferguson, *The Feminist Case against Bureaucracy* (Philadelphia: Temple University Press, 1984); and Luce Irigaray, *Speculum of the Other Woman* (Ithaca: Cornell University Press, 1985).

4. Immanuel Kant, "What is Enlightenment?" in *Foundations of the Metaphysics of Morals* (Indianapolis: Bobbs-Merrill, 1959), 85.

5. For critiques of the mind (reason)/body split, see Naomi Scheman, "Individualism and the Objects of Psychology," in *Discovering Reality: Feminist Perspectives on Epistemology, Metaphysics, Methodology, and Philosophy of Science*, ed. Sandra Harding and Merill B. Hintikka (Boston: D. Reidel Publishing Co., 1983); Susan Bordo, "The Cartesian Masculinization of Thought," *Signs* 11, no. 3 (Spring 1986): 439–56; Nancy C. M. Hartsock, "The Feminist Standpoint: Developing the Ground for a Specifically Feminist Historical Materialism," in Harding and Hintikka, eds.; Caroline Whitbeck, "Afterword to the 'Maternal Instinct,'" in *Mothering: Essays in Feminist Theory*, ed. Joyce Trebilcot (Totowa, N.J. Rowman & Allanheld, 1984); and Dorothy Smith, "A Sociology for Women," in *The Prison of Sex: Essays in the Sociology of Knowledge*, ed. J. Sherman and E. T. Beck (Madison: University of Wisconsin Press, 1979).

6. These questions are suggested by Judith Stacey, "The New Conservative Feminism," *Feminist Studies* 9, no. 3 (Fall 1983): 559–83, and Nancy Chodorow, "Gender, Relation, and Difference in Psychoanalytic Perspective," in *The Future of Difference*, ed. Hester Eisenstein and Alice Jardine (1980, rpt. New Brunswick: Rutgers University Press, 1985).

7. For example, the Marxist treatments of the "woman question" from Engels onward, or existentialist, or Lacanian treatment of woman as the "other" to man.

8. On this point, see Joan Kelly, "The Doubled Vision of Feminist Theory," *Feminist Studies* 6, no. 2 (Summer 1979): 216–27; and also Judith Stacey and Barrie Thorne, "The Missing Feminist Revolution in Sociology," *Social Problems* 32, no. 4 (April 1985): 301–16.

9. Compare Phyllis Marynick Palmer, "White Women/Black Women: The Dualism of Female Identity and Experience in the United States," *Feminist Studies* 9, no. 11 (Spring 1983): 151–70.

10. This is Gayle Rubin's claim in "The Traffic in Women: Notes on the 'Political Economy' of Sex," in *Toward an Anthropology of Women*, ed. Rayna Rapp Reiter (New York: Monthly Review Press, 1975).

11. I develop this argument in "Psychoanalysis as Deconstruction and Myth: On Gender, Narcissism, and Modernity's Discontents," in *The Crisis of Modernity: Recent Theories of Culture in the United States and West Germany*, ed. Kurt Shell (Boulder, CO: Westview Press, 1986).

12. See Isaac D. Balbus, *Marxism and Domination* (Princeton, N.J.: Princeton University Press, 1982) ch. 1, for a further development of these arguments. Despite Balbus's critique of Marx, he still seems to be under Marx's spell on a metatheoretical level when he tries to locate a root of all domination—childrearing practices. I have also discussed the inadequacy of Marxist theories in "Do Feminists Need Marxism?" in *Building Feminist Theory*, ed. Quest Staff (New York: Longman, 1981), and "The Family in Contemporary Feminist Thought: A Critical Re-

view," in *The Family in Political Thought*, ed. Jean Bethke Elshtain (Amherst: University of Massachusetts Press, 1982), 232–39.

13. Marx may replicate rather than deconstruct the capitalist mentality in his emphasis on the centrality of production. Compare Albert O. Hirschman, *The Passions and the Interests* (Princeton: Princeton University Press, 1977) for a very interesting discussion of the historical emergence and construction of a specifically *capitalist* mentality.

14. Annette Kuhn, "Structure of Patriarchy and Capital in the Family," *Feminism and Materialism*, ed. Annette Kuhn and Ann Marie Wolpe, (Boston: Routledge & Kegan Paul, 1978), 53.

15. Ann Ferguson, "Conceiving Motherhood and Sexuality: A Feminist Materialist Approach," in *Mothering* 156–58.

16. The theories of French feminists vary, of course. I am focusing on a predominant and influential approach within the variations. For further discussion of French feminisms, see the essays in *Signs* 7, no. 1 (Autumn 1981) and *Feminist Studies* 7, no. 2 (Summer 1981).

17. Domna Stanton, in "Difference on Trial: A Critique of the Maternal Metaphor in Cixous, Irigaray, and Kristeva," in *The Poetics of Gender*, ed. Nancy Miller (New York: Columbia University Press, 1986), discusses the ontological and essentialist aspects of these writers' work.

18. Catherine MacKinnon, in "Feminism, Marxism, Method, and the State; An Agenda for Theory," *Signs* 7, no. 3 (Spring 1982): 515–44, seems to miss this basic point when she makes claims such as: "The defining theme of the whole is the male pursuit of control over women's sexuality—men not as individuals nor as biological beings, but as a gender group characterized by maleness as socially constructed, of which this pursuit is definitive" (532). On the problem of the Archimedes point, see Myra Jehlen, "Archimedes and the Paradox of Feminist Criticism," *Signs* 6, no. 4 (Summer 1981): 575–601.

19. Compare Michel Foucault, *Power/Knowledge*, ed. Colin Gordon (New York: Random House, 1981).

20. But see the work of Evelyn Fox Keller on the gendered character of our views of the natural world, especially her essays "Gender and Science," in Harding and Hintikka, eds. (Note no. 2), and "Cognitive Repression in Physics," *American Journal of Physics* 47 (1979): 718–21.

21. In *Public Man, Private Woman*, Jean Bethke Elshtain provides an instructive instance of how allegedly natural properties (of infants) can be used to limit what a "reflective feminist" ought to think. In Elshtain's recent writings it becomes (once again) the responsibility of women to rescue children from an otherwise instrumental and uncaring world. Elshtain evidently believes that psychoanalytical theory is exempt from the context-dependent hermeneutics she believes characterize all other kinds of knowledge about social relations. She utilizes psychoanalytic theory as a warrant for absolute or foundational claims about the nature of "real human needs" or "the most basic human relationships" and then bases political conclusions on these "natural" facts. See Jean Bethke Elshtain, *Public Man, Private Woman* (Princeton: Princeton University Press, 1981), 314, 331.

22. See Max Weber, "Science as a Vocation," in *From Max Weber*, ed. H. H. Gerth and C. Wright Mills (New York: Oxford University Press, 1958), and Max Horkheimer and Theodor W. Adorno, *Dialectic of Enlightenment* (New York: Herder and Herder, 1972).

23. I say "until recently" because of developments in medicine such as sex-change operations and new methods of conception and fertilization of embryos.
24. As in the work of Christopher Lasch, *Haven in a Heartless World* (New York: Basic Books, 1977). Lasch's work is basically a repetition of the ideas stated earlier by members of the Frankfurt School, especially Horkheimer and Adorno. See, for example, the essay "The Family" in *Aspects of Sociology*, Frankfurt Institute for Social Research (Boston: Beacon Press, 1972).

SELECTION 25
FROM
Postmodernism and Other Skepticisms

CHRISTINE PIERCE

FEMINIST THEORY, ACCORDING TO some of its practitioners, is a subset of postmodern philosophy.[1] With respect to the possibility of knowledge, Jane Flax, for instance, sets up the choices for feminists as an either/or proposition: postmodernism or the Enlightenment. Feminists, she says, cannot have it both ways: Either what is called "truth" is tainted by history and social practice, as deconstructionist philosophers have shown, or some absolute truth of the whole universe is possible. "We cannot simultaneously claim (1) that the mind, self, and knowledge are socially constituted and that what we can know depends upon our social practices and contexts *and* (2) that feminist theory can uncover the Truth of the Whole once and for all. Such an absolute truth (e.g., the explanation for all gender arrangements at all times is X . . .) would require the existence of an 'Archimedes point' outside of the whole and beyond our embeddedness in it from which we could see (and represent) the whole."[2] Flax's argument follows a recognizable inference schema:

- Postmodern philosophy or Enlightenment philosophy.
- Enlightenment notions are untenable.
- Therefore, "feminist theory . . . belongs in the terrain of postmodern philosophy."[3]

Flax goes on to elaborate this claim: "Feminist notions of the self, knowledge, and truth are too contradictory to those of the Enlightenment to be contained within its categories. The way(s) of feminist future(s) cannot lie in reviving or appropriating Enlightenment concepts of the person or knowledge. . . . [D]espite an understandable attraction to the (apparently) logical, orderly world of the Enlightenment, feminist theory more properly

243

belongs in the terrain of postmodern philosophy."[4]

Without a doubt, Enlightenment philosophers such as Kant were over-confident regarding the powers of reason and promised much more than they could deliver. However, even though both feminists and postmodernists are critical of so-called Enlightenment projects and the universalistic theories associated with those projects, feminist skepticism of the last two decades has been a moderate one compared with the radical skepticism of postmodern philosophy. Moreover, the insight of postmodernism most attractive to recent feminist theory—that advances in knowledge are tentative, limited, constrained by culture, race, class, gender, sexual orientation, and other biases, and applicable only to a fraction of folks—can be salvaged without buying the radical skepticism and relativism of postmodernism.[5]

Flax's own use of the term "contradiction" in her rejection of Enlightenment conceptions indicates that she thinks the notion of contradiction can be employed in some legitimate way despite the dismissal of the principle of noncontradiction by contemporary French feminists Luce Irigaray and and Hélène Cixous as paradigmatically male—penile, to be exact. And since Flax's criticisms of various postmodern thinkers suggest that only some of the conclusions of postmodernism should be saved, it seems equally plausible that some of the ideas of the Enlightenment might be worthwhile as well. If both philosophies can be critiqued for salvageable portions, perhaps feminism ought not to be classified as a subset of either postmodernism or the Enlightenment.

Flax sees feminism and postmodernism as common allies in their criticism of reason—that glory of the Enlightenment—as being ahistoric, transcendental, disembodied, impersonal, and abstract.[6] And in fact, feminists have rightly been concerned with situatedness and the importance of relationships and context in areas such as theories of self. Nevertheless, feminist conceptions of notions in ethical or political theories—justice, for example—can be strengthened by, if not grounded in, certain abstractions. While postmodernists engaged in the unraveling of rational structures cannot take reason as a ground for anything, feminists can appeal to reason unless they choose to abandon it altogether. Which techniques stay and which go can be decided on the basis of relevance. For example, an ahistorical, disembodied concept of the self would be poor psychology; but just such an abstract self in a concept like the "veil of ignorance" might work well to explain justice. The fact that all concrete particular situatedness disappears may be exactly what is needed in order for people to understand what it is like to live in somebody else's shoes. . . .

Explanatory theories such as those found in psychology, history, and metaphysics are under attack by feminists and postmodernists because the generalizations—sometimes referred to as universal or essentialist statements—

they generate inevitably turn out to be false. Explanatory theories are designed to give an account of isolated phenomena, and some theories attempt to account for an extraordinary range of them. Authors Nancy Fraser and Linda Nicholson give as examples the metanarratives of Marx and Enlightenment humanism and the quasi-metanarratives of Nancy Chodorow and Carol Gilligan. Efforts to explain the oppression of women by reference to a single cause, for instance, will unavoidably extrapolate from the experiences of some while leaving out the stories of others. For example, such a theory might single out a domestic life that is typical of white, middle-class, heterosexual women but fails to capture the experiences of lesbians, black women, and working-class women. General claims about gender, in the words of Susan Bordo, create "a false unity out of heterogeneous elements relegating the submerged elements to marginality."[7]

From this enlightened perspective, Gilligan is criticized for ignoring differences in race and class in much the same way as Gilligan criticized Lawrence Kohlberg for ignoring gender differences. Just as Gilligan doubted that Kohlberg's single standard for human moral maturity was really anything of the sort, given that the data for his conclusion included only the moral reasoning of males, so too have some feminists suggested more recently that the type of moral reasoning Gilligan associates with women is better identified with subordinate or minority status.[8] This moderate skepticism regarding universalizing claims is typical of feminist theorizing of the last two decades.

Postmodern skepticism is radical skepticism. Gendered explanations of the kind Gilligan offers are rejected not because she, like Kohlberg, is guilty of false generalization but because of new skepticism about the use of gender as an analytical category.[9] It is not that Gilligan and Kohlberg have the wrong categories; under postmodernism, categories are abolished altogether. Every generalization leaves out something of importance, and our efforts to capture the item left out are endless and lead to a radical particularity. The view is well known: the world as text, subject to endless commentary and particular interpretations, the continual displacement of one text by another. It reminds one of the philosopher Cratylus, who, when convinced of radical skepticism, "did not think it right to say anything but only moved his finger."[10] The feminist celebration of difference that began by discarding false generalizations moves in postmodernism to a radical particularity, what Bordo calls "the view from everywhere." The feminist worry that some stories are marginalized or not told shifts in postmodernism to the view that there are only particular stories, that no rational standards arbitrate between discourses.

The notion of life as literary criticism—ceaseless textual play—has unsurprisingly prompted some feminists to claim that no (practical) politics can come from postmodernism. When one refuses to order thoughts into concepts, categories, and theories, one eliminates politics. If we have no political theory, we have no practical politics. If we have no feminist theory, we have no women's movement. Some feminists have even been tempted to claim there are no "women," following Michel Foucault's idea that "the homosexual" is an invented classification. Teresa de Lauretis, for example, says the subject of feminism is "not only distinct from Woman with the capital letter, the *representation* of an essence inherent in all women . . ., but also distinct from women, the real, historical beings and social subjects who are . . . actually engendered in social relations. The subject of feminism . . . is a theoretical construct . . . not women."[11] Even if academics can understand perfectly well what is meant, one cannot go into the street and talk about a women's movement if there are no women. One might as well join Cratylus in the bending of a finger. But before we become overly pessimistic regarding the possibility of ethics or political theory, it must be noticed that the postmodern disparagement of universalistic claims applies only to discussions that try to capture truths about the world. . . .

REJECTING PRINCIPLES: THE DEMISE
OF EQUALITY AND NONCONTRADICTION

As creator and practitioner respectively of a woman's discourse—*écriture de la femme*—Irigaray and Cixous abandon coherence, consistency, and noncontradiction as reflective of male anatomy. To have a penis is to be the sort of person who would think up such ideas as the principle of identity and the principle of noncontradiction: "Phallic language is based on a sematic economy of 'has' and 'has not,' and endless repetition of the same. . . . The 'one' of the male subject becomes the two of the vaginal lips, constantly in touch with each other in an interaction in which the two are not separated by negation but interact and merge. . . . Instead of the relation of identity, vaginal symbolism suggests contiguity. The law of non-contradiction does not rule because the point is not a repetition of the same. Asked for clarification, a woman cannot answer; she has already moved on, or turned her back on her own thought, in a kind of a vaginal 'fold' within herself."[12] Even as a woman's sexuality is plural, goes the argument, her speech would encompass multiplicity, rejecting rules of grammar, rigid concepts, and boundaries in favor of a language and a philosophy that flow. It is true that the very form of an academic discourse makes ideas such as those of Irigaray and Cixous difficult to described and comprehend, and so they must turn to metaphor to explain. And metaphor is notoriously easy to laugh at; my love is not *really* like a red, red rose at all. But even within the bounds of metaphor, anatomy is poor choice to explain the gendering of language; men have two testicles, after all, and the duplication of organs is basic *human* anatomy. If one is going to accept the possibility of rational discourse, as presumably is axiomatic for scholarship to continue, then one must cite some reason for rejecting the principle of noncontradiction other than genitalia. . . .

Ultimately, philosophy is no freer than any other discipline from the pulls of larger intellectual currents. The struggles of postmodernism and feminism with the heavy weight of rational structures are continuations of the Romantic movement of the early nineteenth century. Milton told the men of the seventeenth-century Enlightenment that reason was their special gift, a gift specifically *not* granted to women. Adam and Eve in Eden are

> Not equal, as their sex not equal seemed.
> For contemplation he and valor formed,
> For softness she and sweet attractive grace:
> He for God only, she for God in him.[13]

The works of thinkers such as Newton and Kant convinced men that reason was their most godlike tool, the facility that would explain the order of the universe if not today, then certainly tomorrow. When Goethe and Rousseau and Blake began to reject the claims of reason, they seemed compelled to reject also its rampant masculinity. Imagination and inspiration became either feminine or androgynous, and reason became the deity of the mechanistic, obviously patriarchal establishment.

Reason, as we have found, makes a bad deity; but it does make a good tool. Physicists who consider Einsteinian relativity and quantum mechanics to be our current best models of the universe still use Newtonian formulas to plot rocket trajectories. Feminist attorneys who understand the origins of civil rights in property protection invented in the capitalistic Renaissance can still use those rights in court to empower minorities.

Where postmodernism will go in its deconstruction of the philosophies of the Enlightenment has yet to be seen. It is easy to understand how the postmodern repudiation of the one true universal story dovetails with much of feminist thought. After all, most of the one true universal stories in Western history, psychology, and so on have been about white, heterosexual men. Patriarchal resistance to multidimensional accounts is at least as big a problem as relativism (some feminists would say greater) in terms of damage to women.[14] Moreover, multidimensional accounts do not entail relativism. To deny that there is a single right view of history, for example, is not to agree that any view of history is as good as any other. But if there are only discourses and no rational way to arbitrate between or among them, then relativism seems to be an obvious consequence. Feminism as a force in the world must keep a balance: understanding the skepticism toward reason as a masculinist, historically weighted method of organizing knowledge while recognizing that not all of the laboriously created works of the past are useless for our own liberation. Certainly you can destroy the master's house with the master's tools.[15]

Notes

My thanks to Beth Timson, Claudia Card, and Sandy Bartky for their ideas and suggestions for this essay.

1. A brief description of postmodern philosophy follows: "Within the last decade, there have emerged . . . radical arguments against claims of objectivity in the academy which have been tied to broad analyses of the limitations of modern Western scholarship. The proponents of such analyses, linked under the label of 'postmodernists,' have argued that the academy's ideal of 'a God's eye view' must be situated within the context of modernity, a period whose organizing principles they claim are on the decline. The postmodernist critique of modernity is wideranging; it focuses on such diverse elements as the modern sense of the self and subjectivity, the idea of history as linear and evolutionary, and the modernist separation of art and mass culture. I will focus, for the moment, on the postmodernist critique of the idea of a transcendent reason.

   "Postmodernists have gone beyond earlier historicist claims about the inevitable 'situatedness' of human thought within culture to focus on the very criteria by which claims to knowledge are legitimized. The traditional historicist claim that all inquiry is inevitably influenced by the values of the inquirer provides a very weak counter to the norm of objectivity. The response can be made that while values and culture might affect the choice of questions the scholar brings to her or his inquiry, they cannot affect the truth or falsity of the answers the scholar gives to such questions. This is because the criteria which determine the truth or falsity of such answers are themselves independent of the specific perspective of the inquirer. But the more radical move in the postmodern turn was to claim that the very criteria demarcating the true and the false, as well as such related distinctions as science and myth or fact and superstition, were internal to the traditions of modernity and could not be legitimized outside of these traditions. . . . Therefore, the postmodern critique has come to focus on philosophy and the very idea of a possible theory of knowledge, justice, or beauty" (Linda J. Nicholson, Introduction, *Feminism/Postmodernism* [New York: Routledge, 1990], 3–4).
2. Jane Flax, "Postmodernism and Gender Relations in Feminist Theory," *Signs: Journal of Women in Culture and Society* 12, no. 4 (Summer 1987): 633.
3. Ibid., 625.
4. Ibid.
5. Robert Paul Wolff makes a similar point about limitations on advances in knowledge, but his remarks are not directed at postmodernists. See "Social Philosophy: The Agenda for the Nineties," *Journal of Social Philosophy* 20, nos. 1, 2 (Spring/Fall 1989): 5.
6. Jane Flax, "Beyond Equality: Gender, Justice, and Difference," lecture at Duke University, Feb. 12, 1990.
7. Susan Bordo, "Feminism, Postmodernism, and Gender-Scepticism," in Nicholson, ed., *Feminism/Postmodernism*, 139.

8. Joan C. Tronto, "Beyond Gender Difference to a Theory of Care," *Signs: Journal of Women in Culture and Society* 12, no. 4 (Summer 1987): 649.

9. See Bordo, "Feminism, Postmodernism, and Gender-Scepticism," 135.

10. Aristotle, *Metaphysics*, 1010a 12, 13; see also 1010a 1–15. Richard McKeon, ed., *The Basic Works of Aristotle* (New York: Random House, 1941), 745–46.

11. Teresa de Lauretis, *Technologies of Gender: Essays on Theory, Film, and Fiction* (Bloomington: Indiana University Press, 1987), 9–10. See also Denise Riley's discussion of the problem in *"Am I That Name?" Feminism and the Category of "Woman" in History* (Minneapolis: University of Minnesota, 1988), chs. 1 and 5.

12. Andrea Nye, *Feminist Theory and the Philosophies of Man* (New York: Routledge, 1989), 194–95.

13. *Paradise Lost*, book 4, in *John Milton's Complete Poems and Major Prose*, ed. Merritt Y. Hughes (New York: Odyssey, 1957), 285.

14. Charlene Haddock Seigfried holds this view. See her "Why Isn't There a Pragmatic Feminism or Feminist Pragmatism?" paper presented at Midwest SWIP, Michigan State University, East Lansing, Feb. 17, 1990.

15. I take issue here with Audre Lorde's often quoted advice to feminists that "the master's tools will never dismantle the master's house." Of course, Lorde did not anticipate in her remarks a deconstructionism that would undercut assertion altogether. See Audre Lorde, *Sister/Outsider: Essays and Speeches* (Trumansburg, NY: Crossing Press, 1984), 112.

SELECTION 26
FROM
Feminism, Postmodernism, and Gender-Skepticism

SUSAN BORDO

CONTEMPORARY FEMINISM AND GENDER-SKEPTICISM

IN THE 1970s, THE feminist imagination was fueled by the insight that the template of gender could disclose aspects of culture and history previously concealed. The male-normative view of the world, feminists argued, had obscured its own biases through its fictions of unity (History, Reason, Culture, Tradition, and so forth). Each of those unities was shown to have a repressed shadow—an *Other* whose material history, values, and perspective had yet to be written.

Today, many feminists are critical of what they now see as the over-simplifications and generalizations of this period in feminism. Challenges have arisen—sometimes emotionally charged—targeted against earlier classics of feminist theory and their gendered readings of culture and history. Where once the prime objects of academic feminist critique were the phallocentric narratives of our male-dominated disciplines, now feminist criticism has turned to its own narratives, finding them reductionist, totalizing, inadequately nuanced, valorizing of gender difference, unconsciously racist, and elitist. It seems possible to discern what may be a new drift within feminism, a new skepticism about the use of gender as an analytical category. . . .

Arising not from monolithic design but from an interplay of factors and forces, it is best understood not as a discrete, definable position which can be adopted or rejected, but as an emerging coherency which is being fed by a variety of currents, sometimes overlapping, sometimes quite distinct.

The first current is the result of a recent academic marriage which has brought indigenous feminist concerns over the ethnocentrisms and unconscious racial biases of gender theory into a theoretical alliance with (a highly programmatic appropriation of) the more historicist, politically oriented wing of poststructuralist thought (e.g., Foucault, Lyotard). This union, I will argue, has contributed to the development of a new feminist "methodologism" which lays claims to an authoritative critical framework, legislating "correct" and "incorrect" approaches to theorizing identity, history, and culture. This methodologism, which eschews generalizations about gender a priori on theoretical grounds, is in danger of discrediting and disabling certain kinds of feminist cultural critique; it also often implicitly (and mistakenly) supposes that the adoption of a "correct" theoretical approach makes it possible to *avoid* ethnocentrism.

The second current is the result of certain feminist appropriations of deconstructionism. Here, a postmodern recognition of *interpretive* multiplicity, of the indeterminacy and heterogeneity of cultural meaning and meaning-production, is viewed as calling for new narrative approaches, aimed at the adequate representation of textual "difference." From this perspective the template of gender is criticized for its fixed, binary structuring of reality and is replaced with a narrative ideal of ceaseless textual play. But this ideal, I will argue, while arising out of a critique of modernist epistemological pretensions to adequately represent reality, remains animated by its *own* fantasies of attaining an epistemological perspective free of the locatedness and limitations of embodied existence—a fantasy that I call a "dream of everywhere."

Through the critical concerns raised in these sections of my chapter, I hope to encourage caution among those who are ready to wholeheartedly celebrate the emergence of "postmodern feminism." The programmatic appropriation of poststructuralist insight, I will argue, in shifting the focus of crucial feminist concerns about the representation of cultural diversity from practical contexts to questions of adequate theory, is highly problematic for feminism. Not only are we thus diverted from attending to the professional and institutional mechanisms through which the politics of exclusion operate most powerfully in intellectual communities, but we also deprive ourselves of still vital analytical tools for critique of those communities and the hierarchical, dualistic power structures that sustain them.[1] . . .

Feminism, appropriately enough, initiated the cultural work of exposing and articulating the *gendered* nature of history, culture, and society. It was a cultural moment of revelation and relief. The category of the "human"—a standard against which all difference translates to lack, insufficiency—was brought down to earth, given a pair of pants, and reminded that it was not the only player in town. Our students still experience this moment of critical and empowering insight when, for example, they learn from Gilligan (1982) and others that the language of "rights" is not the ethical discourse of God or Nature, but the ideological superstructure of a particular construction of masculinity.[2] . . .

The unity of the "gendered human," however, often proved to be as much a fiction as the unity of abstract, universal "man." In responding to the cultural imperative to describe the difference gender makes, gender theorists (along with those who attempted to speak for a "black experience" uninflected by gender or class) often glossed over other dimensions of social identity and location, dimensions which, when considered, cast doubt on the proposed gender (or racial) generalizations. Chodorow (1978), for example, has frequently been criticized for implicitly elevating one pattern of difference between men and women, characteristic at most of a particular historical period and form of family organization, to the status of an essential "gender reality." Since the patterns described in gender analysis have often been based on the experiences of white, middle-class men and women, such accounts are guilty, feminists have frequently pointed out, of perpetuating the same sort of unconscious privilegings and exclusions characteristic of the male-normative theories they criticize. . . .

Certainly, feminist scholarship will benefit from more local, historically specific study and from theoretical projects analyzing the relations of diverse axes of identity. Too often, however (e.g., in grant, program, and conference guidelines and descriptions), this has translated to the coercive, mechanical requirement that *all* enlightened feminist projects attend to "the intersection of race, class, and gender." What happened to ethnicity? Age? Sexual orientation? On the other hand, just how many axes *can* one include and still preserve analytical focus or argument? Even more troubling is the (often implicit, sometimes explicit) dogma that the only "correct" perspective on race, class, and gender is the affirmation of difference; this dogma reveals itself in criticisms which attack gender generalizations as *in principle* essentialist of totalizing. Surely, such charges should require concrete examples of *actual* differences that are being submerged by any particular "totality" in question. . . .

THE VIEW FROM NOWHERE AND THE DREAM OF EVERYWHERE

In theory, deconstructionist postmodernism stands against the ideal of disembodied knowledge and declares that ideal to be a mystification and an impossibility. There is no Archimedean viewpoint; rather, history and culture are texts, admitting an endless proliferation of readings, each of which is itself unstable. I have no dispute with this epistemological critique or with the metaphor of the world-as-text as a means of undermining various claims to authoritative, transcendant insight into the nature of reality. The question remains, however, how the human knower is to negotiate this infinitely perspectival, destabilized world. Deconstructionism answers with constant vigilant suspicion of all determinate readings of culture and a partner aesthetic of ceaseless textual play as an alternative ideal. Here is where deconstruction may slip into its own fantasy of escape from human locatedness—by supposing that the critic can become wholly protean by adopting endlessly shifting, seemingly inexhaustible vantage points, none of which are "owned" by either the critic or the author of a text under examination.

Deconstructionism has profoundly affected certain feminist approaches to gender as a grid for the reading of culture. Such readings, they argue, only reproduce the dualistic logic which has held the Western imagination in its grip. Instead, contemporary feminism should attempt, as Susan Suleiman (1986) describes it, "to get beyond, not only the number one—the number that determines unity of body or of self—but also to get beyond the number two, which determines difference, antagonism and exchange . . ." (24). "One is too few," as Donna Haraway (1989) writes, "but two are too many." (219). The "number one" clearly represents for Suleiman the fictions of unity, stability, and identity characteristic of the phallocentric worldview. The "number two" represents the grid of gender, which feminists have used to expose the hierarchical, oppositional structure of that worldview. "Beyond the number two" is no other number, but "endless complication" and a "dizzying accumulation of narratives." Suleiman here refers to Derrida's often-quoted interview with Christy MacDonald (1982), in which he speaks of "a 'dream' of the innumerable, . . . a desire to escape the combinatory . . . to invent incalculable choreographies" (76).

Such images from Derrida have been used in a variety of ways by feminists. Drucilla Cornel and Adam Thurschwell (1987) present it as a utopian vision of human life no longer organized by gender duality and hierarchy. But Suleiman presents it as offering an *epistemological* or narrative ideal. As such, key contrasts with traditional (most particularly, Cartesian) images of knowing immediately are evident. Metaphors of dance and movement have replaced the ontologically fixing stare of the motionless spectator. The lust for finality is banished. The dream is of "incalculable choreographies," not the clear and distinct "mirrorings" of nature, seen from the heights of "nowhere." But, I would argue, the philosopher's fantasy of transcendence has not yet been abandoned. The historical specifics of the modernist, Cartesian version have simply been replaced with a new postmodern configuration of detachment, a new imagination of disembodiment: a dream of being *everywhere. . . .*

The imagination of "justice" to heterogeneity, entertained as an epistemological (or narrative) goal, devours its own tail. For the appreciation of difference requires the acknowledgment of some *limit* to the dance, beyond which the dancer cannot go. If she were able to go there, there would *be* no difference, nothing which eludes. To deny the unity and stability of identity is one thing. The epistemological fantasy of *becoming* multiplicity—the dream of limitless multiple embodiments, allowing one to dance from place to place and self to self—is another. What sort of body is it that is free to change its shape and location at will, that can become anyone and travel everywhere? If the body is a metaphor for our locatedness in space and time and thus for the finitude of human perception and knowledge, then the postmodern body is no body at all.

The deconstructionist erasure of the body is not affected, as in the Cartesian version, through a trip to "nowhere," but in a resistance to the recognition that one is always *somewhere*, and limited. Here, it becomes clear that to overcome Cartesian hubris, it is not sufficient to replace metaphors of spectatorship with metaphors of dance; it is necessary to relinquish all fantasies of epistemological conquest, not only those that are soberly fixed on necessity and unity but also those that are intoxicated with possibility and plurality. Despite the explicit rejection of conceptions of knowledge that view the mind as a "mirror of nature," deconstructionism reveals a longing for adequate representations—unlike Cartesian conceptions, but no less ambitiously, of a relentlessly heterogeneous reality.[3]

The Retreat from Female Otherness

The preceding discussion of the body as epistemological metaphor for locatedness has focused on deconstructionism's *theoretical* deconstruction of locatedness. In the next sections, I want to shift gears and pursue the issue of locatedness—or rather, the denial of locatedness—in more concrete directions.

It is striking to me that there often is a curious selectivity at work in contemporary feminist criticisms of gender-based theories of identity. The analytics of race and class—the two other giants of modernist social critique—do not seem to be undergoing the same deconstruction. Rather, it is my impression that feminists infrequently demand the same attentiveness to difference, or the same sensitivity to issues of interpretation and textuality, from the analytics of race and class that we do from the analytics of gender. When women of color construct "white feminists" as a unity, without attention to the class, ethnic, and religious differences that situate and divide us, white feminists tend to accept this (as I believe they should) as enabling crucial sorts of criticisms to be made. It is usually acknowledged, too, that the experience of being a person of color in a racist culture creates some similarities of position across class and gender. . . .

I have heard feminists insist, too, that race and class each have a "material base" that gender lacks. When the suggestion is made that perhaps such a material base exists for gender, in women's reproductive role, the wedges of cultural diversity and multiple interpretation suddenly are produced. Women have perceived childbearing, as Jean Grimshaw (1986) points out, "as both the source of their greatest joy and as the root of their worst suffering" (73); she concludes that the differences in various social constructions of reproduction, the vast disparities in women's experiences of childbirth, and so forth preclude that the practices of reproduction can meaningfully be interrogated as a source of insight into the difference gender makes. Why, it must be asked, are we so ready to deconstruct what have historically been the most ubiquitous elements of the gender axis, while so willing to defer to the authority and integrity of race and class axes as fundamentally *grounding?*[4] . . .

A decade ago, the exploration and revaluation of that which has been culturally constructed as "female" set the agenda for academic feminists of many disciplines, at a time when feminism was just entering the (white, male) academy and had not yet been integrated into it or professionalized by it. We were outsiders, of suspect politics (most of us had been "political" feminists before or during our professional training), and inappropriate sex (a *woman* philosopher?). Then, to be a feminist academic was to be constantly aware of one's Otherness; one could not forget that one was a woman even if one tried. The feminist imagination was fueled precisely by what it was never allowed to forget: The analysis of the historical construction of male power and female Otherness became our theoretical task.

Today, on the other hand, we have been "accepted." That is, it has been acknowledged (seemingly) that women can indeed "think like men," and those women who are able to adopt the prevailing standards of professional "balance," critical detachment, rigor, and the appropriate insider mentality have been rewarded for their efforts. Those who are unable or unwilling to do so (along with those men who are similarly unable or unwilling) continue to be denied acceptance, publications, tenure, promotions. At this juncture, women may discover that they have a new investment in combating notions that gender locates and limits.

In such a world any celebration of "female" ways of knowing or thinking may be felt by some to be a dangerous alliance professionally and perhaps a personal regression as well. For, within the masculinist institutions we have entered, relational, holistic, and nurturant attitudes continue to be marked as flabby, feminine, and soft. In this institutional context, as we are permitted "integration" into the public sphere, the category of female Otherness, which has spoken to many feminists of the possibility of institutional and cultural change, of radical transformation of the values, metaphysical assumptions, and social practices of our culture, may become something from which we wish to dissociate ourselves. We need instead to establish our leanness, our critical incisiveness, our proficiency at clear and distinct dissection. . . .

Notes

1. This is not to say that I disdain the insights of poststructuralist thought (which I often apply in my own work). My argument here is addressed to certain programmatic uses of those insights. Much poststructuralist thought (the work of Foucault in particular) is better understood, I would argue, as offering interpretive *tools* and *historical* critique rather than theoretical frameworks for wholesale adoption.
2. It must be noted, however, that Gilligan does *not* view the different "voices" she describes as essentially or only related to gender. She "discovers" them in her clinical work exploring gender difference, but the chief aim of her book, as she describes it, is to "highlight a distinction between two modes of thought" which have been culturally reproduced along (but not only along) genderlines (2).
3. Haraway elides these implications by a constant and deliberate ambiguity about the nature of the body she is describing: It is both "personal" and "collective." Her call for "polyvocality" seems at times to be directed toward feminist culture as a collectivity, at other times, toward individual feminists. The image she ends her piece with, of a "powerful infidel heteroglossia" to replace the old feminist dream of a "common language," sounds like a cultural image—until we come to the next line, which equates this image with that of "a feminist speaking in tongues." I suggest that this ambiguity, although playful and deliberate, nonetheless reveals a tension between her imagination of the Cyborg as liberatory "political myth" and a lingering "epistemologism" which presents the Cyborg as a model of "correct" perspective on reality. I applaud the former and have problems with the latter.
4. In speaking of "the practice of reproduction," I have in mind not only pregnancy and birth, but menstruation, menopause, nursing, weaning, and spontaneous and induced abortion. I do not deny, of course, that all of these have been constructed and culturally valued in diverse ways. But does that diversity utterly invalidate any abstraction of significant points of general contrast between female and male bodily realities? The question, it seems to me, is to be approached through concrete exploration, not decided by theoretical fiat.

References

Chodorow, Nancy. 1978. *The Reproduction of Mothering.* Berkeley: University of California Press.

Cornell, Drucilla, and Adam Thurschwell. 1987. "Feminism, Negativity, Intersubjectivity." In *Feminism as Critique,* ed. Seyla Benhabib and Drucilla Cornell, 143–62. Minneapolis: University of Minnesota Press.

Derrida, Jacques, and Christie V. McDonald. 1982. "Choreographies." *Diacritics* 12 (2): 66–76.

Gilligan, Carol. 1982. *In A Different Voice*. Cambridge: Harvard University Press.
Grimshaw, Jean. 1986. *Philosophy and Feminist Thinking*. Minneapolis: University of Minnesota Press.
Haraway, Donna. 1989. "A Manifesto for Cyborgs: Science, Technology, and Socialist Feminism in the 1980s," in Linda Nicholson, ed., *Feminism/Postmodernism*, 190–233. New York: Routledge, 1990.
Suleiman, Susan. 1986. "(Re)Writing the Body: The Politics and Poetics of Female Eroticism." In *The Female Body in Western Culture*, ed. Susan Suleiman, 7–29. Cambridge: Harvard University Press.

PART V

Ethics and Difference: Care/Justice and Partiality/Impartiality

SELECTION 27
FROM
Noncontractual Society: A Feminist View

VIRGINIA HELD

CONTEMPORARY SOCIETY IS IN the grip of contractual thinking. Realities are interpreted in contractual terms, and goals are formulated in terms of rational contracts. The leading current conceptions of rationality begin with assumptions that human beings are independent, self-interested or mutually disinterested, individuals; they then typically argue that it is often rational for human beings to enter into contractual relationships with each other.

On the side of description, assumptions characteristic of a contractual view of human relations underlie the dominant attempts to view social realities through the lenses of the social sciences.[1] They also underlie the principles upon which most persons in contemporary Western society claim their most powerful institutions to be founded. We are told that modern democratic states rest on a social contract,[2] that their economies should be thought of as a free market where producers and consumers, employers and employees make contractual agreements.[3] And we should even, it is suggested, interpret our culture as a free market of ideas.[4]

On the side of prescription, leading theories of justice and equality, such as those of Rawls, Nozick, and Dworkin, suggest what social arrangements should be like to more fully reflect the requirements of contractual rationality.[5] And various philosophers claim that even morality itself is best understood in contractual terms.[6] . . .

When subjected to examination, the assumptions and conceptions of contractual thinking seem highly questionable. As descriptions of reality they can be seriously misleading. Actual societies are the results of war, exploitation, racism, and patriarchy far more than of social contracts. Economic and political realities are the outcomes of economic strength triumphing over economic weakness more than of a free market. And rather than a

261

free market of ideas, we have a culture in which the loudspeakers that are the mass media drown out the soft voices of free expression. As expressions of normative concern, moreover, contractual theories hold out an impoverished view of human aspiration.

To see contractual relations between self-interested or mutually disinterested individuals as constituting a paradigm of human relations is to take a certain historically specific conception of "economic man" as representative of humanity. And it is, many feminists are beginning to agree, to overlook or to discount in very fundamental ways the experience of women.

I shall try in this paper to look at society from a thoroughly different point of view than that of economic man. I shall take the point of view of women, and especially of mothers, as the basis for trying to rethink society and its possible goals. Certainly there is no single point of view of women; the perspectives of women are potentially as diverse as those of men. But since the perspectives of women have all been to a large extent discounted, across the spectrum, I shall not try to deal here with diversity among such views, but rather to give voice to one possible feminist outlook.

The social contract tradition and bourgeois conceptions of rationality have already been criticized for some time from Marxian and other continental perspectives. These perspectives, however, usually leave out the perspective of mothers as fully as do those they criticize, so I shall not try to deal here with these alternatives either. I shall try instead to imagine what society would look like, for both descriptive and prescriptive purposes, if we replaced the paradigm of "economic man" and substituted for it the paradigm of mother and child. I shall try to explore how society and our goals for it might appear if, instead of thinking of human relations as contractual, we thought of them as *like* relations between mothers and children. What would social relations look like? What would society look like if we would take the relation between mother and child as not just one relation among many, but as the *primary* social relation? And what sorts of aspirations might we have for such a society? . . .

Since it is the practice of mothering with which I shall be concerned in what follows, rather than with women in the biological sense, I shall use the term "mothering person" rather than "mother." A "mothering person" can be male or female. So I shall speak of "mothering persons" in the same gender-neutral way that various writers now try to speak of "rational contractors." If men feel uncomfortable being referred to as, or even more so in being, "mothering persons," this may possibly mirror the discomfort many mothers feel adapting to the norms and practices, and language, of "economic man."

It is important to emphasize that I shall look at the practice of mothering not as it has in fact existed in any patriarchal society, but in terms of what the characteristic features of this practice would be without patriarchal domination. In method this may be comparable to what has been done in developing a concept of rational contracting. This concept of course developed while large segments of society were in fact still feudal, and of course actual human beings are not in fact fully rational. These realities have not prevented the contractual relation from being taken as paradigmatic. . . .

WOMEN AND FAMILY

In the writings of Rousseau, moral principles were to be applied to men and to women in ways thoroughly inconsistent with each other. Rousseau argued that in the polity no man should surrender his freedom. He thought that government could be based on a social contract in which citizens under law will be as free as in the state of nature because they will give the law to themselves.[7] But, he argued, within the household, the man must rule and the woman must submit to this rule.[8] Rousseau maintained that women must be trained from the beginning to serve and to submit to men. Since the essence of being fully human was for Rousseau being free from submission to the will of another, women were to be denied the essential condition for being fully human. And he thought that if women were accorded equality with men in the household (which was the only domain to be open to them) this would bring about the dissolution of society. Human society, Rousseau thought, was incompatible with extending the principles of contractual society to women and the family. . . .

One way in which the dominant patterns of thought have managed to overlook such inconsistencies has been to see women as primarily mothers, and mothering as a primarily biological function. Then it has been supposed that while contracting is a specifically human activity, women are engaged in an activity which is not specifically human. Women have accordingly been thought to be closer to nature than men, to be enmeshed in a biological function involving processes more like those in which other animals are involved than like the rational contracting of distinctively human "economic man." The total or relative exclusion of women from the domain of voluntary contracting has then been thought to be either inevitable or appropriate.

The view that women are more governed by biology than are men is still prevalent. It is as questionable as many other traditional misinterpretations of women's experience. Human mothering is an extremely different activity from the mothering engaged in by other animals. It is as different from the mothering of other animals as is the work and speech of men different from the "work" and "speech" of other animals. Since humans are also animals, one should not exaggerate the differences between humans and other animals. But to whatever extent it is appropriate to recognize a difference between "man" and other animals, so would it be appropriate to recognize a comparable difference between human mothering and the mothering of other animals.

Human mothering shapes language and culture, and forms human social personhood. Human mothering develops morality, it does not merely transmit techniques of survival; impressive as the latter can be, they do not have built into them the aims of morality. Human mothering teaches consideration for others based on moral concern; it does not merely follow and bring the child to follow instinctive tendency. Human mothering creates autonomous persons; it does not merely propagate a species. It can be fully as creative an activity as most other human activities; to create *new* persons, and new types of *persons*, is surely as creative as to make new objects, products, or institutions. Human mothering is no more "natural" than any other human activity. It may include many dull and repetitive tasks, as does farming, industrial production, banking, and work in a laboratory. But degree of dullness has nothing to do with degree of "naturalness." In sum, human mothering is as different from animal mothering as humans are from animals.

On a variety of grounds there are good reasons to have mothering become an activity performed by men as well as by women.[9] We may wish to continue to use the term "mothering" to designate the activity, in recognition of the fact that it has been overwhelmingly women who have engaged in this activity,[10] and because for the foreseeable future it is the point of view of women, including women engaged in mothering, which should be called on to provide a contrast with the point of view of men. A time may come when a term such as "the nurturing of children" would be preferable to "mothering."[11] . . .

THE MOTHER/CHILD RELATION

Let us examine in more detail the relation between mothering person and child. A first aspect of the relation that we can note is the extent to which it is not voluntary and, for this reason among others, not contractual. The ties that bind mothering person and child are affectional and solicitous on the one hand, and emotional and dependent on the other. The degree to which bearing and caring for children has been voluntary for most mothers throughout most of history has been extremely limited; it is still quite limited for most mothering persons. The relation *should* be voluntary for the mothering person but it cannot possibly be voluntary for the young child, and it can only become, gradually, slightly more voluntary.

A woman can have decided voluntarily to have a child, but once that decision has been made, she will never again be unaffected by the fact that she has brought this particular child into existence. And even if the decision to have a child is voluntary, the decision to have this particular child, for either parent, cannot be. Technological developments can continue to reduce the uncertainties of childbirth, but unpredictable aspects are likely to remain great for most parents. Unlike that contract where buyer and seller can know what is being exchanged, and which is void if the participants cannot know what they are agreeing to, a parent cannot know what a particular child will be like. And children are totally unable to choose their parents and, for many years, any of their caretakers.

The recognition of how limited are the aspects of voluntariness in the relation between mothering person and child may help us to gain a closer approximation to reality in our understanding of most human relations, especially at a global level, than we can gain from imagining the purely voluntary trades entered into by rational economic contractors to be characteristic of human relations in other domains.

Society may impose certain reciprocal obligations: on parents to care for children when the children are young, and on children to care for parents when the parents are old. But if there is any element of a bargain in the relation between mothering person and child, it is very different from the bargain supposedly characteristic of the marketplace. If a parent thinks "I'll take care of you now so you'll take care of me when I'm old," it must be based, unlike the contracts of political and economic bargains, on enormous trust and on a virtual absence of enforcement.[12] And few mothering persons have any such exchange in mind when they engage in the activities of mothering. At least the bargain would only be resorted to when the callousness or poverty of the society made the plight of the old person desperate. This is demonstrated in survey after survey; old persons certainly hope not to have to be a burden on their children.[13] And they prefer social arrangements that will allow them to refuse to cash in on any such bargain. So the intention and goal of mothering is to give of one's care without obtaining a return of a self-interested kind. The emotional satisfaction of a mothering person is a satisfaction in the well-being and happiness of another human being, and a satisfaction in the health of the relation between the two persons, not the gain that results from an egoistic bargain. The motive behind the activity of mothering is thus entirely different from that behind a market transaction. And so is, perhaps even more clearly, the motive behind the child's project of growth and development.

A second aspect of the contrast between market relations and relations between mothering person and child is found in the qualities of permanence and nonreplaceability. The market makes of everything, even human labor and artistic expression and sexual desire, a commodity to be bought and sold, with one unit of economic value replaceable by any other of equivalent value. To the extent that political life reflects these aspects of the market, politicians are replaceable and political influence is bought and sold. Though rights may be thought of as outside the economic market, in contractual thinking they are seen as inside the wider market of the social contract, and can be traded against each other. But the ties between parents and children are permanent ties, however strained or slack they become at times. And no person within a family should be a commodity to any other. Although various persons may participate in mothering a given child, and a given person may mother many children, still no child and no mothering person is to the other a merely replaceable commodity. The extent to which more of our attitudes, for instance toward our society's cultural productions, should be thought of in these terms rather than in the terms of the marketplace, should be considered.

A third aspect of the relation between mothering person and child that may be of interest is the insight it provides for our notions of equality. It shows us unmistakably that equality is not equivalent to having equal legal rights. All feminists are committed to equality and to equal rights in contexts where rights are what are appropriately at issue. But in many contexts, concerns other than rights are more salient and appropriate. And the equality that is at issue in the relation between mothering person and child is the equal consideration of persons, not a legal or contractual notion of equal rights. . . .

A fourth important feature of the relation between mothering person and child is that we obviously do not fulfil our obligations by merely leaving people alone. If one leaves an infant alone he will starve. If one leaves a two-year-old alone she will rapidly harm herself. The whole tradition that sees respecting others as constituted by noninterference with them is most effectively shown up as inadequate. It assumes that people can fend for themselves and provide through their own initiatives and efforts what they need. This Robinson Crusoe image of "economic man" is false for almost everyone, but it is totally and obviously false in the case of infants and children, and recognizing this can be salutary. It can lead us to see very vividly how unsatisfactory are those prevalent political views according to which we fulfil our obligations merely by refraining from interference. We ought to acknowledge that our fellow citizens, and fellow inhabitants of the globe, have moral rights to what they need to live—to the food, shelter, and medical care that are the necessary conditions of living and growing— and that when the resources exist for honoring such rights there are few excuses for not doing so. Such rights are not rights to be left to starve unimpeded. Seeing how unsatisfactory rights merely to be left alone are as an interpretation of the rights of children may help us to recognize a similar truth about other persons. And the arguments—though appropriately in a different form—can be repeated for interests as distinct from rights.[14]

A fifth interesting feature of the relation between mothering person and child is the very different view it provides of privacy. We come to see that to be in a position where others are *not* making demands on us is a rare luxury, not a normal state. To be a mothering person is to be subjected to the continual demands and needs of others. And to be a child is to be subjected to the continual demands and expectations of others. Both mothering persons and children need to extricate themselves from the thick and heavy social fabric in which they are entwined in order to enjoy any pockets of privacy at all.

Here the picture we form of our individuality and the concept we form of a "self" is entirely different from the one we get if we start with the self-sufficient individual of the "state of nature." If we begin with the picture of rational contractor entering into agreements with others, the "natural" condition is seen as one of individuality and privacy, and the problem is the building of society and government. From the point of view of the relation between mothering person and child, on the other hand, the problem is the reverse. The starting condition is an enveloping tie, and the problem is individuating oneself. The task is to carve out a gradually increasing measure of privacy in ways appropriate to a constantly shifting interdependency. For the child, the problem is to become gradually more independent. For the mothering person, the problem is to free oneself from an all-consuming involvement. For both, the progression is from society to greater individuality rather than from self-sufficient individuality to contractual ties. . . .

A sixth aspect of the relation between mothering person and child which is noteworthy is the very different view of power it provides. We are accustomed to thinking of power as something that can be wielded by one person over another, as a means by which one person can bend another to his will. An ideal has been to equalize power so that agreements can be forged and conflicts defused. But consider now the very different view of power in the relation between mothering person and child. The superior power of the mothering person over the child is relatively useless for most of what the mothering person aims to achieve in bringing up the child. The mothering person seeks to *empower* the child to act responsibly; she neither wants to "wield" power nor to defend herself against the power "wielded" by the child. The relative powerlessness of the child is largely irrelevant to most of the project of growing up. When the child is physically weakest, as in infancy and illness, the child can "command" the greatest amount of attention and care from the mothering person because of the seriousness of the child's needs.

The mothering person's stance is characteristically one of caring, of being vulnerable to the needs and pains of the child, and of fearing the loss of the child before the child is ready for independence. It is not characteristically a stance of domination. The child's project is one of developing, of gaining ever greater control over his or her own life, of relying on the mothering person rather than of submitting to superior strength. Of course the relation may in a degenerate form be one of domination and submission, but this only indicates that the relation is not what it should be. . . .

MOTHERING AND MORAL THEORY

A final aspect of the relation between mothering person and child about which I would like to speculate is what a focus on this relation might imply for our views of morality itself, and of ethical theory itself. . . .

Mothering persons are vulnerable to the demands and needs of children. We do not know if this is instinctive or innate, or not. Some claim that women lack a mothering instinct. Others claim that the experiences of carrying a child, of laboring and suffering to give birth, of suckling, inevitably cause mothers to be especially sensitive to the cries and needs of a child. Others claim that fathers, placed in the position of being the only persons capable of responding to the needs of a child, develop similar responsiveness. Whatever the truth, one can admit that no one can become a mothering person without becoming sensitive to the needs of relatively helpless or less powerful others. And to become thus sensitive is to become vulnerable. If the vulnerability is chosen, so much the better. Mothering persons become in this way vulnerable to the claims of morality.

It is not, however, the morality of following abstract, universal rules so much as the morality of being responsive to the needs of actual, particular others in relations with us. The traditional view, reasserted in the psychological studies of Lawrence Kohlberg, that women are less likely than men to be guided by the highest forms of morality, would only be plausible if morality were no more than the abstract and rational rules of pure and perfect principle.[15] For traditional morality, increasingly recognizable as developed from a male point of view, there seems to be either the pure principle of the rational lawgiver, or the self-interest of the individual contractor. There is the unreal universality of *all*, or the real *self* of individual interest.

Both views, however, lose sight of acting *for* particular others in actual contexts. Mothering persons cannot lose sight of the particularity of the child being mothered nor of the actuality of the circumstances in which the activity is taking place. Mothering persons may tend to resist harming or sacrificing those particular others for the sake of abstract principles or total faith; on the other hand, it is for the sake of *others*, or for the sake of relationships between persons, rather than to further their own interests, that such resistance is presented by mothering persons. Morality, for mothering persons, must guide us in our relations with actual, particular children, enabling them to develop their own lives and commitments. For mothering persons, morality can never seem adequate if it offers no more than ideal rules for hypothetical situations: Morality must connect with the actual context of real, particular others in need. At the same time, morality, for mothering persons, cannot possibly be a mere bargain between rational contractors. That morality in this context could not be based on self-interest or mutual disinterest directly is obvious; that a contractual escape is unavailable or inappropriate is clear enough. . . .

MODELS FOR SOCIETY

In an earlier paper called "Marx, Sex, and the Transformation of Society,"[16] I looked at the relation between man and woman, if it could be transformed by love into a relation of mutual concern and respect, as a possible model for transformed relations in the wider society. It now seems to me that the relation between man and woman, especially as transformed in the way I suggested, is more special and more limited, as well as far more distant and uncertain, than the relation between mothering person and child. The latter relation seems especially worth exploring to see what implications and insights it might suggest for a transformed society.

There are good reasons to believe that a society resting on no more than bargains between self-interested or mutually disinterested individuals will not be able to withstand the forces of egoism and dissolution pulling such societies apart. Although there may be some limited domains in which rational contracts are the appropriate form of social relations, as a foundation for the fundamental ties which ought to bind human beings together, they are clearly inadequate. Perhaps we can learn from a nonpatriarchal household better than from further searching in the marketplace what the sources might be for justifiable trust, cooperation, and caring. . . .

If the dynamic relation between mothering person and child is taken as the primary social relation, then it is the model of "economic man" that can be seen to be deficient as a model for society and morality, and unsuitable for all but a special context. A domain such as law, if built on no more than contractual foundations, can then be recognized as one limited domain among others; law protects some moral rights when people are too immoral or weak to respect them without the force of law. But it is hardly a majestic edifice that can serve as a model for morality. Neither can the domain of politics, if built on no more than self-interest or mutual disinterest, provide us with a model with which to understand and improve society and morality. And neither, even more clearly, can the market itself.

When we explore the implications of these speculations we may come to realize that instead of seeing the family as an anomalous island in a sea of rational contracts composing economic and political and social life, perhaps it is instead "economic man" who belongs on a relatively small island surrounded by social ties of a less hostile, cold, and precarious kind.

Notes

1. As Carole Pateman writes, "One of the most striking features of the past two decades is the extent to which the assumptions of liberal individualism have permeated the whole of social life." Carole Pateman, *The Problem of Political Obligation: A Critique of Liberal Theory* (Berkeley: University of California Press, 1985), 182–83. All those fields influenced by rational choice theory—and that includes most of the social sciences—thus "hark back to classical liberal contract doctrines," Pateman writes, "and claims that social order is founded on the interactions of self-interested, utility-maximizing individuals, protecting and enlarging their property in the capitalist market" (183).

2. E.g., Thomas Hobbes, *Leviathan*, ed. C. B. Macpherson (Baltimore: Penguin, 1971); John Locke, *Two Treatises of Government*, ed. Peter Laslett (New York: Mentor, 1965); Jean-Jacques Rousseau, *The Social Contract*, ed. Charles Frankel (New York: Hafner, 1947); The U. S. Declaration of Independence; and of course a literature too vast to mention. As Carole Pateman writes of this tradition, "a corollary of the liberal view . . . is that social contract theory is central to liberalism. Paradigmatically, contract is the act through which two free and equal individuals create social bonds, or a collection of such individuals creates the state" (180).

3. E.g., Adam Smith, *The Wealth of Nations*, ed. M. Lerner (New York: Random House, 1937) and virtually the whole of classical and neoclassical economics.

4. The phrase has been entrenched in judicial and social discussion since Oliver Wendell Holmes used it in *Abrams v. United States* (250 U.S. 616, 630 [1919]).

5. E.g., John Rawls, *A Theory of Justice* (Cambridge: Harvard University Press, 1971); Robert Nozick, *Anarchy, State, and Utopia* (New York: Basic Books, 1974); and Ronald Dworkin, *Taking Rights Seriously* (Cambridge: Harvard University Press, 1977).

6. E.g., David A. J. Richards, *A Theory of Reasons for Action* (New York: Oxford University Press, 1971); and David Gauthier, *Morals by Agreement* (New York: Oxford University Press, 1986).

7. J.-J. Rousseau, *The Social Contract*.

8. J.-J. Rousseau, *Emile*, tr. B. Foxley (New York: Dutton, 1911).

9. See especially Nancy Chodorow, *The Reproduction of Mothering: Psychoanalysis and the Sociology of Gender* (Berkeley: University of California Press, 1978); and Joyce Trebilcot, ed., *Mothering: Essays in Feminist Theory* (Totowa, NJ: Rowman and Allanheld, 1984).

10. See, e.g., Susan Peterson, "Against 'Parenting,'" in Trebilcot, *Mothering*.

11. By then "parenting" might also be acceptable to those who find it presently misleading.

12. In some societies, social pressures to conform with the norms of reciprocal care—of children by parents and later of parents by children—can be very great. But these societies are usually of a kind which are thought to be at a stage of development antecedent to that of contractual society.

13. The gerontologist Elaine Brody says about old people that "what we hear over and over again—and I'm talking gross numbers of 80 to 90 percent in survey after survey—is 'I don't want to be a burden on my children.'" Interview by Lindsy Van Gelder, *Ms.* magazine, Jan. 1986, 48.

14. See Virginia Held, *Rights and Goods* (New York: Free Press, 1984).

15. For examples of the view that women are more deficient than men in

understanding morality and acting morally, see, e.g., Mary Mahowald, ed., *Philosophy of Woman: Classical to Current Concepts* (Indianapolis: Hackett, 1978). See also Lawrence Kohlberg, *The Philosophy of Moral Development* (San Francisco: Harper and Row, 1981), and L. Kohlberg and R. Kramer, "Continuities and Discontinuities in Child and Adult Moral Development," *Human Development* 12 (1969): 93–120.

16. Virginia Held, "Marx, Sex, and the Transformation of Society," *Philosophical Forum* 5, nos. 1–2 (Fall–Winter 1973–74).

SELECTION 28
FROM
Moral Orientation and Moral Development

CAROL GILLIGAN

THE DISTINCTION BETWEEN JUSTICE and care as alternative perspectives or moral orientations is based empirically on the observation that a shift in the focus of attention from concerns about justice to concerns about care changes the definition of what constitutes a moral problem, and leads the same situation to be seen in different ways. Theoretically, the distinction between justice and care cuts across the familiar divisions between thinking and feeling, egoism and altruism, theoretical and practical reasoning. It calls attention to the fact that all human relationships, public and private, can be characterized *both* in terms of equality and in terms of attachment, and that both inequality and detachment constitute grounds for moral concern. Since everyone is vulnerable both to oppression and to abandonment, two moral visions—one of justice and one of care—recur in human experience. The moral injunctions, not to act unfairly toward others, and not to turn away from someone in need, capture these different concerns.

The conception of the moral domain as comprised of at least two moral orientations raises new questions about observed differences in moral judgment and the disagreements to which they give rise. Key to this revision is the distinction between differences in developmental stage (more or less adequate positions within a single orientation) and differences in orientation (alternative perspectives or frameworks). The findings reported in this paper of an association between moral orientation and gender speak directly to the continuing controversy over sex differences in moral reasoning. In doing so, however, they also offer an empirical explanation for why previous thinking about moral development has been organized largely within the justice framework.

My research on moral orientation derives from an observation made in the course of studying the relationship between moral judgment and action.

272

Two studies, one of college students describing their experiences of moral conflict and choice, and one of pregnant women who were considering abortion, shifted the focus of attention from the ways people reason about hypothetical dilemmas to the ways people construct moral conflicts and choices in their lives. This change in approach made it possible to see what experiences people define in moral terms, and to explore the relationship between the understanding of moral problems and the reasoning strategies used and the actions taken in attempting to resolve them. In this context, I observed that women, especially when speaking about their own experiences of moral conflict and choice, often define moral problems in a way that eludes the categories of moral theory and is at odds with the assumptions that shape psychological thinking about morality and about the self.[1] This discovery, that a different voice often guides the moral judgments and the actions of women, called attention to a major design problem in previous moral judgment research: namely, the use of all-male samples as the empirical basis for theory construction.

The selection of an all-male sample as the basis for generalizations that are applied to both males and females is logically inconsistent. As a research strategy, the decision to begin with a single-sex sample is inherently problematic, since the categories of analysis will tend to be defined on the basis of the initial data gathered and subsequent studies will tend to be restricted to these categories. Piaget's work on the moral judgment of the child illustrates these problems since he defined the evolution of children's consciousness and practice of rules on the basis of his study of boys playing marbles, and then undertook a study of girls to assess the generality of his findings. Observing a series of differences both in the structure of girls' games and "in the actual mentality of little girls," he deemed these differences not of interest because "it was not this contrast which we proposed to study." Girls, Piaget found, "rather complicated our interrogatory in relation to what we know about boys," since the changes in their conception of rules, although following the same sequence observed in boys, did not stand in the same relation to social experience. Nevertheless, he concluded that "in spite of these differences in the structure of the game and apparently in the players' mentality, we find the same process at work as in the evolution of the game of marbles."[2]

Thus, girls were of interest insofar as they were similar to boys and confirmed the generality of Piaget's findings. The differences noted, which included a greater tolerance, a greater tendency toward innovation in solving conflicts, a greater willingness to make exceptions to rules, and a lesser concern with legal elaboration, were not seen as germane to "the psychology of rules," and therefore were regarded as insignificant for the study of children's moral judgment. Given the confusion that currently surrounds the discussion of sex differences in moral judgment, it is important to emphasize that the differences observed by Piaget did not pertain to girls' understanding of rules per se or to the development of the idea of justice in their thinking, but rather to the way girls structured their games and their approach to conflict resolution—that is, to their use rather than their understanding of the logic of rules and justice.

Kohlberg, in his research on moral development, did not encounter these problems since he equated moral development with the development of justice reasoning and initially used an all-male sample as the basis for theory and test construction. In response to his critics, Kohlberg has recently modified his claims, renaming his test a measure of "justice reasoning" rather than of "moral maturity" and acknowledging the presence of a care perspective in people's moral thinking.[3] But the widespread use of Kohlberg's measure as a measure of moral development together with his own continuing tendency to equate justice reasoning with moral judgment leaves the problem of orientation differences unsolved. More specifically, Kohlberg's efforts to assimilate thinking about care to the six-stage developmental sequence he derived and refined by analyzing changes in justice reasoning (relying centrally on his all-male longitudinal sample), underscores the continuing importance of the points raised in this paper concerning (1) the distinction between differences in developmental stage within a single orientation and differences in orientation, and (2) the fact that the moral thinking of girls and women was not examined in establishing either the meaning or the measurement of moral judgment within contemporary psychology.

An analysis of the language and logic of men's and women's moral reasoning about a range of hypothetical and real dilemmas underlies the distinction elaborated in this paper between a justice and a care perspective. The empirical association of care reasoning with women suggests that discrepancies observed between moral theory and the moral judgments of girls and women may reflect a shift in perspective, a change in moral orientation. Like the figure-ground shift in ambiguous figure perception, justice and care as moral perspectives are not opposites or mirror images of one another, with justice uncaring and care unjust. Instead, these perspectives denote different ways of organizing the basic elements of moral judgment: self, others, and the relationship between them. With the shift in perspective from justice to care, the organizing dimension of relationship changes from inequality/equality to attachment/detachment, reorganizing thoughts, feelings, and language so that words connoting relationship like "dependence" or "responsibility" or even moral terms such as "fairness" and "care" take on different meanings. To organize relationships in terms of attachment rather than in terms of equality changes the way human connection is imagined, so that the images or metaphors of relationship shift from hierarchy or balance to network or web. In addition, each organizing framework leads to a different way of imagining the self as a moral agent.

From a justice perspective, the self as moral agent stands as the figure against a ground of social relationships, judging the conflicting claims of self and others against a standard of equality or equal respect (the Categorical Imperative, the Golden Rule). From a care perspective, the relationship becomes the figure, defining self and others. Within the context of relationship, the self as a moral agent perceives and responds to the perception of need. The shift in moral perspective is manifest by a change in the moral question from "What is just?" to "How to respond?" . . .

The language of the public abortion debate, for example, reveals a justice perspective. Whether the abortion dilemma is cast as a conflict of rights or in terms of respect for human life, the claims of the fetus and of the pregnant woman are balanced or placed in opposition. The morality of abortion decisions thus construed hinges on the scholastic or metaphysical question as to whether the fetus is a life or a person, and whether its claims take precedence over those of the pregnant woman. Framed as a problem of care, the dilemma posed by abortion shifts. The connection between the fetus and the pregnant woman becomes the focus of attention and the question becomes whether it is responsible or irresponsible, caring or careless, to extend or to end this connection. In this construction, the abortion dilemma arises because there is no way not to act, and no way of acting that does not alter the connection between self and others. To ask what actions constitute care or are more caring directs attention to the parameters of connection and the costs of detachment, which become subjects of moral concern.

Finally, two medical students, each reporting a decision not to turn in someone who has violated the school rules against drinking, cast their decision in different terms. One student constructs the decision as an act of mercy, a decision to override justice in light of the fact that the violator has shown "the proper degrees of contrition." In addition, this student raises the question as to whether or not the alcohol policy is just, i.e., whether the school has the right to prohibit drinking. The other student explains the decision not to turn in a proctor who was drinking on the basis that turning him in is not a good way to respond to this problem, since it would dissolve the relationship between them and thus cut off an avenue for help. In addition, this student raises the question as to whether the proctor sees his drinking as a problem.

·This example points to an important distinction, between care as understood or construed within a justice framework and care as a framework or a perspective on moral decision. Within a justice construction, care becomes the mercy that tempers justice; or connotes the special obligations or supererogatory duties that arise in personal relationships; or signifies altruism freely chosen—a decision to modulate the strict demands of justice by considering equity or showing forgiveness; or characterizes a choice to sacrifice the claims of the self. All of these interpretations of care leave the basic assumptions of a justice framework intact: the division between the self and others, the logic of reciprocity or equal respect.

As a moral perspective, care is less well elaborated and there is no ready vocabulary in moral theory to describe its terms. As a framework for moral decision, care is grounded in the assumption that self and other are interdependent, an assumption reflected in a view of action as responsive and, therefore, as arising in relationship rather than the view of action as emanating from within the self and, therefore, "self-governed." Seen as responsive, the self is by definition connected to others, responding to perceptions, interpreting events, and governed by the organizing tendencies of human interaction and human language. Within this framework, detachment, whether from self or from others, is morally problematic, since it breeds moral blindness or indifference—a failure to discern or respond to need. The question of what responses constitute care and what responses lead to hurt draws attention to the fact that one's own terms may differ from those of others. Justice in this context becomes understood as respect for people in their own terms. . . .

These examples are intended to illustrate two crosscutting perspectives that do not negate one another but focus attention on different dimensions of the situation, creating a sense of ambiguity around the question of what is the problem to be solved. Systematic research on moral orientation as a dimension of moral judgment and action initially addressed three questions: (1) Do people articulate concerns about justice and concerns about care in discussing a moral dilemma? (2) Do people tend to focus their attention on one set of concerns and minimally represent the other? and (3) Is there an association between moral orientation and gender? Evidence from studies that included a common set of questions about actual experiences of moral conflict and matched samples of males and females provides affirmative answers to all three questions.

When asked to describe a moral conflict they had faced, fifty-five out of eighty (69 percent) educationally advantaged North American adolescents and adults raised considerations of both justice and care. Two-thirds (fifty-four out of eighty) however, focused their attention on one set of concerns, with focus defined as 75 percent or more of the considerations raised pertaining either to justice or to care. Thus the person who presented, say, two care considerations in discussing a moral conflict was more likely to give a third, fourth, and fifth than to balance care and justice concerns—a finding consonant with the assumption that justice and care constitute organizing frameworks for moral decision. The men and the women involved in this study (high school students, college students, medical students, and adult professionals) were equally likely to demonstrate the focus phenomenon (two-thirds of both sexes fell into the outlying focus categories). There were, however, sex differences in the direction of focus. With one exception, all of the men who focused, focused on justice. The women divided, with roughly one-third focusing on justice and one-third on care.[4]

These findings clarify the different voice phenomenon and its implications for moral theory and for women. First, it is notable that if women were eliminated from the research sample, care focus in moral reasoning would virtually disappear. Although care focus was by no means characteristic of all women, it was almost exclusively a female phenomenon in this sample of educationally advantaged North Americans. Second, the fact that the women were advantaged means that the focus on care cannot readily be attributed to educational deficit or occupational disadvantage—the explanation Kohlberg and others have given for findings of lower levels of justice reasoning in women.[5] Instead, the focus on care in women's moral reasoning draws attention to the limitations of a justice-focused moral theory and highlights the presence of care concerns in the moral thinking of both women and men. In this light, the care/justice group composed of one-third of the women and one-third of the men becomes of particular interest, pointing to the need for further research that attends to the way people organize justice and care in relation to one another—whether, for example, people alternate perspectives, like seeing the rabbit and the duck in the rabbit-duck figure, or integrate the two perspectives in a way that resolves or sustains ambiguity.

Third, if the moral domain is comprised of at least two moral orientations, the focus phenomenon suggests that people have a tendency to lose sight of one moral perspective in arriving at moral decision—a liability equally shared by both sexes. The present findings further suggest that men and women tend to lose sight of different perspectives. The most striking result is the virtual absence of care-focus reasoning among the men. Since the men raised concerns about care in discussing moral conflicts and thus presented care concerns as morally relevant, a question is why they did not elaborate these concerns to a greater extent.

In summary, it becomes clear why attention to women's moral thinking led to the identification of a different voice and raised questions about the place of justice and care within a comprehensive moral theory. It also is clear how the selection of an all-male sample for research on moral judgment fosters an equation of morality with justice, providing little data discrepant with this view. In the present study, data discrepant with a justice-focused moral theory comes from a third of the women. Previously, such women were seen as having a problem understanding "morality." Yet these women may also be seen as exposing the problem in a justice-focused moral theory.

This may explain the decision of researchers to exclude girls and women at the initial stage of moral judgment research. If one begins with the premise that "all morality consists in respect for rules,"[6] or "virtue is one and its name is justice,"[7] then women are likely to appear problematic within moral theory. If one begins with women's moral judgments, the problem becomes how to construct a theory that encompasses care as a focus of moral attention rather than as a subsidiary moral concern. . . .

Kay Johnston suggests that one way of explaining her findings that boys and girls at eleven and fifteen tend to use and prefer different orientations when solving the same moral problems joins Vygotsky's theory of cognitive development with Chodorow's analysis of sex differences in early childhood experiences of relationship.[8] Vygotsky posits that all of the higher cognitive functions originate as actual relations between individuals. Justice and care as moral ideas and as reasoning strategies thus would originate as relationships with others—an idea consonant with the derivation of justice and care reasoning from experiences of inequality and attachment in early childhood. All children are born into a situation of inequality in that they are less capable than the adults and older children around them and, in this sense, more helpless and less powerful. In addition, no child survives in the absence of some kind of adult attachment—or care, and through this experience of relationship children discover the responsiveness of human connection including their ability to move and affect one another.

Through the experience of inequality, of being in the less powerful position, children learn what it means to depend on the authority and the goodwill of others. As a result, they tend to strive for equality of greater power, and for freedom. Through the experience of attachment, children discover the ways in which people are able to care for and to hurt one another. The child's vulnerability to oppression and to abandonment thus can be seen to lay the groundwork for the moral visions of justice and care conceived as ideals of human relationship and defining the ways in which people "should" act toward one another.

Chodorow's work then provides a way of explaining why care concerns tend to be minimally represented by men and why such concerns are less frequently elaborated in moral theory. Chodorow joins the dynamics of gender identity formation (the identification of oneself as male or female) to an analysis of early childhood relationships and examines the effects of maternal child care on the inner structuring of self in relation to others. Further, she differentiates a positional sense of self from a personal sense of self, contrasting a self defined in terms of role or position from a self known through the experience of connection. Her point is that maternal child care fosters the continuation of a relational sense of self in girls, since female gender identity is consonant with feeling connected with one's mother. For boys, gender identity is in tension with mother-child connection, unless that connection is structured in terms of sexual opposition (e.g., as an Oedipal drama). Thus, although boys experience responsiveness or care in relationships, knowledge of care or the need for care, when associated with mothers, poses a threat to masculine identity.[9]. . .

The equation of human with male was assumed in the Platonic and in the Enlightenment tradition as well as by psychologists who saw all-male samples as "representative" of human experience. The equation of care with self-sacrifice is in some ways more complex. The premise of self-interest assumes a conflict of interest between self and other manifest in the opposition of egoism and altruism. Together, the equations of male with human and of care with self-sacrifice form a circle that has had a powerful hold on moral philosophy and psychology. The conjunction of women and moral theory thus challenges the traditional definition of human and calls for a reconsideration of what is meant by both justice and care.

To trace moral development along two distinct although intersecting dimensions of relationship suggests the possibility of different permutations of justice and care reasoning, different ways these two moral perspectives can be understood and represented in relation to one another. For example, one perspective may overshadow or eclipse the other, so that one is brightly illuminated while the other is dimly remembered, familiar but for the most part forgotten. The way in which one story about relationship obscures another was evident in high school girls' definitions of dependence. These definitions highlighted two meanings—one arising from the opposition between dependence and independence, and one from the opposition of dependence to isolation ("No woman," one student observed, "is an island.") As the word "dependence" connotes the experience of relationship, this shift in the implied opposite of dependence indicates how the valence of relationship changes, when connection with others is experienced as an impediment to autonomy or independence, and when it is experienced as a source of comfort and pleasure, and a protection against isolation. This essential ambivalence of human connection provides a powerful emotional grounding for two moral perspectives, and also may indicate what is at stake in the effort to reduce morality to a single perspective.

It is easy to understand the ascendance of justice reasoning and of justice-focused moral theories in a society where care is associated with personal vulnerability in the form of economic disadvantage. But another way of thinking about the ascendance of justice reasoning and also about sex differences in moral development is suggested in the novel *Masks*, written by Fumiko Enchi, a Japanese woman.[10] The subject is spirit possession, and the novel dramatizes what it means to be possessed by the spirits of others. Writing about the Rokujo lady in the *Tales of Genji*, Enchi's central character notes that her soul alternates uncertainly between lyricism and spirit possession, making no philosophical distinction between the self alone and in relation to others, and is unable to achieve the solace of a religious indifference.[11]

The option of transcendance, of a religious indifference or a philosophical detachment, may be less available to women because women are more likely to be possessed by the spirits and the stories of others. The strength of women's moral perceptions lies in the refusal of detachment and depersonalization, and insistence on making connections that can lead to seeing the person killed in war or living in poverty as someone's son or father or brother or sister, or mother, or daughter, or friend. But the liability of women's development is also underscored by Enchi's novel in the women, possessed by the spirits of others, also are more likely to be caught in a chain of false attachments. If women are at the present time the custodians of a story about human attachment and interdependence, not only within the family but also in the world at large, then questions arise as to how this story can be kept alive and how moral theory can sustain this story. In this sense, the relationship between women and moral theory itself becomes one of interdependence.

By rendering a care perspective more coherent and making its terms explicit, moral theory may facilitate women's ability to speak about their experiences and perceptions and may foster the ability of others to listen and to understand. At the same time, the evidence of care focus in women's moral thinking suggests that the study of women's development may provide a natural history of moral development in which care is ascendant, revealing the ways in which creating and sustaining responsive connection with others becomes or remains a central moral concern. The promise in joining women and moral theory lies in the fact that human survival, in the late twentieth century, may depend less on formal agreement than on human connection.

Notes

1. C. Gilligan, "In a Different Voice: Women's Conceptions of Self and of Morality," *Harvard Educational Review* 47 (1982): 481–517; *In a Different Voice: Psychological Theory and Women's Development* (Cambridge: Harvard University Press, 1977).
2. J. Piaget, *The Moral Judgment of the Child* (New York: Free Press paperback ed., 1965), 76–84.
3. L. Kohlberg, *The Psychology of Moral Development* (San Francisco: Harper and Row, 1984).
4. C. Gilligan and J. Attanucci, *Two Moral Orientations*, unpublished ms., Harvard University, 1986.

5. See Kohlberg, *Psychology of Moral Development*; also L. Walker, "Sex Differences in the Development of Moral Reasoning: A Critical Review of the Literature," *Child Development* 55 (3): 677–91.
6. Piaget, *Moral Judgment of the Child*.
7. Kohlberg, *Psychology of Moral Development*.
8. K. Johnston, "Two Moral Orientations—Two Problem-Solving Strategies: Adolescents' Solutions to Dilemmas in Fables," diss., Harvard University, 1985; L. Vygotsky *Mind in Society* (Cambridge: Harvard University Press, 1978); N. Chodorow, "Family Structure and Feminine Personality," in L. M. Rosaldo and L. Lamphere, eds., *Women Culture, and Society* (Stanford: Stanford University Press, 1974); see also N. Chodorow, *The Reproduction of Mothering: Psychoanalysis and the Sociology of Gender* (Berkeley: University of California Press, 1978).
9. Chodorow, op. cit.
10. F. Enchi, *Masks* (New York: Random House, 1983).
11. Ibid., 54.

SELECTION 29
FROM
Women and Caring: What Can Feminists Learn About Morality from Caring?

JOAN C. TRONTO

TWO TYPES OF CARING: CARING
ABOUT AND CARING FOR

THE LANGUAGE OF CARING appears in many settings in our daily language. Caring includes myriad actors and activities. Doing household tasks is taking care of the house. Doctors, nurses, and others provide medical care. We might ask whether a corporation cares for its workers. Someone might ask, who is taking care of this account? Historians care about the past. Judges care about justice. We usually assume that mothers care for their children, that nurses care for their patients, that teachers care for their students, that social workers care for their clients.

What all of these examples share can be distilled: Caring implies some kind of ongoing responsibility and commitment. This notion accords with the original meaning of "care" in English, where care meant a burden; to care is to assume a burden. When a person or a group cares about something or someone, we presume that they are willing to work, to sacrifice, to spend money, to show emotional concern, and to expend energy toward the object of care. Thus, we can make sense of statements such as: he only cares about making money; she cares for her mother; this society does not care about the homeless. To the challenge, You do not care, one responds by showing some evidence of work, sacrifice, or commitment.

If caring involves a commitment, then caring must have an object. Thus, caring is necessarily relational. We say that we care for or about something or someone. We can distinguish "caring about" from "caring for" based on

282

the objects of caring.[1] Caring about refers to less concrete objects; it is characterized by a more general form of commitment. Caring for implies a specific, particular object that is the focus of caring. The boundaries between caring about and caring for are not so neat as these statements imply. Nonetheless, this distinction is useful in revealing something about the way we think of caring in our society because this distinction fits with the engendered category of caring in our society.

Caring for involves responding to the particular, concrete, physical, spiritual, intellectual, psychic, and emotional needs of others. The self, another person, or a group of others can provide care. For example, I take care of myself, a mother cares for the child, a nurse for hospital patients, the Red Cross for victims of the earthquake. These types of care are unified by growing out of the fact that humans have physical and psychic needs (food, grooming, warmth, comfort, etc.) that require activity to satisfy them. These needs are in part socially determined; they are also met in different societies by different types of social practices.

In our society, the particular structures involving caring for grow especially out of the family; caring professions are often construed as a buttress to, or substitute for, care that can no longer be provided within a family. The family may no longer be intact, as a result of death, divorce, distance. Or the family may not be able to provide help; some caring requires expertise. The family may be or may be seen as the source of the problem—for example, families with patterns of substance abuse, incest, violence. Increasingly, then, care has been provided for by the state or in the market. Americans eat fewer meals at home, hire housekeepers, contract for others to wait in a line for them. In response to this increasingly market-oriented version of caring, some thinkers have pulled back in horror and suggested that caring cannot be provided if it disturbs the integrity of the self-other relationship (Elshtain 1981, 330; Noddings 1984). The result is that in modern market society the illusion of caring is often preserved: Providers of services are expected to feign caring (Hochschild 1983).

Caring is engendered in both market and private life. Women's occupations are the caring occupations, and women do the disproportionate amount of caretaking in the private household. To put the point simply, traditional gender roles in our society imply that men care about but women care for.

Because not all caring is moral, another distinction between caring about and caring for becomes obvious. When we wish to know if "caring about" is a moral activity, we inquire about the nature of the object of the care. To care about justice is a moral activity because justice is a moral concern; to care about one's accumulation of vacation days presumably is not a moral activity.

Caring for takes on moral significance in a different way. When we inquire about caring for, it is not enough to know the object of the care;

presumably we must know something about the context of care, perhaps especially about the relationship between the caregiver and recipient of care. A dirty child is not a moral concern for most people, but we might morally disapprove of such a child's mother, who we might think has failed to meet her duty to care for her child. Note, of course, that such judgments are deeply rooted in social, classist, and cultural assumptions about mother's duties, about standards of cleanliness, and so on. The assignment of the responsibility of caring for someone, something, or some group then might be a moral question. Thus, what typically makes "caring for" perceived as moral is not the activity per se but how that activity reflects upon the assigned social duties of the caretaker and who is doing the assigning. . . .

MORAL DIMENSIONS OF THE ACTIVITY OF CARING FOR OTHERS . . .

ATTENTIVENESS

Caring suggests an alternative moral attitude. From the perspective of caring, what is important is not arriving at the fair decision, understood as how the abstract individual in this situation would want to be treated, but at meeting the needs of particular others or preserving the relationships of care that exist (see Gilligan 1982). In this way, moral theory becomes much more closely connected to the concrete needs of others. How we come to know these needs raises several dimensions of concern for moral theory.

KNOWLEDGE. In order to engage in the practice of caring the nature of knowledge needed to act morally changes. At the most obvious level, the mode of philosophical discussion that starts from a philosopher's introspection is an inappropriate starting place to arrive at caring judgments. In the first instance one needs knowledge about others' needs, knowledge that comes from others.

It is not that contemporary moral theory ignores the needs of others, but in most moral discussion the needs of others are taken to reflect the understood needs of the thinking self if only he or she were in another's situation. In contrast, caring rests on knowledge completely peculiar to the particular person being cared for. Proper action for a nurse, faced with a patient who will not finish a meal, depends upon knowing the patient's medical condition, usual eating habits, and tastes. There is no simple way one can generalize from one's own experience to what another needs.

To provide such knowledge, the caring person must devote much attention to learning what the other person might need. Accounts of caring stress that an important part of the process of caring is attentiveness to the needs of others (see Weil 1951, 72–73; Ruddick 1980, 357–58). To achieve the proper frame of mind in which to care, Noddings stresses the need to be receptive to the needs of others (1984, 24). At the moment when one wishes to care, it is impossible to be preoccupied with the self. This kind of selflessness is a key element of what Noddings calls the crucial moral question in caring, that is, how to meet the other morally.

How radically different the epistemological notion of attentiveness is from contemporary ways of thinking can be illustrated by reexamining the long-standing issue about the relationship of knowledge and interests from this perspective. Liberals commonly assume that no one knows your interests as well as you yourself do (see Mill 1975, 187). Marxists and those inspired by Marx believe that a person's interests arise out of the objective circumstances in which one finds oneself or that one can posit some universal, or nearly universal, human interests, for example, "emancipatory interests" (Marx and Engels 1978; Habermas 1971; Cohen 1978). But from the standpoint of caring, these views are equally incomplete. There is some relationship between what the cared-for thinks he or she wants and his or her true interests and needs, although it may not be a perfect correspondence. A patient in the hospital who refuses to get up may be forced to do so. A child who wishes only to eat junk food may be disappointed by parents' reluctance to meet this wish. Genuine attentiveness would presumably allow the caretaker to see through these pseudoneeds and come to appreciate what the other really needs.

Such a commitment to perceiving the genuine needs of the other, though, is not so easy. Alice Miller suggests that many parents act not so much to meet the needs of their children as to work out unmet needs they continue to carry from when they were children (Miller 1981). If a caretaker has deficient self-knowledge about his or her own needs, then there is no way to guarantee that those needs have been removed in looking to see what the other's needs are. It may be very difficult to achieve the state of attentiveness, requiring first a tremendous self-knowledge so that the caretaker does not simply transform the needs of the other into a projection of the self's own needs.[2]

AUTHORITY AND AUTONOMY

The second area where caring raises fundamental questions opposed to contemporary moral theory is another issue that grows out of caring as providing help to meet the needs of others. Because caring occurs in a situation where one person is helping to meet the concrete needs of another, caring raises questions that cannot be easily accommodated by the starting assumption in most contemporary moral philosophy that we are rational, autonomous actors. Many conditions that we usually associate with caregiving belie this view because society does not consider all people we take care of to be rational and autonomous, either in an abstract moral sense (e.g., children) or in a concrete, physical sense (e.g., a bedridden parent, a disabled person) (see Fisher and Galler 1988). Furthermore, if the caregiver is considered rational and autonomous, then the relationship between the parties is unequal, and relationships of authority and dependency are likely to emerge. As I noted earlier, if the caregiver's needs are themselves met by providing care, then the caregiver might desire to keep the cared-for person dependent. How should caregivers understand their authoritative position in relation to those for whom they care?

However, the image of equal adults who rely upon other equal adults for care, not exchange, once again raises questions about what it means to be rational and autonomous. Two people in an equal relationship of care share an awareness of the concrete complications of caring. To maintain such a relationship will often entail making judgments that, from a more abstract point of view, might seem questionable. Is one wrong if one refuses to move for a better job because of an ongoing situation for caring? Again one is forced to considered what autonomy actually means. . . .

Caring challenges the view that morality starts where rational and autonomous individuals confront each other to work out the rules of moral life. Instead, caring allows us to see autonomy as a problem that people must deal with all the time, in their relations with both equals and those who either help them or depend upon them.

PARTICULARITY

Finally, let us consider how the particularity of caring challenges contemporary moral theory. Most contemporary moral theorists require universal moral judgments, that is, that if it is moral for a person to act in a given way in a given situation then it must be moral for any person so situated to act the same way (Kohlberg 1981).[3] Yet the decision we must make about how much care to provide and to whom cannot be so easily generalized or universalized. It is theoretically possible to spend all of one's time caring for others (see Blum 1976); the real decisions everyone will face then are decisions about both when to provide care and when to stop providing care. Because caring varies with the amount of time and kind of effort that a caring individual can expend as well as with the needs of the ones who need care, it is difficult to imagine that rules could ever be specified allowing us to claim that we had applied universal moral principles.

Consider, for example, a rule: Always give aid to a person whose car is broken down on the highway. Suppose you are a nonmechanical woman alone and the stranger is a male? Always take care of your mother. Suppose she and your children rely on your income to keep the household together and caring for her will cost you your job? Thus, the moral judgments made in offering and providing care are much more complex than any set of rules can take into account. Any rule sufficiently flexible to cover all the complexities would probably have to take a form such as "do all that you can to help someone else." Such a form, though, does not serve as any guide to what morality requires. What may be "too much" care for a child to provide an elderly parent may seem too selfishly skimpy to another. This logical objection about the limits of rule-governed morality is familiar, yet it remains a practical difficulty.

The reason that rule-governed behavior is so often associated with moral life, though, is that if we are bound to follow the rules then we are bound to act impartially, not giving special favors to those nearest us. Another problem with caring from a moral point of view, then, is that we might, because of our caring relationship, provide special treatment to those closest to us and ignore others more deserving of care. . . .

To say that we should only care for those things that come within our immediate purview ignores the ways in which we are responsible for the construction of our narrow sphere. When Noddings says that she will respond with caring to the stranger at her door but not to starving children in Africa, she ignores the ways in which the modern world is intertwined and the ways in which hundreds of prior public and private decisions affect where we find ourselves and which strangers show up at our doors. In an affluent community, where affluence is maintained by such decisions as zoning ordinances, the stranger at the door is less of a threat than in a dense city, where the stranger may wish to do you harm. Perhaps Noddings would have no problem with this point because in the city you do not have to care for strangers at the door. But the question then becomes, who does? Questions about the proximity of people to us are shaped by our collective social decisions. If we decide to isolate ourselves from others, we may reduce our moral burden of caring. Yet if moral life is only understood narrowly in the context of the exhibition of caring, then we can be absolved from these broader responsibilities.

One way to answer this objection is to say that the task of moral theory is to set out what the parameters of caring should be. Such an approach would soon blend into questions of social and political life. For caring to be an ongoing activity, it is necessarily bounded by the activities of daily life because the entire complex of social institutions and structures determines with whom we come into contact on a regular enough basis to establish relationships of care.[4]

If caring is used as an excuse to narrow the scope of our moral activity to be concerned only with those immediately around us, then it does have little to recommend it as a moral theory. But the question of whom we should care for is not left entirely to individuals in our society.

A Feminist Approach to Caring: Caring About What We Care For

In the second section of this essay I explored some ways in which caring challenges contemporary moral theory. In each case, I realized that caring seems to provide a richer account of people's moral lives. Nevertheless, caring seems to suffer a fatal moral flaw if we allow it to be circumscribed by deciding that we shall only care for those closest to us. From this perspective, it is hard to see how caring can remain moral, rather than becoming a way to justify inconsideration of others at the expense of those for whom we care.

To solve this problem I must return to the way in which the activity of caring is situated in contemporary society. I noted at the beginning of this essay that the problem of who should care for whom is rooted in (often questionable) social values, expectations, and institutions. We do not hold everyone (anyone?) individually responsible for the homeless. Similarly, we do not hold just anyone responsible for the appearance of a child, but we do hold her mother (and father?) responsible. Nonetheless, I can make at least one generalization about caring in this society: Men care about; women care for. Thus, by definition the traditional script on caring reenacts the division of male and female worlds into public and private. To raise the question about whether caring for is inevitably too particularistic is thus to return as well to the engendered nature of caring in our society and to a consideration of the difference between a feminist and feminine account of caring. . . .

To think of the social world in terms of caring for others radically differs from our present way of conceiving of it in terms of pursuing our self-interest. Because caring emphasizes concrete connections with others, because it evokes so much of the daily stuff of women's lives, and because it stands as a fundamental critique of abstract and often seemingly irrelevant moral theory, it is worthy of the serious attention of feminist theorists.

Notes

1. Note that my distinction between caring for and caring about differs from the distinction drawn by Meyeroff (1971) and Noddings (1984). Meyeroff wishes to conflate caring for ideas with caring for people. Not only does this parallel mask the traditional gender difference, but, as will become clear later, the kinds of activities involved in caring for other people cannot be easily used in this same sense. Noddings distinguishes caring for from caring about on a dimension that tries to get at the degree of commitment. We care more for what we care for than for what we care about (1984, 86, 112), but Noddings also wishes to claim that we can care for ideas. I believe that the way I have formulated the distinc-

tion reveals more about caring and traditional assumptions of gender difference.
2. Nonetheless, in order for caring to occur, there must be more than good intentions and undistorted communication; the acts of caring must also occur. I believe this point may help to distinguish this approach from (at least early versions of) Habermas's approach. For the criticism that Habermas's work is too intellectualized, see Henning Ottmann (1982, 86).
3. See, among other recent authors who question the dominant Kantian form of morality, Lawrence Blum (1980), Alasdair MacIntyre and Stanley Hauerwas (1983), John Kekes (1984), and Peter Winch (1972).
4. I am indebted here to Berenice Fisher's suggestion that one important element of a theory of care is the specification of the limits of caring.

References

Blum, L. 1980. *Friendship, Altruism, and Morality*. Boston: Routledge and Kegan Paul.
Cohen, G. A. 1978. *Karl Marx's Theory of History: A Defence*. Princeton: Princeton University Press.
Elshtain, J. B. 1981. *Public Man, Private Woman*. Princeton: Princeton University Press.
Fisher, B., and R. Galler. 1988. "Friendship and Fairness: How Disability Affects Friendship Between Women." In *Women with Disabilities: Essays in Psychology, Politics, and Policy*, ed. A. Asch and M. Fine. Philadelphia: Temple University Press.
Gilligan, C. 1982. *In a Different Voice*. Cambridge: Harvard University Press.
Habermas, J. 1971. *Knowledge and Human Interests*. Boston: Beacon Press.
Hochschild, A. 1983. *The Managed Heart: Commercialization of Human Feeling*. Berkeley: University of California Press.
Kekes, J. 1984. "Moral Sensitivity." *Philosophy* 59:3–19.
Kohlberg, L. 1981. "From *Is* to *Ought*: How to Commit the Naturalistic Fallacy and Get Away with It in the Study of Moral Development." In his *The Philosophy of Moral Development: Moral Stages and the Idea of Justice*. Vol. 1 of *Essays in Moral Development*. New York: Harper and Row.
MacIntyre, A., and S. Hauerwas, eds. 1983. *Revisions: Changing Perspectives in Moral Philosophy*. Notre Dame: University of Notre Dame Press.
Marx, K., and F. Engels. 1978. "The German Ideology." In *The Marx-Engels Reader*, ed. R. C. Tucker. 2d ed. New York: Norton.
Meyeroff, M. 1971. *On Caring*. New York: Harper and Row.
Mill, J. S. 1975. "Considerations on Representative Government." In *Three Essays*, ed. R. Wollheim. Oxford University Press.
Miller, A. 1981. *The Drama of the Gifted Child*. New York: Basic Books.
Noddings, N. 1984. *Caring: A Feminine Approach to Ethics*. Berkeley: University of California Press.
Ottmann, H. 1982. "Cognitive Interests and Self-Reflection." In *Habermas: Critical Debates*, ed. J. B. Thompson and D. Held. Cambridge: MIT Press.
Ruddick, S. 1980. "Maternal Thinking." *Feminist Studies* 6:342–67.
Weil, S. 1951. "Reflection on the Right Use of School Studies with a View to the Love of God." In *Waiting for God*. Tr. E. Craufurd. New York: Harper.
Winch, P. 1972. *Ethics and Action*. London: Routledge and Kegan Paul.

SELECTION 30
FROM

The Generalized and the Concrete Other

SEYLA BENHABIB

CAN THERE BE A feminist contribution to moral philosophy? That is to say, can those men and women who view the gender-sex system of our societies as oppressive, and who regard women's emancipation as essential to human liberation, criticize, analyze, and when necessary replace the traditional categories of moral philosophy in order to contribute to women's emancipation and human liberation? By focusing on the controversy generated by Carol Gilligan's work, this chapter seeks to outline such a feminist contribution to moral philosophy.[1] . . .

THE KOHLBERG-GILLIGAN CONTROVERSY

In a 1980 article on "Moral Development in Late Adolesence and Adulthood: A Critique and Reconstruction of Kohlberg's Theory," Murphy and Gilligan note that moral-judgment data from a longitudinal study of twenty-six undergraduates scored by Kohlberg's revised manual replicate his original findings that a significant percentage of subjects appear to regress from adolescence to adulthood.[2] The persistence of this relativistic regression suggests a need to revise the theory. In this article they propose a distinction between "postconventional formalism" and "postconventional contextualism." While the postconventional type of reasoning solves the problem of relativism by constructing a system that derives a solution to all moral problems from concepts like social contract or natural rights, the second approach finds the solution in that "while no answer may be objectively right in the sense of being context-free, some answers and some ways of thinking are better than others" (ibid., 83). The extension of the original paradigm from postconventional formalist to postconventional contextual then leads Gilligan to see some other discrepancies in the theory in a new light, and most notably among these, women's persistently low score when compared with their male peers. Distinguishing between the ethics of justice and rights and the ethics of care and responsibility allows her to account for women's moral development and the cognitive skills they show in a new way. Women's moral judgment is more contextual, more immersed in the details of relationships and narratives. It shows a greater propensity to take the standpoint of the "particular other," and women appear more adept at revealing feelings of empathy and sympathy required by this. Once these cognitive characteristics are seen not as deficiencies, but as essential components of adult moral reasoning at the postconventional stage, then women's apparent moral confusion of judgment becomes a sign of their strength. Agreeing with Piaget that a developmental theory hangs from its vertex of maturity, "the point towards which progress is traced," a change in "the definition of maturity," writen Gilligan, "does not simply alter the description of the highest stage but recasts the understanding of development, changing the entire account."[3] The contextuality, narrativity, and specificity of women's moral judgment is not a sign of weakness or deficiency, but a manifestation of a vision of moral maturity that views the self as a being immersed in a network of relationships with others. According to this vision, the respect for each other's needs and the mutuality of effort to satisfy them sustain moral growth and development. . . .

I want to define two premises as constituents of feminist theorizing. First, for feminist theory the gender-sex system is not a contingent but an essential way in which social reality is organized, symbolically divided, and lived through experientially. By the "gender-sex" system I understand the social-historical, symbolic constitution and interpretation of the anatomical differences of the sexes. The gender-sex system is the grid through which the self develops an *embodied* identity, a certain mode of being in one's body and of living the body. The self becomes an I in that it appropriates from the human community a mode of psychically, socially, and symbolically experiencing its bodily identity. The gender-sex system is the grid through which societies and cultures reproduce embodied individuals.[4]

Second, the historically known gender-sex systems have contributed to the oppression and exploitation of women. The task of feminist critical theory is to uncover this fact, and to develop a theory that is emancipatory and reflective, and which can aid women in their struggles to overcome oppression and exploitation. Feminist theory can contribute to this task in two ways: by developing an *explanatory-diagnostic analysis* of women's oppression across history, culture, and societies, and by articulating an *anticipatory-utopian critique* of the norms and values of our current society and culture, such as to project new modes of togetherness, of relating to ourselves and to nature in the future. Whereas the first aspect of feminist theory requires critical, social-scientific research, the second is primarily normative and philosophical: It involves the clarification of moral and political principles, both at the metaethical level with respect to their *logic of justification* and at the substantive, normative level with reference to their concrete content.[5]

In this chapter I shall be concerned with articulating such an anticipatory-utopian critique of universalistic moral theories from a feminist perspective. I want to argue that the *definition* of the moral domain, as well as the ideal of *moral autonomy*, not only in Kohlberg's theory but in universalistic, contractarian theories from Hobbes to Rawls, lead to a *privatization of* women's experience and to the exclusion of its consideration from a moral point of view. In this tradition, the moral self is viewed as a *disembedded* and *disembodied* being. This conception of the self reflects aspects of male experience; the "relevant other" in this theory is never the sister but always the brother. This vision of the self, I want to claim, is incompatible with the very criteria of reversibility and universalizability advocated by defenders of universalism. A universalistic moral theory restricted to the standpoint of the "generalized other" falls into epistemic incoherencies that jeopardize its claim to adequately fulfill reversibility and universalizability.

Universalistic moral theories in the Western tradition from Hobbes to Rawls are *substitutionalist*, in the sense that the universalism they defend is defined surreptitiously by identifying the experiences of a specific group of subjects as the paradigmatic case of the human as such. These subjects are invariably white, male adults who are propertied or at least professional. I want to distinguish *substitutionalist* from *interactive* universalism. Interactive universalism acknowledges the plurality of modes of being human, and differences among humans, without endorsing all these pluralities and differences as morally and politically valid. While agreeing that normative disputes can be settled rationally, and that fairness, reciprocity, and some procedure of universalizability are constituents, that is, necessary conditions of the moral standpoint, interactive universalism regards difference as a starting point for reflection and action. In this sense "universality" is a regulative ideal that does not deny our embodied and embedded identity, but aims at developing moral attitudes and encouraging political transformations that can yield a point of view acceptable to all. Universality is not the ideal consensus of fictitiously defined selves, but the concrete process in politics and morals of the struggle of concrete, embodied selves, striving for autonomy. . . .

This split between the public sphere of justice, in which history is made, and the atemporal realm of the household, in which life is reproduced, is internalized by the male ego. The dichotomies are not only without but within. He himself is divided into the public person and the private individual.

Within his chest clash the law of reason and the inclination of nature, the brilliance of cognition and the obscurity of emotion. Caught between the moral law and the starry heaven above and the earthly body below,[6] the autonomous self strives for unity. But the antagonism—between autonomy and nurturance, independence and bonding, sovereignty of the self and relations to others—remains. In the discourse of modern moral and political theory, these dichotomies are reified as being essential to the constitution of the self. While men humanize outer nature through labor, inner nature remains ahistorical, dark, and obscure. I want to suggest that contemporary universalist moral theory has inherited this dichotomy between autonomy and nurturance, independence and bonding, the sphere of justice and the domestic, personal realm. This becomes most visible in its attempt to restrict the moral point of view to the perspective of the "generalized other."

THE GENERALIZED VS. THE CONCRETE ORDER

Let me describe two conceptions of self-other relations that delineate both moral perspectives and interactional structures. I shall name the first the standpoint of the "generalized"[7] and the second that of the "concrete" other. In contemporary moral theory these conceptions are viewed as incompatible, even as antagonistic. These two pespectives reflect the dichotomies and splits of early modern moral and political theory between autonomy and nurturance, independence and bonding, the public and the domestic, and more broadly, between justice and the good life. The content of the generalized as well as the concrete other is shaped by this dichotomous characterization, which we have inherited from the modern tradition.

The standpoint of the generalized other requires us to view each and every individual as a rational being entitled to the same rights and duties we would want to ascribe to ourselves. In assuming the standpoint, we abstract from the individuality and concrete identity of the other. We assume that the other, like ourselves, is a being who has concrete needs, desires, and affects, but that what constitutes his or her moral dignity is not what differentiates us from each other, but rather what we, as speaking and acting rational agents, have in common. Our relation to the other is governed by the norms of *formal equality* and *reciprocity*: Each is entitled to expect and to assume from us what we can expect and assume from him or her. The norms of our interactions are primarily public and institutional ones. If I have a right to X, then you have the duty not to hinder me from enjoying X and conversely. In treating you in accordance with these norms, I confirm in your person the rights of humanity and I have a legitimate claim to expect that you will do the same in relation to me. The moral categories that accompany such interactions are those of right, obligation, and entitlement, and the corresponding moral feelings are those of respect, duty, worthiness, and dignity.

The standpoint of the concrete other, by contrast, requires us to view each and every rational being as an individual with a concrete history, identity, and affective-emotional constitution. In assuming this standpoint, we abstract from what constitutes our commonality. We seek to comprehend the needs of the other, his or her motivations, what s/he searches for, and what s/he desires. Our relation to the other is governed by the norms of *equity* and *complementary reciprocity*: Each is entitled to expect and to assume from the other forms of behavior through which the other feels recognized and confirmed as a concrete, individual being with specific needs, talents, and capacities. Our differences in this case complement rather than exclude one another. The norms of our interaction are usually private, noninstitutional ones. They are norms of friendship, love, and care. These norms require in various ways that I exhibit more than the simple assertion of my rights and duties in the face of your needs. In treating you in accordance with the norms of friendship, love, and care, I confirm not only your *humanity* but your human *individuality*. The moral categories that accompany such interactions are those of responsibility, bonding, and sharing. The corresponding moral feelings are those of love, care, and sympathy and solidarity. . . .

Through an immanent critique of the theories of Kohlberg and Rawls, I want to show that ignoring the standpoint of the concrete other leads to epistemic incoherence in universalistic moral theories. The problem can be stated as follows: According to Kohlberg and Rawls, moral reciprocity involves the capacity to take the standpoint of the other, to put oneself imaginatively in the place of the other, but under conditions of the "veil of ignorance," the *other as different from the self* disappears. Unlike in previous contract theories, in this case the other is not constituted through projection, but as a consequence of total abstraction from his or her identity. Differences are not denied; they become irrelevant. The Rawlsian self does not know

> his place in society, his class position or status; nor does he know his fortune in the distribution of natural assets and abilities, his intelligence strength, and the like. Nor, again, does anyone know his conception of the good, the paticulars of his rational plan of life, or even the special features of his psychology such as his aversion to risk or liability to optimism or pessimism.[8]

Let us ignore for a moment whether such selves who also do not know "the particular circumstances of their own society" can know anything at all that is relevant to the human condition, and ask instead, are these individuals *human selves* at all? In his attempt to do justice to Kant's conception of noumenal agency, Rawls recapitulates a basic problem with the Kantian conception of the self, namely, that noumenal selves cannot be *individuated*. If all that belongs to them as embodied, affective, suffering creatures, their memory and history, their ties and relations to others, are to be subsumed unde the phenomenal realm, then what we are left with is an empty mask that is everyone and no one. Michael Sandel points our that the difficulty in Rawls's conception derives from his attempt to be consistent with the Kantian concept of the autonomous self, as a being freely choosing his or her own ends in life.[9] However, this moral and political concept of autonomy slips into a metaphysics accordings to which it is meaningful to define a self independently of *all* the ends it may choose and all and any conceptions of the good it may hold (Sandel, *Liberalism and the Limits of Justice*, 47 ff.). At this point we must ask whether the *identity* of any human self can be defined with reference to its capacity for agency alone. Identity does not refer to my potential for choice alone, but to the actuality of my choices, namely, to how I as a finite, concrete, embodied individual shape and fashion the circumstances of my birth and family, linguistic, cultural, and gender identity into a coherent narrative that stands as my life's story. Indeed, if we recall that every autonomous being is one born of others and not, as Rawls, following Hobbes, assumes, a being "not bound by prior moral ties to another,"[10] the question becomes: How does this finite, embodied creature constitute into a coherent narrative those episodes of choice and limit, agency and suffering, initiative and dependence? The self is not a thing, a substrate, but the protagonist of a life's tale. The conception of selves who can be individuated prior to their moral ends is incoherent. We could not know if such a being was a human self, an angel, or the Holy Spirit. . . .

If selves who are epistemologically and metaphysically prior to their individuating characteristics, as Rawls takes them to be, cannot be human selves at all; if, therefore, there is no human *plurality* behind the veil of ignorance but only *definitional identity*, then this has consequences for criteria of reversibility and universalizability said to be constituents of the moral point of view. Definitional identity leads to *incomplete reversibility*, for the primary requisite of reversibility, namely, a coherent distinction between me and you, the self and the other, cannot be sustained under these circumstances. Under conditions of the veil of ignorance, the other disappears. . . .

I conclude that a definition of the self that is restricted to the standpoint of the generalized other becomes incoherent and cannot individuate among selves. Without assuming the standpoint of the concrete other, no coherent universalizability test can be carried out, for we lack the necessary epistemic information to judge my moral situation to be "like" or "unlike" yours. . . .

A Communicative Ethic of Need Interpretations
and the Relational Self

This distinction between the generalized and the concrete other raises questions in moral and political theory. It may be asked whether, without the standpoint of the generalized other, it would be possible to define a moral point of view at all. Since our identities as concrete others are what distinguish us from each other according to gender, race, class, cultural differentials, as well as psychic and natural abilities, would a moral theory restricted to the standpoint of the concrete other not be a racist, sexist, cultural relativist, discriminatory one? Furthermore, without the standpoint of the generalized other, it may be argued, a political theory of justice suited for modern, complex societies is unthinkable. Certainly rights must be an essential component in any such theory. Finally, the perspective of the "concrete other" defines our relations as private, noninstitutional ones, concerned with love, care, friendship, and intimacy. Are these activities so gender-specific? Are we not all "concrete others"?

The distinction between the "generalized" and the "concrete other," as drawn in this chapter so far, is not a *prescriptive* but a *critical* one. My goal is not to prescribe a moral and political theory consonant with the concept of the "concrete other." For, indeed, the recognition of the dignity and worthiness of the generalized other is a *necessary*, albeit not *sufficient*, condition to define the moral standpoint in modern societies. In this sense, the concrete other is a critical concept that designates the *ideological* limits of universalistic discourse. It signifies the *unthought*, the *unseen*, and the *unheard* in such theories. . . .

From a metaethical and normative standpoint, I would argue, therefore, for the validity of a moral theory that allows us to recognize the dignity of the generalized other through an acknowledgment of the moral identity of the concrete other. The point is not to juxtapose the generalized to the concrete other or to see normative validity in one or another standpoint. The point is to think through the ideological limitations and biases that arise in the discourse of universalist morality through this unexamined opposition. I doubt that an easy integration of both points of view, of justice and of care, is possible, without first clarifying the moral framework that would allow us to question both standpoints and their implicit gender presuppositions.

For this task a model of communicative need interpretations suggests itself. Not only is such an ethic, as I interpret it, compatible with the dialogic, interactive generation of universality, but most significant, such an ethic provides the suitable framework within which moral and political agents can define their own concrete identities on the basis of recognizing each other's dignity as generalized others. Questions of the most desirable and just political organization, as well as the distinction between justice and the good life, the public and the domestic, can be analyzed, renegotiated, and redefined in such a process. Since, however, all those affected are participants in this process, the presumption is that these distinctions cannot be drawn in such a way as to privatize, hide, and repress the experiences of those who have suffered under them, for only what all could consensually agree to be in the best interest of each could be accepted as the outcome of this dialogic process.

One consequence of this communicated ethic of need interpretations is that the object domain of moral theory is so enlarged that not only rights but needs, not only justice but possible modes of the good life, are moved into an anticipatory-utopian perspective. What such discourses can generate are not only universalistically prescribable norms, but also intimations of otherness in the present that can lead to the future.

Notes

1. Earlier versions of this chapter were read at the Conference on "Women and Morality," SUNY at Stony Brook, March 22–24, 1985, and at the "Philosophy and Social Science" Course at the Inter-University Center in Dubrovnik, Yugoslavia, April 2–4, 1985. I would like to thank participants at both conferences for their criticisms and suggestions. Larry Blum and Eva Feder Kittay have made valuable suggestions for corrections. Nancy Fraser's commentary on this work, "Toward a Discourse Ethic of Solidarity," *Praxis International* 5 no. 4 (Jan. 1986): 425–30, as well as her paper "Feminism and the Social State," *Salmagundi* (forthcoming) have been crucial in helping me articulate the political implications of the position developed here. A slightly altered version of this chapter has appeared in the Proceedings of the Women and Moral Theory Conference, ed. E. F. Kittay and Diana T. Meyers, *Women and Moral Theory* (New Jersey: Rowman and Littlefeld, 1987), 154–78.
2. John Michael Murphy and Carol Gilligan, "Moral Development in Late Adolescence and Adulthood: A Critique and Reconstruction of Kohlberg's Theory," *Human Development* 23 (1980): 77–104.
3. Carol Gilligan, *In a Different Voice: Psychological Theory and Women's Development* (Cambridge: Harvard University Press, 1982), 18–19.
4. Let me explain the status of this premise. I would characterize it as a "second-order research hypothesis" that both guides concrete research in the social sciences and that can, in turn, be falsified by them. It is not a statement of faith about the way the world is: The cross-cultural and transhistorical universality of the sex-gender system is an empirical fact. It is also most definitely not a normative proposition about the way the world *ought* to be. To the contrary, feminism radically challenges the validity of the sex-gender system in organizing societies and cultures, and advocates the emancipation of men and women from the unexamined and oppressive grids of this framework. The historian

. Kelly-Gadol succinctly captures the meaning of this premise for empirical research:

> Once we look to history for an understanding of woman's situation, we are, of course, already assuming that woman's situation is a social matter. But history, as we first come to it, did not seem to confirm this awareness... The moment this is done—the moment that one assumes that women are part of humanity in the fullest sense—the period or set of events with which we deal takes on a wholly different character or meaning from the normally accepted one. Indeed what emerges is a fairly regular pattern of relative loss of status for women precisely in those periods of so-called progressive change... Our notions of so-called progressive developments, such as classical Athenian civilization, the Renaissance and the French Revolution, undergo a startling reevaluation... Suddenly we see these ages *with a new, double vision—and each eye sees a different picture.* ("The Social Relations of the Sexes: Methodological Implications of Women's History," Signs 1, no.4 (1976): 81–11; emphasis mine)

5. For further clarification of these two aspects of critical theory, see part 2, "The Transformation of Critique," in my *Critique, Norm, and Utopia: A Study of the Foundations of Critical Theory* (New York: Columbia University Press, 1986).
6. Kant, "Critique of Practical Reason," in *Critique of Practical Reason and Other Writings in Moral Philosophy*, tr. and ed. and with an introduction by Louis White Beck (Chicago: University of Chicago Press, 1949), 258.
7. Although the term "generalized other" is borrowed from George Herbert Mead, my definition of it differs from this. Mead defines the "generalized other" as follows: "The organized community or social group which gives the individual his unity of self may be called the 'generalized other.' The attitude of the generalized other is the attitude of the whole community." George Herbert Mead, *Mind, Self, and Society: From the Standpoint of a Social Behaviorist*, ed. and with introduction by Charles W. Morris (Chicago: University of Chicago Press, 1955), 154. Among such communities Mead includes a ball team as well as political clubs, corporations, and other more abstract social classes or subgroups such as the class of debtors and the class of creditors (ibid., 157). Mead himself does not limit the concept of the "generalized other" to what is described in the text. In identifying the "generalized other" with the abstractly defined, legal, and juridical subject, contract theorists and Kohlberg depart from Mead. Mead criticizes the social contract tradition precisely for distorting the psychosocial genesis of the individual subject, cf. ibid., 233.
8. John Rawls, *A Theory of Justice*, 2d ed. (Cambridge: Harvard University Press, 1971), 137.
9. Michael J. Sandel, *Liberalism and the Limits of Justice* (Cambridge: Harvard University Press, 1982), 9.
10. Rawls, *A Theory of Justice*, 128.

SELECTION 31
FROM
Maternal Thinking

SARA RUDDICK

IN RECENT DECADES SEVERAL philosophers have elaborated a "practicalist" conception of "truth." They have argued negatively that there is no truth by which all truths can be judged nor any foundation of truths nor any total and inclusive narrative of all true statements. Positively they have claimed that distinctive ways of knowing and criteria of truth arise out of practices. I use this general philosophical view—which makes no mention of either women or mothers—to describe the relation between mothering and thinking. I therefore begin by outlining very briefly certain tenets of practicalism that I assume.[1]

THINKING AND PRACTICE

From the practicalist view, thinking arises from and is tested against practices. Practices are collective human activities distinguished by the aims that identify them and by the consequent demands made on practitioners committed to those aims. The aims or goals that define a practice are so central or "constitutive" that in the absence of the goal you would not have that practice. I express this intrinsic dependency when I say that to engage in a practice means to be committed to meeting its demands. People more or less consciously create a practice as they simultaneously pursue certain goals and make sense of their pursuit. Understanding shapes the end even as the practical pursuit of the end shapes the understanding. Horse racing, for example, is defined by the goal of winning a race by means of riding a horse over a finish line. In a particular culture, horse racers refine their concept of the race and the means of victory as questions about meaning or policy arise. A horse racing riderless past the wire, and a jockey slowing her mount in the interests of its beauty, are not engaged in horse racing. Natural science is defined by its goal of understanding nature's workings so that they may be explained, predicted, and, in so far as possible, controlled. Central to scientific control is replication by experiment. A chemist who created only beautiful reactions, invented her results, or was uninterested in replicating a reaction would not be doing chemistry. . . .

On the practicalist view, thought does not transcend its social origins. There is no truth to be apprehended from a transcendental perspective, that is, from no perspective at all. Practicalists reject a recurrent philosophic fantasy of finding a language free from the limits of any language in which to speak of the limits of all language. Limit and pespective are intrinsic to language and to thought, not a deficiency of them. . . .

Truth is perspectival, relative to the practices in which it is made. To say that true statements are relative in this sense does not mean that their truth is a matter of the opinion of communities of speakers. The statement that Mount Baldy is ten feet high is false, whatever any like-minded group of people may think. The point is that it is possible to make the false statement (and the alternative true one) because some people have identified mountains and invented a vocabulary of measurement. To speak, name, and measure means to act in social contexts in which geography and height matter to us. . . .

It is only within a practice that thinkers judge which questions are sensible, which answers are appropriate to them, and which criteria distinguish between better and worse answers. . . .

In sum, any discipline will distinguish true from false, will take some matters on faith, others on evidence, will judge evidence inadequate or faith misplaced. The practicalist's point is that the criteria for truth and falsity, the nature of evidence, and the role of faith will vary with the practice, whether the practice be religious, scientific, critical—or maternal.

MATERNAL PRACTICE

Maternal practice begins in a response to the reality of a biological child in a particular social world. To be a "mother" is to take upon oneself the responsibility of child care, making its work a regular and substantial part of one's working life.

Mothers, as individuals, engage in all sorts of other activities, from farming to deep sea diving, from astrophysics to elephant training. Mothers as individuals are not defined by their work; they are lovers and friends; they watch baseball, ballet, or the soaps; they run marathons, play chess, organize church bazaars and rent strikes. Mothers are as diverse as any other humans and are equally shaped by the social milieu in which they work. In my terminology they are "mothers" just because and to the degree that they are committed to meeting demands that define maternal work.

Both her child and the social world in which a mother works make these demands. "Demands" is an artificial term. Children demand all sorts of things— to eat ice cream before dinner, stay up all night, take the subway alone, watch the latest horror show on TV. A mother's social group demands of her all sorts of behavior—that she learn to sew or get a high school degree, hold her tongue or speak wittily in public, pay her taxes or go to jail for refusing to do so, sit ladylike in a restaurant or sit in at a lunch counter. A mother will decide in her own way which of these demands she will meet.

But in my discussion of maternal practice, I mean by "demands" those requirements that are imposed on anyone doing maternal work, in the way respect for experiment is imposed on scientists and racing past the finish line is imposed on jockeys. In this sense of demand, children "demand" that their lives be preserved and their growth fostered. In addition, the primary social groups with which a mother is identified, whether by force, kinship, or choice, demand that she raise her children in a manner accept- able to them. These three demands—for *preservation, growth,* and *social acceptability*—constitute maternal work; to be a mother is to be committed to meeting these demands by works of preservative love, nurturance, and training.

Conceptually and historically, the preeminent of these demands is that of preservation. As a species, human children share prolonged physical fra- gility and therefore prolonged dependence on adults for their safety and well-being. In all societies, children need protective care, though the causes and types of fragility and the means of protection vary widely. This univer- sal need of human children creates and defines a category of human work. A mother who callously endangers her child's well-being is simply not do- ing maternal work. (This does not mean that she is a bad person. She may sacrifice maternal work out of desperation or in a noble cause.)

The demand for protection is both epistemological and practical. Meet- ing the demand presupposes a minimal attentiveness to children and an awareness that their survival depends upon protective care. Imaginatively grasping the significance of children's biological vulnerability is necessary but not sufficient for responding to them. The perception that someone is in need of care may lead to caring; but then again it may lead to running away. In the settings where I first encountered polliwogs and goldfish (usu- ally in jars and bowls where I'd managed to put them), they were exceed- ingly vulnerable. When I was young, I saw that these little creatures were vulnerable and I cared for them. Much later, when I was dealing with my children's attachment to them, I found the vulnerability and total unpredictability of goldfish merely an annoyance. I cared for them because I cared for my children but, given the total inadequacy of our caring, I would have been delighted if my children had forgotten them altogether.

Now I almost never think about goldfish and never want to care for one the rest of my life.

Given the passions that we have for children, comparing them to goldfish may seem frivolous. When you *see* children as demanding care, the reality of their vulnerability and the necessity of a caring response seem unshakable. But I deliberately stress the optional character first of perceiving "vulnerability" and then of responding with care. Maternal responses are complicated acts that social beings make to biological beings whose existence is inseparable from social interpretations. Maternal practice begins with a double vision—seeing the fact of biological vulnerability as socially significant and as demanding care. Neither birth nor the actual presence of a vulnerable infant guarantees care. In the most desperate circumstances mothers are more apt to feed their babies than to let them sicken and starve. Yet when infants were dependent solely on mothers' milk, biological mothers could refuse the food their children needed, for example, sending them away to wet-nurses, although this was known to have a high risk of illness and even death.[2] To be committed to meeting children's demand for preservation does not require enthusiasm or even love; it simply means to see vulnerability and to respond to it with care rather than abuse, indifference, or flight. Preserving the lives of children is the central constitutive, invariant aim of maternal practice; the commitment to achieving that aim is the constitutive maternal act.

The demand to preserve a child's life is quickly supplemented by the second demand, to nurture its emotional and intellectual growth. . . .

This demand to foster children's growth appears to be historically and culturally specific to a degree that the demand for preservation is not. To be aware of children's need for nurturance depends on a belief, prevalent in my social milieu, that children have complicated lives, that their minds and psyches need attending. But even in social groups I know firsthand, some people—in my experience more often men—claim that if children are protected and trained, growth takes care of itself. On the other hand, it is difficult to judge what mothers themselves really believe about the conditions of growth. Some mothers who say that children simply grow and need little nurturance nonetheless act in ways that indicate they believe their children are complex and needy beings. . . .

The third demand on which maternal practice is based is made not by children's needs but by the social groups of which a mother is a member. Social groups require that mothers shape their children's growth in "acceptable" ways. What counts as acceptable varies enormously within and among groups and cultures. The demand for acceptability, however, does not vary, nor does there seem to be much dissent from the belief that children cannot "naturally" develop in socially correct ways but must be "trained." I use the neutral, though somewhat harsh, term "training" to underline a mother's active aims to make her children "acceptable." Her training strategies may be persuasive, manipulative, educative, abusive, seductive, or respectful and are typically a mix of most of these.

A mother's group is that set of people with whom she identifies to the degree that she would count failure to meet their criteria of acceptability as her failure. The criteria of acceptability consist of the group values that a mother has internalized as well as the values of group members whom she feels she must please. Acceptability is not merely a demand imposed on a mother by her group. Indeed, mothers themselves as part of the larger social group formulate its ideals and are usually governed by an especially stringent form of acceptability that nonmothers in the group may not necessarily adhere to. Mothers want their children to grow into people whom they themselves and those closest to them can delightedly appreciate. This demand gives an urgency—sometimes exhilarating, sometimes painful—to mothers' daily lives. . . .

To protect, nurture, and train—however abstract the schema, the story is simple. A child leans out of a high-rise window to drop a balloon full of water on a passerby. She must be hauled in from the window (preservation) and taught not to endanger innocent people (training), and the method used must not endanger her self-respect or confidence (nurturance). In any mother's day, the demands of preservation, growth, and acceptability are intertwined. Yet a reflective mother can separately identify each demand, partly because they are often in conflict. If a child wants to walk to the store alone, do you worry about her safety or applaud her developing capacity to take care of herself? If you overhear your son hurling insults at a neighbor's child, do you rush to instill decency and compassion in him, or do you let him act on his own impulses in his need to overcome shyness? If your older child, in her competitive zeal, pushes ahead of your younger, smaller child while climbing a high slide, do you inhibit her competitive pleasure or allow an aggressiveness you cannot appreciate? Should her younger brother learn to fight back? And if he doesn't, is he bowing too easily to greater strength? Most urgently, whatever you do, is somebody going to get hurt? Love may make these question painful; it does not provide the answers. Mothers must *think*.

Maternal Thinking

Daily, mothers think out strategies of protection, nurturance, and training. Frequently conflicts between strategies or between fundamental demands provoke mothers to think about the meaning and relative weight of preservation, growth, and acceptability. In quieter moments, mothers reflect on their practice as a whole. As in any group of thinkers, some mothers are more ambitiously reflective than others, either out of temperamental thoughtfulness, moral and political concerns, or, most often, because they have serious problems with their children. However, maternal thinking is no rarity. Maternal work itself demands that mothers think; out of this need for thoughtfulness, a distinctive discipline emerges.

I speak about a mother's thought—the intellectual capacities she develops, the judgments she makes, the metaphysical attitudes she assumes, the values she affirms. . . .

If thinking arises in and is tested by practice, who is qualified to judge the intellectual strength and moral character of a practice as a whole? It is sometimes said that only those who participate in a practice can criticize its thinking. Accordingly, it might be argued that it is not possible to evaluate maternal thinking without practicing maternal work or living closely and sympathetically with those who do. When mothers engage in self-criticism, their judgments presuppose a knowledge of the efforts required to respond to children's demands that those unpracticed in tending to children do not have. Maternal criticisms are best left to those who know what it means to attempt to protect, nurture, and train, just as criticism of scientific or—to use a controversial example—psychoanalytic thinking should be left to those who have engaged in these practices.

There are moral grounds for critical restraint. People who have not engaged in a practice or who have not lived closely with a practitioner have no right to criticize. Although any group might make this claim, the point is particularly apt for maternal thinkers. Mothers have been a powerless group whose thinking, when it has been acknowledged at all, has most often been recognized by people interested in interpreting and controlling rather than in listening. Philosophically minded mothers have only begun to articulate the precepts of a thought whose existence other philosophers do not recognize. Surely, they should have time to think among and for themselves. . . .

One should not, however, conflate epistemological restraint with critical silence. The practical origins of reason do not preclude radical self-criticism. Indeed, developing vocabularies and standards of self-criticism is a central intellectual activity in most practices. More important, although all criticism arises from some practice or other, interpractice criticism is both possible and necessary for change. It is common sense epistemologically that alternative perspectives offer distinctive critical advantages. A historian, medical ethicist, and peace activist—especially if they themselves were conversant with science—might claim to have a better sense than a scientist not only of the limits but also of the character of scientific discipline. Militarists criticize maternal thinkers for insufficient respect for abstract causes, while peacemakers criticize them for the parochial character of maternal commitment.

Interpractice criticism is possible and often desirable; yet there is no privileged practice capable of judging all other practices. To criticize is to act on one's practical commitments, not to stand above them. Maternal thinking is one discipline among others, capable of criticizing and being criticized. It does not offer nor can it be judged from a standpoint uncontaminated by practical struggle and passion.

Notes

1. The philosophers on whom I draw most closely are Ludwig Wittgenstein, especially *Philosophical Investigations* (New York: Macmillan, 1953) and *On Certainty*, ed. G. E. M. Anscombe and G. H. von Wright (Oxford: Basil Blackwell, 1969), and Peter Winch, especially "Understanding a Primitive Society," in *Ethics and Action* (London: Routledge and Kegan Paul, 1972). In my earliest work on maternal thinking I was directly indebted to Jurgen Habermas, *Knowledge and Human Interests* (Boston: Beacon Press, 1971), and influenced by Jean-Paul Sartre, *Being and Nothingness* (New York: Philosophical Library, 1956). In the last several years, there has been considerable philosophical discussion of the social construction of knowledge and its relation to relativism. An excellent account of some of this discussion is Richard Bernstein, *Beyond Objectivism and Relativism* (Philadelphia: University of Pennsylvania Press, 1983). I have found the following works and discussions of them useful: Richard Rorty, *Philosophy and the Mirror of Nature* (Princeton: Princeton University Press, 1979) and *Consequences of Pragmatism* (Minneapolis: University of Minnesota Press, 1982); Jean-François Lyotard, *The Post-Modern Condition: A Report on Knowledge* (Minneapolis: University of Minnesota Press, 1984). I do not, however, enter into the subtleties of philosophic argument here.
2. The example is from Elisabeth Badinter, *Mother Love: Myth and Reality* (New York: Macmillan, 1980).

SELECTION 32
FROM
The Social Self and the Partiality Debates

MARILYN FRIEDMAN

THE PARTIALITY/IMPARTIALITY DEBATES AND THE SOCIAL CONCEPTION OF THE SELF: A SUMMARY

IT HAS BECOME A commonplace of contemporary mainstream ethics that we are each entitled to show favoritism, preferential treatment, partiality toward loved ones. Some philosophers would say even more strongly that we have the *obligation* to show such treatment, that it is not simply an option or a prerogative. This notion of partiality toward loved ones is lately gaining wide philosophical acclaim. (Ordinary people, fortunately, have held this view for quite some time.)

Although the appropriateness of partiality toward loved ones is itself uncontested, there is a lively debate growing in ethics over its theoretical justification. One of the hottest questions is whether partiality toward loved ones can adequately be justified by any of the dominant impartialist theories of modern moral philosophy. In the past two decades, both feminist and nonfeminist philosophers have been disputing the adequacy of those traditions to account for the moral value of personal relationships. The feature of these theories that seems to deny the legitimacy of partiality is their requirement of moral *impartiality*—the requirement to show equal consideration, in some specified sense, toward all persons. . . .

From the *impartial* standpoint, one is to reason about moral matters detached from the influence of one's own specific contingencies—one's wants, needs, loyalties, and so on. The impartial attitude is supposed to overcome what is traditionally regarded as the pervasive human tendency toward *self-serving* partiality and *egoism*. From the impartialist point of view, one is permitted to take account of one's own particularities—but only as contextual details of the moral matter under consideration, a sort of "grist" for the mill of moral judgment. One is not to reason *from* those particularities, that is, from a perspective that at the outset prejudicially favors those interests. . . .

But this is hardly the way to treat loved ones. And so critics of moral impartialism charge that impartial theories call for attitudes that are alienating in close personal relationships—attitudes such as detachment from personal concerns and loyalties, disinterest, dispassion, and a regard for the generalized moral equality of all persons that abstracts from their particularity and uniqueness. Close relationships call instead for personal concern, loyalty, interest, passion, and responsiveness to the uniqueness of loved ones, to their specific needs, interests, history, and so on. In a word, personal relationships call for partiality rather than impartiality. . . .

Partialists have attacked moral impartialism and defended partiality with a variety of additional arguments. John Cottingham insists that partiality toward loved ones is essential to human integrity and fulfillment. John Kekes describes how the nature of intimacy renders impartiality inappropriate. Lawrence Blum and Charles Fried see intrinsic value in benefiting one's own friends and loved ones. In the opinion of Bernard Williams, devoting oneself preferentially to one's own ground projects, including personal relationships, is necessary in order to have character, integrity, motive force to face one's future, and reason for living. Andrew Oldenquist warns that equal concern for the whole of humanity is simply too weak a sentiment, in any case, to be effective as moral motivation.[1]

Those are typical nonfeminist arguments. Feminists, such as Sara Ruddick,[2] have generally endorsed partiality not so much for its own sake but rather as part of a larger project. This is the project of promoting esteem for the caring and nurturing activities that women have traditionally undertaken in such areas of life as family and health care. Those caring activities have essentially involved moral attention and responsiveness to the specific wants and needs of particular persons.

As if that entire array of charges against impartiality were not formidable enough,[3] some critics of moral impartiality—nonfeminists such as Alasdair MacIntyre and Michael Sandel and feminists such as Iris Young—have denied the very possibility of impartial reasoning.[4] (Young urges, further, that the rhetoric of impartiality should be distrusted because it has been used in practice by dominant social groups to disguise their de facto political and cultural hegemony.)[5] All three of these theorists argue that no self can reason as if dissociated from the contingencies that make her the self she is. There is no escape from the specifics of one's embodiment, historical situation, and relational connections to others. Impartial reasoning is impossible; the self is inherently partial.

Indeed, for MacIntyre, Sandel, and Young, the self is inherently *social* to some degree or other. In its identity, character, interests, and preferences, it is constituted by, and in the course of, relationships to particular others, including the network of relationships that locate it as a member of certain communities or social groups. This is the social conception of the self. According to Sandel's version of it, we each have "loyalties and convictions whose moral force consists partly in the fact that living by them is inseparable from understanding ourselves as the particular persons we are— as members of this family or community or nation or people, as bearers of this history, as sons and daughters of that revolution, as citizens of this republic."[6] For MacIntyre as well "we all approach our own circumstances as bearers of a particular social identity. I am someone's son or daughter, someone else's cousin or uncle; I am a citizen of this or that city, a member of this or that guild or profession; I belong to this clan, that tribe, this nation."[7] Relationships to others are intrinsic to identity, preferences, and so on, and the self can only reason *as* the social being she is.

The social conception of the self fits comfortably into the feminist project of incorporating women's moral perspectives into ethical theorizing. Caroline Whitbeck and Virginia Held argue that the social conception of the self, with its emphasis on the primacy of relationships, coincides with women's traditional experiences as mothers and caregivers.[8] The concept of the social self also provides a theoretical underpinning for the feminist view that gender in particular is a socially constructed aspect of human identity, one that may, therefore, diverge from our present gender arrangements of pervasive male dominance.

In addition, a social conception of the self makes a concern for other persons fundamental to the self and does not reduce it to a mere variety of self-concern. Indeed, the social conception of the self tends somewhat to blur the distinction between self and other. If my relationship to someone or some group is internal to who I am, then she or they are somehow a part of me—admittedly, a metaphor that needs substantial clarification. In my partiality for those who are in this way near and dear to me, I show a moral attitude that is neither egoism nor self-denying altruism. The flourishing of loved ones promotes my own well-being, yet my motivation to care for them does not require me to compute how their well-being will further my own interests; I simply am interested in them. . . .

THE FLAVOR OF THE PARTIALITY DEBATES . . .

There are at least two . . . features of the partiality debates that are noteworthy from a feminist perspective. First, in mainstream ethics, partiality means favoritism or preferential treatment. Mainstream discussions presuppose a context of competing interests. The emphasis is on what I do for my wife or child *at the expense of* someone else, including other wives, other children.

Hypothetical disasters abound as thought experiments in these discussions. The moral world of mainstream ethics is a nightmare of plane crashes, train wrecks, and sinking ships! Wives and children drown in this literature at an alarming rate. The nonfeminist impartiality critics never acknowledge how infrequent these emergencies are in daily moral life, nor, therefore, how rare is the need to sacrifice someone else's wife in order to save one's own. And for these infrequent occasions, the nonfeminist impartiality critics never discuss the possibility of investing our moral energies in efforts to *reduce beforehand* those breathtaking contests for survival and love—for example, by better FAA regulation of airline safety.

Second, although there is broad consensus about the legitimacy of partiality toward family members and friends, there is no consensus about other special relationships. Some theorists defend partiality toward the members of one's local and national communities, such as neighborhood, city, and nation. Communitarians, as we have seen, especially favor these examples.[9] (It is astonishing how few nonfeminist participants in the partiality debates mention gender or race; those few who do are usually *defenders* of moral impartialism, who point out that some forms of partiality are unjustified and who cite racism and sexism as examples.)[10]

My point is that beyond the realm of close relationships, there is no consensus on the legitimacy of partiality. Note, however, that those who do defend partiality toward local or national communities ironically pay no attention to the historical specifics of interrelationships among communities and social groups—the hierarchies of group domination, the institutionalized oppressions, the imperialistic policies. Group loyalty is a form of partiality that covers a wide spectrum—for example, ethnic pride and group solidarity in the face of oppression, but also white supremacism, male chauvinism, and heterosexism. The moral worth of group loyalty varies with the relative needs, interests, powers, privileges, and history of the social group in question. At any rate, this issue has yet to find adequate treatment in the partiality debates. . . .

ON BEING PARTIAL BUT NOT PAROCHIAL: GLOBAL MORAL CONCERN

I mentioned earlier that moral impartiality is currently understood in terms of giving equal consideration to all persons. As interpreted by most nonfeminist critics of impartiality, this requirement calls for the moral agent to devote literally equal amounts of time, energy, and resources to all persons. I should not be buying my own child such luxuries as toys when there are children (and adults) across town, or across the oceans, who don't even have food to eat. An equality of global moral concern, then, is an important part of what impartiality represents or entails for nonfeminist impartiality critics and is a primary target for them.

In opposing that view, many nonfeminist critics defend partiality with the fervor of political activists fighting for a social cause. In this case, the cause is "taking care of one's own." These philosophers have been especially troubled by the demand that we always consider the interests of all strangers and unloved acquaintances equally with the interests of loved ones. On the nonfeminist partialist view, the special obligations we have to those who are close to us have overriding moral priority when compared with general obligations to show concern for distant peoples. Nonfeminist partialists argue that special obligations to those who are close to us, to those who are "our own," should virtually eclipse those distant obligations in our moral attention.[11]

It should be noted that only a few moral *im*partialists have explicitly stated the requirement of impartiality in these demanding terms. William Godwin and Peter Singer are convenient targets for the partialists because they each profess an uncompromisingly thoroughgoing impartiality.[12] Peter Singer, especially in his earlier writings, argues that proximity and close relationship carry no moral weight and that moral responsibilities—for example, to those who are starving—extend equally to all members of the global village.[13]

William Godwin (ironically, the husband of the late-eighteenth-century British feminist Mary Wollstonecraft) was the one who invited us to consider this philosophically (in)famous dilemma: Should I rescue my beloved but socially worthless parent, a mere valet or chambermaid (depending on which edition one consults)? Or should I rescue instead François de Salignac de La Mothe-Fénelon, the archbishop of Cambray, in a disaster that prevents me from rescuing both? Godwin urges us to opt for the eminent archbishop. "What magic is there is the pronoun 'my,'" he asks, "that should justify us in overturning the decision of impartial truth?"[14] It is noteworthy how few such extreme defenders of the impartiality requirement there really are. (This suggests that moral impartiality means something else to most of its defenders and that its critics attack a straw person. But that is a discussion for another occasion.)

The point to emphasize here is that feminists who dispute the requirement of moral impartiality are not usually challenging the idea of global moral concern.[15] Global concerns and international connections among feminists have nourished our wider movement. Most feminists would insist on the importance of a cross-cultural variety of women's issues and of forging cross-cultural connections and solidarity among women. The responsibility to be concerned about distant peoples, then, is one implication of moral impartiality that, I think, most feminists would wish to retain. It is not in this respect that the notion of moral impartiality has worried feminists.

It is important to beware of possible equivocations over the notion of global moral concern. The difference between nonfeminist and feminist impartiality critics on this point is subtle. Some nonfeminists, such as John Cottingham, are quick to point out that they do not oppose, for example, giving money to Oxfam. What Cottingham opposes is the idea that morality requires giving nearly *all* one's money to Oxfam, down to the point at which one has no more money than any of the starving beneficiaries of Oxfam relief—a radical divestment that he thinks is the ultimate logical outcome of the impartialist's insistence on giving equal weight to everyone's interests.[16]

However, even feminists with money to burn and whose charity-giving histories are second to none are not usually relinquishing their resources at such a rate. So what exactly is the point at issue? The dispute seems to concern a matter of degree and a matter of what is honored and who the heroes are. Nonfeminist partialists, some of them at any rate, concede that it is all right to be charitable toward distant peoples; but on the whole, they downplay the importance of global concern and instead idealize favoring "one's own." By contrast, feminist partialists devote much more theoretical attention to developing concern for those who are not "one's own." This is the significance of all work that feminists put into theorizing "difference" and into trying to incorporate a diversity of racial and class consciousness into feminist theory. Cross-cultural connections, theoretical and practical, are highly revered feminist achievements. Thus for feminists, "global moral concern" does not mean the practice of exactly equal consideration of the interests of all individuals; but it does mean substantially more concern for distant or different peoples than is common in our culture and our time.

However, global moral concern raises a unique problem for the social conception of the self. A self whose identity is defined in terms of relationships to certain others is capable of having immediate and direct moral concern for those others. Her moral concern for them does not need to be mediated by calculations of how their well-being might serve her own interests. The question raised by the issue of global moral concern is whether concern for distant and unknown peoples is an immediate moral motivation of the social self.

The likeliest source of such a motivation is group identity and consciousness.[17] We are familiar with the sort of group consciousness that attaches to racial, ethnic, and national communities. What about consciousness of membership in the human community? Unfortunately, it is not clear just what role it plays in self-identity. Philosophy has been of no help on this question. Philosophical works that have inquired into what it means for us to be "men" and not brutes aim to clarify how we are different from (nonhuman) animals but not to foster among all human beings a sense of globally shared mutual interest. Human group consciousness is an aspect of the social conception of the self that awaits further clarification.

Virginia Held suggests that we acquire concern for, say, starving children elsewhere by *learning* to empathize with them.[18] One learns what it is like for children close to home to starve, and one recognizes that distant children are like those close to home. One's empathic capacities, developed in relationships with persons known closely, are engaged by more distant peoples through recognition of their similarity to those whom we know. This approach, however, does not spring solely from motives that are rooted in self-identity but requires, in addition, reasoning and analogical insight.

Interpreted in this way, global moral concern is a rational achievement but not an immediate motivation, and it is an achievement only for some selves. It is a result of moral thinking that has no necessary motivational source in the self and so not everyone will find it convincing. (Think about those who *fail to see* the similarity between "them" and "us.") Since so many people appear to lack global moral concern, Held's view is certainly plausible—regrettably so.

This result does not threaten the social conception of the self. However, it brings us face-to-face with one important limit of that concept: its inability to ground the widest sort of concern for others in unmediated constituents of the self. Thus we confront the apparent fragility of the human motivation of global concern.

Notes

1. Citations, in the order of appearance, are to John Cottingham, "Ethics and Impartiality," *Philosophical Studies* 43 (1983): 87, 94; John Kekes, "Morality and Impartiality," *American Philosophical Quarterly* 18, no. 4 (Oct. 1981): 299–302; Lawrence Blum, *Friendship, Altruism, and Morality* (London: Routledge and Kegan Paul, 1980), ch. 3; Charles Fried, *Right and Wrong* (Cambridge: Harvard University Press, 1978), 172; Bernard Williams, *Utilitarianism: For and Against* (Cambridge: Cambridge University Press, 1973), 108–18, and "Persons, Character, and Morality," in Williams, *Moral Luck: Philosophical Debates, 1973–1980* (Cambridge: Cambridge University Press, 1981), 1–19, and Andres Oldenquist, "Loyalties," *Journal of Philosophy* 79, no. 4 (April 1982): 181.

2. See Sara Ruddick, *Maternal Thinking: Toward a Politics of Peace* (Boston: Beacon Press, 1989).

3. Impartialists have responded to these charges in several ways. One prevalent theme, which appears in both deontological and consequentialist writings, is the view that moral thinking is two-leveled. Impartiality is a requirement only of the higher level of moral thinking at which moral rules, practices, or insti-

tutions are to be justified. At this level, some practices of partiality are justifiable, such as taking special care of one's own children—albeit in impartialist terms. At the lower level of moral thinking, which involves the application of moral rules or the implementation of practices, one may, therefore, show partiality in the justified ways. There are other impartialist rejoinders as well, but it is beyond the scope of this essay to discuss them or their adequacy; however, see my entry on partiality in Lawrence Becker, ed., *Encyclopedia of Ethics* (New York: Garland Publishing, 1992).

4. See Alasdair MacIntyre, *After Virtue* (Notre Dame: University of Notre Dame Press, 1981); Michael J. Sandel, *Liberalism and the Limits of Justice* (Cambridge: Cambridge University Press, 1982); and Iris Marion Young, "Impartiality and the Civic Public: Some Implications of Feminist Critiques of Moral and Political Theory," *Praxis International* 5, no. 4 (Jan. 1985): 381–401. See also Marilyn Friedman, "The Impracticality of Impartiality," *Journal of Philosophy* 86, no. 11 (Nov. 1989): 645–56.

5. Young, "Impartiality and the Civic Public," 385–86. The notion of the "rhetoric" of impartiality comes from Margaret Walker, "Partial Consideration: Some Images of Impartiality Re-Examined," unpublished manuscript presented at the Conference on the Partiality/Impartiality Debates sponsored by *Ethics* and held at Hollins College, Roanoke, Virginia, June 1990.

6. Sandel, *Liberalism and the Limits of Justice*, 179.

7. MacIntyre, *After Virtue*, 204–5.

8. Caroline Whitbeck, "A Different Reality: Feminist Ontology," in *Beyond Domination*, ed. Carol Gould (Totowa, NJ: Rowman and Allanheld, 1984), 64–88; and Virginia Held, "Non-Contractual Society," in *Science, Morality, and Feminist Theory*, ed. Marsha Hanen and Kai Nielsen (Calgary: University of Calgary Press, 1987), 111–38.

9. See MacIntyre, *After Virtue*; Sandel, *Liberalism and the Limits of Justice*; and Oldenquist, "Loyalties."

10. See Alan Gewirth, "Ethical Univeralism and Particularism," *Journal of Philosophy* 85, no. 6 (June 1988): 298. John Cottingham is a singular example of a nonfeminist partialist who argues that not all partialities are justified and who worries about racism and sexism (see his "Partiality, Favouritism, and Morality," *Philosophical Quarterly* 36, no. 144 [1986]: 357–73).

11. See Williams, *Moral Luck*; Oldenquist, "Loyalties"; and Christina Hoff Sommers, "Filial Morality," *Journal of Philosophy* 83, no. 8 (Aug. 1986): 439–56.

12. William Godwin, *Enquiry Concerning Political Justice*, ed. K. Codell Carter (Oxford: Clarendon Press, 1971); and Peter Singer, *Practical Ethics* (Cambridge: Cambridge University Press, 1979), 10–11.

13. Singer, *Practical Ethics*, 10–11; and Singer, "Famine, Affluence, and Morality," *Philosophy and Public Affairs* 1, no. 3 (Spring 1972): 229–43.

14. Godwin, *Enquiry Concerning Political Justice*, 71; Carter notes that Godwin's first edition used the terms "mother," "sister," and "chambermaid," whereas the later edition substitutes "father," "brother," and "valet" (see Carter's editorial note 2, ibid.).

15. But see the skepticism expressed over the notion of universal moral concern in Nel Noddings, *Caring: A Feminine Approach to Ethics and Moral Education* (Berkeley: University of California Press, 1984), 91–94. It is noteworthy that Noddings uses the word "feminine" rather than "feminist" in her subtitle.

16. Cottingham, "Ethics and Impartiality," 91.

17. On the moral nature and importance of group identity, see Larry May, *The Morality of Groups* (Notre Dame: University of Notre Dame Press, 1987).

18. Virginia Held, "Feminism and Moral Theory," in *Women and Moral Theory*, ed. Eva Feder Kittay and Diana T. Meyers (Totowa, NJ: Rowman and Allanheld, 1987), 118.

PART VI

Gender in Democracy
and Politics

SELECTION 33
FROM
The Sexual Contract

CAROLE PATEMAN

TELLING STORIES OF ALL kinds is the major way that human beings have endeavored to make sense of themselves and their social world. The most famous and influential political story of modern times is found in the writings of the social contract theorists. The story, or conjectural history, tells how a new civil society and a new form of political right is created through an original contract. An explanation for the binding authority of the state and civil law, and for the legitimacy of modern civil government, is to be found by treating our society as if it had originated in a contract. The attraction of the idea of an original contract and of contract theory in a more general sense, a theory that claims that free social relations take a contractual form, is probably greater now than at any time since the seventeenth and eighteenth centuries when the classic writers told their tales. But today, invariably, only half the story is told. We hear an enormous amount about the *social* contract; a deep silence is maintained about the *sexual* contract.

The original contract is a sexual-social pact, but the story of the sexual contract has been repressed. Standard accounts of social contract theory do not discuss the whole story and contemporary contract theories give no indication that half the agreement is missing. The story of the sexual contract is also about the genesis of political right, and explains why exercise of the right is legitimate—but this story is about political right as *patriarchal right* or sex-right, the power that men exercise over women. The missing half of the story tells how a specifically modern form of patriarchy is established. The new civil society created through the original contract is a patriarchal social order.

Social contract theory is conventionally presented as a story about freedom. One interpretation of the original contract is that the inhabitants of the state of nature exchange the insecurities of natural freedom for equal,

317

civil freedom which is protected by the state. In civil society freedom is universal; all adults enjoy the same civil standing and can exercise their freedom by, as it were, replicating the original contract when, for example they enter into the employment contract or the marriage contract. Another interpretation, which takes into account conjectural histories of the state of nature in the classic texts, is that freedom is won by sons who cast off their natural subjection to their fathers and replace paternal rule by civil government. Political right as paternal right is inconsistent with modern civil society. In this version of the story, civil society is created through the original contract after paternal rule—or patriarchy—is overthrown. The new civil order, therefore, appears to be antipatriarchal or postpatriarchal. Civil society is created through contract so that contract and patriarchy appear to be irrevocably opposed.

These familiar readings of the classic stories fail to mention that a good deal more than freedom is at stake. Men's domination over women, and the right of men to enjoy equal sexual access to women, is at issue in the making of the original pact. The social contract is a story of freedom; the sexual contract is a story of subjection. The original contract constitutes both freedom and domination. Men's freedom and women's subjection are created through the original contract—and the character of civil freedom cannot be understood without the missing half of the story that reveals how men's patriarchal right over women is established through contract. Civil freedom is not universal. Civil freedom is a masculine attribute and depends upon patriarchal right. The sons overturn paternal rule not merely to gain their liberty but to secure women for themselves. Their success in this endeavor is chronicled in the story of the sexual contract. The original pact is a sexual as well as a social contract: It is sexual in the sense of patriarchal—that is, the contract establishes men's political right over women—and also sexual in the sense of establishing orderly access by men to women's bodies. The original contract creates what I shall call, following Adrienne Rich, "the law of male sex-right."[1] Contract is far from being opposed to patriarchy; contract is the means through which modern patriarchy is constituted.

One reason why political theorists so rarely notice that half the story of the original contract is missing, or that civil society is patriarchal, is that "patriarchy" is usually interpreted patriarchally as paternal rule (the literal meaning of the term). So, for example, in the standard reading of the theoretical battle in the seventeenth century between the patriarchalists and social contract theorists, patriarchy is assumed to refer only to paternal right. Sir Robert Filmer claimed that political power was paternal power and that the procreative power of the father was the origin of political right. Locke and his fellow contract theorists insisted that paternal and political power were not the same and that contract was the genesis of political right. The contract theorists were victorious on this point; the standard interpretation is on firm ground—as far as it goes. Once more, a crucial portion of the story is missing. The true origin of political right is overlooked in this interpretation; no stories are told about its genesis.

Political right originates in sex-right or conjugal right. Paternal right is only one, and not the original, dimension of patriarchal power. A man's power as a father comes after he has exercised the patriarchal right of a man (a husband) over a woman (wife). The contract theorists had no wish to challenge the original patriarchal right in their onslaught on paternal right. Instead, they incorporated conjugal right into their theories and, in so doing, transformed the law of male sex-right into its modern contractual form. Patriarchy ceased to be paternal long ago. Modern civil society is not structured by kinship and the power of fathers; in the modern world, women are subordinated to men *as men*, or to men as a fraternity. The original contract takes place after the political defeat of the father and creates modern *fraternal patriarchy*.

Another reason for the omission of the story of the sexual contract is that conventional approaches to the classic texts, whether those of mainstream political theorists or their socialist critics, give a misleading picture of a distinctive feature of the civil society created through the original pact. Patriarchal civil society is divided into two spheres, but attention is directed to one sphere only. The story of the social contract is treated as an account of the creation of the public sphere of civil freedom. The other, private, sphere is not seen as politically relevant. Marriage and the marriage contract are, therefore, also deemed politically irrelevant. To ignore the marriage contract is to ignore half the original contract. In the classic texts, as I shall show in some detail, the sexual contract is displaced onto the marriage contract. The displacement creates a difficulty in retrieving and recounting the lost story. All too easily, the impression can be given that the sexual contract and the social contract are two separate, albeit related, contracts, and that the sexual contract concerns the private sphere. Patriarchy then appears to have no relevance to the public world. On the contrary, patriarchal right extends throughout civil society. The employment contract and (what I shall call) the prostitution contract, both of which are entered into in the public, capitalist market, uphold men's right as firmly as the marriage contract. The two spheres of civil society are at once separate and inseparable. The public realm cannot be fully understood in the absence of the private sphere, and, similarly, the meaning of the original contract is misinterpreted without both, mutually dependent, halves of the story. Civil freedom depends on patriarchal right.

My interest in the sexual contract is not primarily in interpreting texts, although the classic works of social contract theory figure largely in my discussion. I am resurrecting the story in order to throw light onto the present-day structure of major social institutions in Britain, Australia, and the United States—societies which, we are told, and properly be seen as if they had originated in a social contract. The sense in which these societies are patriarchal can be elucidated through the full story of the original contract; they have enough in common historically and culturally to enable the same story to be told (and many of my general arguments will also be relevant to other developed Western countries). The manner in which patriarchal domination differs from other forms of domination in the late twentieth century becomes much clearer once the sexual contract has been retrieved from oblivion. The connection between patriarchy and contract has been little explored, even by feminists, despite the fact that, in modern civil society, crucially important institutions are constituted and maintained through contract.

The relationship between employer and worker is contractual, and for many contract theorists the employment contract is the exemplary contract. Marriage also begins in a contract. Feminists have been greatly concerned with the marriage contract but their writings and activities have been ignored for the most part, even by most socialist critics of contract theory and the employment contract who might have been expected to be keenly interested in feminist arguments. . . . My concern is with contract as a principle of social association and one of the most important means of creating social relationships, such as the relation between husband and wife or capitalist and worker. Nor is my argument about property in the sense in which "property" commonly enters into discussions of contract theory. Proponents and critics of contract theory tend to concentrate on property either as material goods, land, and capital, or as the interest (the property) that individuals can be said to have in civil freedom. The subject of all the contracts with which I am concerned is a very special kind of property, the property that individuals are held to own in their persons.

Some knowledge of the story of the sexual contract helps explain why singular problems arise about contracts to which women are a party. The problems are never mentioned in most discussions of the classic texts or by contemporary contract theorists. Feminist have been pointing out the peculiarities of the marriage contract for at least a century and a half, but to no avail. The standard commentaries on the classic stories of the original contract do not usually mention that women are *excluded* from the original pact. Men make the original contract. The device of the state of nature is used to explain why, given the characteristics of the inhabitants of the natural condition, entry into the original contact is a rational act. The crucial point that is omitted is that the inhabitants are sexually differentiated and, for all the classic writers (except Hobbes), a difference in rationality follows from natural sexual difference. Commentaries on the texts gloss over the fact that the classic theorists construct a patriarchal account of masculinity and femininity, of what it is to be men and women. Only masculine beings are endowed with the attributes and capacities necessary to enter into contracts, the most important of which is ownership of property in the person; only men, that is to say, are "individuals". . . .

The construction of the difference between the sexes as the difference between freedom and subjection is not merely central to a famous political story. The structure of our society and our everyday lives incorporates the patriarchal conception of sexual difference. I shall show how the exclusion of women from the central category of the "individual" has been given social and legal expression and how the exclusion has structured the contracts with which I am concerned. . . .

To tell the story of the sexual contract is to show how sexual difference, what it is to be a "man" or "woman," and the construction of sexual difference as political difference, is central to civil society. Feminism has always been vitally concerned with sexual difference and feminists now face a very complex problem. In modern patriarchy the difference between the sexes is presented as the quintessentially natural difference. Men's patriarchal right over women is presented as reflecting the proper order of nature. How then should feminists deal with sexual difference? The problem is that, in a period when contract has a wide appeal, the patriarchal insistence that sexual difference is politically relevant all too easily suggests that arguments that refer to women *as women* reinforce the patriarchal appeal to nature. The appropriate feminist response then seems to be to work for the elimination of all reference to the difference between men and women in political life; so, for example, all laws and policies should be "gender-neutral." I shall say something about the now ubiquitous terminology of "gender" in the final chapter. Such a response assumes that "individuals" can be separated from sexually differentiated bodies. Contract doctrine relies on the same assumption in order to claim that all examples of contract involving property in the person establish free relations. The problem is that the assumption relies on a political fiction.

When feminism uncritically occupies the same terrain as contract, a response to patriarchy that appears to confront the subjection of women head-on also serves to consolidate the peculiarly modern form of patriarchal right. To argue that patriarchy is best confronted by endeavoring to render sexual difference politically irrelevant is to accept the view that the civil (public) realm and the "individual" are uncontaminated by patriarchal subordination. Patriarchy is then seen as a private familial problem that can be overcome if public laws and policies treat women as if they were exactly the same as men. However, modern patriarchy is not, first and foremost, about women's familial subjection. Women engage in sexual relations with men and are wives before they become mothers in families. The story of the sexual contract is about (hetero)sexual relations and women as embodied sexual beings. The story helps us understand the mechanisms through which men claim right of sexual access to women's bodies and claim right of command over the use of women's bodies. Moreover, heterosexual relations are not confined to private life. The most dramatic example of the public aspect of patriarchal right is that men demand that women's bodies are for sale as commodities in the capitalist market; prostitution is a major capitalist industry.

Some feminists fear that references to "men" and "women" merely reinforce the patriarchal claim that "Woman" is a natural and timeless category, defined by certain innate, biological characteristics. To talk about Woman, however, is not all the same thing as talking about women. "The eternal Woman" is a figment of the patriarchal imagination. The constructions of the classical contract theorists no doubt are influenced by the figure of Woman and they have a good deal to say about natural capacities. Nonetheless, they develop a social and political, albeit patriarchal, construction of what it means to be masculine or feminine in modern civil society. To draw out the way in which the meaning of "men" and "women" has helped structure major social institutions is not to fall back on purely natural categories. Nor is it to deny that there are many important differences between women and that, for example, the life of a young Aboriginal woman in inner Sydney will be markedly different from the life of the wife of a wealthy white banker in Princeton. At various points in my argument I shall make specific reference, say, to working-class women, but, in an exploration of contract and patriarchal right, the fact that women are *women* is more relevant than the differences between them. . . .

Sex is central to the original contract. The brothers make the agreement to secure their natural liberty, part of which consists in the patriarchal right of men, the right of one sex. Only one sex has the capacity to enjoy civil freedom. Civil freedom includes right of sexual access to women and, more broadly, the enjoyment of mastery of a sex—not a gender. The germ "gender" is now ubiquitous but frequently lies idle, used merely as an often not very apt synonym for "women." "Gender" was introduced as a crucial weapon in the struggle against patriarchy. The patriarchal claim is that women are naturally subject to men, subject, that is, because of their biology, their sex. To refer to gender instead of sex indicates that women's position is not dictated by nature, by biology or sex, but is a matter of social and political contrivance. True; what men and women are, and how relations between them are structured, depends on a good deal more that their natural physiology and biology. It is also true, however, that the meaning of men's and women's natures, even the depiction of male and female skeletons and physiology, has depended on the political significance accorded to manhood and womanhood. To use the language of gender reinforces the language of the civil, the public, and the individual, language that depends on the repression of the sexual contract.

The meaning of the "individual" remains intact only so long as the dichotomies (internal to civil society) between natural/civil, private/public, women/individual—and sex/gender—remain intact. Women's inclusion into civil society as members of a gender, as individuals, is also their inclusion as member of a sex, as women. The new surrogacy contract illustrates the mutual dependence of sex and the individual/gender in the most dramatic fashion. Two sexually indifferent individuals (owners, representatives of the genders) must be party to the contract or the contract will be illegitimate, nothing more than a case of baby selling. On the other hand, the surrogacy contract is only possible at all because one party is a woman; only a woman has the requisite capacity (property) to provide the service demanded, a capacity integral to (natural to) her sex.

For feminists to argue for the elimination of nature, biology, sex in favor of the "individual" is to play the modern patriarchal game and to join in a much wider onslaught on nature within and beyond the boundaries of civil societies. Nature is represented not only by women, but also, for example, by land, indigenous peoples, the descendants of the slaves whom the Reverend Seabury imagined to have contracted with their masters, and animals (and the latter may become property in a new fashion; the Patent and Trademark Office in the United States will now take applications for patents for genetically altered animals, which are being given the same status as any other human invention). To suppose that the patriarchal appeal to nature and natural, sexual difference implies that patriarchal theories and institutions follow directly from what is given by nature (from physiology, from biology, from sex) is to remain locked within patriarchal confines. The classic contract theorists are instructive here; they did not simply take their pictures of the state of nature and the natural inhabitants of the original condition from nature. Nothing about political relations can be read directly from the two natural bodies of humankind that must inhabit the body politic. The state of nature is drawn by each theorist in a manner that enables him to reach "the desired solution"—the political solution he has already formulated. Sexual difference in the classic contract theories is, and can only be, a political construct.

To ask whether sexual difference is politically significant is to ask the wrong question; the question is always how the difference is to be expressed. One reason why the wrong question is so often posed is that a good deal of contemporary feminist argument assumes that a choice has to be made between femininity as subordination and the ostensibly sex-neuter "individual." In modern patriarchy, as a (re)reading of the texts of classic contract theory makes clear, these are *not alternatives*; to choose one is to choose the other too. . . .

Note

1. A. Rich, "Compulsory Heterosexuality and Lesbian Existence," *Signs* 5, no. 4 (1980): 645.

SELECTION 34
FROM
Feminism and Democratic Community Revisited

CAROL C. GOULD

WHAT CONTRIBUTION CAN FEMINIST theory make to the conception of a democratic community? In recent years, feminists have drawn on women's experiences as the basis for a reconstructed political theory. They have sought to revise or replace the models of contract, or of the marketplace, or of formal justice with alternative models derived from the relations of care and mothering and from women's experiences of inequality and domination.[1] Some feminist theorists have also put in question what they regard as a prevailing Western model of rationality, sometimes characterized as logocentric, which they see as underlying the political conceptions. But there have been few attempts to articulate the connection between feminism and the important part of political philosophy that may be characterized as democratic theory.

In this context, Jane Mansbridge, is her essay "Feminism and Democratic Community," offers a useful and detailed summary of the feminist literature focusing on two central contributions that bear on the concept of democratic community: namely, feminism's sensitivity to the phenomenon of unequal power, and the distinctive emphasis on the dimension of care and commonality that derives in part from the experience of mothering. She advances a perceptive critique of gratuitous gendering and of gender coding. She also points to the need for a notion of democracy as not simply atomistic or adversarial, which is a theme she has developed at length in her earlier work. Her essay, therefore, provides a point of entry for an analysis of the contributions that feminist theory can make to democracy and of some of the limitations of the contemporary debate. . . .

Here, I wish to explore some of the contributions that feminist theorizing concerning the care perspective and the critique of domination can make

to democratic theory and to the concept of democratic community in particular. However, I wish to be more critical than Mansbridge about the
limits of the mothering/familial model for politics. . . .

BEYOND DOMINATION: WOMEN'S EXPERIENCE AND DEMOCRATIC COMMUNITY

A major area of women's experience that is clearly relevant to democratic
community is domination. This presumably is what Mansbridge refers to in
her discussion of women's experience of unequal power. But unequal power
is one thing and domination another. Though this may be a minor point of
difference, there would seem to be a distinction between having less or greater
power than another to effect one's ends and exercising power over another
for one's ends. For example, we may say that a parent has more power than
the child, but it does not follow by virtue of this alone that the parent
stands in a relation of domination toward the child. Unequal power is a
necessary but not a sufficient condition for domination.

Mansbridge's account has the advantage of generality and objectivity in
describing the inequalities in power between men and women in various
contexts. But a description of unequal power omits reference to the social
relations of domination between men and women in personal contexts or
through the functioning of institutions. Domination, as distinguished from
coercion on the one hand and unequal power on the other, involves control or delimitation of the actions of another through control over the conditions of action, objective or subjective. Such domination is not necessarily
fully conscious or deliberate, and may be implicit in the way certain social
institutions or customs operate. Of course, many of the relations between
men and women are not characterized by domination, but it remains a serious problem nonetheless, which tends to be slighted if described only in
terms of inequalities of power.

The critique of domination presupposes a norm of equal freedom and a
requirement of reciprocal recognition of equal agency. That is, individuals
have equal rights to exercise their agency in the development of their capacities and the pursuit of long-term projects. This entails prima facie equal
right to the conditions for such activity and requires recognition by others
of these rights.[2] Though this much follows directly from the critique of
domination, what may be less obvious is how this critique bears on the
requirement for democracy. Equal agency, presupposed by the critique of
domination, entails in general an equal right of self-determination of one's
activity, within the constraints of respect for these equal rights of others.
And where one's activity is common and shared, as it would be in a polity,
or in economic or social institutions, it entails an equal right to participate

in joint decision making concerning this activity. But this is in effect the requirement for democracy. If, by contrast, others determine the range or direction of one's activity, or control the conditions necessary for carrying out the activity, whether this activity is individual or shared as in the institutional contexts of social, economic, or political life, then this is, in one degree or another, a case of domination in the exercise of unequal power. It may in a certain sense seem obvious that the critique of domination, of which women's experience is a paradigmatic case, maps onto an institutional requirement for democracy, but the intrinsic relation between these concepts is not often articulated.

These implications for democracy of the norm of equal freedom inplicit in the critique of domination also bear on the question of individual rights, that is, on the protection of individuals from interference with their liberties or from domination, either by other individuals or by the community as a whole. And it also suggests the need for certain positive rights. For if individuals are to be equally free, their basic freedom of choice needs to be protected by civil liberties and political rights from undue interference; and their power to effect their choices needs to be supported by positive rights to the conditions for their agency.

This view conflicts with the position recently taken by some feminists that rights-based theories of ethics and politics are misguided and ought to be replaced by theories based on caring and particular obligations. A care perspective, they argue, emerges from women's experience, in contrast to the rights and justice perspective held to be drawn from men's experience in the public sphere. Whatever the merits of this emphasis on care, which I consider shortly, I would argue that some conception of equal rights is both implicit in the critique of domination and essential to the justification of democracy. In this way, preservation or further development of an approach that includes rights should not be abandoned by feminist theorists. Such an approach to rights may well need to be developed beyond traditional liberal conceptions. . . .

Likewise, the principle of equal positive freedom, which is implied in the critique of domination, constitutes a principle of distributive justice, namely, that individuals have prima facie equal rights to the conditions necessary for their differentiated self-development. Thus, justice, which has been denigrated as the male gender-coded value in social and political theory, may itself be seen to have a source in the critique of domination that grows out of women's experience.

This interpretation supports not only a norm of equal rights but one of reciprocity as well. By reciprocity I mean a relation characterized by a shared understanding and free agreement that the actions of each individual with respect to the other(s) are equivalent. However, the form of reciprocity

that I have in mind goes beyond what I have called instrumental reciprocity or what has been characterized by others as return for benefit done or as
"tit for tat." This is the externalized form of a relation stripped of its richer
aspects. Rather, the reciprocity that I believe grows out of the feminist critique
of domination in an intentional relation of reciprocal recognition in which
each recognizes the other as free and self-developing, hence as unique.[3]

This mode of reciprocity is most obviously applicable to face-to-face relations among individuals. But something like this may also be seen to be an
essential feature of a democratic decision process in which each agent affords the other reciprocal recognition as a free and distinctive individual,
and in which their differences are respected. . . .

The relation of reciprocity is most obviously characteristic of participatory democratic processes. But it applies to other modes of democratic deliberation and decision making as well. In representative contexts, recognition
of equal political rights and liberties—voting, eligibility for office, free speech,
and so forth—entails tacit, if not explicit, recognition by each citizen of
the other's equal rights. However, I wish to distinguish this sort of reciprocity from that which is sometimes adduced of the care and mothering relation. This latter is a more problematic sense of reciprocity for politics, as I
note later.

These reflections bear on the import of the feminist critique of domination, and of what Mansbridge refers to as women's experience of unequal
power, for questions of individual freedom and rights. Some feminists, however, have criticized such an emphasis as implying an atomistic conception
of individuals,[4] which in turn suggests an adversarial model of democracy.
But this interpretation of freedom and equal rights seems to me mistaken.
And it would be a further mistake to suggest that an emphasis on individual freedom and equal rights entails an atomistic conception of democracy. In fact, the slide from individual freedom and rights to atomic or
abstract individualism may derive from a kind of dichotomous thinking that
sees individuals and relations, or again justice and care, as mutually exclusive categories rather than as closely related aspects of a complex social
reality. By contrast, I have argued that the basic entities that make up social life should be construed as individuals-in-relations or social individuals;[5]
and that justice and care are complementary, rather than conflicting frameworks.[6] Moreover, emphasis on individual freedom and equal rights, when
so understood, certainly does not entail an atomistic or adversarial conception of democracy, but in fact is entirely congruent with the concept of
democratic community. . . .

IS CARE AN ADEQUATE MODEL OF DEMOCRATIC COMMUNITY?

The second major domain of women's experience that has increasingly been adduced as a normative model for ethics and politics is that of care, especially as it relates to the practice of mothering.[7] Care is held to emcompass a range of characteristic dispositions, such as concern for the other not out of duty or obligation but out of feeling or sympathy; attention or attentiveness; sensitivity to the needs of others, and more strongly, taking the others' interests as equal to or more important than one's own; concern for the growth and enhancement of the other; and an orientation to the common interest of the family or of those who are close or related to one. These feelings and dispositions are directed to particular others rather than universally, and so contrast with traditional notions of universal and impartial principles and obligations. Although some of the feminist literature associates these characteristics exclusively with a gender-defined experience or mothering, some feminists, including Mansbridge, rightly see these features as not exclusively gender-related—and therefore I would say perhaps better characterized as related to parenting—although it is clear that the culturally dominant expression of these traits has heretofore been identified with the role of experience of women.

There is a presumption that these experiences lend support to notions of community and hence to a richer conception of democracy. The question is how to interpret these dispositions of caring and attentiveness and the concern with the common interest of the family for the case of democracy. In one sense this seems obvious: These ways of expressing concern for others and for their needs that characterize the relation of care in intimate personal relations and in certain familial relations would seem to match the democratic community's requirement for relations of reciprocity and especially for reciprocal respect, though not all relations of care are reciprocal, as I discuss below. Further, the notion of a common interest seems to be easily extrapolated from the commonality of family feeling to a larger polity or community.

Indeed, the elements of what I have called democratic personality include just such features as a disposition to reciprocity, and receptivity or attentiveness to the views of others.[8] In addition, a shared or common interest both provides the context for democratic decision making and is elaborated in the process of deliberation.[9] I think that the experience of caring and concern that is characteristically taken to belong to women facilitates an awareness of common interest that is fundamental to the possibility of a democratic community. In addition, I also believe that the typical concern for providing for the specific needs of others associated with mothering or parenting or with family relations more generally can usefully be imported into the larger democratic community in terms of a focus on meeting the differentiated needs of individuals and not simply protecting their negative liberties. Thus, care is this context translates into responsiveness to the particular needs and interests of individuals or groups instead of treating them all in the very same way. It also connotes a concern for providing the economic and social means for the development of individuals and not only refraining from impeding their choices. So far so good.

However, the notion of care as a model for democratic community has serious limitations. But to deal with them, I think it important to draw some distinctions in the concept of care that have been overlooked in the feminist discussion. In the recent literature, the idea of care seems to be drawn mainly from two sources of models, which are most often blended together. However, important differences exist between them, even though they are related. The first of these sources is mothering or parenting, in which care manifests itself largely as nurturance or concern for the vulnerable child and for its development. Care in this sense of nurturance is nonreciprocal, because in this relation, the parent takes care of the young child but, at this stage at least, the child is not in a position reciprocally to take care of the parent, even though they reciprocally care *about* each other and reciprocally adjust their responses to each other. The child is initially utterly dependend on the parent and the parent provides for, teaches, and has responsibility for the child. Of course, as Virginia Held points out, the mothering relation is aimed at raising an equal in the child so that the relation with the child becomes reciprocal with maturation;[10] and it is already reciprocal in that parent and child love each other. But qua mothering or parenting, the care is nonreciprocal. A somewhat related context of nonreciprocal relation is care for others who are vulnerable or dependent by virtue of their weakness, illness, or deprivation. Here, common models are nursing and welfare.

The nonreciprocal relation of care as nurturance may be characterized as a case of benign nonreciprocity by contrast with what we might call malignant nonreciprocity. The latter refers to nonreciprocal relations of domination or exploitation, in which one controls the actions of another and thus inhibits the other's freedom or benefits at the other's expense.

The second main source for the feminist concept of care is that of love or intimate personal relation, which entails, ideally, a reciprocal or mutual concern of each for the other. Feminist theorists have most often interpreted this as involving mutuality, in a sense that connotes not only reciprocal recognition of the individuality of the other and respect for the other's needs, but beyond this, enhancement by each of the other, by altruistic actions. The distinction between the two models of care based on these two rather different sources, mothering and love, has largely been disregarded in the literature. But it remains a significant distinction between a nonreciprocal and a reciprocal relation.

Where care involves a reciprocal relation, as in the case of love or intimate personal connection, we need a further distinction between the strong case of mutuality, as a relation in which each individual consciously undertakes to enhance the other, and the more minimal model of care involved in social reciprocity of the reciprocity of respect. In this latter type of reciprocity, each recognizes the distinctive individuality of the other and has concern for the differences in the other's needs, and for their satisfaction. We have a relation of sympathy or understanding of the other but not yet the active engagement in enhancing the other that characterizes mutuality. A relation of reciprocal sympathy and understanding, or concern for the other, is clearly a feature of the relation of love or indeed of friendship. But it may also characterize a social relation among members of a community who are neither lovers nor friends. For example, among members of a tribal or ethnic or political community, there may be relations of such reciprocal sympathy, as a type of care.

In addition to the two sources for the conception of care, the maternal and the love relation, one should mention a third source for this concept in the feminist literature. This is the family as a model of common concern or a common good that relates all of the members to each other.[11] In addition to caring for each other, as in the case of love, on this model they are bound by a common interest in the well-being of the family unit that is not identical with the care they have for each other as individuals. In such a case, we may speak of cooperative reciprocity as a relation among individuals engaged in activities toward common ends. It is easy to see how such a familial model could be interpreted for political community. The family metaphor is commonplace in the history of political thought, though most often with a patriarchal interpretation, the King or the State as Father.

The limitations on the extension of the concept of care to the democratic community can be seen from this account of the various models of care. The maternal or parental model has obvious limitations in any extrapolation to political or institutional contexts of democratic communities. Even though it includes elements of reciprocity, parenting is more fundamentally a nonreciprocal relation. A democratic community, by contrast, is based on reciprocal relations among equals who share authority by virtue of their equal rights to participate in decision making. This is not to say that the elements of personal care that characterize both parenting and care for the indigent or ill are irrelevant to democratic community. On the contrary, concern for specific needs and individual differences is one of the features that marks off democratic community from a society of abstract equality.

Another limitation of the maternal or parental model is the particularism and exclusivity that are characteristic of the caring concern for the child in the family. Though appropriate in that context, it can hardly provide a model for the democratic community, because in this case fairness requires equal rights and equal consideration of interests, independent of any particular feelings of care for given individuals. In fact, it is an acknowledged violation of democratic equality to act on the basis of favoritism, or of special interests, or to permit personal alliances to violate requirements of fairness. The same limitation holds for the model of love or intimate personal connection, as well as for the model of the family, which are characterized by particularism and exclusivity of care.

Yet it should be granted that the domain of politics, like those of the economy and social life, has its own modes of exclusivity and particularism, some warranted and some not. For example, citizenship itself is an exclusionary category, at least as states are now constituted. And the criteria of membership in social institutions more generally is a live issue in contemporary political and social debate. Similarly, ethnicity connotes not only belonging but exclusion as well. Nonetheless, at the political/institutional level, membership or exclusion ought not to be on the basis of personal feelings that are relevant in the contexts of care. Similarly, universality and equality are norms for politics in the context of law and rights in ways that are inappropriate for the domain of personal relations.

The models of loving care and of the family in their extrapolation to political or other institutional contexts have the further problem that it would be misplaced or wrong to require in a democratic community that people act toward others out of feelings of love or even affection, or that they aim at the enhancement of particular others. Such mutuality is appropriate in interpersonal relations of love, family, or in the case of friendship, but cannot be expected or normatively required at an institutional level. It may be observed that the models of both mothering and intimate personal connection display the same problem as does the friendship model of democracy that has so often been drawn on,[12] namely, the problem of attempting to extrapolate what is appropriate for a two-person relation to institutional relations. More generally, I suggest that a norm like mutuality that is fully appropriate as an ethical desideratum in certain relations among individuals does not map onto the political level as an appropriate value, where instead we need to speak of the value of reciprocity, along with freedom, equality, and democracy. Further, the more complex norm of care cannot be simply taken over whole into political or institutional contexts of democracy. This does not rule out that certain personal relations and traits of character, as well as certain specifically ethical norms, may themselves be conditions for the development of democratic community. Additionally, there may well be specific forms of family or personal relations, for example, shared child raising between parents, that are more conducive to democratic community than are other arrangements.

Despite these limitations, some features of these models of care can usefully be extrapolated to the larger context of democratic community. We may point to three relevant aspects: first, the concern for the specific individuality and differences of the other that is involved in social reciprocity or the reciprocity of respect. This type of reciprocity is, as we have seen, a prime feature of democratic community. It expresses a relation of care inasmuch as it involves a sympathetic understanding of the perspective of the other and the other's concrete individuality. In deliberation or decision making in politics, or the workplace, social relations of this sort help to distinguish a democratic community from the merely procedural form of decisions by voting. However, reciprocal concern does not either presuppose or require that the individuals have any personal affection for each other. We are speaking of what we might call political feelings rather than personal sentiments or even moral feelings.

A second type of care that relates to democratic community, whether in politics, the economy, or social life more generally, is that involved in cooperative reciprocity. In this case, the concern that individuals have for each other is defined by their participation in a common activity oriented to shared ends, or to what they take to be a common good. The care in this case is therefore aimed at the achievement of this good that in turn requires their concern for each other's participation in this common activity and concern about their own responsibility for the joint undertaking.

The third type of political or social care is concern for the vulnerable that we have characterized as a benign form of nonreciprocity. In a democratic community, this concern expresses itself in support of and participation in those programs that provide for the welfare of the sick, the aged, the unemployed, and the otherwise dependent members of the community. Here, as in mothering, the aim of care is the elimination where possible of the conditions of dependence.

We have considered the contributions that the perspective of care makes to the concept of democratic community, and also the limitations of this perspective displayed in attempts to extrapolate it to the political/institutional level. However, other aspects of women's experience, in the contexts of mothering, love, and family life, must be recognized as negative and as potentially having a distorting effect on the concepts of care and democratic community. First, as Mansbridge observes, the ideal model of the caring mother, concerned with the good of the child, is not always realized in practice, for the relation is sometimes marked by domination or even abuse. Likewise, care in family relations between men and women is sometimes distorted by the subordination of the interests or the personality of one to the other. In consequence, women's experience may generate indifference to or even embarassment over the exercise of effective power in social or political contexts, as if it were exclusively a male prerogative and therefore to be eschewed. This leads to a distortion of the idea of democratic community, where in fact the proper uses of power have an important place, and where effectiveness in reaching goals is as central as concern for others.

Another negative element in women's experience tends to be left out of discussion in some uncritical or romanticized accounts of care. In our culture there is a tendency to overlook the degree to which women are socialized to adopt the prevailing norms of competitive and possessive individualism, which may well describe contexts of the family and mothering, as well as work. Consumerism and self-seeking, antagonistic attitudes toward others, including other women or families, are not absent from women's contemporary experience. Where women act in these ways, whether at home or at work, it is not simply that they are emulating men, as it is frequently suggested, but these modes may be part of their own upbringing as well.

Moreover, it would be a mistake to focus the import of women's experience for democratic community exclusively on the domains of mothering, love, or family. This would make it appear that the context of work and of social engagement outside these personal relations is not a distinctive source of women's experience that is relevant to the concept of democratic community or indeed to the model of caring itself.

Beyond this, I suggest that the exclusive association of the model of care with women's experience overlooks the degree to which caring is also a deep feature of human experience generally. One is reminded of the early Heidegger's view that the Being of *Dasein* is care.[13] The term "care" obviously has wider connotations than the more limited notion of maternal concern. This has been noted by some feminists who distinguish different connotations of the term.[14] A further analysis of the concept, and the various concrete caring relations in the experience of men as well as of women, would lead to a more nuanced view of care, while recognizing the centrality of parenting and love.

In an earlier essay, I proposed that what was needed was what I called "political androgyny," that is, an importation into the public domain of politics, economics, and social life of the range of capacities, concerns, and values deriving from women's historical experience, as a corrective for the predominance in public life of historically male concerns and values.[15] What is needed is a synthesis of these two, which would integrate considerations of care with those of justice, and of individuality with those of community. Here, I have tried to suggest some of these mediations. The gendering of these concepts, though historically important (as well as in most ways historically unfortunate), is incidental to their normative content. Nonetheless, only through an explicit study of women's experience that is the main source of the norm of care itself can we realize the full depth of the concept and work out its relations to the concepts of justice, power, and democratic community.

One consequence of my analysis is that the conception of a democratic community cannot involve a reduction to a set of personal relations, nor should it be understood in terms of a holistic or organic community imposed on a set of indifferent individuals. Instead, I propose that democratic community is constituted by what I have called individuals-in-relations, who reciprocally recognize each other, share some ends, and take themselves to be members of the community. Further, in a democratic community, this same joint intentionality constitutes what comes to be represented as the common interest, but that is the beginning of another story.

Notes

1. Cf., for example, Virginia Held, "Non-Contractual Society: A Feminist View," in M. Hanen and K. Nielsen, eds., *Science, Morality, and Feminist Theory* (Calgary: University of Calgary Press, 1987); Sara Ruddick, *Maternal Thinking* (Boston: Beacon Press, 1989); and Iris M. Young, *Justice and the Politics of Difference* (Princeton: Princeton University Press, 1990).
2. Cf. Carol C. Gould, *Rethinking Democracy: Freedom and Social Cooperation in Politics, Economy and Society* (Cambridge: Cambridge University Press, 1988), ch. 1.
3. Carol C. Gould, "Beyond Causality in the Social Sciences: Reciprocity as a Model of Non-Exploitative Social Relations," in R. S. Cohen and M. W. Wartofsky, eds., *Epistemology, Methodology, and the Social Sciences: Boston Studies in the Philosophy of Science*, vol. 71 (Boston and Dordrecht: D. Reidel, 1983), 53–88; and Gould, *Rethinking Democracy*, 71–80.
4. See, for example, Carol Gilligan, "Moral Orientation and Moral Development," in E. F. Kittay and D. T. Meyers, eds., *Women and Moral Theory* (Totowa, NJ: Rowman and Littlefield, 1987), 19–33.
5. Gould, *Rethinking Democracy*, ch. 2; and *Marx's Social Ontology* (Cambridge, MA: MIT Press, 1978), ch. 1.
6. Cf. Carol C. Gould, "Philosophical Dichotomies and Feminist Thought: Towards a Critical Feminism," in H. Nagl, ed., *Feministische Philosophie*, Wiener Reihe, Band 4 (Vienna: R. Oldenbourg Verlag, 1990), 184–90.
7. Cf., for example, Held, "Non-Contractual Society"; Sara Ruddick, *Maternal Thinking*; Carol Gilligan, *In a Different Voice* (Cambridge: Harvard University Press, 1982); Nel Noddings, *Caring: A Feminine Approach to Ethics and Moral Education* (Berkeley: University of California Press, 1984); and the essays in Kittay and Meyers, eds., *Women and Moral Theory*.
8. Gould, *Rethinking Democracy*, ch. 10.
9. Cf. Carol C. Gould, "On the Conception of the Common Interest: Between Procedure and Substance," in M. Kelly, ed., *Hermeneutics and Critical Theory in*

Ethics and Politics (Cambridge: MIT Press, 1990), 253–73.

10. Held, "Non-Contractual Society," 131.

11. By family here, I do not exclusively mean family by marriage or in terms of blood relations.

12. Most recently by Jacques Derrida, "The Politics of Friendship," *Journal of Philosophy* 85, no. 12 (1988) 632–45.

13. Martin Heidegger, *Being and Time*, tr. J. Macquarrie and E. Robinson (New York: Harper and Row, 1962), 225–73.

14. Cf. Joan C. Tronto, "Women and Caring: What Can Feminists Learn about Morality from Caring?" in A. M. Jaggar and S. R. Bordo, eds., *Gender/Body/Knowledge* (New Brunswick: Rutgers University Press, 1984), 172–87; and Noddings, *Caring*.

15. Carol C. Gould, "Private Rights and Public Virtues: Women, the Family, and Democracy," in C. Gould, ed., *Beyond Domination: New Perspectives on Women and Philosophy* (Totowa, NJ: Rowman and Allanheld, 1984), 3–18.

SELECTION 35
FROM
Justice, Gender, and the Family
SUSAN MOLLER OKIN

THE CONSTRUCTION OF GENDER

DUE TO FEMINISM AND feminist theory, gender is coming to be recognized as a social factor of major importance. Indeed, the new meaning of the word reflects the fact that so much of what has traditionally been thought of as sexual difference is now considered by many to be largely socially produced.[1] . . .

During the same two decades in which feminists have been intensely thinking, researching, analyzing, disagreeing about, and rethinking the subject of gender, our political and legal institutions have been increasingly faced with issues concerning the injustices of gender and their effects. These issues are being decided within a fundamentally patriarchal system, founded in a tradition in which "individuals" were assumed to be male heads of households. Not surprisingly, the system has demonstrated a limited capacity for determining what is just, in many cases involving gender. Sex discrimination, sexual harassment, abortion, pregnancy in the workplace, parental leave, child care, and surrogate mothering have all become major and well-publicized issues of public policy, engaging both courts and legislatures. Issues of family justice, in particular—from child custody and terms of divorce to physical and sexual abuse of wives and children—have become increasingly visible and pressing, and are commanding increasing attention from the police and court systems. There is clearly a major "justice crisis" in contemporary society arising from issues of gender.

· THEORIES OF JUSTICE AND THE NEGLECT OF GENDER

During these same two decades, there has been a great resurgence of theories of social justice. Political theory, which had been sparse for a period before the late 1960s except as an important branch of intellectual history, has become a flourishing field, with social justice as its central concern. Yet, remarkably, major contemporary theorists of justice have almost without exception ignored the situation I have just described. They have displayed little interest in or knowledge of the findings of feminism. They have largely bypassed the fact that the society to which their theories are supposed to pertain is heavily and deeply affected by gender, and faces difficult issues of justice stemming from its gendered past and present assumptions. Since theories of justice are centrally concerned with whether, how, and why persons should be treated differently from one another, this neglect seems inexplicable. These theories are *about* which initial or acquired characteristics or positions in society legitimize differential treatment of persons by social institutions, laws, and customs. They are *about* how and whether and to what extent beginnings should affect outcomes. The division of humanity into two sexes seems to provide an obvious subject for such inquiries. But, as we shall see, this does not strike most contemporary theorists of justice, and their theories suffer in both coherence and relevance because of it. . . .

THE HIDDEN GENDER-STRUCTURED FAMILY

In the past, political theorists often used to distinguish clearly between "private" domestic life and the "public" life of politics and the marketplace, claiming explicitly that the two spheres operated in accordance with different principles. They separated out the family from what they deemed the subject matter of politics, and they made closely related, explicit claims about the nature of women and the appropriateness of excluding them from civil and political life. Men, the subjects of the theories, were able to make the transition back and forth from domestic to public life with ease, largely because of the functions performed by women in the family.[2] When we turn to contemporary theories of justice, superficial appearances can easily lead to the impression that they are inclusive of women. In fact, they continue the same "separate spheres" tradition, by ignoring the family, its division of labor, and the related economic dependency and restricted opportunities of most women. The judgment that the family is "nonpolitical" is implicit in the fact that it is simply not discussed in most works of political theory today. In one way or another almost all current theorists continue to assume that the "individual" who is the basic subject of their theories is the male head of a fairly traditional household. Thus the application of principles of justice to relations between the sexes, or within the household, is frequently, though tacitly, ruled out from the start. In the most influential of all twentieth-century theories of justice, that of John Rawls, family life is not only assumed, but is assumed to be just—and yet the prevalent gendered division of labor within the family is neglected, along with the associated distribution of power, responsibility, and privilege.

Moreover, this stance is typical of contemporary theories of justice. They persist, despite the wealth of feminist challenges to their assumptions, in their refusal even to discuss the family and its gender structure, much less to recognize the family as a political institution of primary importance. Recent theories that pay even less attention to issues of family justice than Rawl's include Bruce Ackerman's *Social Justice in the Liberal State*, Ronald Dworkin's *Taking Rights Seriously*, William Galston's *Justice and the Human Good*, Alasdair MacIntyre's *After Virtue* and *Whose Justice? Who Rationality?*, Robert Nozick's *Anarchy, State, and Utopia*, and Roberto Unger's *Knowledge and Politics* and *The Critical Legal Studies Movement*.[3] Philip Green's *Retrieving Democracy* is a welcome exception.[4] Michael Walzer's *Spheres of Justice*, too, is exceptional in this regard, but the conclusion that can be inferred from his discussion of the family—that its gender structure is unjust—does not sit at all easily with his emphasis on the shared understandings of a culture as the foundation of justice.[5] For gender is one aspect of social life about which clearly, in the United States in the latter part of the twentieth century, there are no shared understandings.

What is the basis of my claim that the family, while neglected, is *assumed* by theorists of justice? One obvious indication is that they take mature, independent human beings as the subjects of their theories without any mention of how they got to be that way. We know, of course, that human beings develop and mature only as a result of a great deal of attention and hard work, by far the greater part of it done by women. But when theorists of justice talk about "work," they mean paid work performed in the marketplace. They must be assuming that women, in the gender-structured family, continue to do their unpaid work of nurturing and socializing the young and providing a haven of intimate relations—otherwise there would be no moral subjects for them to theorize about. But these activities apparently take place outside the scope of their theories. Typically, the family itself is not examined in the light of whatever standard of justice the theorist arrives at.[6]

The continued neglect of the family by theorists of justice flies in the face of a great deal of persuasive feminist argument. Scholars have clearly revealed the interconnections between the gender structure inside and outside the family and the extent to which the personal is political. They have shown that the assignment of primary parenting to women is crucial, both in forming the gendered identities of men and women and in influencing their respective choices and opportunities in life. Yet, so far, the simultaneous assumption and neglect of the family has allowed the impact of these arguments to go unnoticed in major theories of justice. . . .

The combined effect of the omission of the family and the falsely gender-neutral language in recent political thought is that most theorists are continuing to ignore the highly political issue of gender. The language they use makes little difference to what they actually do, which is to write about men and about only those women who manage, in spite of the gendered structures and practices of the society in which they live, to adopt patterns of life that have been developed to suit the needs of men. The fact that human beings are born as helpless infants—not as the purportedly autonomous actors who populate political theories—is obscured by the implicit assumption of gendered families, operating outside the range of the theories. To a large extent, contemporary theories of justice, like those of the past, are about men with wives at home.

GENDER AS AN ISSUE OF JUSTICE

For three major reasons, this state of affairs is unacceptable. The first is the obvious point that women must be fully included in any satisfactory theory of justice. The second is that equality of opportunity, not only for women but for children of both sexes, is seriously undermined by the current gender injustices of our society. And the third reason is that, as has already been suggested, the family—currently the linchpin of the gender structure—must be just if we are to have a just society, since it is within the family that we first come to have that sense of ourselves and our relations with others that is at the root of moral development. . . .

COUNTING WOMEN IN

Unfortunately, much feminist intellectual energy in the 1980s has gone into the claim that "justice" and "rights" are masculinist ways of thinking about morality that feminists should eschew or radically revise, advocating a morality of care.[7] The emphasis is misplaced, I think, for several reasons. First, what is by now a vast literature on the subject shows that the evidence for differences in women's and men's ways of thinking about moral issues is not (at least yet) very clear; neither is the evidence about the source of whatever differences there might be.[8] It may well turn out that any differences can be readily explained in terms of roles, including female primary parenting, that are socially determined and therefore alterable. There is certainly no evidence—nor could there be, in such a gender-structured society—for concluding that women are somehow naturally more inclined toward contextuality and away from universalism in their moral thinking, a false concept that unfortunately reinforces the old stereotypes that justify separate spheres. The capacity of reactionary forces to capitalize on the "different moralities" strain in feminism is particularly evident in Pope John Paul II's recent Apostolic Letter, "On the Dignity of Women," in which he refers to women's special capacity to care for others in arguing for confining them to motherhood or celibacy.[9]

Second, I think the distinction between an ethic of justice and an ethic of care has been overdrawn. The best theorizing about justice, I argue, has integral to it the notions of care and empathy, of thinking of the interests and well-being of others who may be very different from ourselves. It is, therefore, misleading to draw a dichotomy as though they were two contrasting ethics. The best theorizing about justice is not some abstract "view from nowhere," but results from the carefully attentive consideration of *everyone's* point of view. This means, of course, that the best theorizing about justice is not good enough if it does not, or cannot readily be adapted to, include women and their points of view as fully as men and their points of view.

THE FAMILY AS A SCHOOL OF JUSTICE

One of the things that theorists who have argued that families need not or cannot be just, or who have simply neglected them, have failed to explain is how, within a formative social environment that is *not* founded upon principles of justice, children can learn to develop that sense of justice they will require as citizens of a just society. Rather than being one among many coequal institutions of a just society, a just family is its essential foundation.

It may seem uncontroversial, even obvious, that families must be just because of the vast influence they have on the moral development of children. But this is clearly not the case. I shall argue that unless the first and most formative example of adult interaction usually experienced by children is one of justice and reciprocity, rather than one of domination and manipulation or of unequal altruism and one-sided self-sacrifice, and unless they themselves are treated with concern and respect, they are likely to be considerably hindered in becoming people who are guided by principles of justice. Moreover, I claim, the sharing of roles by men and women, rather than the division of roles between them, would have a further positive impact because the experience of *being* a physical and psychological nurturer—whether of a child or of another adult—would increase that capacity to identify with and fully comprehend the viewpoints of others that is important to a sense of justice. In a society that minimized gender this would be more likely to be the experience of all of us. . . .

The position that justice within the family is irrelevant to the development of just citizens was not plausible even when only men were citizens. John Stuart Mill, in *The Subjection of Women*, takes an impassioned stand against it. He argues that the inequality of women within the family is deeply subversive of justice in general in the wider social world, because it subverts the moral potential of men. Mill's first answer to the question, "For whose good are all these changes in women's rights to be undertaken?" is: "the advantage of having the most universal and pervading of all human relations regulated by justice instead of injustice." Making marriage a relationship of equals, he argues, would transform this central part of daily life from "a school of despotism" into "a school of moral cultivation."[10] . . . Mill both saw clearly and had the courage to address what so many other political philosophers either could not see, or saw and turned away from.

Despite the strength and fervor of his advocacy of women's rights, however, Mill's idea of a just family structure falls far short of that of many feminists even of his own time, including his wife, Harriet Taylor. In spite of the fact that Mill recognized both the empowering effect of earnings on one's position in the family and the limiting effect of domestic responsibility on women's opportunities, he balked at questioning the traditional division of labor between the sexes. For him, a woman's choice of marriage was parallel to a man's choice of a profession: Unless and until she had fulfilled her obligations to her husband and children, she should not undertake anything else. But clearly, however equal the legal rights of husbands and wives, this position largely undermines Mill's own insistence upon the importance of marital equality for a just society. His acceptance of the traditional division of labor, without making any provision for wives who were thereby made economically dependent upon their husbands, largely undermines his insistence upon family justice as the necessary foundation for social justice.

Thus even those political theorists of the past who have perceived the family as an important school of moral development have rarely acknowledged the need for congruence between the family and the wider social order, which suggests that families themselves need to be just. Even when they have, as with Mill, they have been unwilling to push hard on the traditional division of labor within the family in the name of justice or equality.

Contemporary theorists of justice, with few exceptions, have paid little or no attention to the question of moral development—of how we are to *become* just. Most of them seem to think, to adapt slightly Hobbes's notable phrase, that just men spring like mushrooms from the earth.[11] Not surprisingly, then, it is far less often acknowledged in recent than in past theories that the family is important for moral development, and especially for instilling a sense of justice. As I have already noted, many theorists pay no attention at all to either the family or gender. In the rare case that the issue of justice within the family is given any sustained attention, the family is not viewed as a potential school of social justice.[12] In the rare case that a theorist pays any sustained attention to the development of a sense of justice or morality, little if any attention is likely to be paid to the family.[13] Even in the rare event that theorists pay considerable attention to the family *as* the first major locus of moral socialization, they do not refer to the fact that families are almost all still thoroughly gender-structured institutions.[14]

Among major contemporary theorists of justice, John Rawls alone treats the family seriously as the earliest school of moral development. He argues that a just, well-ordered society will be stable only if its members continue to develop a sense of justice. And he argues that families play a fundamental role in the stages by which this sense of justice is acquired. From the parents' love for their child, which comes to be reciprocated, comes the child's "sense of his own value and the desire to become the sort of person that they are."[15] The family, too, is the first of that series of "associations" in which we participate, from which we acquire the capacity, crucial for a sense of justice, to see things from the perspectives of others. This capacity— the capacity for empathy—is essential for maintaining a sense of justice of the Rawlsian kind. For the perspective that is necessary for maintaining a sense of justice is not that of the egoistic or disembodied self, or of the dominant few who overdetermine "our" traditions or "shared understandings," or (to use Nagel's term) of "the view from nowhere," but rather the perspective of every person in the society for whom the principles of justice are being arrived at. As I shall argue, the problem with Rawls's rare and interesting discussion of moral development is that it rests on the unexplained *assumption* that family institutions are just. If gendered family institutions are *not* just, but are, rather, a relic of caste or feudal societies in which responsibilities, roles, and resources are distributed, not in accordance with the principles of justice he arrives at or with any other commonly respected values, but in accordance with innate differences that are imbued with enormous social significance, then Rawls's theory of moral development would seem to be built on uncertain ground. This problem is exacerbated by suggestions in some of Rawls's most recent work that families are "private institutions," to which it is not appropriate to apply standards of justice. But if families are to help form just individuals and citizens, surely they must be *just families*.

In a just society, the structure and practices of families must give women the same opportunities as men to develop their capacities, to participate in political power and influence social choices, and to be economically secure. But in addition to this, families must be just because of the vast influence that they have on the moral development of children. The family is the primary institution of formative moral development. And the structure and practices of the family must parallel those of the larger society if the sense of justice is to be fostered and maintained. While many theorists of justice, both past and present, appear to have denied the importance of at least one of these factors, my own view is that both are absolutely crucial. A society that is committed to equal respect for all of its members, and to justice in social distributions of benefits and responsibilities, can neither neglect the family nor accept family structures and practices that violate these norms, as do current gender-based structures and practices. It is essential that children who are to develop into adults with a strong sense of justice and commitment to just institutions spend their earliest and most formative years in an environment in which they are loved and nurtured, *and* in which principles of justice are abided by and respected. What is a child of either sex to learn about fairness in the average household with two full-time working parents, where the mother does, at the very least, twice as much family work as the father? What is a child to learn about the value of nurturing and domestic work in a home with a traditional division of labor in which the father either subtly or not so subtly uses the fact that he is the wage earner to "pull rank" on or to abuse his wife? What is a child to learn about responsibility for others in a family in which, after many years of arranging her life around the needs of her husband and children, a woman is faced with having to provide for herself and her children but is totally ill-equipped for the task by the life she agreed to lead, has led, and expected to go on leading? . . .

Notes

1. As Joan Scott has pointed out, *gender* was until recently used only as a grammatical term. See "Gender: A Useful Category of Historical Analysis," in Joan Wallach Scott, *Gender and the Politics of History* (New York: Columbia University Press, 1988), 28, citing Fowler's *Dictionary of Modern English Usage.*
2. There is now an abundant literature on the subject of women, their exclusion from nondomestic life, and the reasons given to justify it, in Western political theory. See, for example, Lorenne J. Clark and Lynda Lange, eds., *The Sexism of Social and Political Thought* (Toronto: University of Toronto Press, 1979); Jean Bethke Elshtain, *Public Man, Private Woman: Women in Social and Political Thought* (Princeton: Princeton University Press, 1981); Genevieve Lloyd, *The Man of Reason: "Male" and "Female" in Western Philosophy* (Minneapolis: University of Minnesota Press, 1984); Mary O'Brien, *The Politics of Reproduction* (London: Routledge and Kegan Paul, 1981); Susan Moller Okin, *Women in Western Political Thought* (Princeton: Princeton University Press, 1979); Carole Pateman, "Feminist Critiques of the Public/Private Dichotomy," in *Public and Private in Social Life*, ed. S. Benn and G. Gaus (London: Croom Helm, 1983); Carole Pateman and Elizabeth Gross, eds., *Feminist Challenges: Social and Political Theory* (Boston: Northeastern University Press, 1987); Carole Pateman, *The Sexual Contract* (Stanford: Stanford University Press, 1988); Carole Pateman and Mary L. Shanley, eds., *Feminist Critiques of Political Theory* (Oxford: Polity Press, in press).
3. Bruce Ackerman, *Social Justice in the Liberal State* (New Haven: Yale University Press, 1980); Ronald Dworkin, *Taking Rights Seriously* (Cambridge: Harvard University Press, 1977); William Galston, *Justice and the Human Good* (Chicago: University of Chicago Press, 1980); Alasdair MacIntyre, *After Virtue* (Notre Dame: University of Notre Dame Press, 1981), and *Whose Justice? Which Rationality?* (Notre Dame: University of Notre Dame Press, 1988); Robert Nozick, *Anarchy, State, and Utopia* (New York: Basic Books, 1974); Roberto Unger,

Knowledge and Politics (New York: Free Press, 1975), and *The Critical Legal Studies Movement* (Cambridge: Harvard University Press, 1986).

4. Philip Green, in *Retrieving Democracy: In Search of Civic Equality* (Totowa, NJ: Rowman and Allanheld, 1985), argues that the social equality that is prerequisite to real democracy is incompatible with the current division of labor between the sexes. See 96–108.

5. Michael Walzer, *Spheres of Justice* (New York: Basic Books, 1983).

6. This is commented on and questioned by Francis Schrag. "Justice and the Family," *Inquiry* 19 (1976): 200, and Walzer, *Spheres of Justice*, ch. 9.

7. This claim, originating in the moral development literature, has significantly influenced recent feminist moral and political theory. Two central books are Carol Gilligan, *In a Different Voice* (Cambridge: Harvard University Press, 1982); and Nel Noddings, *Caring: A Feminine Approach to Ethics and Moral Education* (Berkeley: University of California Press, 1984). For the influence of Gilligan's work on feminist theory, see, for example, Seyla Benhabib, "The Generalized and the Concrete Other: The Kohlberg-Gilligan Controversy and Feminist Theory," in *Feminism as Critique*, ed. Benhabib and Drucilla Cornell (Minneapolis: University of Minnesota Press, 1987); Lawrence Blum, "Gilligan and Kohlberg: Implications for Moral Theory," *Ethics* 98, no. 3 (1988); and Eva Kittay and Diana Meyers, eds., *Women and Moral Theory* (Totowa, NJ: Rowman and Allenheld, 1986). For a valuable alternative approach to the issues, and an excellent selective list of references to what has now become a vast literature, see Owen Flanagan and Kathryn Jackson, "Justice, Care, and Gender: The Kohlberg-Gilligan Debate Revisited," *Ethics* 97, no. 3 (1987).

8. See, for example, John M. Broughton, "Women's Rationality and Men's Virtues: A Critique of Gender Dualism in Gilligan's Theory of Moral Development," *Social Research* 50, no. 3 (1983); Owen Flanagan, *Varieties of Moral Personality: Ethics and Psychological Realism* (Cambridge: Harvard University Press, forthcoming), ch. 8; Catherine G. Greeno and Eleanor E. Maccoby, "How Different Is the 'Different Voice'?" and Gilligan's reply, *Signs* 11, no. 2 (1986); Debra Nails, "Social-Scientific Sexism: Gilligan's Mismeasure of Man," *Social Research* 50, no. 3 (1983); Joan Tronto, "'Women's Morality': Beyond Gender Difference to a Theory of Care," *Signs* 12, no. 4 (1987); Lawrence J. Walker, "Sex Differences in the Development of Moral Reasoning: A Critical Review," *Child Development* 55 (1984).

9. See extracts from the Apostolic Letter in *New York Times*, October 1, 1988, pp. A1 and 6. On the reinforcement of the old stereotypes in general, see Susan Moller Okin, "Thinking Like a Woman," in Deborah L. Rhode, ed., *Theoretical Perspectives on Sexual Difference* (New Haven and London: Yale University Press, 1990).

10. John Stuart Mill, *The Subjection of Women* (1869), in *Collected Works*, ed. J. M. Robson (Toronto: University of Toronto Press, 1984), 21:324, 293–95. At the time Mill wrote, women had no political rights and coverture deprived married women of most legal rights, too. He challenges all this in his essay.

11. Hobbes writes of "men . . . as if but even now sprung out of the earth . . . like mushrooms." "Philosophical Rudiments Concerning Government and Society," in *The English Works of Thomas Hobbes*, ed. Sir William Molesworth (London: John Bohn, 1966), 2:109.

12. For example, Walzer, *Spheres of Justice*, ch. 9, "Kinship and Love."

13. See Alan Gewirth, *Reason and Morality* (Chicago: University of Chicago Press,

1978). He discusses moral development from time to time, but places families within the broad category of "voluntary associations" and does not discuss gender roles within them.

14. This is the case with both Rawls's *A Theory of Justice* (Cambridge: Harvard University Press, 1971), discussed here and in ch. 5, and Phillips's sociologically oriented *Toward a Just Social Order*, as discussed above.

15. Rawls, Theory, 465.

SELECTION 36
FROM
On Racism and Sexism

RICHARD A. WASSERSTROM

VIEWED FROM THE PERSPECTIVE of social reality it should be clear . . . that racism and sexism should not be thought of as phenomena that consist simply in taking a person's race or sex into account, or even simply in taking a person's race or sex into account in an arbitrary way. Instead, racism and sexism consist in taking race and sex into account in a certain way, in the context of a specific set of institutional arrangements and a specific ideology which together create and maintain a specific *system* of institutions, role assignments, beliefs, and attitudes. That system is one, and has been one, in which political, economic, and social power and advantage is concentrated in the hands of those who are white and male.

The evils of such systems are, however, not all of a piece. For instance, sometimes people say that what was wrong with the system of racial discrimination in the South was that it took an irrelevant characteristic, namely race, and used it systematically to allocate social benefits and burdens of various sorts. The defect was the irrelevance of the characteristic used, i.e., race, for that meant that individuals ended up being treated in a manner that was arbitrary and capricious.

I do not think that was the central flaw at all—at least of much of the system. Take, for instance, the most hideous of the practices, human slavery. The primary thing that was wrong with the institution was not that the particular individuals who were assigned the place of slaves were assigned there arbitrarily because the assignment was made in virtue of an irrelevant characteristic, i.e., their race. Rather, it seems to me clear that the primary thing that was and is wrong with slavery is the practice itself—the fact of some individuals being able to own other individuals and all that goes with that practice. It would not matter by what criterion individuals were assigned; human slavery would still be wrong. And the same can be said for many of the other discrete practices and institutions that comprised the

347

system of racial discrimination even after human slavery was abolished. The practices were unjustifiable—they were oppressive—and they would have been so no matter how the assignment of victims had been made. What made it worse, still, was that the institutions and ideology all interlocked to create a system of human oppression whose effects on those living under it were as devastating as they were unjustifiable.

Some features of the system of sexual oppression are like this and others are different. For example, if it is true that women are socialized to play the role of servers of men and if they are in general assigned that position in the society, what is objectionable about that practice is the practice itself. It is not that women are being arbitrarily or capriciously assigned the social role of server, but rather that such a role is at least prima facie unjustifiable as a role in a decent society. As a result, the assignment on any basis of individuals to such a role is objectionable.

The assignment of women to primary responsibility for childrearing and household maintenance may be different; it may be objectionable on grounds of unfairness of another sort. That is to say, if we assume that these are important but undesirable aspects of social existence—if we assume that they are, relatively speaking, unsatisfying and unfulfilling ways to spend one's time, then the objection is that women are unduly and unfairly allocated a disproportionate share of unpleasant, unrewarding work. Here the objection, if it is proper, is to the degree to which the necessary burden is placed to a greater degree than is fair on women, rather than shared equally by persons of both sexes.

Even here, though, it is important to see that the essential feature of both racism and sexism consists in the fact that race or sex is taken into account in the context of a specific set of arrangements and a specific ideology which is systemic and which treats and regards persons who are nonwhite or female in a comprehensive, systemic way. Whether it would be capricious to take either a person's race or a person's sex into account in the good society because race and sex were genuinely irrelevant characteristics is a question that can only be answered after we have a clearer idea of what the good society would look like in respect either to race or sex. . . .

IDEALS

The second perspective . . . which is also important for an understanding and analysis of racism and sexism, is the perspective of the ideal. Just as we can and must ask what is involved today in our culture in being of one race or of one sex rather than the other, and how individuals are in fact viewed and treated, we can also ask different questions: namely, what would the good or just society make of race and sex, and to what degree, if at all, would racial and sexual distinctions ever be taken into account? Indeed, it could plausibly be argued that we could not have an adequate idea of whether a society was racist or sexist unless we had some conception of what a thoroughly nonracist or nonsexist society would look like. This perspective is an extremely instructive as well as an often neglected one. Comparatively little theoretical literature that deals with either racism or sexism has concerned itself in a systematic way with this perspective.

In order to ask more precisely what some of the possible ideals are of desirable racial or sexual differentiation, it is necessary to see that we must ask: "In respect to what?" And one way to do this is to distinguish in a crude way among three levels or areas of social and political arrangements and activities. These correspond very roughly to the matters of status, role, and temperament. . . . First, there is the area of basic political rights and obligations, including the rights to vote and to travel, and the obligation to pay income taxes. Second, there is the area of important, nongovernmental institutional benefits and burdens. Examples are access to and employment in the significant economic markets, the opportunity to acquire and enjoy housing in the setting of one's choice, the right of persons who want to marry each other to do so, and the duties (nonlegal as well as legal) that persons acquire in getting married. And third, there is the area of individual, social interaction, including such matters as whom one will have as friends, and what aesthetic preferences one will cultivate and enjoy.

As to each of these three areas we can ask, for example, whether in a nonracist society it would be thought appropriate ever to take the race of the individuals into account. Thus, one picture of a nonracist society is that which is captured by what I call the assimilationist ideal: A nonracist society would be one in which the race of an individual would be the functional equivalent of the eye color of individuals in our society today.[1] In our society no basic political rights and obligations are determined on the basis of eye color. No important institutional benefits and burdens are connected with eye color. Indeed, except for the mildest sort of aesthetic preferences, a person would be thought odd who even made private, social decisions by taking eye color into account. And for reasons that we could fairly readily state we could explain why it would be wrong to permit anything but the mildest, most trivial aesthetic preference to turn on eye color. The reasons would concern the irrelevance of eye color for any political or social institution, practice, or arrangement. According to the assimilationist ideal, a nonracist society would be one in which an individual's race was of no more significance in any of these three areas than is eye color today.

The assimilationist ideal in respect to sex does not seem to be as readily plausible and obviously attractive here as it is in the case of race. In fact, many persons invoke the possible realization of the assimilationist ideal as a reason for rejecting the Equal Rights Amendment and indeed the idea of women's liberation itself. My own view is that the assimilationist ideal may be just as good and just as important an ideal in respect to sex as it is in respect to race. But many persons think there are good reasons why an assimilationist society in respect to sex would not be desirable.

To be sure, to make the assimilationist ideal a reality in respect to sex would involve more profound and fundamental revisions of our institutions and our attitudes than would be the case in respect to race. On the institutional level we would have to alter radically our practices concerning the family and marriage. If a nonsexist society is a society in which one's sex is no more significant than eye color in our society today, then laws that require the persons who are getting married to be of different sexes would clearly be sexist laws.

And on the attitudinal and conceptual level, the assimilationist ideal would require the eradication of all sex-role differentiation. It would never teach about the inevitable or essential attributes of masculinity or femininity; it would never encourage or discourage the ideas of sisterhood or brotherhood; and it would be unintelligible to talk about the virtues as well as disabilities of being a woman or a man. Were sex like eye color, these things would make no sense. Just as the normal, typical adult is virtually oblivious to the eye color of other persons for all major interpersonal relationships, so the normal, typical adult in this kind of nonsexist society would be indifferent to the sexual, physiological differences of other persons for all interpersonal relationships.

To acknowledge that things would be very different is, of course, hardly to concede that they would be undesirable. But still, perhaps the problem is with the assimilationist ideal. And the assimilationist ideal is certainly not the only possible, plausible ideal.

There are, for instance, two others that are closely related, but distinguishable. One I call the ideal of diversity; the other, the ideal of tolerance. Both can be understood by considering how religion, rather than eye color, tends to be thought about in our culture. According to the ideal of diversity, heterodoxy in respect to religious belief and practice is regarded as a positive good. On this view there would be a loss—it would be a worse society—were everyone to be a member of the same religion. According to the other view, the ideal of tolerance, heterodoxy in respect to religious belief and practice would be seen more as a necessary, lesser evil. On this view there is nothing intrinsically better about diversity in respect to religion, but the evils of achieving anything like homogeneity far outweigh the possible benefits.

Now, whatever differences there might be between the ideals of diversity and tolerance, the similarities are more striking. Under neither ideal would it be thought that the allocation of basic political rights and duties should take an individual's religion into account. And we would want equalitarianism even in respect to most important institutional benefits and burdens—for example, access to employment in the desirable vocations. Nonetheless, on both views it would be deemed appropriate to have some institutions (typically those that are connected in an intimate way with these religions) that do in a variety of ways take the religion of members of the society into account. For example, it might be thought permissible and appropriate for members of a religious group to join together in collective associations which have religious, educational, and social dimensions. And on the individual, interpersonal level, it might be thought unobjectionable, or on the diversity view, even admirable, were persons to select their associates, friends, and mates on the basis of their religious orientation. So there are two possible and plausible ideals of what the good society would look like in respect to religion in which religious differences would be to some degree maintained because the diversity of religions was seen either as an admirable, valuable feature of the society, or as one to be tolerated. The picture is a more complex, less easily describable one than that of the assimilationist ideal.

It may be that in respect to sex (and conceivably, even in respect to race) something more like either of these ideals in respect to religion is the right one. But one problem then—and it is a very substantial one—is to specify with a good deal of precision and care what that ideal really comes to. Which legal, institutional, and personal differentiations are permissible and which are not? Which attitudes and beliefs concerning sexual identification and differences are properly introduced and maintained and which are not? Part, but by no means all, of the attractiveness of the assimilationist ideal is its clarity and simplicity. In the good society of the assimilationist sort we would be able to tell easily and unequivocally whether any law, practice, or attitude was in any respect either racist or sexist. Part, but by no means all, of the unattractiveness of any pluralistic ideal is that it makes the question of what is racist or sexist a much more difficult and complicated one to answer. But although simplicity and lack of ambiguity may be virtues, they are not the only virtues to be taken into account in deciding among competing ideals. We quite appropriately take other considerations to be relevant to an assessment of the value and worth of alternative nonracist and nonsexist societies.

Nor do I even mean to suggest that all persons who reject the assimilationist ideal in respect to sex would necessarily embrace either something like the ideal of tolerance or the ideal of diversity. Some persons might think the right ideal was one in which substantially greater sexual differentiation and sex-role identification was retained than would be the case under either of these conceptions. Thus, someone might believe that the good society was, perhaps, essentially like the one they think we now have in respect to sex: equality of political rights, such as the right to vote, but all of the sexual differentiation in both legal and nonlegal institutions that is characteristic of the way in which our society has been and still is ordered. And someone might also believe that the usual ideological justifications for these arrangements are the correct and appropriate ones.

This could, of course, be regarded as a version of the ideal of diversity, with the emphasis upon the extensive character of the institutional and personal difference connected with sexual identity. Whether it is a kind of ideal of diversity or a different ideal altogether turns, I think, upon two things: first, however pervasive the sexual differentiation is; second, whether the ideal contains a conception of the appropriateness of significant institutional and interpersonal inequality, e.g., that the woman's job is in large measure to serve and be dominated by the male. The more this latter feature is present, the clearer the case for regarding this as ideal, distinctively different from any of those described by me so far. . . .

Despite appearances, the case of sex is more like that of race than is often thought. What opponents of assimilationism seize upon is that sexual difference appears to be a naturally occurring category of obvious and inevitable social relevance in a way, or to a degree, which race is not. The problems with this way of thinking are twofold. To begin with, an analysis of the social realities reveals that it is the socially created sexual differences which tend in fact to matter the most. It is sex-role differentiation, not gender per se,[2] that makes men and women as different as they are from each other, and it is sex-role differences which are invoked to justify most sexual differentiation at any of the levels of society.[3]

More important, even if naturally occurring sexual difference were of such a nature that they were of obvious prima facie social relevance, this would by no means settle the question of whether in the good society sex should or should not be as minimally significant as eye color. Even though there are biological differences between men and women in nature, this fact does not determine the question of what the good society can and should make of these differences. I have difficulty understanding why so many persons seem to think that it does settle the question adversely to anything like the assimilationist ideal. They might think it does settle the question for two different reasons. In the first place, they might think the differences are of such a character that they substantially affect what would be possible within a good society of human persons. Just as the fact that humans are mortal necessarily limits the features of any possible good society, so, they might argue, the fact that males and females are physiologically different limits the features of any possible good society.

In the second place, they might think the differences are of such a character that they are relevant to the question of what would be desirable in the good society. That is to say, they might not think that the differences *determine* to a substantial degree what is possible, but that the differences ought to be taken into account in any rational construction of an ideal social existence.

The second reason seems to me to be a good deal more plausible than the first. For there appear to be very few, if any, respects in which the ineradicable, naturally occurring differences between males and females *must* be taken into account. The industrial revolution has certainly made any of the general differences in strength between the sexes capable of being ignored by the good society in virtually all activities.[4] And it is sex-role acculturation, not biology, that mistakenly leads many persons to the view that women are both naturally and necessarily better suited than men to be assigned the primary responsibilities of childrearing. Indeed, the only fact that seems required to be taken into account is the fact that reproduction of the human species requires that the fetus develop in utero for a period of months. Sexual intercourse is not necessary, for artificial insemination is available. Neither marriage nor the family is required for conception or childrearing. Given the present state of medical knowledge and the natural realities of female pregnancy, it is difficult to see why any important institutional or interpersonal arrangements *must* take the existing gender difference of in utero pregnancy into account.

But, as I have said, this is still to leave it a wholly open question to what degree the good society *ought* to build upon any ineradicable gender differences to construct institutions which would maintain a substantial degree of sexual differentiation. The arguments are typically far less persuasive for doing so than appears upon the initial statement of this possibility. Someone might argue that the fact of menstruation, for instance, could be used as a premise upon which to predicate different social roles for females than for males. But this could only plausibly be proposed if two things were true: first, that menstruation would be debilitating to women and hence relevant to social role even in a culture which did not teach women to view menstruation as a sign of uncleanliness or as a curse;[5] and second, that the way in which menstruation necessarily affected some or all women was in fact related in an important way to the role in question. But even if both of these were true, it would still be an open question whether any sexual differentiation ought to be built upon these facts. The society could still elect to develop institutions that would nullify the effect of the natural differences. And suppose, for example, what seems implausible—that some or all women will not be able to perform a particular task while menstruating, e.g., guard a border. It would be easy enough, if the society wanted to, to arrange for substitute guards for the women who were incapacitated. We know that

persons are not good guards when they are sleepy, and we make arrangements so that persons alternate guard duty to avoid fatigue. The same could
be done for menstruating women, even given these implausibly strong assumptions about menstruation. At the risk of belaboring the obvious, what
I think it important to see is that the case against the assimilationist ideal—
if it is to be a good one—must rest on arguments concerned to show why
some other ideal would be preferable; it cannot plausibly rest on the claim
that it is either necessary or inevitable.

There is, however, at least one more argument based upon nature, or at
least the "natural," that is worth mentioning. Someone might argue that
significant sex-role differentiation is natural not in the sense that it is biologically determined but only in the sense that it is a virtually universal
phenomenon in human culture. By itself, this claim of virtual universality,
even if accurate, does not directly establish anything about the desirability
or undesirability of any particular ideal. But it can be made into an argument
by the addition of the proposition that where there is a virtually universal
social practice, there is probably some good or important purpose served by
the practice. Hence, given the fact of sex-role differentiation in all, or
almost all, cultures, we have some reason to think that substantial sex-role
differentiation serves some important purpose for and in human society.

This is an argument, but I see no reason to be impressed by it. The
premise which turns the fact of sex-role differentiation into any kind of a
strong reason for sex-role differentiation is the premise of conservatism. And
it is no more convincing here than elsewhere. There are any number of
practices that are typical and yet upon reflection seem without significant
social purpose. Slavery was once such a practice; war perhaps still is.

More to the point, perhaps, the concept of "purpose" is ambiguous. It
can mean in a descriptive sense "plays some role" or "is causally relevant."
Or it can mean in a prescriptive sense "does something desirable" or "has
some useful function." If "purpose" is used descriptively in the conservative
premise, then the argument says nothing about the continued desirability
of sex-role differentiation or the assimilationist ideal. If "purpose" is used
prescriptively in the conservative premise, then there is no reason to think
that premise is true.

To put it another way, the question is whether it is desirable to have a
society in which sex-role differences are to be retained at all. The straightforward way to think about that question is to ask what would be good and
what would be bad about a society in which sex functioned like eye color
does in our society. We can imagine what such a society would look like
and how it would work. It is hard to see how our thinking is substantially
advanced by reference to what has typically or always been the case. If it is
true, as I think it is, that the sex-role differentiated societies we have had

so far have tended to concentrate power in the hands of males, have developed institutions and ideologies that have perpetuated that concentration and have restricted and prevented women from living the kinds of lives that persons ought to be able to live for themselves, then this says far more about what may be wrong with any nonassimilationist ideal than does the conservative premise say what may be right about any nonassimilationist ideal.

Nor is this all that can be said in favor of the assimilationist ideal. For it seems to me that the strongest affirmative moral argument on its behalf is that it provides for a kind of individual autonomy that a nonassimilationist society cannot attain. Any nonassimilationist society will have sex roles. Any nonassimilationist society will have some institutions that distinguish between individuals in virtue of their gender, and any such society will necessarily teach the desirability of doing so. Any substantially nonassimilationist society will make one's sexual identity an important characteristic, so that there are substantial psychological, role, and status differences between persons who are males and those who are females. Even if these could be attained without systemic dominance of one sex over the other, they would, I think, be objectionable on the ground that they necessarily impaired an individual's ability to develop his or her own characteristics, talents, and capacities to the fullest extent to which he or she might desire. Sex roles, and all that accompany them, necessarily impose limits—restrictions on what one can do, be, or become. As such, they are, I think, at least prima facie wrong.

To some degree, all role-differentiated living is restrictive in this sense. Perhaps, therefore, all role-differentiation in society is to some degree troublesome, and perhaps all strongly role-differentiated societies are objectionable. But the case against sexual differentiation need not rest upon this more controversial point. For one thing that distinguishes sex roles from many other roles is that they are wholly involuntarily assumed. One has no choice whatsoever about whether one shall be born a male or female. And if it is a consequence of one's being born a male or a female that one's subsequent emotional, intellectual, and material development will be substantially controlled by this fact, then substantial, permanent, and involuntarily assumed restraints have been imposed on the most central factors concerning the way one will shape and live one's life. The point to be emphasized is that this would necessarily be the case, even in the unlikely event that substantial sexual differentiation could be maintained without one sex or the other becoming dominant and developing institutions and an ideology to support that dominance.

I do not believe that all I have said in this section shows in any conclusive fashion the desirability of the assimilationist ideal in respect to sex. I have tried to show why some typical arguments against the assimilationist ideal are not persuasive,[6] and why some of the central ones in support of that ideal are persuasive. But I have not provided a complete account, or a complete analysis. At a minimum, what I have shown is how thinking about this topic ought to proceed, and what kinds of arguments need to be marshaled and considered before a serious and informed discussion of alternative conceptions of a nonsexist society can even take place. Once assembled, these arguments need to be individually and carefully assessed before any final, reflective choice among the competing ideals can be made. There does, however, seem to me to be a strong presumptive case for something very close to, if not identical with, the assimilationist ideal.

Notes

1. There is a danger in calling this ideal the "assimilationist" ideal. That term suggests the idea of incorporating oneself, one's values, and the like into the dominant group and its practices and values. I want to make it clear that no part of that idea is meant to be captured by my use of this term. Mine is a stipulative definition.

2. The term "gender" may be used in a number of different senses. I use it to refer to those anatomical, physiological, and other differences (if any) that are naturally occurring in the sense described above. Some persons refer to these differences as "sex differences," but that seems to me confusing. In any event, I am giving a stipulative definition to "gender".

3. See, e.g., Hochschild, A Review of Sex Role Research, 78 Am. J. Soc. 1011 (1973), which reviews and very usefully categorizes the enormous volume of literature on this topic. See also Stewart, Social Influences on Sex Differences in Behavior, in Sex Differences 138 (M. Teitelbaum, ed., 1976); Weitzman, Sex Role Socialization, in Women: A Feminist Perspective 105 (J. Freeman, ed.) 1975. . . .

   "These three situations [the cultures of the Anapesh, the Mundugumor, and the Tchambuli] suggest, then, a very definite conclusion. If those temperamental attitudes which we have traditionally regarded as feminine—such as passivity, responsiveness, and a willingness to cherish children—can so easily be set up as the masculine pattern in one tribe, and in another to be outlawed for the majority of women as well as for the majority of men, we no longer have any basis for regarding such aspects of behavior as sex-linked. . . .

   ". . . We are forced to conclude that human nature is almost unbelievably malleable, responding accurately and contrastingly to contrasting cultural conditions. . . . Standardized personality differences between the sexes are of this order, cultural creations to which each generation, male and female, is trained to conform" (190–91).

   A somewhat different view is expressed in J. Sherman, On the Psychology of Women (1971). There, the author suggests there are "natural" differences of a psychological sort between men and women, the chief ones being aggressiveness and strength of sex drive (238). However, even if she is correct as to these biologically based differences, this does little to establish what the good society should look like.

   Almost certainly the most complete discussion of this topic is E. Macoby and

C. Jacklin, *The Psychology of Sex Differences* (1974). The authors conclude that the sex differences which are, in their words, "fairly well established," are: (1) that girls have greater verbal ability than boys; (2) that boys excel in visual-spatial ability; (3) that boys excel in mathematical ability; and (4) that males are more aggressive (351–52). They conclude, in respect to the etiology of these psychological sex differences, that there appears to be a biological component to the greater visual-spatial ability of males and to their greater aggressiveness (360).

4. As Sherman observes: "Each sex has its own special physical assets and liabilities. The principal female liability of less muscular strength is not ordinarily a handicap in a civilized, mechanized, society. . . . There is nothing in the biological evidence to prevent women from taking a role of equality in a civilized society" (*On the Psychology of Women*, 11).

There are, of course, some activities that would be sexually differentiated in the assimilationist society; namely, those that were specifically directed toward, say, measuring unaided physical strength. Thus, I think it likely that even in this ideal society, weight-lifting contests and boxing matches would in fact be dominated, perhaps exclusively so, by men. But it is hard to find any *significant* activities or institutions, that are analogous. And it is not clear that such insignificant activities would be thought worth continuing, especially since sports function in existing patriarchal societies to help maintain the dominance of males. See K. Millett, *Sexual Politics* (Garden City, NY: Doubleday, 1970), 23–58.

It is possible that there are some nontrivial activities or occupations that depend sufficiently directly upon unaided physical strength that most if not all women would be excluded. Perhaps being a lifeguard at the ocean is an example. Even here, though, it would be important to see whether the way lifeguarding had traditionally been done could be changed to render such physical strength unimportant. If it could be changed, then the question would simply be one of whether the increased cost (or loss of efficiency) was worth the gain in terms of equality and the avoidance of sex-role differentiation. In a nonpatriarchal society very different from ours, where sex was not a dominant social category, the argument from efficiency might well prevail. What is important once again, is to see how infrequent and peripheral such occupational cases are.

5. See, e.g., Paige, "Women Learn to Sing the Menstrual Blues," in *The Female Experience* 17 (C. Tavis, ed., 1973).

"I have come to believe that the 'raging hormones' theory of menstrual distress simply isn't adequate. All women have the raging hormones, but not all women have menstrual symptoms, nor do they have the same symptoms for the same reasons. Nor do I agree with the 'raging neurosis' theory, which argues that women who have menstrual symptoms are merely whining neurotics, who need only a kind pat on the head to cure their problems.

"We must instead consider the problem from the perspective of women's subordinate social position, and of the cultural ideology that so narrowly defines the behaviors and emotions that are appropriately 'feminine.' Women have perfectly good reasons to react emotionally to reproductive events. Menstruations, pregnancy and childbirth—so sacred, yet so unclean—are the woman's primary avenues of achievement and self-expression. Her reproductive abilities define her femininity; other routes to success are only second-best is this society. . . .

". . . My current research on a sample of 114 societies around the world indicates that ritual observances and taboos about menstruation are a method of controlling women and their fertility. Men apparently use such rituals, along with those surrounding pregnancy and childbirth, to assert their claims to women and their children.

"... The hormone theory isn't giving us much mileage, and it's time to turn it in for a better model, one that looks to our beliefs about menstruation and women. It is no mere coincidence that women get the blue meanies along with an event they consider embarrassing, unclean—and a curse" (21).

6. Still other arguments against something like the assimilationist ideal and in favor of something like the idea of diversity are considered by Jaggar and shown by her to be unpersuasive. See Jaggar, supra note 20, at 281–91.

SELECTION 37
FROM
The Ideal of Impartiality and the Civic Public

IRIS MARION YOUNG

A GROWING BODY OF feminist-inspired moral theory has challenged the paradigm of moral reasoning as defined by the discourse of justice and rights. In this paradigm moral reasoning consists in adopting an impartial and impersonal point of view on a situation, detached from any particular interests at stake, weighing all interests equally, and arriving at a conclusion which conforms to general principles of justice and rights, impartially applied to the case at hand. Critics argue that this paradigm describes not moral reasoning as such, but the specific moral reasoning called for in the impersonal public contexts of law, bureaucracy, and the regulation of economic competition. This "ethic of rights" corresponds poorly to the social relations typical of family and personal life, whose moral orientation requires not detachment from but engagement in and sympathy with the particular parties in a situation; it requires not principles that apply to all people in the same way, but a nuanced understanding of the particularities of the social context, and the needs particular people have and express within it. Philosophers should recognize that the paradigm of moral reasoning as the impartial application of general principles describes only a restricted field of moral life, and develop moral theories adequate to the private, personal, and informal contexts it ignores (Gilligan 1982; Blum 1980, 1988; Friedman 1986; Noddings 1984).

More recently some feminist theorists have begun to question this opposition between justice and care (Friedman 1987; Okin 1989). In this chapter I extend this line of argument. The feminist critiques of traditional moral theory retain a distinction between public, impersonal institutional roles in which the ideal of impartiality and formal reason applies, on the one hand, and private, personal relations which have a different moral structure. In-

359

stead of retaining this public/private dichotomy, these criticisms of an ethic of rights should lead us to question the ideal of impartiality itself, as an appropriate ideal for any concrete moral context.

I argue that the ideal of impartiality in moral theory expresses a logic of identity that seeks to reduce differences to unity. The stances of detachment and dispassion that supposedly produce impartiality are attained only by abstracting from the particularities of situation, feeling, affiliation, and point of view. These particularities still operate, however, in the actual context of action. Thus the ideal of impartiality generates a dichotomy between universal and particular, public and private, reason and passion. It is, moreover, an impossible ideal, because the particularities of context and affiliation cannot and should not be removed from moral reasoning. Finally, the ideal of impartiality serves ideological functions. It masks the ways in which the particular perspectives of dominant groups claim universality, and helps justify hierarchical decision-making structures.

The ideal of impartial moral reason corresponds to the Enlightenment ideal of the public realm of politics as attaining the universality of a general will that leaves difference, particularity, and the body behind in the private realms of family and civil society. Recent attempts to revive republican thinking appeal to the ideal of a civic public which transcends particularities of interest and affiliation to seek a common good. I followed this new republican initiative in criticizing the depoliticized public life of interest-group pluralism, and agreed with its proponents that politics should involve public forums of deliberation and collective decisionmaking. In this chapter, however, I argue that the modern ideal of the civic public is inadequate. The traditional public realm of universal citizenship has operated to exclude persons associated with the body and feeling—especially women. Blacks, American Indians, and Jews. Many contemporary theorists of participatory democracy retain the ideal of a civic public in which citizens leave behind their particularity and differences. Because such a universalist ideal continues to threaten the exclusion of some, the meaning of "public" should be transformed to exhibit the positivity of group differences, passion, and play. . . .

The ideal of impartiality is an idealist fiction. It is impossible to adopt an unsituated moral point of view, and if a point of view is situated, then it cannot be universal, it cannot stand apart from and understand all points of view. It is impossible to reason about substantive moral issues without understanding their substance, which always presupposes some particular social and historical context; and one has no motive for making moral judgments and resolving moral dilemmas unless the outcome matters, unless one has a particular and passionate interest in the outcome. As Bernard Williams points out, the difference between factual or scientific reflection and practical or moral reflection is precisely that the former is impersonal while the latter is not:

Practical deliberation is in every case first-personal, and the first person is not derivative or naturally replaced by *anyone*. The action I decide on will be mine, and its being mine means not just that it will be arrived at by this deliberation, but that it will involve changes in the world of which I shall be empirically the cause, and of which these desires and this deliberation itself will be, in some part, the cause. (Williams 1985, 68)

Some writers who agree with this critique of the dichotomy between reason and feeling, general and particular, generated by the traditional ideal of impartiality in moral theory suggest that rather than think of impartiality as a view from nowhere, one can arrive at the same results by thinking of the view from everywhere. Susan Okin, for example, reconstructs Rawls's idea of the original position as a reasoning process that takes account of all the particular positions and perspectives in the society in order to arrive at the just outcome. Unlike a more universalist Kantian approach, she suggests, this idea of taking the point of view of everyone does not oppose reason to feeling or exclude particularity. Indeed, it depends on the ability of the moral reasoner to be sympathetic with every particular position and point of view (Okin 1989; cf. Sunstein 1988).

This move to particularize impartiality retains a totalizing urge, however, and is no more possible than its more universalistic counterpart. The idea remains that *one* subject, the impartial reasoner, can adopt the point of view of everyone. This construction of a particularist notion of impartiality assumes that from my particular perspective, with my particular history and experience, I can nevertheless empathize with the feelings and perspectives of others differently situated. This assumption denies the difference among subjects. To be sure, subjects are not opaque to one another, their difference is not absolute. But especially when class, race, ethnicity, gender, sexuality, and age define different social locations, one subject cannot fully emphathize with another in a different social location, adopt her point of view; if that were possible then the social locations would not be different (cf. Friedman 1989, 649–53).

Some might object that by rejecting the universality of the ideal of impartiality I am rejecting the very possibility of moral reflection itself. Such an objection rests on an identification of reflection with impartiality, and this is the very identification I deny. Moral reason certainly does require reflection, an ability to take some distance from one's immediate impulses, intuitions, desires, and interests in order to consider their relation to the demands of others, their consequences if acted upon, and so on. This process of reflection, however, does not require that one adopt a point of view emptied of particularity, a point of view that is the same for everyone; indeed, it is hard to see how such a universal point of view could aid reflection that leads to action at all (Williams 1985, 63–69, 110–11; cf. Walzer 1987, 48–56). . . .

THE LOGIC OF IDENTITY IN THE
IDEAL OF THE CIVIC PUBLIC

The dichotomy between reason and desire also appears in modern political theory in the distinction between the universal, public realm of sovereignty and the state, on the one hand, and the particular, private realm of needs and desires, on the other. Modern normative political theory and political practice aim to embody impartiality in the public realm of the state. Like impartial moral reason, this public realm attains its generality only by the exclusion of particularity, desire, feeling, and those aspects of life associated with the body. In modern political theory and practice the civic public associated with this realm achieves a unity in particular by the exclusion of women and others associated with nature and the body. . . .

Recent feminist analyses of the dichotomy between public and private in modern political theory imply that the ideal of the civic public as impartial and universal is itself suspect. Modern political theorists and politicians proclaimed the impartiality and generality of the public and at the same time quite consciously found it fitting that some persons, namely, women, nonwhites, and sometimes those without property, should be excluded from participation in that public. If this was not just a mistake, it suggests that the ideal of the civic public as expressing the general interest, the impartial point of view of reason, itself results in exclusion. By assuming that reason stands opposed to desire, affectivity, and the body, this conception of the civic public excludes bodily and affective aspects of human existence. In practice this assumption forces homogeneity upon the civic public, excluding from the public those individuals and groups that do not fit the model of the rational citizen capable of transcending body and sentiment. This exclusion has a twofold basis: the tendency to oppose reason and desire, and the association of these traits with kinds of persons.

In the social scheme expounded by Rousseau, and Hegel after him, women must be excluded from the public realm of citizenship because they are the caretakers of affectivity, desire, and the body. Allowing appeals to desires and bodily needs to move public debates would undermine public deliberation by fragmenting its unity. Even within the domestic realm, moreover, women must be dominated. Their dangerous, heterogeneous sexuality must be kept chaste and confined to marriage. Enforcing chastity on women will keep each family a separated unity, preventing the chaos and blood mingling that would be produced by illegitimate children. Only then can women be the proper caretakers of men's desire, by tempering its potentially disruptive impulses through moral education. Men's desire for women itself threatens to shatter and disperse the universal rational realm of the public, as well as to disrupt the neat distinction between the public and the private. As guardians of the private realm of need, desire, and affectivity, women must ensure that men's impulses do not remove them from the universality of reason. The moral neatness of the female-tended hearth, moreover, will temper the possessively individualistic impulses of the particularistic realm of business and commerce, which like sexuality constantly threatens to explode the unity of society (see Okin 1978, part 3; Lange 1979; Elshtain 1981, ch. 4; Pateman 1988, ch. 4).

The bourgeois world instituted a moral division of labor between reason and sentiment, identifying masculinity with reason and femininity with sentiment and desire (Glennon 1979; Lloyd 1984). The sphere of family and personal life is as much a modern creation as the modern realm of state and law, and comes about as part of the same process (Nicholson 1986, ch. 4; cf. Okin 1981). The impartiality and rationality of the state depend on containing need and desire in the private realm of the family. The public realm of citizens achieves unity and universality only by defining the civil individual in opposition to the disorder of womanly nature, which embraces feeling, sexuality, birth and death, the attributes that concretely distinguish persons from one another. The universal citizen is disembodied, dispassionate (male) reason (Pateman 1986, 1988, chs. 1–4).

The universal citizen is also white and bourgeois. Women have not been the only persons excluded from participation in the modern civic public. In Europe until recently in many nations both Jews and working-class people were excluded from citizenship. In the United States the designers of the Constitution specifically restricted the access of the laboring class to the rational public, and of course excluded slaves and Indians from participation in the civic public as well. George Mosse (1985) and Ronald Takaki (1979) expose the structure of such exclusion in bourgeois republican life in Europe and the United States respectively. The white male bourgeoisie conceived republican virtue as "respectability." The "respectable" man was rational, restrained, and chaste, unyielding to passion, sentimental attachments, or the desire for luxury. The respectable man should be straight, dispassionate, rule-bound. The bodily, sexual, uncertain, disorderly aspects of existence in these cultural images were and are identified with women, homosexuals, blacks, Indians, Jews, and Orientals.

The idea of the unified nation which developed in Europe in the nineteenth century, Mosse argues, depended precisely on opposing manly virtue to the heterogeneity and uncertainty of the body, and associating despised groups with the body, setting them outside the homogeneity of the nation (cf. Anderson 1983). Takaki shows that early American republicans were quite explicit about the need for the homogeneity of citizens, a need which from the earliest days of the republic involved the relationship of the white republicans to the black and Indian peoples (cf. Herzog 1985). These republican

fathers, such as Jefferson, identified the red and black people in their terri-
tories with wild nature and passions, just as they feared that women outside
the domestic realm were wanton and avaricious. They defined moral, civilized
republican life in opposition to this backward-looking, uncultivated desire
they identified with women and nonwhites. Most important, they explicitly
justified the restriction of citizenship to white men on the grounds that the
unity. of the nation depended on homogeneity and dispassionate reason.

To summarize, the ideal of normative reason, moral sense, stands opposed to desire and affectivity. Impartial civilized reason characterizes the
virtue of the republican man who rises above passion and desire. Instead of
cutting bourgeois man entirely off from the body and affectivity, however,
the culture of the rational public confines them to the domestic sphere,
which also confines women's passions and provides emotional solace to men
and children. Indeed, within this domestic realm sentiments can flower,
and each individual can recognize and affirm his particularity. Precisely because the virtues of impartiality and universality define the civic public,
that public must exclude human particularity. Modern normative reason
and its political expression in the idea of the civic public, then, attain
unity and coherence through the expulsion and confinement of everything
that would threaten to invade the polity with differentiation: the specificity
of women's bodies and desire, differences of race and culture, the variability
and heterogeneity of needs, the goals and desires of individuals, the ambiguity and changeability of feeling. . . .

The repoliticization of public life does not require the creation of a unified public realm in which citizens leave behind their particular group affiliations, histories, and needs to discuss a mythical "common good." In a society
differentiated by social groups, occupations, political positions, differences
of privilege and oppression, regions, and so on, the perception of anything
like a common good can only be an outcome of public interaction that
expresses rather than submerges particularities. Those seeking the democratization of politics in our society, in my view, should reconceptualize the
meaning of public and private and their relation, to break decisively with
the tradition of Enlightenment republicanism. While there are good theoretical and practical reasons to maintain a distinction between public and
private, this distinction should not be constructed as a hierarchical opposition corresponding to oppositions between reason and feeling, masculine
and feminine, universal and particular.

The primary meaning of public is what is open and accessible. The public is in principle not exclusionary. While general in that sense, this conception of a public does not imply homogeneity or the adoption of some
general or universal standpoint. Indeed, in open and accessible public spaces
and forums, one should expect to encounter and hear from those who are

different, whose social perspectives, experience, and affiliations are different. To promote a politics of inclusion, then, participatory democrats must promote the ideal of a heterogeneous public, in which persons stand forth with their differences acknowledged and respected, though perhaps not completely understood, by others.

The private, as Hannah Arendt (1958, 58–67) points out, is etymologically related to deprivation. The private, as traditionally conceived, is what should be hidden from view, or what cannot be brought to view. It is connected with shame and incompleteness. As Arendt points out, this notion of the private implies the exclusion of bodily and affective aspects of human life from the public.

Instead of defining the private as what the public excludes, I suggest, the private should be defined, as in one strain of liberal theory, as that aspect of his or her life and activity that any person has a right to exclude others from. The private in this sense is not what public institutions exclude, but what the individual chooses to withdraw from public view. With the growth of both state and nonstate bureaucracies, the protection of privacy has become a burning public issue. In welfare capitalist society, the defense of personal privacy has become not merely a matter of keeping the state out of certain affairs, but of calling for positive state regulation to ensure that both its own agencies and nonstate organizations, such as corporations, respect the claims of individuals to privacy.

This manner of formulating the concepts of public and private, which is inspired by feminist confrontations with traditional political theory, does not deny their distinction. It does deny, however, a social division between public and private spheres, each with different kinds of institutions, activities, and human attributes. The concept of a heterogeneous public implies two political principles: (a) no persons, actions, or aspects of a person's life should be forced into privacy; and (b) no social institutions or practices should be excluded a priori from being a proper subject for public discussion and expression.

The modern conception of the public, I have argued, creates a conception of citizenship which excludes from public attention most particular aspects of persons. Public life is supposed to be "blind" to sex, race, age, and so on, and all persons are supposed to enter the public and its discussion on identical terms. This conception of the public has resulted in the exclusion of persons and aspects of persons from public life.

Ours is still a society that forces persons or aspects of persons into privacy. Repression of homosexuality is perhaps the most striking example. In the United States today most people seem to hold the liberal view that persons have a right to be gay as long as they keep their activities private. Calling attention in public to the fact that one is gay, making public displays of gay affection, or even publicly asserting gay needs and rights, provokes ridicule and fear in many people. Our society is only beginning to change the practice of keeping the physically and mentally disabled out of public view. For almost a century "respectable" women have had access to public spaces and public expression, but prevailing norms still pressure us to privatize the most obvious manifestations of our femaleness—menstruation, pregnancy, lactation—to keep these out of public speech, public view, and public consideration. By extension, children should be kept out of public view, and of course their voices should not receive public expression.

The feminist slogan "the personal is political" expresses the principle that no social practices or activities should be excluded as improper subjects for public discussion, expression, or collective choice. The contemporary women's movement has made public issues out of many practices claimed to be too trivial or private for public discussion: the meaning of pronouns, domestic violence against women, the practice of men's opening doors for women, the sexual assault of women and children, the sexual division of housework, and so on.

Socialist and populist politics call for making public issues out of many actions and activities deemed properly private, such as how individuals and enterprises invest their money, what they produce, and how they produce it. Welfare corporate society allows many large institutions whose actions have an enormous impact on many people to define their activity as private, and thus gives them the right to exclude others. Participatory democrats interested in undermining economically caused oppressions such as exploitation and marginalization usually call for bringing some or all of the activities of such institutions under the purview of public democratic decisions.

These examples show that public and private do not easily correspond to institutional spheres, such as work versus family, or state versus economy. In democratic politics, where the line of privacy should be drawn itself becomes a public issue (Cunningham 1987, 120). The purpose of protecting privacy is to preserve liberties of *individual* action, opportunity, and participation. The claim of any institution or collective to privacy, to the right to exclude others, can be justified only on grounds of enabling a justified range of individual privacy.

As I suggested at the beginning of this chapter, challenging the traditional opposition between public and private that aligns it with oppositions between universality and particularity, reason and affectivity, implies challenging a conception of justice that opposes it to care. A theory that limits justice to formal and universal principles that define a context in which each person can pursue her or his personal ends without hindering the ability of others to pursue theirs entails not merely too limited a conception of social life, as Michael Sandel (1982) suggests, but too limited a conception of justice. As a virtue, justice cannot stand opposed to personal need, feeling, and desire, but names the institutional conditions that enable people to meet their needs and express their desires. Needs can be expressed in their particularity in a heterogeneous public. . . .

References

Anderson, Benedict. 1983. *Imagined Communities: Reflections on the Origin and Spread of Nationalism.* London: New Left Books.

Arendt, Hannah. 1958. *The Human Condition.* Chicago: University of Chicago Press.

Blum, Lawrence. 1980. *Friendship, Altruism, and Morality.* London: Routledge and Kegan Paul.

———. 1988. "Gilligan and Kohlberg: Implications for Moral Theory." *Ethics* 97 (April): 472–91.

Cunningham, Frank. 1987. *Democratic Theory and Socialism.* Cambridge: Cambridge University Press.

Elshtain, Jean. 1981. *Public Man, Private Woman.* Princeton: Princeton University Press.

Friedman, Marilyn. 1985. "Care and Context in Moral Reasoning." In Carol Harding, ed., *Moral Dilemmas: Philosophical and Psychological Issues in the Development of Moral Reasoning.* Chicago: Precedent.

———. 1987. "Beyond Caring: The De-Moralization of Gender." In Marsha Hanen and Kai Nielsen, eds. *Science, Morality, and Feminist Theory.* Calgary: University of Calgary Press.

———. 1989. "Impracticality of Impartiality." *Journal of Philosophy* 86 (Nov.) 645–56.

Gilligan, Carol. 1982. *In a Different Voice.* Cambridge: Harvard University Press.

Glennon, Lynda. 1979. *Women and Dualism.* New York: Longman.

Herzog, Don. 1986. "Some Questions for Republicans." *Political Theory* 14 (Aug.) 473–93.

Lange, Lynda. 1979. "Rousseau: Women and the General Will." In Lynda Lange and Lorenne M. G. Clark, eds., *The Sexism of Social and Political Theory.* Toronto: University of Toronto Press.

Lloyd, Genevieve. 1984. *The Man of Reason: "Male" and "Female" in Western Philosophy.* Minneapolis: University of Minnesota Press.

Mosse, George. 1985. *Nationalism and Sexuality.* New York: Fertig.

Nicholson, Linda. 1986. *Gender and History.* New York: Columbia University Press.

Noddings, Nel. 1984. *Caring—A Feminine Approach to Ethics and Moral Education.* Berkeley: University of California Press.

Okin, Susan. 1978. *Women in Western Political Thought.* Princeton: Princeton University Press.

———. 1989. "Reason and Feeling in Thinking about Justice." *Ethics* 99 (Jan.) 229–49.

Pateman, Carole. 1986. "Feminism and Participatory Democracy: Some Reflections on Sexual Difference and Citizenship." Paper presented at the American Philosophical Association Western Division meeting, St. Louis, April.

———. 1988. *The Sexual Contract.* Stanford: Stanford University Press.

Sandel, Michael. 1982. *Liberalism and the Limits of Justice.* Cambridge: Cambridge University Press.

Sunstein, Cass R. 1988. "Beyond the Republican Revival." *Yale Law Journal* 97 (July): 1539–90.

Takaki, Ronald. 1979. *Iron Cages: Race and Culture in Nineteenth-Century America.* New York: Knopf.

Walzer, Michael. 1987. *Interpretation and Social Criticism.* Cambridge: Harvard University Press.

Williams, Bernard. 1985. *Ethics and the Limits of Philosophy.* Cambridge: Harvard University Press.

SELECTION 38

FROM

Rethinking the Public Sphere: A Contribution to the Critique of Actually Existing Democracy

NANCY FRASER

OPEN ACCESS, PARTICIPATORY PARITY, AND SOCIAL EQUALITY

HABERMAS'S ACCOUNT OF THE bourgeois conception of the public sphere stresses its claim to be open and accessible to all. Indeed, this idea of open access is one of the central meanings of the norm of publicity. Of course, we know both from revisionist history and from Habermas's account that the bourgeois public's claim to full accessibility was not in fact realized. Women of all classes and ethnicities were excluded from official political participation on the basis of gender status, while plebeian men were formally excluded by property qualifications. Moreover, in many cases women and men of racialized ethnicities of all classes were excluded on racial grounds.

What are we to make of this historical fact of the nonrealization in practice of the bourgeois public sphere's ideal of open access? One approach is to conclude that the ideal itself remains unaffected, since it is possible in principle to overcome these exclusions. And in fact, it was only a matter of time before formal exclusions based on gender, property, and race were eliminated.

This is convincing enough as far as it goes, but it does not go far enough. The question of open access cannot be reduced without remainder to the presence or absence of formal exclusions. It requires us to look also at the process of discursive interaction within formally inclusive public arenas. Here we should recall that the bourgeois conception of the public sphere requires bracketing inequalities of status. This public sphere was to be an arena in

369

which interlocutors would set aside such characteristics as differences in birth and fortune and speak to one another as if they were social and economic peers. The operative phrase here is "as if." In fact, the social inequalities among the interlocutors were not eliminated but only bracketed.

But were they really effectively bracketed? The revisionist historiography suggests they were not. Rather, discursive interaction within the bourgeois public sphere was governed by protocols of style and decorum that were themselves correlates and markers of status inequality. These functioned informally to marginalize women and members of the plebeian classes and to prevent them from participating as peers.

Here we are talking about informal impediments to participatory parity that can persist even after everyone is formally and legally licensed to participate. That these constitute a more serious challenge to the bourgeois conception of the public sphere can be seen from a familiar contemporary example. Feminist research has documented a syndrome that many of us have observed in faculty meetings and other mixed-sex deliberative bodies: Men tend to interrupt women more than women interrupt men; men also tend to speak more than women, taking more turns and longer turns; and women's interventions are more often ignored or not responded to than men's. In response to the sorts of experiences documented in this research, an important strand of feminist political theory has claimed that deliberation can serve as a mask for domination. Theorists like Jane Mansbridge have argued that "the transformation of 'I' into 'we' brought about through political deliberation can easily mask subtle forms of control. Even the language people use as they reason together usually favors one way of seeing things and discourages others. Subordinate groups sometimes cannot find the right voice or words to express their thoughts, and when they do, they discover they are not heard. [They] are silenced, encouraged to keep their wants inchoate, and heard to say 'yes' when what they have said is 'no.'"[1] Mansbridge rightly notes that many of these feminist insights into ways in which deliberation can serve as a mask for domination extend beyond gender to other kinds of unequal relations, like those based on class or ethnicity. They alert us to the ways in which social inequalities can infect deliberation, even in the absence of any formal exclusions.

Here I think we encounter a very serious difficulty with the bourgeois conception of the public sphere. Insofar as the bracketing of social inequalities in deliberation means proceeding as if they don't exist when they do, this does not foster participatory parity. On the contrary, such bracketing usually works to the advantage of dominant groups in society and to the disadvantage of subordinates. In most cases it would be more appropriate to *unbracket* inequalities in the sense of explicitly thematizing them—a point that accords with the spirit of Habermas's later communicative ethics.

The misplaced faith in the efficacy of bracketing suggests another flaw in the bourgeois conception. This conception assumes that a public sphere is or can be a space of zero degree culture, so utterly bereft of any specific ethos as to accommodate with perfect neutrality and equal ease interventions expressive of any and every cultural ethos. But this assumption is counterfactual, and not for reasons that are merely accidental. In stratified societies, unequally empowered social groups tend to develop unequally valued cultural styles. The result is the development of powerful informal pressures that marginalize the contributions of members of subordinated groups both in everyday contexts and in official public spheres.[2] Moreover, these pressures are amplified, rather than mitigated, by the peculiar political economy of the bourgeois public sphere. In this public sphere the media that constitute the material support for the circulation of views are privately owned and operated for profit. Consequently, subordinated social groups usually lack equal access to the material means of equal participation.[3] Thus political economy enforces structurally what culture accomplishes informally. . . .

EQUALITY, DIVERSITY, AND MULTIPLE PUBLICS

So far I have been discussing what we might call "intrapublic relations," that is, the character and quality of discursive interactions within a given public sphere. Now I want to consider what we might call "interpublic relations," that is, the character of interactions among different publics.

Let me begin by recalling that Habermas's account stresses the singularity of the bourgeois conception of the public sphere, its claim to be *the* public arena, in the singular. In addition, his narrative tends in this respect to be faithful to that conception, since it casts the emergence of additional publics as a late development signaling fragmentation and decline. This narrative, then, like the bourgeois conception itself, is informed by an underlying evaluative assumption, namely, that the institutional confinement of public life to a single, overarching public sphere is a positive and desirable state of affairs, whereas the proliferation of a multiplicity of publics represents a departure from, rather than an advance toward, democracy. It is this normative assumption that I now want to scrutinize. In this section I shall assess the relative merits of a single, comprehensive public versus multiple publics in two kinds of modern sciences: stratified societies and egalitarian, multicultural societies.[4]

First, let me consider the case of stratified societies, by which I mean societies whose basic institutional framework generates unequal social groups in structural relations of dominance and subordination. I have already argued that in such societies, full parity of participation in public debate and deliberation is not within the reach of possibility. The question to be addressed here then is, What form of public life comes closest to approaching that ideal? What institutional arrangements will best help narrow the gap in participatory parity between dominant and subordinate groups?

I contend that in stratified societies, arrangements that accommodate contestation among a plurality of competing publics better promote the ideal of participatory parity than does a single, comprehensive, overarching public. This follows from the argument of the previous section. There I argued that it is not possible to insulate special discursive arenas from the effects of societal inequality and that where societal inequality persists, deliberative processes in public spheres will tend to operate to the advantage of dominant groups and to the disadvantage of subordinates. Now I want to add that these effects will be exacerbated where there is only a single, comprehensive public sphere. In that case, members of subordinated groups would have no arenas for deliberation among themselves about their needs, objectives, and strategies. They would have no venues in which to undertake communicative processes that were not, as it were, under the supervision of dominant groups. In this situation they would be less likely than otherwise to "find the right voice or words to express their thoughts" and more likely than otherwise "to keep their wants inchoate." This would render them less able than otherwise to articulate and defend their interests in the comprehensive public sphere. They would be less able than otherwise to expose modes of deliberation that mask domination by, in Mansbridge's words, "absorbing the less powerful into a false 'we' that reflects the more powerful."

This argument gains additional support from revisionist historiography of the public sphere, up to and including that of very recent developments. This historiography records that members of subordinated social groups—women, workers, peoples of color, and gays and lesbians—have repeatedly found it advantageous to constitute alternative publics. I propose to call these *subaltern counterpublics* in order to signal that they are parallel discursive arenas where members of subordinated social groups invent and circulate counterdiscourses to formulate oppositional interpretations of their identities, interests, and needs.[5] Perhaps the most striking example is the late-twentieth-century U.S. feminist subaltern counterpublic, with its variegated array of journals, bookstores, publishing companies, film and video distribution networks, lecture series, research centers, academic programs, conferences, conventions, festivals, and local meeting places. In this public sphere, feminist women have invented new terms for describing social reality, including "sexism," "the double shift," "sexual harassment," and "marital, date, and acquaintance rape." Armed with such language, we have recast our needs and identities, thereby reducing, although not eliminating, the extent of our disadvantage in official public spheres.[6] . . .

Let me now consider the relative merits of multiple publics versus a single public for egalitarian, multicultural societies. By "egalitarian societies" I mean nonstratified societies, societies whose basic framework does not generate unequal social groups in structural relations of dominance and subordination. Egalitarian societies, therefore, are societies without classes and without gender or racial divisions of labor. However, they need not be culturally homogeneous. On the contrary, provided such societies permit free expression and association, they are likely to be inhabited by social groups with diverse values, identities, and cultural styles, and hence to be multicultural. My question is, Under conditions of cultural diversity in the absence of structural inequality, would a single, comprehensive public sphere be preferable to multiple publics?

To answer this question, we need to take a closer look at the relationship between public discourse and social identities. *Pace* the bourgeois conception, public spheres are not only arenas for the formation of discursive opinion; in addition, they are arenas for the formation and enactment of social identities.[7] This means that participation is not simply a matter of being able to state propositional contents that are neutral with respect to form of expression. Rather, as I argued in the previous section, participation means being able to speak in one's own voice, and thereby simultaneously to construct and express one's cultural identity through idiom and style.[8] . . .

It follows that public life in egalitarian, multicultural societies cannot consist exclusively in a single, comprehensive public sphere. That would be tantamount to filtering diverse rhetorical and stylistic norms through a single, overarching lens. Moreover, since there can be no such lens that is genuinely culturally neutral, it would effectively privilege the expressive norms of one cultural group over others and thereby make discursive assimilation a condition for participation in public debate. The result would be the demise of multiculturalism (and the likely demise of social equality). In general, then, we can conclude that the idea of an egalitarian, multicultural society only makes sense if we suppose a plurality of public arenas in which groups with diverse values and rhetorics participate. By definition, such a society must contain a multiplicity of publics. . . .

In general, I have been arguing that the ideal of participatory parity is better achieved by a multiplicity of publics than by a single public. This is true both for stratified societies and for egalitarian, multicultural societies, albeit for different reasons. In neither case is my argument intended as a simple postmodern celebration of multiplicity. Rather, in the case of stratified societies, I am defending subaltern counterpublics formed under conditions of dominance and subordination. In the other case, by contrast, I am defending the possibility of combining social equality, cultural diversity, and participatory democracy. . . .

Notes

1. Jane Mansbridge, "Feminism and Democracy," *The American Prospect*, no. 1 (Spring 1990): 127.
2. In *Distinction: A Social Critique of the Judgment of Pure Taste* (Cambridge: Harvard University Press, 1979) Pierre Bourdieu has theorized these processes in an illuminating way in terms of the concept of "class habitus."
3. As Habermas notes, this tendency is exacerbated with the concentration of media ownership in late capitalist societies. For the steep increase in concentration in the United States in the late twentieth century, see Ben H. Bagdikian, *The Media Monopoly* (Boston: Beacon Press, 1983) and "Lords of the Global Village," *The Nation* (June 12, 1989). This situation contrasts in some respects with countries with television owned and operated by the state. But even there it is doubtful that subordinated groups have equal access. Moreover, political and economic pressures have recently encouraged privatization of media in several of these countries. In part, this reflects the problems of state networks having to compete for "market share" with private channels airing U.S.-produced mass entertainment.
4. My argument in this section is deeply indebted to Joshua Cohen's perceptive comments on an earlier draft of this paper in "Comments on Nancy Fraser's 'Rethinking the Public Sphere.'"
5. I have coined this expression by combining two terms that other theorists have recently effectively used for purposes consonant with my own. I take the term "subaltern" from Gayatri Spivak, "Can the Subaltern Speak?" in *Marxism and the Interpretation of Culture*, ed. Cary Nelson and Larry Grossberg (Chicago: University of Illinois Press, 1988), 271–313. I take the term "counterpublic" from Rita Felski, *Beyond Feminist Aesthetics* (Cambridge: Harvard University Press, 1989).
6. For an analysis of the political import of oppositional feminist discourses about needs, see Nancy Fraser, "Struggle over Needs: Outline of a Socialist-Feminist Critical Theory of Late-Capitalist Political Culture," in Nancy Fraser, *Unruly Practices—Power, Discourse and Gender in Contemporary Social Theory* (Minneapolis: University of Minnesota Press, 1991).
7. It seems to me that public discursive arenas are among the most important and underrecognized sites in which social identities are constructed, deconstructed, and reconstructed. My view stands in contrast to various psychoanalytic accounts of identity formation, which neglect the formative importance of post-Oedipal discursive interaction outside the nuclear family and which therefore cannot explain identity shifts over time. It strikes me as unfortunate that so much of contemporary feminist theory has taken its understanding of social identity from psychoanalytic models, while neglecting to study identity construction in relation to public spheres. The revisionist historiography of the public sphere discussed earlier can help redress the imbalance by identifying public spheres as loci of identity reconstruction. For an account of the discursive character of social identity and a critique of Lacanian psychoanalytic approaches to identity, see Nancy Fraser, "The Uses and Abuses of French Discourse Theories for Feminist Politics," *boundary* 2, 17, no. 2 (Summer 1990): 82–101.
8. For another statement of this position, see Nancy Fraser, "Toward a Discourse Ethic of Solidarity," *Praxis International* 5, no. 4 (Jan. 1986): 425–29. See also Iris Young, "Impartiality and the Civic Public: Some Implications of Feminist Critiques of Moral and Political Theory," in *Feminism as Critique*, ed. Seyla Benhabib and Drucilla Cornell (Minneapolis: University of Minnesota Press, 1987), 56–76.

SELECTION 39
FROM
The Power and the Promise of Ecological Feminism

KAREN J. WARREN

ECOFEMINISM AS A FEMINIST AND
ENVIRONMENTAL ETHIC

A FEMINIST ETHIC INVOLVES a twofold commitment to critique male bias in ethics wherever it occurs, and to develop ethics which are not male-biased. Sometimes this involves articulation of values (e.g., values of care, appropriate trust, kinship, friendship) often lost or underplayed in mainstream ethics.[1] Sometimes it involves engaging in theory building by pioneering in new directions or by revamping old theories in gender-sensitive ways. What makes the critiques of old theories or conceptualizations of new ones "feminist" is that they emerge out of sex-gender analyses and reflect whatever those analyses reveal about gendered experience and gendered social reality.

As I conceive feminist ethics in the prefeminist present, it rejects attempts to conceive of ethical theory in terms of necessary and sufficient conditions, because it assumes that there is no essence (in the sense of some transhistorical, universal, absolute abstraction) of feminist ethics. While attempts to formulate joint necessary and sufficient conditions of a feminist ethic are unfruitful, nonetheless, there are some necessary conditions, what I prefer to call "boundary conditions," of a feminist ethic. These boundary conditions clarify some of the minimal conditions of a feminist ethic without suggesting that feminist ethics has some ahistorical essence. They are like the boundaries of a quilt or collage. They delimit the territory of the piece without dictating what the interior, the design, the actual pattern of the piece looks like. Because the actual design of the quilt emerges from the multiplicity of voices of women in a cross-cultural context, the design will change over time. It is not something static.

What are some of the boundary conditions of a feminist ethic? First, nothing can become part of a feminist ethic—can be part of the quilt—that promotes sexism, racism, classism, or any other "isms" of social domination. Of course, people may disagree about what counts as a sexist act, racist attitude, classist behavior. What counts as sexism, racism, or classism may vary cross-culturally. Still, because a feminist ethic aims at eliminating sexism and sexist bias, and sexism is intimately connected in conceptualization and in practice to racism, classism, and naturism, a feminist ethic must be antisexist, antiracist, anticlassist, antinaturist, and opposed to any "ism" which presupposes or advances a logic of domination.

Second, a feminist ethic is a *contextualist* ethic. A contextualist ethic is one which sees ethical discourse and practice as emerging from the voices of people located in different historical circumstances. A contextualist ethic is properly viewed as a *collage* or *mosaic*, a *tapestry* of voices that emerges out of felt experiences. Like any collage or mosaic, the point is not to have *one picture* based on a unity of voices, but a *pattern* which emerges out of the very different voices of people located in different circumstances. When a contextualist ethic is *feminist*, it gives a central place to the voices of women.

Third, since a feminist ethic gives central significance to the diversity of women's voices, a feminist ethic must be structurally pluralistic rather than unitary or reductionistic. It rejects the assumption that there is "one voice" in terms of which ethical values, beliefs, attitudes, and conduct can be assessed.

Fourth, a feminist ethic reconceives ethical theory as theory in process which will change over time. Like all theory, a feminist ethic is based on some generalizations.[2] Nevertheless, the generalizations associated with it are themselves a pattern of voices within which the different voices emerging out of concrete and alternative descriptions of ethical situations have meaning. The coherence of a feminist theory so conceived is given within a historical and conceptual context, i.e., within a set of historical, socio-economic circumstances (including circumstances of race, class, age, and affectional orientation) and within a set of basic beliefs, values, attitudes, and assumptions about the world.

Fifth, because a feminist ethic is contextualist, structurally pluralistic, and "in-process," one way to evaluate the claims of a feminist ethic is in terms of their *inclusiveness*: Those claims (voices, patterns of voices) are morally and epistemologically favored (preferred, better, less partial, less biased) which are more inclusive of the felt experiences and perspectives of oppressed persons. The condition of inclusiveness requires and ensures that the diverse voices of women (as oppressed persons) will be given legitimacy in ethical theory building. It thereby helps to minimize empirical bias, e.g., bias rising from faulty or false generalizations based on stereotyping, too small a sample size, or a skewed sample. It does so by ensuring that any generalizations which are made about ethics and ethical decision making include—indeed cohere with—the patterned voices of women.[3]

Sixth, a feminist ethic makes no attempt to provide an "objective" point of view, since it assumes that in contemporary culture there really is no such point of view. As such, it does not claim to be "unbiased" in the sense of "value-neutral" or "objective." However, it does assume that whatever bias it has as an ethic centralizing the voices of oppressed persons is a *better bias*—"better" because it is more inclusive and therefore less partial—than those which exclude those voices.[4]

Seventh, a feminist ethic provides a central place for values typically unnoticed, underplayed, or misrepresented in traditional ethics, e.g., values of care, love, friendship, and appropriate trust.[5] Again, it need not do this at the exclusion of considerations of rights, rules, or utility. There may be many contexts in which talk of rights or of utility is useful or appropriate. For instance, in contracts or property relationships, talk of rights may be useful and appropriate. In deciding what is cost-effective or advantageous to the most people, talk of utility may be useful and appropriate. In a feminist qua contextualist ethic, whether or not such talk is useful or appropriate depends on the context; *other values* (e.g., values of care, trust, friendship) are *not* viewed as reducible to or captured solely in terms of such talk.[6]

Eighth, a feminist ethic also involves a reconception of what it is to be human and what it is for humans to engage in ethical decision making, since it rejects as either meaningless or currently untenable any gender-free or gender-neutral description of humans, ethics, and ethical decision making. It thereby rejects what Alison Jaggar calls "abstract individualism," i.e., the position that it is possible to identify a human essence or human nature that exists independently of any particular historical context.[7] Humans and human moral conduct are properly understood essentially (and not merely accidentally) in terms of networks or webs of historical and concrete relationships.

All the props are now in place for seeing how ecofeminism provides the framework for a distinctively feminist and environmental ethic. It is a feminism that critiques male bias wherever it occurs in ethics (including environmental ethics) and aims at providing an ethic (including an environmental ethic) which is not male-biased—and it does so in a way that satisfies the preliminary boundary conditions of a feminist ethic.

First, ecofeminism is quintessentially antinaturist. Its antinaturism consists in the rejection of any way of thinking about or acting toward nonhuman nature that reflects a logic, values, or attitude of domination. Its antinaturist, antisexist, antiracist, anticlassist (and so forth, for all other "isms" of social domination) stance forms the outer boundary of the quilt: Nothing gets on the quilt which is naturist, sexist, racist, classist, and so forth.

Second, ecofeminism is a contextualist ethic. It involves a shift *from* a conception of ethics as primarily a matter of rights, rules, or principles predetermined and applied in specific cases to entities viewed as competitors in the contest of moral standing, *to* a conception of ethics as growing out of what Jim Cheney calls "defining relationships," i.e., relationships conceived in some sense as defining who one is.[8] As a contextualist ethic, it is not that rights, or rules, or principles are *not* relevant or important. Clearly they are in certain contexts and for certain purposes.[9] It is just that what *makes* them relevant or important is that those to whom they apply are entities *in relationship with* others.

Ecofeminism also involves an ethical shift *from* granting moral consideration to nonhumans *exclusively* on the grounds of some similarity they share with humans (e.g., rationality, interests, moral agency, sentiency, right-holder status) *to* "a highly contextual account to see clearly what a human being is and what the nonhuman world might be, morally speaking, *for* human beings."[10] For an ecofeminist, *how* a moral agent is in relationship to another becomes of central significance, not simply *that* a moral agent is a moral agent or is bound by rights, duties, virtue, or utility to act in a certain way.

Third, ecofeminism is structurally pluralistic in that it presupposes and maintains difference—difference among humans as well as between humans and at least some elements of nonhuman nature. Thus, while ecofeminism denies the "nature/culture" split, it affirms that humans are both members of an ecological community (in some respects) and different from it (in other respects). Ecofeminism's attention to relationships and community is not, therefore, an erasure of difference but a respectful acknowledgment of it.

Fourth, ecofeminism reconceives theory as theory in process. It focuses on patterns of meaning which emerge, for instance, from the storytelling and first-person narratives of women (and others) who deplore the twin dominations of women and nature. The use of narrative is one way to ensure that the content of the ethic—the pattern of the quilt—may/will change over time, as the historical and material realities of women's lives change and as more is learned about women-nature connections and the destruction of the nonhuman world.[11]

Fifth, ecofeminism is inclusivist. It emerges from the voices of women who experience the harmful domination of nature and the way that domination is tied to their domination as women. It emerges from listening to the voices of indigenous peoples such as Native Americans who have been dislocated from their land and have witnessed the attendant undermining of such values as appropriate reciprocity, sharing, and kinship that characterize traditional Indian culture. It emerges from listening to voices of those who, like Nathan Hare, critique traditional approaches to environmental ethics as white and bourgeois, and as failing to address issues of "black ecology" and the "ecology" of the inner city and urban spaces.[12] It also emerges out of the voices of Chipko women who see the destruction of "earth, soil and water" as intimately connected with their own inability to survive economically.[13] With its emphasis on inclusivity and difference, ecofeminism provides a framework for recognizing that what counts as ecology and what counts as appropriate conduct toward both human and nonhuman environments is largely a matter of context.

Sixth, as a feminism, ecofeminism makes no attempt to provide an "objective" point of view. It is a social ecology. It recognizes the twin dominations of women and nature as social problems rooted both in very concrete, historical, socioeconomic circumstances and in oppressive patriarchal conceptual frameworks which maintain and sanction these circumstances.

Seventh, ecofeminism makes a central place for values of care, love, friendship, trust, and appropriate reciprocity—values that presuppose that our relationships to others are central to our understanding of who we are.[14] It thereby gives voice to the sensitivity that in climbing a mountain, one is doing something in relationship with an "other," an "other" whom one can come to care about and treat respectfully.

Last, an ecofeminist ethic involves a reconception of what it means to be human, and in what human ethical behavior consists. Ecofeminism denies abstract individualism. Humans are who we are in large part by virtue of the historical and social contexts and the relationships we are in, including our relationships with nonhuman nature. Relationships are not something extrinsic to who we are, not an "add on" feature of human nature; they play an essential role in shaping what it is to be human. Relationships of humans to the nonhuman environment are, in part, constitutive of what it is to be a human.

By making visible the interconnections among the dominations of women and nature, ecofeminism shows that both are feminist issues and that explicit acknowledgment of both is vital to any responsible environmental ethic. Feminism *must* embrace ecological feminism if it is to end the domination of women because the domination of women is tied conceptually and historically to the domination of nature.

A responsible environmental ethic also *must* embrace feminism. Otherwise, even the seemingly most revolutionary, liberational, and holistic ecological ethic will fail to take seriously the interconnected dominations of nature and women that are so much a part of the historical legacy and conceptual framework that sanctions the exploitation of nonhuman nature. Failure to make visible these interconnected, twin dominations results in an inaccurate account of how it is that nature has been and continues to be dominated and exploited and produces an environmental ethic that lacks the depth necessary to be truly *inclusive* of the realities of persons who at least in dominant Western culture have been intimately tied with that exploitation, viz., women. Whatever else can be said in favor of such holistic ethics, a failure to make visible ecofeminist insights into the common denominators of the twin oppressions of women and nature is to perpetuate, rather than overcome, the source of that oppression.

This last point deserves further attention. It may be objected that as long as the end result is "the same"—the development of an environmental ethic which does not emerge out of or reinforce an oppressive conceptual framework—it does not matter whether that ethic (or the ethic endorsed in getting there) is feminist or not. Hence, it simply is *not* the case that any adequate environmental ethic must be feminist. My argument, in contrast, has been that it *does* matter, and for three important reasons. First, there is the scholarly issue of accurately representing historical reality, and that, ecofeminists claim, requires acknowledging the historical feminization of nature and naturalization of women as part of the exploitation of nature. Second, I have shown that the conceptual connections between the domination of women and the domination of nature are located in an oppressive and, at least in Western societies, patriarchal conceptual framework characterized by a logic of domination. Thus, I have shown that failure to notice the nature of this connection leaves at best an incomplete, inaccurate, and partial account of what is required of a conceptually adequate environmental ethic. An ethic which *does not* acknowledge this is simply *not* the same as one that does, whatever else the similarities between them. Third, the claim that, in contemporary culture, one can have an adequate environmental ethic which is *not* feminist assumes that, in contemporary culture, the label *feminist* does not add anything crucial to the nature or description of environmental ethics. I have shown that at least in contemporary culture this is false, for the word *feminist* currently helps to clarify just *how* the domination of nature is conceptually linked to patriarchy and, hence, how the liberation of nature, is conceptually linked to the termination of patriarchy. Thus, because it has critical bite in contemporary culture, it serves as an important reminder that in contemporary sex-gendered, raced, classed, and naturist culture, an unlabeled position functions as a privileged and "unmarked" position. That is, without the addition of the word *feminist*, one presents environmental ethics as if it has no bias, including male-gender bias, which is just what ecofeminists deny: Failure to notice the connections between the twin oppressions of women and nature *is* male-gender bias.

One of the goals of feminism is the eradication of all oppressive sex-gender (and related race, class, age, affectional preference) categories and the creation of a world in which *difference does not breed domination*—say, the world of 4001. If in 4001 an "adequate environmental ethic" is a "feminist environmental ethic," the word *feminist* may then be redundant and unnecessary. However, this is *not* 4001, and in terms of the current histori-cal and conceptual reality the dominations of nature and of women are intimately connected. Failure to notice or make visible that connection in 1990 perpetuates the mistaken (and privileged) view that "environmental ethics" is *not* a feminist issue, and that *feminist* adds nothing to environ-mental ethics.[15]

CONCLUSION

I have argued in this paper that ecofeminism provides a framework for a distinctively feminist and environmental ethic. Ecofeminism grows out of the felt and theorized-about connections between the domination of women and the domination of nature. As a contextualist ethic, ecofeminism refocuses environmental ethics on what nature might mean, morally speaking, *for* humans, and on how the relational attitudes of humans to others—humans as well as nonhumans—sculpt both what it is to be human and the nature and ground of human responsibilities to the nonhuman environment. Part of what this refocusing does is to take seriously the voices of women and other oppressed persons in the construction of that ethic.

A Sioux elder once told me a story about his son. He sent his seven-year-old son to live with the child's grandparents on a Sioux reservation so that he could "learn the Indian ways." Part of what the grandparents taught the son was how to hunt the four-leggeds of the forest. As I heard the story, the boy was taught "to shoot your four-legged brother in his hind area, slowing it down but not killing it. Then, take the four-legged's head in your hands, and look into his eyes. The eyes are where all the suffering is. Look into your brother's eyes and feel his pain. Then, take your knife and cut the four-legged under his chin, here, on his neck, so that he dies quickly. And as you do, ask your brother, the four-legged, for forgiveness for what you do. Offer also a prayer of thanks to your four-legged kin for offering his body to you just now, when you need food to eat and clothing to wear. And promise the four-legged that you will put yourself back into the earth when you die, to become nourishment for the earth, and for the sister flowers, and for the brother deer. It is appropriate that you should offer this blessing for the four-legged and, in due time, reciprocate in turn with your body in this way, as the four-legged gives life to you for your survival." As I reflect upon that story, I am struck by the power of the environmental ethic that grows out of and takes seriously narrative, con-text, and such values and relational attitudes as care, loving perception, and appropriate reciprocity, and doing what is appropriate in a given situa-tion—however that notion of appropriateness eventually gets filled out. I am also struck by what one is able to see, once one begins to explore some of the historical and conceptual connections between the dominations of women and of nature. A *re-conceiving* and *re-visioning* of both feminism and environmental ethics, is, I think, the power and promise of ecofeminism.

Notes

1. This account of a feminist ethic draws on my paper "Toward an Ecofeminist Ethic."
2. Marilyn Frye makes this point in her illuminating paper, "The Possibility of Feminist Theory," read at the American Philosophical Association Central Division Meetings in Chicago, April 29–May 1, 1986. My discussion of feminist theory is inspired largely by that paper and by Kathryn Addelson's paper "Moral Revolution," in *Women and Values: Reading in Recent Feminist Philosophy*, ed. Marilyn Pearsall (Belmont, CA: Wadsworth, 1986) 291–309.
3. Notice that the standard of inclusiveness does not exclude the voices of men. It is just that those voices must cohere with the voices of women.
4. For a more in-depth discussion of the notions of impartiality and bias, see my paper, "Critical Thinking and Feminism," *Informal Logic* 10, no. 1 (Winter 1988): 31–44.
5. The burgeoning literature on these values is noteworthy. See, e.g., Carol Gilligan, *In a Different Voice: Psychological Theories and Women's Development* (Cambridge: Harvard University Press, 1982); *Mapping the Moral Domain: A Contribution of Women's Thinking to Psychological Theory and Education*, ed. Carol Gilligan, Janie Victoria Ward, and Jill McLean Taylor, with Betty Bardige (Cambridge: Harvard University Press, 1988); Nel Noddings, *Caring: A Feminine Approach to Ethics and Moral Education* (Berkeley: University of California Press, 1984); Maria Lugones and Elizabeth V. Spelman, "Have We Got a Theory for You! Feminist Theory, Cultural Imperialism, and the Women's Voice," *Women's Studies International Forum* 6 (1983): 573–81; Maria Lugones, "Playfulness"; Annette C. Baier, "What Do Women Want in a Moral Theory?" *Nous* 19 (1985): 53–63.
6. Jim Cheney would claim that our fundamental relationships to one another as moral agents are not as moral agents to rights holders, and that whatever rights a person properly may be said to have are relationally defined rights, not rights possessed by atomistic individuals conceived as Robinson Crusoes who do not exist essentially in relation to others. On this view, even rights talk itself is properly conceived as growing out of a relational ethic, not vice versa.
7. Alison Jaggar, *Feminist Politics and Human Nature* (Totowa, NJ: Rowman and Allanheld, 1980) 42–44.
8. Henry West has pointed out that the expression "defining relations" is ambiguous. According to West, "the 'defining' as Cheney uses it is an adjective, not a principle—it is not that ethics defines relationships; it is that ethics grows out of conceiving of the relationships that one is in as defining what the individual is."
9. For example, in relationships involving contracts or promises, those relationships might be correctly described as that of moral agent to rights holders. In relationships involving mere property, those relationships might be correctly described as that of moral agent to objects having only instrumental value, "relationships of instrumentality." In comments on an earlier draft of this paper, West suggested that possessive individualism, for instance, might be recast in

such a way that an individual is defined by his or her property relationships.

10. Jim Cheney, "Ecofeminism and Deep Ecology," *Environmental Ethics* 9 (1987): 115–45.

11. One might object that such permission for change opens the door for environmental exploitation. This is not the case. An ecofeminist ethic is antinaturist. Hence, the unjust domination and exploitation of nature is a "boundary condition" of the ethic; no such actions are sanctioned or justified on ecofeminist grounds. What it *does* leave open is some leeway about what counts as domination and exploitation. This, I think, is a strength of the ethic, not a weakness, since it acknowledges that *that* issue cannot be resolved in any practical way in the abstract, independent of a historical and social context.

12. Nathan Hare, "Black Ecology," in *Environmental Ethics*, ed. K. S. Shrader-Frechette (Pacific Grove, CA: Boxwood Press, 1981), 229–36.

13. For an ecofeminist discussion of the Chipko movement, see my "Toward an Ecofeminist Ethic," and Shiva's *Staying Alive*.

14. See Cheney, "Eco-Feminism and Deep Ecology," 122.

15. I offer the same sort of reply to critics of ecofeminism such as Warwick Fox who suggest that for the sort of ecofeminism I defend, the word *feminist* does not add anything significant to environmental ethics and, consequently, that an ecofeminist like myself might as well call herself a deep ecologist. He asks: "Why doesn't she just call it [i.e., Warren's vision of a transformative feminism] deep ecology? Why specifically attach the label *feminist* to it . . .?" (Warwick Fox, "The Deep Ecology-Ecofeminism Debate and Its Parallels," *Environmental Ethics* 11, no. 1 [1989]: 14, n. 22). Whatever the important similarities between deep ecology and ecofeminism (or, specifically, my version of ecofeminism)—and, indeed, there are many—it is precisely my point here that the word *feminist* does add something significant to the conception of environmental ethics, and that any environmental ethic (including deep ecology) that fails to make explicit the different kinds of interconnections among the domination of nature and the domination of women will be, from a feminist (and ecofeminist) perspective such as mine, inadequate.

SELECTION 40
Human Rights as Men's Rights

HILARY CHARLESWORTH

ALTHOUGH THERE IS NO doubt that the apartheid of gender is considerably more pervasive than the apartheid of race, it has never provoked the same degree of international concern or opprobrium. The international community usually couches discussion of the advancement of women in terms of the acquisition and implementation of rights particular to women. While this is certainly an important and valuable project, it can also obscure some basic elements contributing to the oppression of women. My central argument is that the current international human rights structure itself and the substance of many norms of human rights law create obstacles to the advancement of women. Because the lawmaking institutions of the international legal order have always been, and continue to be, dominated by men, international human rights law has developed to reflect the experiences of men and largely to exclude those of women, rendering suspect the claim of the objectivity and universality of international human rights law. Until the gendered nature of the human rights system itself is recognized and transformed, no real progress for women can be achieved.

There are problems in speaking about women and their experiences in a global context. Obviously, differences of class, wealth, race, and nationality will lead to differing power relationships among women. Some feminists of color and women from developing nations have questioned attempts to universalize a particular understanding of feminism, charging white Western feminists with inappropriately assuming that their particular concerns are shared worldwide.[1] But patriarchy and the devaluing of women, although manifested differently within different societies, are almost universal. As Peggy Antrobus, director of the Women and Development Program at the University of the West Indies, told the 1991 World Women's Congress for a Healthy Planet in Florida:

Although we are divided by race, class, culture, and geography, our hope lies in our commonalities. All women's unremunerated household work is

384

exploited, we all have conflicts in our multiple roles, our sexuality is exploited by men, media, and the economy, we struggle for survival and dignity, and, rich or poor, we are vulnerable to violence. We share our "otherness," our exclusion from decision making at all levels.[2]

Certainly no monolithic "women's point of view" can be assumed, but it is also important to acknowledge commonalities across cultures. In analyzing other cultures, we must interrogate our own assumptions and tools, acknowledge the partialness of our perspective, and regard women from other cultures with, in Maria Lugones's words, "loving perception" rather than as objects for theory.[3]

THE INTERNATIONAL LEGAL STRUCTURE

The structure and institutions of the international legal order set up under the United Nations reflect and ensure the continued dominance of a male perspective. In the primary subjects of international law—nation-states and, increasingly, international organizations—the invisibility of women is striking. Power structures within governments are overwhelmingly masculine: Very few states have women in significant positions of power, and even in those states that do, the numbers are extremely small.[4] Women are either unrepresented or underrepresented in the national and global decision-making processes: The global average of women's representation in parliaments is less than 10 percent.[5]

International organizations have the same problem. Their structures replicate those of states, with women restricted to insignificant and subordinate roles. Wherever, in international institutions, major decisions are made concerning global policies and guidelines, women are almost completely absent, despite the often disparate impact of those decisions upon women.[6] This is of course the case in the Secretariat of the United Nations and its specialized agencies, despite the terms of Article 8 of the Charter, which states:[7] "The United Nations shall place no restriction on the eligibility of men and women to participate in any capacity and under conditions of equality in its principal and subsidiary organs." Although over 40 percent of Secretariat staff are women, very few women are in management positions.[8] Since the 1985 Nairobi conference, there have been some improvements in this respect.[9] It has been estimated, however, that at the current rate of change it will take until the year 2021 for women to hold half of the United Nations professional jobs.

The silence and invisibility of women is also a feature of those bodies with special functions in creating and progressively developing international law. Only one woman has sat as a judge on the International Court of

Justice,[10] and no woman has ever been elected to the International Law Commission. Although the question of human rights has typically been regarded as an appropriate area in which attention can be directed toward women, women are still vastly underrepresented in the specialized United Nations human rights bodies. Apart from the Committee on the Elimination of Discrimination against Women, all of whose members are women, in 1993 there was only one woman (out of eighteen members) on the Committee on the Elimination of Racial Discrimination, two (out of eighteen) on the Economic, Social, and Cultural Rights Committee, three (out of eighteen) on the Human Rights Committee, and two (out of ten) on the Committee against Torture.[11] Strikingly, the only occasion on which imbalance in gender representation was ever the subject of an official criticism was when the Economic and Social Council called on states parties to nominate both men and women for election to the Committee on the Elimination of Discrimination Against Women.[12]

Why is it problematic that all the major institutions of the international legal order are peopled by men? What is the value of insisting on the need for significant representation of women? Long-term male domination of all bodies wielding political power nationally and internationally means that issues traditionally of concern to men are seen as *general* human concerns; "women's concerns," by contrast, are regarded as a distinct and limited category. Because men generally are not the victims of sex discrimination, domestic violence, or sexual degradation and violence, for example, these matters are often relegated to a specialized and marginalized sphere and are regulated, if at all, by weaker methods. Unless the experiences of women contribute directly to the mainstream international legal order, beginning with women's equal representation in lawmaking forums, international human rights law loses its claim to universal applicability: It should be more accurately characterized as international *men's* rights law.

The United Nations system has already accepted the importance of balanced representation among nations of differing political and economic structure and power in all aspects of its work. It is acknowledged that the international legal system cannot simply reproduce the concerns of a particular set of states—that its effectiveness depends precisely on its reflection of truly global interests. Although women make up more than half of the world's population, this sensitivity has never been extended to the accommodation of alternative gender perspectives, producing an impoverished, ineffective, and lopsided jurisprudence.

THE SUBSTANCE OF INTERNATIONAL
HUMAN RIGHTS LAW

Many generally applicable international human rights principles are inherently biased against women. An important aspect of international human rights law is that, like many national legal systems, it operates primarily in the public sphere, that is, within the world of government, politics, economics, and the workplace, areas traditionally associated with men. Its contrast is the private sphere of home, hearth, and family, the traditional province of women, which is generally regarded as outside the scope of both national laws and international human rights laws. And yet the most pervasive harm against women tends to occur within the inner sanctum of the private realm, within the family.

The following examples of what I suggest are male "human" rights principles are drawn from each of the so-called generations of rights. The priority to be enjoyed by each generation of rights has, of course, been a matter of great controversy, the North typically giving prominence to the first generation of civil and political rights, the South emphasizing the importance of the second and third generations. It is striking, however, that the three generations have in common the exclusion of the experiences of women.

FIRST GENERATION RIGHTS

The primacy traditionally given to civil and political rights by developed nations is directed toward protection of men within public life, in their relationship with government. But this is not the arena in which women most need protection. The operation of a public/private distinction at a gendered level is seen most clearly in the definition of those civil and political rights concerned with protection of the individual from violence.

An example of this, often regarded as the most important of all human rights, is the right to life set out in Article 6 of the *International Covenant on Civil and Political Rights*. The right is concerned with the arbitrary deprivation of life through public action. But protection from arbitrary deprivation of life or liberty through public action, important as it is, does not address the ways in which being a woman is in itself life-threatening and the special ways in which women need legal protection to be able to enjoy their right to life. From conception to old age, womanhood is full of risks: of abortion and infanticide because of the social and economic pressure in some cultures to have sons; of malnutrition because social practices give men and boys priority with respect to food; of less access to health care than men; of endemic violence against women in all states. Yet the right to life is not regarded as extending to these threats to women's lives.

A similar myopia can be detected in the international prohibition on torture. A central feature of the international legal definition of torture is that it takes place in the public realm: It must be "inflicted by or at the instigation of or with the consent or acquiescence of a public official or other person acting in an official capacity."[13] Although many women are victims of torture in this "public" sense,[14] by far the greatest violence against women occurs in the "private," nongovernmental sphere. This is left untouched by the international definition of torture.

In a wide range of cultures, significant forms of violence against women such as wife murder, battery, and rape, are, through (for example) nonprosecution or comparatively lower sentencing practices, treated less seriously than other violent crimes.[15] One reason for the official toleration of violence against women worldwide is the both explicitly and implicitly held view that it is a "private" matter, not within the proper scope of national criminal justice systems.[16] And yet if violence against women is understood not just as aberrant "private" behavior but as part of the structure of the universal subordination of women, it can never be considered a purely "private" issue: The distinction between "public" and "private" action in the context of violence against women is a not a useful or meaningful one. Yet it is by no means clear that the traditional rules of state responsibility can be invoked to hold states internationally accountable for legal and social systems in which violence and discrimination against women are endemic and in which such actions are trivialized or discounted.

The traditional construction of civil and political rights, then, obscures the most consistent harms done to women. While recent developments such as the United Nations' *Declaration on the Elimination of Violence against Women*[17] indicate international concern on this issue, they do not directly challenge the inability of human rights law generally to respond to injuries sustained constantly by women worldwide. Apart from a brief preambular reference, the Declaration does not define violence against women as a human rights violation, but presents it implicitly as a discrete category of harm, on a different (and lesser) plane than serious human rights violations.

SECOND GENERATION RIGHTS

It might be thought that "second" generation rights—economic, social, and cultural rights—by their nature transcend the dichotomy between public and private spheres of life and thus offer more to women's lives. But the definition of these rights, set out in the *International Covenant on Economic, Social, and Cultural Rights*, indicates the tenacity of a distinction between public and private worlds in human rights law.[18] The Covenant does not touch on the economic, social, and cultural contexts in which most women live, since the crucial economic, social, and cultural power relationship for most women is not one directly with the state but with men—fathers, husbands, or brothers—whose authority is supported by patriarchal state structures. For example, the definition of the right to just and favorable conditions of work in Article 7 is confined to work in the public sphere. Marilyn Waring has documented the tremendous amount of economic activity by women that is rendered invisible precisely because it is performed by women without pay and within the private, domestic sphere.[19] Article 7's guarantee to women of "conditions of work not inferior to those enjoyed by men, with equal pay for equal work" thus sounds rather hollow in light of the international myopia with respect to the extent and economic value of women's work.

Moreover, notions of cultural and religious rights can often reinforce a distinction between public and private worlds that operates to the disadvantage of women: Culture and religion can be seen as spheres protected from legal regulation even though they are often the sites for oppression of women by men. While the right to gender equality, on the one hand, and religious and cultural rights, on the other, can be reconciled by limiting the latter,[20] in political practice cultural and religious freedom tend to be accorded much higher priority nationally and internationally.

THIRD GENERATION RIGHTS

The philosophical basis of group rights rests on a primary commitment to the welfare of the community over and above the interests of particular individuals. It might seem that such rights would hold particular promise for women, whose lives typically center more on the family, the group, and the community than the individual. There has been much controversy over the legal status of such rights, but from a woman's perspective, they are, in fundamental ways, little different from the first and second generations of rights, since they too have developed in an androcentric way.

The theoretical and practical development of third generation rights has, in fact, delivered very little to women. The right to development, for example, is both defined and implemented internationally to support male economic dominance.[21] The subordination of women to men does not enter the traditional development calculus: "Development" conceived as economic growth is not concerned with the lack of benefits or disadvantageous effects this growth may have on half of the society it purports to benefit. Indeed, the position of many women in developing countries has deteriorated over the last two decades: Women's access to economic resources has been reduced, their health and educational status has declined, and their work burdens have increased.[22] The generality and apparently universal applicability of the right to development as formulated in the UN *Declaration on the Right to Development* is undermined by the fundamentally androcentric nature of the international economic system, which accords far greater value to work conducted in the public (male) sphere than to women's work in the private sphere. The problematic nature, for Third World women, of current development practice cannot of course be attributed solely to the international legal formulation of the right to development. But the rhetoric of international law both reflects and reinforces a system that contributes to the subordination of women. More recent UN deliberations on development have paid greater attention to the role of women.[23] However, these concerns are usually presented as quite distinct (soluble by the application of special protective measures) rather than as crucial to the notion of development itself.[24]

So, too, the right to self-determination, allowing "all peoples" to "freely determine their political status and freely pursue their economic, social and cultural development," has been invoked and supported recently in a number of contexts and ultimately to the disadvantage of women. The oppression of women within groups claiming the right of self-determination has never been considered relevant to the validity of such claims or to the form self-determination should take. In this sense, the right to self-determination is relevant only in the most public of contexts: male political life. The right to self-determination attaches to "peoples"—entities defined ethnically or culturally—even if half the persons who make up the "people" have little or no power in the community.[25] In many cases (the Afghani Mujihadeen and "liberated" Kuwait are well-documented examples), the oppression of women within the self-determining unit is ignored. In practice, then, the "people" to whom the right of self-determination attaches are men.

STRATEGIES FOR CHANGE

Most United Nations work relating to the advancement of women is centered on the Commission on the Status of Women and the *Convention on the Elimination of All Forms of Discrimination against Women*. The Commission and the Women's Convention have provided a valuable, if underresourced, focus for women's interests in the international system, but, ironically, the creation of a specialized branch of women's human rights law has also allowed its marginalization. "Mainstream" human rights bodies have tended to ignore the application of general human rights norms to women.

I have argued that both the process and substance of international law is gendered, and thus is partial in its effectiveness and authority. It is important, as a strategy for the advancement of women, to ensure that women's voices and experiences are included in the definition of all human rights norms. The United Nations' concern for balanced geographical and ideological representation should be extended to gender: The critical importance of having equality of representation of women in all international lawmaking forums must be recognized and acted on so that international law can claim truly global applicability. Training in equal opportunity issues should be mandatory for both state representatives and civil servants in international forums. Effective affirmative action programs need to be designed for the United Nations Secretariat to counter its resistance to gender equality. A commitment to gender-inclusive language in all United Nations work (especially in human rights instruments) is a good way of starting the task of reducing the overtly masculine culture of international lawmaking.

Most fundamentally, the boundaries of "mainstream" international law must be reoriented to incorporate women's experiences. One method of doing this in the context of human rights law is to challenge the gendered dichotomy of (and to reshape doctrines based on) public and private worlds. The expert committees established under the major human rights treaties should be encouraged to consider issues of gender in their work, and to use techniques, such as the issuing of general comments, to broaden the traditionally androcentric scope of rights.

The Second World Conference on Human Rights held in Vienna in 1993 responded to the well-organized lobbying by women's groups by declaring that "the full and equal enjoyment by women of all human rights" be a priority for national governments and the United Nations. It urged that women's rights be integrated into the mainstream of United Nations activity. The effect such encouragement will have is as yet uncertain. Although there remains much to be done within the deeply androcentric United Nations, redefining the traditional scope of international human rights law so as to acknowledge the interests of women may lead international actors to pursue change that will allow for the reimagination of gender difference.

Notes

1. E.g., Maria Lugones and Elizabeth Spelman, "Have We Got a Theory for You," *Women's Studies International Forum* 6 (6): 573.
2. Peggy Antrobus, paper presented to the World Women's Congress for a Healthy Planet, Miami, FL, November 8–12, 1991.
3. Maria Lugones, "Playfulness, World Traveling, and Loving Perception," *Hypatia* 2 (2): 3. See also Isabel Guning, "Arrogant Perception, World-Traveling, and Multicultural Feminism: The Case of Female Genital Surgeries," *Columbia Human Rights Law Review* 23 (1991–92): 189; Annie Bunting, "Theorizing Women's Cultural Diversity in Feminist International Human Rights Strategies," in *Feminist Theory and Legal Strategy*, ed. Anne Bottomly and Joanne Conaghen (Oxford, UK, and Cambridge, MA: Blackwell, 1993), 6.
4. United Nations, *Women in Politics and Decision-Making in the Late Twentieth Century* (Dordrecht: Martinus Nijhoff, 1992). UN Sales No. E.91.IV.3.
5. Ibid.
6. See Hilary Charlesworth, Christine Chinkin, and Shelley Wright, "Feminist Approaches to International Law," *American Journal of International Law* 85 (613): 623 n. 60 (1991).

7. Charter of the United Nations, Article 8, 1945.
8. The Secretary-General's report, *Review and Appraisal of the Implementation of the Nairobi Forward-Looking Strategies for the Advancement of Women*, UN Doc. E/CN. 6/1990/5, indicates that between 1984 and 1988 the total increase in the representation of women in professional and management positions in the UN was 3.6 percent, to a total of 21 percent of professional staff. At the senior management level in 1988, however, only 4 percent of staff were women (ibid., 84–86).
9. In 1985 the Secretary-General appointed a Coordinator for the Improvement of the Status of Women for twelve months. This position was subsequently extended.
10. Mme. Suzanne Bastid was Judge ad hoc in *Application for Revision and Interpretation of the Judgment of 24 February 1982 in the Case Concerning the Continental Shelf (Tunisia/Libyan Arab Jamahiriya)* [1985], ICJ Rep. 4.
11. See A. Byrnes, "The 'Other' Human Rights Treaty Body: The Work of the Committee on the Elimination of Discrimination Against Women," *Yale Journal of International Law* 14, no. 1 (1989):8 n. 26. The Sub-Commission on Prevention of Discrimination and Protection of Minorities has six women out of twenty-six members.
12. Charlesworth, Chinkin, and Wright, "Feminist Approaches," 624.
13. United Nations, General Assembly, *Convention against Torture and Other Cruel, Inhuman or Degrading Treatment or Punishment*, General Assembly Resolution 39/46, Article 1 (1), (Dec. 10, 1984). UN Doc. A/RES/39/46(1984).
14. See, e.g., Amnesty International, *Women in the Front Line: Human Rights Violations against Women* (London: Amnesty International, 1991). Even given the limited international definition of torture, recent research suggests that the torture of women receives considerably less attention than the torture of men. See International Human Rights Law Group, *Token Gestures* (Washington, DC: International Human Rights Law Group, 1993), which examines the work of the United Nations Special Rapporteur on Torture. The report argued that the Special Rapporteur failed adequately to investigate and condemn many well-documented cases of systematic torture of women.
15. See, for example, Margaret Schuler, ed., *Freedom from Violence: Women's Strategies from around the World* (New York: Unifem, 1992).
16. See Americas Watch, *Criminal Injustice: Violence against Women in Brazil* (Washington, DC: International Human Rights Law Group, 1991); and Dorothy Thomas and Michele Beasley, "Domestic Violence as a Human Rights Issue," *Human Rights Quarterly* 15 (1993): 36.
17. UN Doc. E/CN.6/WG.2/1992/L.3 (Sept. 3, 1992).
18. Shelley Wright, "Economic Rights and Social Justice: A Feminist Analysis of Stone International Human Rights Conventions," *Australian YearBook of International Law* 12 (1992): 242.
19. Marilyn Waring, *Counting for Nothing* (Sydney: Allen and Unwin, 1988).
20. See Donna Sullivan, "Gender Equality and Religious Freedom: Toward a Framework for Conflict Resolution," *New York University Journal of International Law and Politics* 24 (1992): 795.
21. This argument is more fully pursued in Hilary Charlesworth, "The Public/Private Distinction and the Right to Development," *Australian YearBook of International Law* 12 (1992): 190.
22. See United Nations, *World Survey on the Role of Women in Development* 19–20 (New York: United Nations, 1986).

23. E.g., *Analytical Compilation of Comments and Views on the Implementation of the Declaration on the Right to Development Prepared by the Secretary-General*, UN Doc E/CN.4/AC.39/1988/L.2, paras. 59–63; *Report Prepared by the Secretary-General on the Global Consultation on the Realization of the Right to Development as a Human Right*, UN Doc E/Cn.4/1990/9, paras. 15, 42, 51, 52, 59.

24. The section of the Secretary-General's report dealing with "Obstacles to the Implementation of the Right to Development as a Human Right," for example, mentions failure to respect the right of peoples to self-determination, racial discrimination, apartheid, foreign occupation, restrictions on transfers of technology, and the consumption patterns of industrialized countries as serious barriers to the realization of the right to development; it contains no reference to sex discrimination. Ibid., paras. 27–35. Compare the detail of Article 14 of the Women's Convention. UN Doc. A/RES/34/180 (1980).

25. See C. Chinkin, "A Gendered Perspective to the International Use of Force," *Australian YearBook of International Law* 12 (1992): 142.

This paper is a revised version of an address to the Third Committee of the United Nations General Assembly, New York, on October 27, 1992. An expanded account of the argument in the paper is to be published in *The Human Rights of Women: National and International Perspectives*, ed. Rebecca Cook, University of Pennsylvania Press (forthcoming).

PART VII

Law and Difference: Privacy, Pornography, and Reproductive Rights

SELECTION 41
FROM
Making All the Difference

MARTHA MINOW

FEMINISM, RELATIONAL THOUGHT, AND LAW

INSPIRED BY THE MOVEMENT for women's rights and by feminist scholarship in other fields, feminist legal scholarship began in the 1970s to challenge the overt exclusion or subordination of women.[1] Legal scholars argued that gender distinctions in law lacked justification for denying equal treatment, given basic similarities between men's and women's abilities and interests. By the late 1970s feminist legal scholarship was specifically criticizing the pretense of neutrality in legal standards that use male experience as the benchmark for universal human experience and, in effect, marginalize women or treat as deviant any difference drawn in relation to men.[2] Some feminist legal scholars have sought to validate women's experiences and differences as new starting points for equality analysis;[3] others emphasize the systematic, gender-based oppression and subordination embedded in both social structures and the legal rules available to challenge them.[4] Some have urged reflection on women's experiences as the grounding for legal norms and legal strategies;[5] others have explored images of women in legal texts as powerful, unstated messages and frameworks affecting decisions.[6] In both kinds of work, feminists challenge the presupposition that there is a neutral norm against which to judge experience, and the accompanying assumption that male experience and perceptions conform to that neutral norm.

Little of the feminist work in law has yet reached beyond the legal treatment of women to deal with other issues.[7] Yet relational ideas of the self and relational theories of knowledge and reasoning offer much to legal thought and to the legal treatment of "differences" that include but are not limited to gender differences. Explicit relational strategies may contribute to the legal treatment of disabled persons and of members of racial and religious minorities—or even to legal theories of rights and of the relationships between branches of government. . . .

For legal analysis, relational approaches may best be articulated as imperatives to engage an observer—a judge, a legislator, or a citizen—in the problems of difference: *Notice* the mutual dependence of people. *Investigate* the construction of difference in light of the norms and patterns of interpersonal and institutional relationships which make some traits matter. *Question* the relationship between the observer and the observed in order to situate judgments in the perspective of the actual judge. *Seek out* and *consider* competing perspectives, especially those of people defined as the problem. *Locate* theory within context; *criticize* practice in light of theoretical commitments; and *challenge* abstract theories in light of their practical effects. *Connect* the parts and the whole of a situation; *see* how the frame of analysis influences what is assumed to be given.

Some lawyers and judges have already drawn on relational insights, especially in legal challenges to socially assigned statuses that yield isolation and stigma. I have called hints of this development the social-relations approach in several Supreme Court opinions in the Cleburne case. There, Justice Stevens and Justice Marshall, in different ways, questioned the assignment of difference that the community had treated as obvious. They sought out the perspective of the mentally retarded persons involved and considered the isolation and stigma those persons had experienced because of zoning restrictions. They looked at the social practices that had isolated mentally retarded people and allowed fears about them to grow. They questioned the motives, self-interest, and misconceptions behind the zoning ordinance. They asked why members of the residential community did not want a group of mentally retarded people living in their midst and what the objections indicated about relationships in this community.

Some may doubt the utility of a judicial review of such questions. What can or should a court do with the perception that neighborhood residents are frightened and uncomfortable about living close to people who seem different? What good will talking about this do? The hope of relational approaches is that if we talk about these things, the people behind the labels will become more vivid to those who would exclude them. The community's negative attitude toward those they call different will be itself conceived as part of the problem, rather than as an immutable given.[8] Notions of difference will no longer be the end but rather the beginning of an inquiry about how all people, with all their differences, should live. . . .

A MISUNDERSTANDING AND A RESTATEMENT

One misunderstanding arises when scholars try to accommodate the feminist notions of care, borrowed particularly from Gilligan's work. Doing so risks a kind of simplistic and wooden reasoning, and it is especially disappointing if the tactic simply injects compassion or sympathy into an otherwise resilient structure of legal analysis and institutions. Simply transporting an ethic of care into the legal system can leave in place the system's established rules about what counts as a conflict, its adversary method, and its assumptions about human personality. Moreover, conceptions of care may ignore the significance of power differentials which the legal framework of rights more explicitly acknowledges.[9] Simply adding an emphasis on caretaking responsibility and compassion neglects the profound challenge to conventional legal understandings introduced by the relational methods of feminist theories.

Thus, the challenge presented by feminist strategies is not just to deepen an interest in "responsibility" or "care," contrasted with "fairness" or "rights." The challenge is to maintain a steady inquiry into the interpersonal and political relationships between the known and the knower; a concern for the relations between wholes and parts; a suspicion of abstractions, which are likely to hide under claims of universality what is in fact the particular point of view and experience of those in power; and a respect for particularity, concreteness, reflection on experience, and dialogue. Through these relational themes, feminist methodologies frame the issues in ways that avoid the constraining assumptions behind the dilemma of difference.[10] Both historical and sociological strategies identify "difference" as a function of contingent patterns of relationships; literary and psychological strategies help to articulate the naming of difference in relationships of disparate power.[11] Many feminists urge recasting issues of "difference" as problems of dominance or subordination in order to disclose the social relationships of power within which difference is named and enforced.[12] In sum, feminist strategies question the assignment of difference to the "different person" by locating difference within relationships of differential power.

Further, by questioning the choice of the norm, theory, or context within which difference has been named and assigned, feminist theorists force the statement of those norms that have remained implicit. What has been taken for granted must be stated. And once stated, norms based on the male experience become a subject for contest; alternative norms can be articulated and defended. For example, "maternal thinking" can be freed from the "private sphere" of family and transposed to the "public sphere" of politics as a basis for critique and reform.[13] Similarly, rather than assuming that women must adjust to a workplace designed for men, one can advocate designing a workplace for both men and women.[14] The idea of an unsituated perspective on issues of difference fails amid repeated demonstrations of the influence of the observer on the observed. Feminist critics note that the legal definitions of rape, for example, adopt a male perspective and ignore female perceptions: Thus, the observer's situation influences what is observed.[15]

Similarly, previously ignored perspectives become plausible contestants for illuminating and debating the legal treatment of divorce, child custody, domestic violence, and pregnancy and the workplace.[16]

When those who have been considered "different" become the source of information about a critical but previously suppressed perspective on the legal issues affecting them, the social and institutional patterns that ignore this perspective themselves become questionable. The status quo no longer seems natural and inevitable but is revealed instead as a reflection of choices made and choices that can be remade. Individualized solutions that leave the status quo in place—by accommodating one person, or making an exception—no longer appear unproblematic. By challenging the classifications drawn on gender lines that have been taken for granted in legal rules because they mirror social practices, feminist legal theorists open the way for more creative alternatives to the exclusion of or impositions on women based on legal rules that either ignore or acknowledge "their" difference. New strategies include acknowledging more fundamental similarities between people, such as the interests shared by men and women in combining work and family duties. Another strategy explores the pervasive differences distinguishing each individual and the possibilities of responding to a variety of traits rather than simply classifying people as "normal" or "abnormal."[17] Still another is to devise inclusive solutions: to include within the basic design of social institutions the facilities and treatments that respond to those who have been marginalized in the past.[18]

These strategies are not simply expressions of empathy, altruism, or an ethos of care toward the "different" person. Those impulses may be helpful, but they fundamentally preserve the pattern of relationships in which some people enjoy the power and position from which to consider—as a gift or act of benevolence—the needs of others without having to encounter their own implication in the social patterns that assign the problems to those others.

Feminist psychology highlights each person's dependence on others for a sense of self; feminist literary theory illuminates the reliance of any apparently dominating category on a relationship with what it excludes or devalues. These relational insights show a mutual dependence between "normal" and "abnormal" people, and between male norms and women who do not fit them. Hierarchical pairings that deny the mutual dependence of both elements provide clues to deeper motives that makes oppression and degradation seem natural and inevitable. Such patterns deposit on some people the fears of all of us about vulnerability and danger. The relational turn in feminist work asks us instead to examine the connections between what seems disconnected, the larger patterns that conjoin what has seemed different. The conception of each self as fundamentally relational carries implications for the enterprise of judging as well as for the content of norms for judgment.[19] For no longer can the act of judgment—whether done with dispassion or compassion—seem possible from an unsituated perspective or from a person with no relationship to the one being judged. The act of judgment depends on and simultaneously forges a relationship. What qualities that relationship should attain becomes the important question for law, informed by feminist theory.

AN EXAMPLE AND NEW QUESTIONS

A short story first published by Susan Keating Glaspell in 1917, "A Jury of Her Peers," illuminates promising and troubling dimensions of relational thought in conjunction with problems of legal rights, legal duties, and legal judgments.[20] In the story, the district attorney and the sheriff go to a farmhouse to investigate a farmer's murder. The sheriff's wife and a friend come along to gather some belongings for the farmer's widow, who is being held in jail as a suspect in the case. While the sheriff and district attorney tramp through the house and barn looking for clues, the two women in the kitchen find themselves imagining the movements of the farmer's wife and reviewing her entire life experience. Through keen observation and efforts to place themselves in her shoes, they locate clues the men would never have discovered: a half-spilled sugar pot; pieces of a quilt with one stretch of poor stitches amid the otherwise careful sewing; an empty birdcage; and a dead pet bird with a broken neck, wrapped in a piece of silk and hidden in a sewing box. From these curious and unobtrusive items—and through their own efforts to identify with the farmer's wife—the two women construct a story of her harsh and lonely life. They imagine how she was badgered by an unsympathetic and cold husband, how she delighted in her pet bird, how her husband strangled the bird, and how she responded with anger, desperation, and finally murder. They blame themselves for never visiting her and thus contributing to her isolation. One of them almost absentmindedly fixes the stitches in the quilt piece, picking up where the farmer's wife left off.

The two women do not always see eye to eye. Indeed, they seem awkward and uncomfortable in exchanging their thoughts. The process of empathizing and identifying with the absent woman, then, is presented as something that obviously takes work, not as the natural result of something that all women always feel toward one another.

The women decide to share neither their clues nor their conclusions with the men. They hide the dead canary and wait quietly while the men belittle as "trifles" their conversation about the quilt pieces. Besides trying to view the world from the perspective of the absent woman and besides discerning facts missed by the men, the two women form a judgment that implicitly distinguishes them from the men. But what is this judgment? Have the women tried the farmer's wife and either excused or exonerated her? I think not. Instead, they conclude that they themselves are implicated in her act, and in her life, by their failures to attend to her needs earlier. Believing that the formal legal system—the men's justice—would not understand what they now understand, they decline to share their knowledge or otherwise assist the men's search for a clinching motive. This does not seem an easy decision for them; especially for the sheriff's wife, someone "married to the law," resistance to the system takes courage.

The women finally decide to deceive even the widow herself through a comforting lie. She had worried about the jam she had just jarred before she was arrested, and the two women find that it has burst and spilled from most of the jars, as sometimes happens. But there is one unbroken jar, and they decide to take it to the widow to assure her that all has gone well.

Glaspell wrote "A Jury of Her Peers" as an argument for allowing women to serve on juries. It may seem a curious argument, however. The story seems to say that women see facts, events, and emotions differently from men, and that women act on values that differ from—that are indeed at odds with—the prevailing justice system run by men. In a sense, the argument underlying the story echoes the ideology of separate spheres: the historical idea that men belong in the public and women in the private sphere and that members of each gender are experts and sovereigns in their separate domains. Until women are allowed to judge women, suggests the story, women should not be judged; a formal legal order that excludes some points of view cannot comprehend those points of view when they do appear. Excluded people should not be judged by the rules of the game but should instead resist the risk of being misunderstood by refusing to participate altogether. Implicit in this conception is the claim that women should be included as jurors because they are different from men, not because they are the same. The story depicts women as profoundly different from men, whether the difference is due to biology or social experience. The women's outlook on the world, their methods of knowing, and their bases for judgment differ from those of the men. Thus, the story explores relationships between knowledge and power, between who does the judging and what that person can and cannot understand. Suppressed points of view may look deviant from the perspective of the dominant system, but the dominant norms may look wrong or insensitive from the perspective of those marginalized by it.

On yet another level, the story suggests that the task of judgment should be not the application of general principles to a problem but instead a process of taking the perspective of another. Those who would judge should reflect on their own relationships to the one they would judge, not just the actions and motives of that other person. Moreover, the story implies that people's actions and motives are formed not autonomously but in relationship to others and may even result from the failure of others to attend to a person who lands in trouble. The desperation of the farmer's wife had something, although not everything, to do with the other women's failure to visit her. The two women use their own positions of relative powerlessness in the formal legal system and in their society to keep silent about what they have discovered and even tell a comforting lie to the widow. They operate according to a moral code different from the prevailing social rules and affirm their own connections to each other in the process.

Some may worry that the story—and many versions of relational thought—condone a kind of relativism, a suspension of judgment about right and wrong. The women seem to excuse or forgive the murder of a man apparently committed by his wife after he killed her pet bird. Even if it does not condone any act, the story does demonstrate the power of contrasting points of view and the power of interpersonal relationships on the qualities of people's lives and on human moral judgments. Like current relational frames in scholarship, the story declares that knowledge and identities are forged in relationship and that meaning is social rather than natural, mutable rather than fixed. Scholars pursuing these themes invite charges of indifference to truth. Once one participant in the debate says, "All claims of knowledge carry a perspective: None is based in an unchanging reality," then anyone else who claims to know an unchanging reality at least becomes vulnerable to the challenge, "What is the perspective that so entitles you or so blinds you to make such a claim?" Once there is more than one point of view, no point of view can be treated as not a point of view. Such relational concerns prompt worries about relativism and worries about obligations without limits.[21] Relational approaches even invite the charge that the relational view itself is simply a point of view. There is no end to a process of continual debate among competing points of view. Relational concerns do not "tell us what to do" in times of conflict and difficulty. The admonition to care and to connect does not dictate whether to lie to the widow or to tell her the truth, whether to hold her responsible for her act or excuse her in some formal or informal way. Indeed, relational approaches reject the whole idea that principles, norms, or abstractions can or should "tell us" anything.

The response defending relational views will not satisfy objectors, because it calls for shifting the frame of reference, the very criterion for judging normative judgments. The response starts by challenging the pretense that abstract norms ever "tell us" what to do. Norms seem clear only when they have subtracted all that makes a given context unique. Norms seem unproblematic only when they implicitly embody, or else ignore, the features of a given context that they leave unstated. The contrasting approach, an emphatic attention to contextual details, does not reject normative considerations or alter them on a premise that any value is as good as another.

As the women in "Jury of Her Peers" demonstrate, there can be normative dimensions in a commitment to paying closer attention to the relationship between particular contexts and particular values.[22] Denying the multiplicity of moral perspectives and demands does not make them go away; instead, it marks a rigid either/or thinking that constrains moral understanding.[23] . . .

Notes

1. See Barbara Babcock, Ann Freedman, Eleanor Holmes Norton, and Susan Ross, *Sex Discrimination* (Boston: Little, Brown, 1975). Elizabeth Schneider, "Task Force Reports on Women in the Courts: The Challenge for Legal Education," *J. Legal Educ.* 38 (1988): 87, 89–90, describes the 1972 Symposium on the Law School Curriculum and the Legal Rights of Women.
2. Lucinda Finley, "Transcending Equality Theory: A Way Out of the Maternity and the Workplace Debate," *Colum. L. Rev.* 86 (1986): 1118; Ann Freedman, "Sex Equality, Sex Differences, and the Supreme Court," *Yale L. J.* 92 (1983): 913: Mary Joe Frug, "Securing Job Equality for Women: Labor Market Hostility to Working Mothers," *B. U. L. Rev.* 50 (1979): 55; Nancy Gertner, "Bakke on Affirmative Action for Women: Pedestal or Cage?" *Harv. C. R.–C. L. L. Rev.* 14 (1979): 173; Sylvia Law, "Rethinking Sex and the Constitution," *Pa. L. Rev.* 132 (1984): 955; Christine Littleton, "Reconstructing Sexual Equality," *Calif. L. Rev.* 75 (1987): 1267; Frances Olsen, "Statutory Rape: A Feminist Critique of Rights Analysis," *Tex. L. Rev.* 63 (1984): 387; Catharine MacKinnon, "Feminism, Marxism, Method, and the State: Toward Feminist Jurisprudence," *Signs* 8 (1983): 635; Ann Scales, "The Emergence of Feminist Jurisprudence: An Essay," *Yale L. J.* 95 (1986): 1373.
3. Carrie Menkel-Meadow, "Portion in a Different Voice: Speculations on a Women's Lawyering Process," *Berkeley Women's L. J.* 1 (1985): 39; Kenneth Karst, "Women's Constitution," *Duke L. J.* 1984 (1984): 447; Herma Hill Kay, "Equality and Difference: The Case of Pregnancy," *Berkeley Women's L. J.* 1 (1985): 1; Paul Spiegelman, "Court-Ordered Hiring Quotas after Stotts: A Narrative on the Role of the Moralities of the Web and the Ladder in Employment Discrimination Doctrine," *Harv. C. R.–C. L. L. Rev.* 20 (1985): 339; Robin West, "Women's Hedonic Lives," *Wis. Women's L. J.* 3 (1987): 81.
4. Ruth Colker, "Anti-Subordination above All: Sex, Race, and Equal Protection," *N. Y. U. L. Rev.* 61 (1986): 1003; MacKinnon, "Feminism, Marxism, Method, and the State"; Janet Rifkin, "Toward a Theory of Law and Patriarchy," *Harv. Women's L. J.* 3 (1980): 83; Diane Polan, "Toward a Theory of Law and Patriarchy," in *The Politics of Law: A Progressive Critique*, ed. David Kairys (New York: Pantheon Books, 1982), 294.
5. Elizabeth Schneider, "The Dialectic of Rights and Politics," *N. Y. U. L. Rev.* 61 (1986): 589; Catharine MacKinnon, *Sexual Harassment of Working Women: A Case of Sex Discrimination* (New Haven: Yale University Press, 1979), 233–35.
6. Leslie Bender, "A Lawyer's Primer on Feminist Theory and Tort," *J. Legal Educ.* 38 (1988): 3; Mary Joe Frug, "Re-Reading Contracts: A Feminist Analysis of a Contracts Casebook," *Am. U. L. Rev.* 34 (1985): 1065; Clare Dalton, "An Essay in the Deconstruction of Contract Doctrine," *Yale L. J.* 94 (1985): 997.
7. Recent scholarship has addressed gender and law teaching; see, e.g., Patricia

Cain, "Teaching Feminist Legal Theory at Texas: Listening to Difference and Exploring Connections," *J. Legal Educ.* 38 (1988): 165; Catharine W. Hantzis, "Kingsfield and Kennedy: Reappraising the Male Models of Law School Teaching," *J. Legal Educ.* 38 (1988): 155; Sallyanne Payton, "Releasing Excellence: Erasing Gender Zoning from the Legal Mind," *Ind. L. Rev.* 18 (1985): 629; Toni Pickard, "Experience as Teacher: Discovering the Politics of Law Teaching," *U. Toronto L. J.* 33 (1983): 279; Jennifer Jaff, "Frame-Shifting: An Empowering Methodology for Teaching and Learning Legal Reasoning," *J. Legal Educ.* 36 (1986): 249. Ann Scales has recently turned to issues of pacifism; see her "Feminism and Peace" (University of New Mexico School of Law, unpublished manuscript, 1988). Mari Matsuda's work importantly combines feminist methods with attention to minority race experiences; see "Looking to the Bottom: Critical Legal Studies and Reparations," *Harv. C. R.–C. L. L. Rev.* 22 (1987): 323. Interestingly, work that began as a critique of the treatment of women in a given legal area has also turned to more broadly gauged analyses of those fields. See, e.g., Bender, "Lawyer's Primer," 3; Lucinda Finley, "A Break in the Silence: Including Women's Issues in a Torts Course," *Yale J. Law and Feminism* 1 (1989), 41. Margaret June Radin, "Market-Inalienability," *Harv. L. Rev.* 100 (1987): 1849, a critique of commodification, includes distinctively feminist concerns. And Robin West has powerfully employed feminist strategies to critique patterns of arguments between feminist theorists and between feminist and other legal theorists; see "Jurisprudence and Gender," *Chi. L. Rev.* 55 (1987): 1.

8. Cf. the law-and-economics approach, in chapter 6 of *Making All the Difference.*
9. See Schneider, "Dialectic of Rights and Politics"; Lisa Lerman, "Mediation in Wife Abuse Cases: The Adverse Impact of Informal Dispute Resolution on Women," *Harv. Women's L. J.* 7 (1984): 57; and Janet Rifkin, "Mediation from a Feminist Perspective: Promise and Problems," *Law and Inequality* 2 (1984): 21. Carol Gilligan, "Do Changes in Women's Rights Change Women's Moral Judgment?" in *The Challenge of Change: Perspectives on Family, Work, and Education*, ed. Matina Horner, Carol Nadelson, and Malka Notman (New York: Plenum Press, 1983), 39, shows how women incorporate conceptions of legal rights into conceptions of caretaking and responsibility.
10. Feminists emphasize the need for multiple accounts and methodologies, given the partiality of any one approach or point of view. See Flax, "Postmodernism and Gender Relations," 621; Nancy Fraser and Linda Nicholson, "Social Criticism without Philosophy: An Encounter between Feminism and Postmodernism," in *The Institution of Philosophy: A Discipline in Crisis?* ed. Avner Cohen and Marcelo Descal (La Salle, IL: Open Court, 1988); Sandra Harding, "The Instability of the Analytic Categories of Feminist Theory," *Signs* 11 (1986): 645; Deborah Rhode, "Gender and Jurisprudence: An Agenda for Research," *U. Cin. L. Rev.* 56 (1987): 521.
11. See Dale Spender, *Man Made Language*, 2d ed. (London: Routledge and Kegan Paul, 1985), 163–90.
12. See Colker, "Anti-Subordination above All"; MacKinnon, "Feminism, Marxism, Method, and the State."
13. See Lynn Henderson, "Legality and Empathy," *Mich. L. Rev.* 85 (1987): 1574; Sarah Ruddick, *Maternal Thinking* (Boston: Beacon Press, 1989), and the discussion of Jane Addams in ch. 8 of *Making all the Difference.*
14. Doing so would accommodate not only pregnancy and child-care duties but

also health and safety features. E.g., employers in industrial settings that have proved hazardous to women's reproductive conditions have refused to hire any woman who would not "voluntarily" agree to sterilization. An alternative to this draconian solution would be to make the workplace safe for women. The additional cost might be warranted not only to avoid charges of discrimination but also because there is some possibility that those settings have been unsafe for men too. See Judith Areen, *Family Law*, 2d ed. (Mineola, NY: Foundation Press, 1985), 876.

15. See Susan Estrich, "Rape," *Yale L. J.* 95 (1986): 1087. Susan Brownmiller has argued that "penetration" is the name for the male experience that a woman might instead call "enclosure" (*Against Our Will: Men, Women and Rape* [New York: Simon and Schuster, 1977], 334). See also Olsen, "Statutory Rape," 387, 424, arguing that pervasive male sexual aggression, rather than women's vulnerability to it, is the problem to be addressed by rape laws.

16. See Frug, "Securing Job Equality for Women," 55; Kathleen Lahey, " . . . Until Women Themselves Have Told All That They Have to Tell . . .," *Osgoode Hall L. J.* 23 (1985): 519; Nancy Polikoff, "Why Mothers Are Losing: A Brief Analysis of Criteria Used in Child Custody Determinations," *Women's Rights L. Rep.* 7 (1982): 235; Elizabeth Schneider, "Equal Rights to Trial for Women: Sex Bias in the Law of Self Defense," *Harv. C. R.–C. L. L. Rev.* 15 (1980): 623. Women's perceptions may be complicated and may engage women in debates among themselves about equality and victimization. See Martha Fineman, "Implementing Equality: Ideology, Contradiction, and Social Change," *Wis. L. Rev.* 1983 (1983): 789.

17. Attention to language and the hidden assumptions in the prevailing terms of debate also characterize feminist work. See, e.g., Marie Ashe, "Law-Language of Maternity: Discovered Holding Nature in Contempt," *New Eng. L. Rev.* 22 (1988): 521.

18. Making sidewalks and other facilities accessible to wheelchairs and treating all patients with the precautions suited to someone with the AIDS virus are the examples here. See also Finley, "Transcending Equality Theory"; Christine Littleton, "Equality across Difference: A Place for Rights Discourse?" *Wis. Women's L. J.* 3 (1987): 189.

19. See Judith Resnik, "On the Bias: Feminist Reconsiderations of the Aspirations for Our Judges," *S. Calif. L. Rev.* 61 (1988): 1877; Robin West, "The Authoritarian Impulse in Constitutional Law," *Miami L. Rev.* 2 (1988): 531.

20. Susan Glaspell, "A Jury of Her Peers," *Every Week*, March 5, 1917, rpt. in *The Best Short Stories of 1917*, ed. Edward O'Brien (Boston: Small, Maynard, 1918), 256. Glaspell, a member of the Provincetown Players, also cast the story as a play called *Trifles*. For analysis by contemporary literary critics, see, e.g., Annette Kolodny, "A Map for Rereading: Gender and the Interpretation of Literary Texts," in *The New Feminist Criticism: Essays on Women, Literature, and Theory*, ed. Elaine Showalter (New York: Pantheon Books, 1985), 46, 55–58. The story has been used as a teaching vehicle for college students, law students, law professors, and judges. See Carol Weisbrod, "Images of the Women Juror," *Harv. Women's L. J.* 9 (1986): 59.

21. Widespread debates about the attractions and risks of relativism have accompanied the recognition of plural sources of knowledge and values in many fields. See, e.g. *Rationality and Relativism*, ed. Martin Hollis and Steven Lukes (Cambridge: MIT Press, 1984).

22. See Jeffrey Stout, *Ethics after Babel: The Languages of Morals and Their Discontents* (Boston: Beacon Press, 1988), 82–105; Charles Larmore, *Patterns of Moral Complexity* (Cambridge: Cambridge University Press, 1987), 1–21.

23. See Martha Nussbaum, *The Fragility of Goodness: Luck and Ethics in Greek Tragedy and Philosophy* (Cambridge: Cambridge University Press, 1986); Geertz, "Anti-Anti Relativism."

SELECTION 42

FROM

Feminist Critical Theories

DEBORAH L. RHODE

WHATEVER THE RISKS OF other generalizations, one threshold observation is difficult to dispute: Feminism takes gender as a central category of analysis, while the core texts of critical legal studies do not.[1] To be sure, many of these texts make at least some reference to problems of sex-based subordination, and to the existence (if not the significance) of feminist scholarship. Yet most critical legal theory and the traditions on which it relies have not seriously focused on gender inequality. Why then should feminists continue participating in enterprises in which their perspectives are added but not integrated, rendered separate but not equal?

Efforts to provide the "woman's point of view" also risk contributing to their own marginalization. In effect, feminists are invited to explain how their perspectives differ from others associated with critical legal studies or with more mainstream bodies of legal theory. Such invitations impose the same limitations that have been characteristic for women's issues in conventional legal ideology. Analysis has fixated on how women are the same or different from men; men have remained the unstated standard of analysis.[2]

In recent years, these concerns have increasingly emerged within the critical legal studies [CLS] movement. During the last decade, issues of gender as well as race and ethnicity dominated the agendas of several national CLS conferences, and feminist theorists organized regional groups around common interests. A growing body of feminist and critical race scholarship also developed along lines that paralleled, intersected, and challenged critical legal theory.[3] . . .

The following discussion focuses on a body of work that may be loosely identified as feminist critical theories. Although they differ widely in other respects, these theories share three central commitments. On a political level, they seek to promote equality between women and men. On a substantive level, feminist critical frameworks make gender a focus of analysis;

408

their aim is to reconstitute legal practices that have excluded, devalued, or undermined women's concerns. On a methodological level, these frameworks aspire to describe the world in ways that correspond to women's experience and they identify the fundamental social transformations necessary for full equality between the sexes. These commitments are for the most part mutually reinforcing, but they occasionally pull in different directions. This essay explores various ways that feminists have sought to fuse a political agenda that is dependent on both group identity and legalist strategies with a methodology that is in some measure skeptical of both.

What distinguishes feminist critical theories from other analysis is both the focus on gender equality and the conviction that it cannot be obtained under existing ideological and institutional structures. This theoretical approach partly overlaps, and frequently draws upon, other critical approaches, including CLS and critical race scholarship. At the most general level, these traditions share a common goal: to challenge existing distributions of power. They also often employ similar deconstructive or narrative methodologies aimed at similar targets—certain organizing premises of conventional liberal legalism. Each tradition includes both internal and external critiques. Some theorists focus on the inadequacy of conventional legal doctrine in terms of its own criteria for coherence, consistency, and legitimacy. Other commentators emphasize the role of legal ideology in legitimating unjust social conditions. Yet these traditions also differ considerably in their theories about theory, in their critiques of liberal legalism, in their strategies for change, and in their alternative social visions.

THEORETICAL PREMISES

Critical feminism, like other critical approaches, builds on recent currents in social theory that have made theorizing increasingly problematic. Postmodern and poststructural traditions that have influenced Left legal critics presuppose the social construction of knowledge.[4] To varying degrees, critics within these traditions deny the possibility of any universal foundations for critique. Taken as a whole, their work underscores the cultural, historical, and linguistic construction of human identity and social experience.[5]

Yet such a theoretical stance also limits its own aspirations to authority. For feminists, this postmodern paradox creates political as well as theoretical difficulties. Adherents are left in the awkward position of maintaining that gender oppression exists while challenging our capacity to document it.[6] Such awkwardness is, for example, especially pronounced in works that assert as unproblematic certain "facts" about the pervasiveness of sexual abuse while questioning the possibility of any objective measure.[7] . . .

Although responses to this dilemma vary widely, the most common feminist strategies bear mention. The simplest approach is to decline to address the problem—at least at the level of abstraction at which it is customarily formulated. The revolution will not be made with slogans from Lyotard's *Postmodern Condition*, and the audiences that are most in need of persuasion are seldom interested in epistemological anxieties. Critiques of existing ideology and institutions can proceed under their own standards without detailed discussions of the philosophy of knowledge. Yet, even from a purely pragmatic view, it is helpful to have some self-consciousness about the grounding for our claims about the world and the tensions between our political and methodological commitments.

Critical feminism's most common response to questions about its own authority has been reliance on experiential analysis. This approach draws primarily on techniques of consciousness-raising in contemporary feminist organizations, but also on pragmatic philosophical traditions. A standard practice is to begin with concrete experiences, integrate these experiences into theory, and rely on theory for a deeper understanding of the experiences.[8] One distinctive feature of feminist critical analysis is, as Katharine Bartlett emphasizes, a grounding in practical problems and a reliance on "practical reasoning."[9] Rather than working deductively from abstract principles and overarching conceptual schemes, such analysis builds from the ground up. Many feminist legal critics are also drawn to narrative styles that express the personal consequences of institutionalized injustice.[10] Even those commentators most wedded to broad categorical claims usually situate their works in the lived experience of pornography or sexual harassment rather than, for example, in the deep structure of Blackstone's *Commentaries* or the fundamental contradictions in Western political thought.[11]

In part, this pragmatic focus reflects the historical origins and contemporary agenda of feminist legal theory. Unlike critical legal studies, which began as a movement within the legal academy and took much of its inspiration from the Grand Theory of contemporary Marxism and the Frankfurt School, feminist legal theories emerged against the backdrop of a mass political movement. In America, that struggle has drawn much of its intellectual inspiration not from overarching conceptual schemes, but from efforts to provide guidance on particular substantive issues. As Carrie Menkel-Meadow has argued, the strength of feminism "originates" in the experience of "*being* dominated, not just in thinking about domination," and in developing concrete responses to that experience.[12] Focusing on women's actual circumstances helps reinforce the connection between feminist political and analytic agendas, but it raises its own set of difficulties. How can critics build a unified political and analytical stance from women's varying perceptions of their varying experiences? And what entitles that stance to special authority?

The first question arises from a long-standing tension in feminist methodology. What gives feminism its unique force is the claim to speak from women's experience. But that experience counsels sensitivity to its own diversity across such factors as time, culture, class, race, ethnicity, sexual orientation, and age. As Martha Minow has noted, "[c]ognitively we need simplifying categories, and the unifying category of 'woman' helps to organize experience, even at the cost of denying some of it."[13] Yet to some constituencies, particularly those who are not white, heterosexual, and economically privileged, that cost appears prohibitive since it is their experience that is most often denied.

A variation of this problem arises in discussions of "false consciousness." How can feminists wedded to experiential analysis respond to women who reject feminism's basic premises as contrary to *their* experience? . . .

The issue deserves closer attention particularly since contemporary survey research suggests that the vast majority of women do not experience the world in the terms that most critical feminists describe.[14] Nor do these feminists agree among themselves about which experiential accounts of women's interests should be controlling in disputes involving, for example, pornography, prostitution, surrogate motherhood, or maternity leaves.[15] . . .

RIGHTS

One central difference between critical feminism and other critical legal theory involves the role of rights. Although both bodies of work have challenged liberal legalism's reliance on formal entitlements, feminist accounts, like those of minority scholars, have tended more toward contextual analysis than categorical critique.

Most CLS scholarship has viewed rights-based strategies as an ineffective and illusory means of progressive social change. While sometimes acknowlededging the importance of basic political liberties in preserving opportunities for dissent, critical legal theorists have generally presented the liberal rights agenda as a constraint on individual consciousness and collective mobilization.[16] Part of the problem arises from the indeterminacy noted earlier. Feminist commentators such as Fran Olsen have joined other critical theorists in noting that rights discourse cannot resolve social conflict but can only restate it in somewhat abstract, conclusory form. A rights-oriented framework may distance us from necessary value choices and obscure the basis on which competing interests are accommodated.[17]

According to this critique, too much political energy has been diverted into battles that cannot promise significant gains. For example, a decade's experience with state equal rights amendments reveals no necessary correlation between the standard of constitutional protection provided by legal tribunals and the results achieved.[18] It is unlikely that a federal equal rights amendment would have insured the vast array of substantive objectives that its proponents frequently claimed. Supporters' tendencies to cast the amendment as an all-purpose prescription for social ills—the plight of displaced homemakers, the feminization of poverty, and the gender gap in earnings— have misdescribed the problem and misled as to the solution.[19]

A related limitation of the liberal rights agenda involves its individualist premises and restricted scope. A preoccupation with personal entitlements can divert concern from collective responsibilities. Rights rhetoric too often channels individuals' aspirations into demands for their own share of protected opportunities and fails to address more fundamental issues about what ought to be protected. Such an individualistic framework ill serves the values of cooperation and empathy that feminists find lacking in our current legal culture.[20]

Nor are mandates guaranteeing equality in formal rights adequate to secure equality in actual experience as long as rights remain restricted to those that a predominately white upper-middle-class male judiciary has been prepared to regard as fundamental. No legal structure truly committed to equality for women would end up with a scheme that affords extensive protection to the right to bear arms or to sell violent pornography, but not to control our reproductive lives.[21]

In a culture where rights have been defined primarily in terms of "freedoms from" rather than "freedoms to," many individuals lack the resources necessary for exercising rights to which they are formally entitled. Such problems are compounded by the costs and complexities of legal proceedings and the maldistribution of legal services available to enforce formal entitlements or prevent their curtailment.[22] By channeling political struggles into legal disputes, rights-based strategies risk limiting aspirations and reinforcing dependence on legal decision-makers.

Yet while acknowledging these limitations, critical feminism has also emphasized certain empowering dimensions of rights strategies that other CLS work discounts. As theorists including Kimberlé Crenshaw, Christine Littleton, Elizabeth Schneider, and Patricia Williams have argued, legal rights have a special resonance in our culture.[23] The source of their limitations is also the source of their strength. Because claims about rights proceed within established discourse, they are less readily dismissed than other progressive demands. By insisting that the rule of law make good on its own aspirations, rights-oriented strategies offer a possibility of internal challenge that critical theorists have recognized as empowering in other contexts. . . .

Whatever its inadequacies, rights rhetoric has been the vocabulary most effective in catalyzing mass progressive movements in this culture. It is a discourse that critical feminists are reluctant to discard in favor of ill-defined or idealized alternatives. The central problem with rights-based frameworks is not that they are inherently limiting but that they have operated within a limited institutional and imaginative universe. Thus, critical feminism's central objective should be not to delegitimate such frameworks but rather to recast their content and recognize their constraints. Since rights-oriented campaigns can both enlarge and restrict political struggle, evaluation of their strategic possibilities requires historically situated contextual analysis.

On this point, feminists join other critical theorists in seeking to build on the communal, relational, and destabilizing dimensions of rights-based arguments.[24] Claims to self-determination can express desires not only for autonomy but also for participation in the communities that shape our existence. If selectively invoked, the rhetoric of rights can empower subordinate groups to challenge the forces that perpetuate their subordination. . . .

Notes

1. See Carrie Menkel-Meadow, "Feminist Legal Theory, Critical legal Studies, and Legal Education or 'The Fem-Crits Go to Law School,'" 38 *J. Legal Educ.* 61 (1988); Robin West, "Deconstructing the CLS-Fem Split," 2 *Wis. Women's L. J.* 85 (1986). Early collections of critical legal scholarship did not explore gender issues and included no, or only a token number of, essays focusing on feminist concerns. For the relevant omissions, see, e.g., D. Kairys, ed., *The Politics of Law: A Progressive Critique* (1982); "Critical Legal Studies Symposium," 36 *Stan. L. Rev.* 1 (1984); 6 *Cardozo L. Rev.* 691 (1985) (Critical Legal Studies Symposium).
2. For a discussion of the marginalization and homogenization of feminist perspectives in legal circles, see, e.g., Deborah L. Rhode, "The 'Woman's Point of View,'" 38 *J. Legal Educ.* 39 (1988) and companion articles in that symposium, as well as in "Gender and the Law," 40 *Stan. L. Rev.* 1163 (1988). For problems with the sameness/difference approach toward gender issues, see Catharine A. MacKinnon, *Feminism Unmodified* (1987), 32–45; Deborah L. Rhode, *Justice and Gender* (1989), 117–25; Deborah L. Rhode, "Definitions of Difference," in *Theoretical Perspectives on Sexual Difference*, ed. D. Rhode (1990), 197; Lucinda M. Finley, "Transcending Equality Theory: A Way Out of the Maternity and the Workplace Debate," 86 *Colum. L. Rev.* 1118 (1986); Ann E. Freedman, "Sex Equality, Sex Differences, and the Supreme Court," 92 *Yale L. J.* 913 (1983); Herma Hill Kay, "Models of Equality," 1985 *U. Ill. L. Rev.* 39; Sylvia A. Law, "Rethinking Sex and the Constitution," 132 *U. Pa. L. Rev.* 955 (1984); Christine A. Littleton, "Reconstructing Sexual Equality," 75 *Calif. L. Rev.* 1279 (1987); Stephanie M. Wildman, "The Legitimation of Sex Discrimination: A Critical Response to Supreme Court Jurisprudence," 63 *Or. L. Rev.* 265 (1984).
3. See Menkel-Meadow, *Feminist Legal Theory;* "Minority Critiques of the Critical Legal Studies Movement," 22 *Harv. C.R.–C.L. L. Rev.* 297 (1987); "Voices of Experience: New Responses to Gender Discourse," 24 *Harv. C.R.–C.L. L. Rev.* 1 (1989).
4. Critics such as François Lyotard invoke the term postmodernism to describe the present age's collapse of faith in traditional Grand Narratives. Since the Enlightenment, these metanarratives have sought to develop principles of objective

science, universal morality, and autonomous art. For discussion of postmodernism's denial that categorical, noncontingent, abstract theories derived through reason or human nature can serve as the foundation for knowledge, see Jean-François Lyotard, *The Postmodern Condition* (1984); J. Rajchman and C. West, eds., *Post-Analytic Philosophy* (1985); Nancy Fraser and Linda Nicholson, "Social Criticism without Philosophy: An Encounter between Feminism and Postmodernism," in *Universal Abandon?: The Politics of Postmodernism*, ed. A. Ross (1988), 83; Sandra Harding, "The Instability of the Analytical Categories of Feminist Theory," *Signs* 11 (1986): 645; David Luban, "Legal Modernism," 84 *Mich. L. Rev.* 1656 (1986); Robin West, "Feminism, Critical Social Theory, and Law," 1989 *U. Chi. Legal F.* 59.

Poststructuralism, which arises from and contributes to this postmodern tradition, refers to theories of interpretation that view meaning as a cultural construction mediated by arrangements of language or symbolic form. What distinguishes poststructuralism from other interpretive schools is the premise that these arrangements are unstable and contradictory, and that readers create rather than simply discover meaning. For a useful overview, see Christopher Norris, *Deconstruction: Theory and Practice* (1982); Peter Fitzpatrick and Alan Hunt, "Critical Legal Studies: Introduction," 14 *J. L. and Soc'y* 1 (1987); David Kennedy, "Critical Theory, Structuralism, and Contemporary Legal Scholarship," 21 *New Eng. L. Rev.* 209 (1986).

5. J.-F. Lyotard, *Postmodern Condition*; Jane Flax, "PostModernism and Gender Relations in Feminist Theory," *Signs* 12 (1987): 621. Critical legal studies scholars have responded in varying ways, ranging from Roberto Unger's and Jürgen Habermas's continued embrace of universalist claims, to Duncan Kennedy's reliance on deconstructive technique. Compare Roberto Mangabeira Unger, *Knowledge and Politics* (1975) and Jürgen Habermas, *Legitimation Crisis* (1975), with Peter Gabel and Duncan Kennedy, "Roll Over Beethoven," 36 *Stan. L. Rev.* 1 (1984).

6. As Nancy Cott notes, "in deconstructing categories of meaning, we deconstruct not only patriarchal definitions of 'womanhood' and 'truth' but also the very categories of our own analysis—'woman' and 'feminism' and 'oppression.'" Quoted in Frances E. Macia-Lees, Patricia Sharpe, and Colleen Ballerino Cohen, "The Postmodernist Turn in Anthropology: Cautions from a Feminist Perspective," *Signs* 15, no. 7 (1989).

7. Compare MacKinnon, *Feminism Unmodified*, 81–92 (discussing the social construction of rape and sexual violence) with ibid., 23 (asserting "facts" about its prevalence). See also Catharine A. MacKinnon, *Toward a Feminist Theory of the State* (1989), 100 (acknowledging without exploring the difficulty).

8. According to Catharine MacKinnon, "Consciousness raising is the major technique of analysis, structure of organization, method of practice, and theory of social change of the women's movement," Catharine A. MacKinnon, "Feminism, Marxism, Method and the State: An Agenda for Theory," *Signs* 7 (1982): 515, 519; see also Nancy Hartsock, "Fundamental Feminism: Process and Perspective," *Quest* 2 (1975): 67, 71–79; Elizabeth M. Schneider, "The Dialectic of Rights and Politics: Perspectives from the Women's Movement," 61 *NYU L. Rev.* 589, 602–3 (1986).

9. See, for example, the work of Amelie Rorty, discussed in Katharine T. Bartlett, "Feminist Legal Methods," 103 *Harv. L. Rev.* 829 (1990); Margaret Jane Radin, "The Pragmatist and the Feminist," 63 *S. Cal. L. Rev* (1990).

10. See, e.g., Patricia Williams, "Spirit Murdering the Messenger: The Discourse of Fingerpointing as the Law's Response to Racism," 42 *U. Miami L. Rev.* 127 (1987); Mari J. Matsuda, "Public Response to Racist Speech: Considering the Victim's Story," 87 *Mich. L. Rev.* 2320 (1989); Robin L. West, "The Difference in Women's Hedonic Lives: A Phenomenological Critique of Feminist Legal Theory," 3 *Wis. Women's L. J.* 81 (1987).

11. See Duncan Kennedy, "The Structure of Blackstone's Commentaries," 28 *Buffalo L. Rev.* 205 (1979); R. M. Unger, *Knowledge and Politics*.

12. Menkel-Meadow, *Feminist Legal Theory*, 61; see also MacKinnon, "Feminism, Marxism"; West, "Difference in Women's Hedonic Lives."

13. Martha Minow, "Feminist Reason: Getting It and Losing It," 38 *J. Legal Educ.* 47, 51 (1988).

14. See, e.g., Rhode, *Justice and Gender*, 66; Lisa Belkin, "Bars to Equality of Sexes Seen as Eroding Slowly," *New York Times*, Aug. 20, 1989, 1, 16 (61 percent of wives felt husbands did less than fair share of housework; 70 percent of women with full-time jobs felt women had equal or better chance of promotion than men where they worked; and only 39 percent of black women and 22 percent of white women believed organized women's groups had made their lives better); "Rosy Outlook among Women Ages 18 to 44," *San Francisco Examiner*, Aug. 23, 1988, A7, col. 3 (finding that nearly 90 percent of women of childbearing ages are satisfied with their lives). For more qualitative research, see F. Crosby, ed., *Spouse, Parent, Worker: On Gender and Multiple Roles* (1987).

15. For differences on pornography, compare West, "Difference in Women's Hedonic Lives," 134–39, with MacKinnon, *Feminism Unmodified*, 127–213. For differences on maternity policies, compare Finley, "Transcending Equality Theory," Herma Hill Kay, "Equality and Difference: The Case of Pregnancy," 1 *Berkeley Women's L. J.* 1 (1985), and Reva B. Siegel, "Employment Equality under the Pregnancy Discrimination Act of 1978," 94 *Yale L. J.* 929 (1984–85) (student author) with Nadine Taub, "From Parental Leaves to Nurturing Leaves," 13 *NYU Rev. L. and Soc. Change* 381 (1985) and Wendy W. Williams, "Equality's Riddle: Pregnancy and the Equal Treatment/Special Treatment Debate," 13 *NYU Rev. L. and Soc. Change* 325 (1984–85). For differences on prostitution, see sources cited in Rhode, *Justice and Gender*, 157–62. For differences on surrogate motherhood, see ibid., 223–29, and Martha A. Field, *Surrogate Motherhood* (1988).

16. See Peter Gabel, "The Phenomenology of Rights-Consciousness and the Pact of the Withdrawn Selves," 62 *Tex. L. Rev.* 1563 (1984); Mark Tushnet, "An Essay on Rights," 62 *Tex. L. Rev.* 1363, 1382–84 (1984).

17. See generally sources cited in notes 16 and 24; Kairys, ed., *Politics of Law*; Adelaide Villamore, "The Left's Problems with Rights," 9 *Legal Stud. F.* 39 (1985).

18. See generally Dawn-Marie Driscoll and Barbara J. Rouse, "Through a Glass Darkly: A Look at State Equal Rights Amendments," 12 *Suffolk U. L. Rev.* 1282, 1308 (1978); Rhode, *Justice and Gender*, 92.

19. See Rhode, *Justice and Gender*; Catharine A. MacKinnon, "Unthinking ERA Thinking," book review, 54 *U. Chi. L. Rev.* 759 (1987).

20. Michael Ignatieff, *The Needs of Strangers* (1984), 13.

21. Compare U. S. Constitution, Amendment 2, and *American Booksellers Ass'n. v. Hudnut*, 771 F.2d 323 (7th Cir. 1985), aff'd, 475 U.S. 1001 (1986), with *Webster v. Reproductive Health Servs.*, 109 S. Ct. 3040 (1989), and *Harris v. McRae*, 448 U. S. 297 (1980).

22. Richard Abel, *American Lawyers* (1989); Richard L. Abel. "United States: The Contradictions of Professionalism," in R. Abel and P. Lewis, eds., *Lawyers in Society: The Common Law World* (1988), 186; Stuart A. Scheingold, *The Politics of Rights: Lawyers, Public Policy, and Political Change* (1974), 172; Deborah L. Rhode, "The Rhetoric of Professional Reform," 45 *Md. L. Rev.* 274, 281–82 (1986).

23. Kimberlé Williams Crenshaw, "Race, Reform, and Retrenchment: Transformation and Legitimation in Antidiscrimination Law," 101 *Harv. L. Rev.* 1331, 1366–69 (1988); Schneider, "Dialectics of Rights and Politics"; Patricia J. Williams, "Alchemical Notes: Reconstructing Ideals from Deconstructed Rights," 22 *Harv. C.R.–C.L. L. Rev.* 401 (1987).

24. See Staughton Lynd, "Communal Rights," 62 *Tex. L. Rev.* 1417 (1984) Roberto Mangabeira Unger, "The Critical Legal Studies Movement," 96 *Harv. L. Rev.* 561, 612–16 (1983).

SELECTION 43
FROM
Women and Their Privacy: What Is at Stake?

ANITA L. ALLEN

INTRODUCTION

PRIVACY IS AN OBSCURE object of desire. Widely regarded as command-ing legal protection in a just liberal state, privacy and its value are never-theless poorly understood. There is considerable disagreement about the theoretical basis and extent of the privacy rights recognized by our laws, social practices, and moral theories.

To a great extent the sphere we call "private" overlaps the traditional sphere of women's concerns: marriage, home, and family. Under the yoke of their traditional roles, however, women have been less able than men to secure privacy for themselves, and have been less able to enjoy and benefit from any privacy they *have* been able to secure.

In response to ongoing philosophical and jurisprudential efforts to under-stand the right to privacy and the interests it protects, I want to identify the special privacy interests of women. I also want to consider whether some of the more recent formulations of the right to privacy take into ac-count the full range of women's special privacy interests. By "special" pri-vacy interests I mean those interests women have in virtue of traits, roles, and experiences mainly or exclusively belonging to women in our society. These are apt to be overlooked or understressed in theoretical arguments for the protection of privacy rights.

For present purposes it is unnecessary to argue what Ruth Gavison and many others have argued extensively: that the law should recognize a per-sonal right to privacy, and that the state as well as individuals have an interest in the protection of privacy.[1] . . .

Ruth Gavison's analysis of privacy is a useful, straightforward catalogue

of interests protected and promoted by privacy. Her analysis seeks to de-
mystify the concept of privacy in a way that is theoretically cogent and
consistent with common theoretical understandings of cognate concepts.
Gavison defined privacy straightforwardly as "limited accessibility." Privacy
and accessibility, on her characterization, are inversely proportional. The
more privacy an individual has, the less accessibility; the more accessibility,
the less privacy. Secrecy, anonymity, and solitude are the three chief dimensions of privacy. Secrecy (or confidentiality) is limited accessibility in
the sense of *limited information about a person*; anonymity is limited accessibility in the sense of *limited attention paid to a person*; and solitude is limited
accessibility in the sense of *limited contact with or sensing of a person*. The
distinction between anonymity and solitude is important. The anonymity
interest is an interest in not having attention drawn to us, not being singled out or identified when we wish otherwise. Anonymity may be desired
when solitude is not. Anonymity is a kind of privacy we may desire, and
reasonably desire, even in a public place. On the other hand, as film stars
know very well, anonymity is sometimes impossible without retreat to a
solitude that seals one off from others. A breach of secrecy may have as its
consequence a loss of the possibility of either anonymity or solitude. . . .

I will use Gavison's analysis of privacy, limited accessibility, to structure
my examination of the ways in which privacy functions to protect the interests of women. By pointing out the special privacy interests of women
through the windows of Gavison's tripartite analysis, two things will be
made clear. First, Gavison's analysis contains an important theoretical inadequacy that relates directly to the privacy interests of women. Second,
other existing privacy theories are similarly inadequate.

WOMEN AND INFORMATIONAL PRIVACY

The general value of informational privacy has been much discussed by
lawyers and philosophers in the privacy literature. I want only to identify
the interest of women that their right to limited information access (i.e.,
secrecy of confidentiality) could be expected to protect. Legal informational
privacy rights protect by providing judicial remedies and deterring invasions. Moral informational privacy rights protect insofar as they become the
basis of legal rights, and through their power as individually and socially
effective action guides.

An important class of informational privacy interests relate to employment.[2] Female job applicants and employees are commonly asked to supply
information about their marital or family status, which has no direct bearing on job qualifications or performance. Invasions of privacy of this type
can occur during personal interviews or because of sex biases built into
standard application forms. The invasions occur where women are presumed

less independent or less dependable in light of their sex or of the roles they are presumed to have in their families. They also occur where being female or unmarried is improperly treated as a qualification for employment by a male employer or personnel officer who may anticipate sexual favors. Premised on female inferiority and subservience, these invasions are demeaning. But female victims of these invasions also suffer material consequences, such as loss of self-esteem and emotional distress. Substantial career and economic losses may accrue, as well, where a woman's employment is contingent upon her marital status or sexual availability.

Women commonly suffer unwarranted losses of informational privacy in the hands of the state.[3] In some states female rape victims still have inadequate statutory protection of their informational privacy rights, with the result that prosecutors are permitted to grill them about irrelevant aspects of their sexual histories. Women seeking welfare aid from the state are also asked irrelevant questions about their sexual lives and have an informational privacy interest in not answering them. Some disclosure of information is indeed necessary to the determination of qualifications and the prevention of fraud. But the state's interest in effective programs does not absolutely and automatically override the privacy interests of needy women and their families. Even if it were conceded that humiliation in the hands of the state's judicial and administrative officials has some justification, given the important goals of the criminal justice and welfare systems, women's interests in not suffering humiliation would not lose their relevance in the determination of what are acceptable practices.

Female students in colleges and universities have their privacy interests compromised by male instructors who press them under the guise of authority for information they would not seek to elicit from male students. Female students who are unwilling to disclose personal information to their professors risk retaliation in the form of low grades and lost educational opportunities. Physical forms of sexual harassment in the university and in the workplace are typically accompanied by prying questions.[4] This verbal harassment is another form of informational privacy invasion.

Discrimination against women by banks and lending institutions has been a much-discussed phenomenon to which the legal system has begun to address itself. Even so, widespread use of computerized information sources facilitate unfair expropriations and the exchange of financial histories by bad-faith lenders and creditors. Historic economic deprivations have resulted in institutions and prejudices that make women more likely than men to be disadvantaged by these practices.[5]

Injury to a woman's career, financial losses, losses of self-esteem, and emotional distress can follow invasions of her informational privacy. Emotional distress can include "fright, horror, grief, shame, humiliation, embarassment, anger, chagrin, [and] worry."[6] Explicit legal provisions and the existence of legal remedies cannot eliminate all the informational privacy invasions to which women are routinely subjected. Some of these are bad-faith invasions out of reach of the legal system. Suppose, for example, that in a one-on-one employment interview a woman is asked irrelevant personal questions in violation of law and company policy. Whether blatant or clothed in ambiguity, the invasion is one the interviewee will be unable to prove; she is unlikely to have the time or financial resources to seek redress; she may wrongly blame herself for the invasion. To bring about an end to this kind of informational privacy invasion it is necessary to strike a blow to the source of attitudinal sexism. Both small-scale "consciousness-raising" efforts and fundamental changes in social and legal institutions will be required to eliminate discriminatory attitudes. Personnel officer-training programs could teach men—and women—with hiring responsibilities ways to avoid informational privacy invasions. Public discussion and media exposure of these practices and their effects on women could work attitudinal changes.

The philosophical rationale for promoting change to protect these privacy interests of women can be couched in the terms of either a deontological or an instrumental ethic. From a Kantian deontological perspective, protecting these interests is in keeping with respecting them as full and equal moral persons. By protecting these interests, what some feminists term the ideology of sexual hierarchy and male domination is supplanted by respect for individuals. A society which so dignifies women is to that extent on the road to becoming a just society. Instrumentally, the special privacy interests of women promote their emotional and economic well-being, which in turn can be expected to promote the aggregate well-being of society.

ANONYMITY FOR WOMEN

Anonymity privacy invasions are commonly experienced by women in public places. Women of all ages are approached by men seeking their names, phone numbers, or other personal information. Women are followed, taunted, and mocked. Fearful, resentful, and distressed, women come to accept not being left alone. They come to accept deprivations of informational privacy (being questioned about personal matters by strangers) and anonymity (being singled out by strangers) as a way of life. But acceptance has a cost. Its cost is to be measured by its cumulative effects on the victimized women, and on the quality of the social life of their communities. One evident effect of continual invasions of anonymity is that women come to believe they are "fair game" if they venture into public places into which men may go to find repose. This can only lead to a perpetuation of the hostility and mistrust many women have for men. . . .

WOMEN AND SOLITUDE

Enjoying privacy in public has been a problem for women; but so has enjoying privacy at home. Limited accessibility within their homes is perhaps the most important—and most complex—privacy interest of women. Women have not always had the freedom, nor the independence of mind, needed to secure solitude and enjoy it once secured.

To begin, the traditional caretaker functions of women have allowed them little time for themselves. The enjoyment of privacy becomes possible for women only as they yield certain traditional family roles. The roles to be yielded are not their roles as mothers and wives per se. As psychologist Jean Baker Miller has pointed out, most women do not want an autonomy which

> carries the implication—and for women therefore the threat—that one should be able to pay the price of giving up affiliations in order to become a separate and self-directed individual. . . . Women are quite validly seeking something more complete than autonomy as it is defined for men, a fuller not a lesser ability to encompass relationships to others, simultaneous with the fullest development of oneself.[7]

If this is correct, it is clear why the quest for solitude has been particularly difficult for women unwilling to eschew the family. With modern standards of nurture and education, motherhood can be the antithesis of solitude. Moreover, women's often-unreciprocated, often-subservient caretaking functions with respect to their husbands have denied them both the *opportunity* for solitude and the *ability* to enjoy and exploit the modicum of privacy their lives as wives and mothers afforded. . . .

Thus, the problem of privacy for women has been in part the problem of achieving a degree of solitude notwithstanding their roles and responsibilities; and upon achieving it through shared parenting, egalitarian marriages, or total abrogation of traditional life-styles, using it to formulate and further their ends.

Women have a special privacy interest in a solitude that affords them the possibility of the full development of their unique personalities. And this implies yet a further special privacy interest, namely, the freedom to choose when and to what extent the privacy-limiting experiences of motherhood and marriage are undertaken. Thus, although there can be no legal right to domestic solitude enforceable against a woman's children and spouse, her interests in domestic solitude can be legally protected indirectly, through the protection of her freedom to choose when and to what extent the privacy-limiting experiences of motherhood and traditional marriage are undertaken.

Sexual politics and politics proper reveal that men and the state are cochoosers and regulators of the choices women make. Questions concerning the precise extent to which men and women, husbands and wives, ought to have equal voice in decisions relating to childbearing and child nurturance remain some of the most difficult. Social and political morality also pose unanswered questions about the just limit of state regulation of sexual relations and parenting. . . .

PRIVACY AND CHOICE

Free choice is an important means by which privacy interests may be promoted in a liberal society. If women cannot choose among motherhood, marriage, and their alternatives, they will continue to find it difficult to secure privacy and conditions requisite to the meaningful enjoyment of privacy. Sexual inequality is perpetuated if women are choiceless and thereby confined to roles that have historically denied them the opportunity for and ability to enjoy privacy. Free to choose, women enjoy privacy in the sense of *limited control by others of matters affecting their sexual and familial life.*

Thus women's privacy interests can be seen as falling into two classes: (a) liberty interests, or interests in limiting their accessibility to others through nonregulation and noncontrol by others of their sexual and familial lives; and (b) privacy per se interests, or, interests in limiting their accessibility to others through secrecy, anonymity, and solitude. Ideally, a right to privacy would protect both classes of women's privacy interests. For women have *both* kinds of privacy interests at stake. . . .

Theoretical difficulties are posed by a right to privacy inclusive enough to protect both class (a) and class (b) interests. But other difficulties are posed by the fiat of declaring class (a) interests to be "really" liberty interests, rather than genuine privacy interests. For the fact of the matter is that they are *both* privacy interests. Liberty in the area of sexual and familial concerns and privacy per se are interrelated privacy interests. This interrelatedness is one of the things those who seek to explain our privacy interests must explain.

The foregoing discussion has made some progress in that direction. The interrelatedness of privacy and a certain kind of liberty has been explained by showing that privacy as solitude in one's home, so important for the continued development of women as persons, often depends upon freedom or liberty to choose one's life-style. Thus, while solitude outside the home depends upon a privacy right to anonymity, confidentiality, and solitude in Gavison's sense, a woman's solitude in her home will depend much more on a privacy right to choice.

We are left with the difficult problem of articulating the standards, legal and moral, of justifying limitations on a woman's free choice in matters affecting her sexual and familiar life. Whatever else is true, the standards would be expected to reflect an egalitarian conception of men and women. Yet, *many* life-styles and family forms are consistent with the social ideal of sexual egalitarianism. Meaningful moral standards would have to be formulated in relation to particular life-styles and family forms, and the particular vows and commitments of the parties involved. . . .

CONCLUSION

As attempts to articulate moral and constitutional rights to privacy continue, the privacy interests of women must not be overlooked or underemphasized. Women have special privacy interests in what Gavison called secrecy, anonymity, and solitude. But they also have a special privacy interest in freedom of choice in marital, sexual, and reproductive concerns. Women need this freedom of choice to structure their lives in ways that afford the domestic solitude requisite for their continued development as persons. A legal right to privacy must protect all of privacy's dimensions—secrecy, anonymity, solitude, *and* choice—if women's privacy interests are to be adequately protected. A society which protects these interests shields women from low self-esteem, emotional distress, and loss of opportunities and income. Liberal ideals such as liberty, equality, equal opportunity, and personal productivity are more surely advanced where women are treated with respect and they are free from discriminatory legal institutions, social policy, and customs.

Notes

1. Ruth Gavison, "Privacy and the Limits of Law," *Yale Law Journal* 89, no. 3 (1980): 421–71.
2. See Catherine MacKinnon, *Sexual Harassment of Working Women* (New Haven: Yale University Press, 1979); Lin Farley, *Sexual Shakedown: The Sexual Harassment of Women on the Job* (New York: McGraw Hill, 1978); see also Alice Montgomery, "Sexual Harassment in the Work Place," *Golden Gate University Law Review* 10, no. 1 (1980): 879–928; Barbara M. White, "Job-Related Sexual Harassment and Union Women: What Are Their Rights?" *Golden Gate University Law Review* 10, no. 1 (1980): 929–62.
3. Mary Dunlap, "Where the Person Ends, Does the State Begin? An Exploration of Present Controversies Concerning 'The Right to Privacy,'" *Lincoln Law Review* 12, no. 2 (1981): 47–75; Andra M. Pearldaughter and Vivian Schneider, "Women and Welfare: The Cycle of Female Poverty," *Golden Gate University Law Review* 10, no. 1 (1980): 1043–86; J. F. Handler and M. K. Roseheim, "Privacy in Welfare," *Law and Contemporary Problems* 31, no. 31 (1966): 377; J. F. Handler and E. J. Hollingsworth, "Stigma, Privacy, and Other Attitudes of Welfare Recipients," *Stanford Law Review* 22, no. 1 (1969): 1.
4. White, "Sexual Harassment," 937.
5. See Andrew Cuomo, "Equal Credit," *Journal of Legislation* 8, no. 4 (1981): 121–39.
6. Montgomery, "Sexual Harassment in the Work Place," 889.
7. Jean Baker Miller, *Toward a New Psychology of Women* (Boston: Beacon Press, 1976), 94–95.

SELECTION 44
FROM
Pornography and the Erotics of Domination

EVA FEDER KITTAY

PORNOGRAPHY IS A FEMINIST issue. This means that it is also a moral and political issue. Like other moral issues, it requires reflection and inquiry to understand the proper grounds for its condemnation; like other political issues, its analysis does not stand apart from a political position. Some feminists have claimed that pornography has a causal efficacy in maintaining patriarchy; others have argued that pornography is merely the symptom of deeper underlying social ills. But feminist issues, perhaps because of the historically long-standing and culturally pervasive nature of the subordinate position of women, do not fit easily into a "disease model" of social issues. In particular, I believe, there is no one underlying cause of women's oppression such that by removing it, all the symptomatic manifestations of oppression will be relieved. If this is so, feminist issues such as pornography must be regarded as being simultaneously symptom and cause.

As symptom, pornography is reflective of certain social and political relations between men and women; although as a mirror, it reflects through hyperbolic distortions. As a cause, pornography is a contributing factor, perpetuating a social order in which men dominate. In its causal aspect, pornography is hate literature (where "literature" is meant to cover not merely the written word but spoken, graphic, and cinemagraphic materials as well) and is morally wrong, for it contributes to a political and moral injustice. As such, it deserves the same moral and legal sanctions as other defamatory materials. In its aspect as symptom, we can see the disturbing reflections of a mode of social interaction so prevalent that the pornographic hyperbolic image is not only tolerated, but is experienced as an occasion for sexual, that is pleasurable, arousal for many.

The aim of this essay is twofold: first, to explore the moral-political questions concerning the objectionable nature of pornography in its causal aspect as hate literature, and as hate literature with a sexual charge; and second, to consider the conceptual-political questions concerning pornography in its symptomatic aspect, asking what we can learn about sexual relations in a sexist society by looking at the limiting case of pornography. . . .

IDENTIFYING THE PORNOGRAPHIC

EROTIC VERSUS PORNOGRAPHIC

. . . We may provide a *provisional characterization* of pornography:

> *Pornography deals in the representation of violence, degradation, or humiliation of some persons (most frequently female) for the sexual gratification of other persons (almost exclusively male).*

This is not a *definition* of pornography, for a definition will, of necessity, be not specific as to the descriptive content of pornography. To see why, we need to consider Joel Feinberg's analysis of the term "obscene."

Under the Moral Penal Code, obscenity is defined as the "shameful or morbid interest in nudity, sex, or excretion."[1] But Feinberg argues that the Penal Code is ultimately useless in determining what is obscene, because the term "obscene" is not purely descriptive. We cannot simply pick out or somehow find the elements of what constitutes obscenity in the work or behavior which we so designate. Borrowing a notion from P. H. Nowell-Smith, Feinberg calls "obscene" an "aptness" word, that is, a word that "indicates that an object has certain properties which are apt to arouse a certain emotion or range of emotions."[2] In using an aptness word, we generally mean to say that when the given word is applied to some particular entity, it predicts of others, expresses of ourselves (unless we explicitly disavow it), and endorses as correct and appropriate certain reactions to our seeing or experiencing that to which the word is applied. In the case of obscenity, we find the obscene thing to be "disgusting," "shocking," "revolting."

I would like to claim that "pornographic" is also an aptness term, as is the term "erotic," which I want to contrast with pornographic. When we claim a work to be "erotic," we mean to express, predict, and endorse as appropriate a response of what I will call "sexual interest," that is, sexual arousal or satisfaction. To call a work erotic is to focus, specifically, on the following condition:

> *That we regard it as being apt to evoke what we think to be the appropriate response of sexual interest which is more sensuous and voluptuous than lewd or prurient.*

When we say that something is pornographic, we are also saying that it is apt to arouse certain feelings in us. Here, however, it is less clear what those feelings might be and what we might endorse as an appropriate response. In the case of pornography, I think that we have in mind something like the following:

> That we regard the work as having certain characteristics which are apt to arouse an intended (the intention being on the part of those responsible for the work) response of sexual interest which we now qualify not as sensuous but as lewd and licentious.

That which is licentious is that which is lawless—is taken to be illegitimate. Every society, from the most austere to the most free, makes some distinction between a legitimate and an illegitimate sexuality. What we call erotic as opposed to pornographic, sensuous as opposed to lewd, is expressive of this distinction (though it may not be coincident with what the prevailing ideology holds to be legitimate), a distinction one may regard as part of the "sex/gender system" inherent in a given society at a given historical moment.[3]

LEGITIMATE VERSUS ILLEGITIMATE SEXUALITY

Where the lines between the erotic and the pornographic are legally or morally or aesthetically drawn varies from culture to culture. This is perhaps because almost anything can trigger sexual desire, providing only that it has been eroticized at some time in a person's history (and each person's individual history is both reflective of and a part of a culture). . . .

Regardless of how we draw the line between a legitimate and illegitimate sexuality, it appears that there are nonsexual grounds, purely moral considerations which apply to human actions and intentions, that render some sexual acts illegitimate—illegitimate by virtue of the moral impermissibility of harming another person and particularly for the purpose of obtaining pleasure or other benefit from the harm another incurs. Such a moral injunction is but a particular statement of the Kantian imperative not to treat persons as means only. Therefore, I maintain that sexual activity involving the violation of such moral imperatives is necessarily illegitimate. And because what I have termed "sexual interest" is itself sexual activity, sexual interest in necessarily illegitimate sexual activity is also necessarily illegitimate sexuality. I leave aside the issue of whether it ought to be the only form of sexuality we consider illegitimate. I am concerned here only to indicate that a prima facie case can be made for the view that, regardless of the general relativity of the distinction between legitimate and illegitimate sexuality, at least some sexual activity has a claim to be considered universally and necessarily illegitimate—an illegitimacy that derives not from any

particular sex/gender system, but from a universal moral imperative.[4] . . .
We are now ready to provide a definition of pornography:

> *Pornography is a depiction or enactment which has characteristics apt to arouse sexual interest because of the actual or intimated sexual illegitimacy of what is portrayed, and endorsing as an appropriate response the arousal of sexual interest by virtue of the illegitimacy of its sexuality. It may, either instead of or in addition to such intended effects, also arouse feelings of disgust and revulsion, i.e., feelings appropriate to obscenity as defined above.*

The above definition is meant to incorporate much of what is often called "hard-core" pornography, but also some of what is generally labeled "soft-core," and it is meant to capture the relation between what is obscene and what is pornographic. I believe that the definition is consonant with what Rosemary Tong has called "thanatic" as opposed to "erotic" pornography, in an attempt to tie the former to the idea of death as opposed to love. Thanatica, writes Tong,

> represent sexual exchanges devoid or nearly devoid of mutual or self-respect; they display sexual exchanges which are degrading in the sense and to the degree that the desires and experiences of at least one participant are not regarded by the other participant(s) as having a validity and a subjective importance equal to his/her/their own.[5]

My formulation may be still stronger in that I explicitly tie the depictions to a sexual activity that is to be censured as morally impermissible, on nonsexual grounds, although it casts the net wider in that it encompasses depictions that are not necessarily depictions of sexual exchanges as such. I will, however, adopt the term "thanatic" pornography for the phenomena with which I am here concerned. . . .

PORNOGRAPHY AS HATE LITERATURE

In defamatory material we see the oppressed group portrayed in humiliating or demeaning ways. Violence directed against the victims is seen as justified by their own presumed weakness, evilness, or vileness. The humiliating portrayals are sometimes masked as scientific or sociological fact and sometimes as the exercise of good fun on the part of the propagators of the hate literature. The violence, shown as justifiable and satisfying, is thereby implicitly advocated—sometimes the advocacy is forthright. In racist hate literature, the hate and the consequent abuse are justified on the basis of racial characteristics. Pornography justifies the abuse of women on the basis of their sexual characteristics.

But in pornography the pernicious message comes in sheep's clothing. Hedonistic celebration of sexual pleasure should not blind us to what is more than a mere analogy between hate literature and pornography. In pornography one's gender, usually female, is a sufficient condition for one's use and abuse, just as in hate literature a person's race or national identity is a sufficient condition for his/her use and abuse. . . .

THE HARM OF PORNOGRAPHY CONSIDERED AS HATE LITERATURE

Only the morally blind would not recognize the moral evil of hate literature. To the extent that hate literature has as its aim the advocacy of abusive behavior toward certain groups of people, its moral evil lies in its intent to cause injury to innocent persons. Not only are the ends of hate literature objectionable, but also its means, for the expression of the hatred normally results in false and misleading portrayals of the objects of the hate. Thus, hate literature is usually libelous. To the extent that our concept of some entity influences our behavior toward such an entity, these false and misleading portrayals, if believed, can be supposed eventually to influence behavior directed to the entity in question. In this causal relation between our beliefs and our actions, the intent to harm is seen in defamatory materials. . . .

Hate literature may be immoral in still another way. For it is not only characterized by the advocacy of injury to others and the intentional propagation of libelous claims; it also often panders to those who derive pleasure in witnessing the real or fictive abuse of the despised group. Insofar as pornography by definition aims at arousal and pleasure from its depictions, it clearly shares this feature with other hate literature. . . .

PORNOGRAPHY AND THE LAW

I have argued that thanatic pornography is hate literature and have give some arguments concerning the moral sanctions appropriate to hate literature. As hate literature reflects, promulgates, and endorses the morally repugnant attitudes of those who produce, believe, and enjoy it, it is harmful and inimical to a just society. As such, one might well argue that such materials ought to be legally sanctioned, and look for the appropriate legal grounds on which to censure them. Because of the stringent requirements for censorship established by the First Amendment, such legal grounds are difficult to establish without at once jeopardizing the protections enjoined by the First Amendment. Whether we are dealing with hate literature of the usual sort or with pornography, the central question is whether the material under consideration is "protected speech." Speech is not protected under the Constitution if it is obscene or if it constitutes "a clear and present danger" to others. Nor are libel and slander protected speech. . . .

In recent years feminists have been more likely to argue that pornography ought not to be protected under the First Amendment because it constitutes a "clear and present danger." Rosemary Tong has distinguished three stances feminists have taken in arguing the harmfulness of thanatic pornography:

(1) Although such thanatic material may not be harmful per se, it causes people to engage in harmful behavior; (2) Thanatic material does not have to be harmful in order to be constitutionally censorable; and (3) Thanatic material is harmful.[6]

She claims, correctly I believe, that the third is the strongest argument, that the first is the weakest, and that the second might be useful in making pornographic material less visible. . . .

In arguing that pornography is a form of defamation and arguing the immorality of such materials, I am also arguing for the view that hate material and thanatic pornography are harmful per se. Do these arguments provide a ground for a legal sanction against pornography? In arguing that pornography is hate literature, can we use whatever sanctions exist against defamation to apply to pornography? Legal sanctions against defamatory materials do not, unfortunately, provide us with clear models we can adopt for the case of pornography. The difficulty centers on the issue of "group libel" as a viable legal concept. As Tong points out, quoting Zechariah Chafee, the concept of "group libel" has proved embarrassing for legal theorists because of its close association with the sedition laws of English common law, laws which made it illegal to make statements construed as hostile or injurious to the state or as intending to "promote feelings of ill will and hostility between different classes.[7] Recall that the First Amendment was framed against the background of the English common law. Tong writes (10–11), "legal theorists are not likely to turn to the criminal law to forge a group-libel doctrine. . . . Consequently, the only salvation for the notion of group libel would seem to be the civil law."

As long as the libel is distributive over all the members of the class who are libeled, that is, as long as the defamatory remarks claim that a certain fact or characteristic holds for all members of the libeled class, any particular woman can engage in a civil suit claiming a defamation of her character due to libelous claims.

This may indeed sound promising, but I fear that this course of action may promise more than it can deliver. For a statement to be libelous it must be a statement of fact that can be proven to be false. The libelous content of much pornography does not easily lend itself to such proof, particularly when much of it (a) is so widely assumed to be true and (b) is also believed to be the sort of thing that a woman will not easily admit to it. Take, for example, the implicit or explicit claim that women want to be raped as a characteristic but libelous claim found in much pornography. Within our culture, men and women alike think that a woman saying "no" does not justify a belief that she means "no," and girls are still taught that they ought not to be open and honest about their sexual feelings. Under such social conditions, a defendant can argue that regardless of what any individual woman claims, any presumably seductive behavior warrants the conclusion that she "secretly" desires to be forced to engage in sexual intercourse. Precisely these sorts of presuppositions make it difficult to prosecute actual rape cases. Efforts to establish legal resolutions to pornography suffer by virtue of the fact that the legal system itself is embedded within a patriarchical society; even if the abstract system of rules can be made free of patriarchical bias, the implementation of those laws still depends on persons who are largely male and largely insensitive to the oppressive nature of our sexual relations. The woman taking the witness stand in such a suit against libelous pornographic claims would be subject to the sort of mental rape endured by the woman who testifies against her rapist, and the fate of the suit would most likely be as unsuccessful as that of attempts to prosecute rapists. . . .

THE LIMITS OF THE EROTIZATION OF DOMINATION

It seems clear that violence expressed sexually reveals to us the frighteningly destructive possibilities of the same sexuality that is often the source of our most intense pleasure and the binding of loves and friendships. The legitimatization of sexuality in marriage may be seen as the societal harnessing of the binding force of sexual attachments. To see how sexuality is linked with violence, and why this linkage can be exploited in a $4 billion a year industry, we need to examine the relation between eroticism and power.

Most pertinent is the extent to which we have eroticized the relations of power. We have done so in a manner consonant with the dominant power relations between men and women, so that women generally seek male sexual partners who are their superiors, while men regard as erotic women who are their inferiors. The parameters may be height, age, social status, wealth, education, intellect, physical strenght, or whatever other qualities are regarded as salient hierarchical differentiations. Women eroticize being possessed, conquered, overwhelmed, etc. Men have eroticized the conquering, possessing, subduing. . . .

To be in a position of dependency is to be in a position in which another can exert power over you. That power may involve the potential exercise of physical force or psychological coercion. The exercise of that power in its extreme forms involves the capacity to inflict pain and injury on another. Physical violence (and in some cases psychological violence) is the exercise of the ultimate power over life and limb. If the direct proportionality of power and eroticism was not in any way bounded, then we should expect to find a great deal of violence in our sexual relations. And perhaps there *is* more than we care to admit. There are, however, good reasons to suppose that, in real life experiences, the increase in the polarity of power has limits to its erotic potential. . . .

CONCLUSION

As a symptom, as a reflection of the society in which it thrives, pornography displays an extreme in the erotization of domination. It portrays a fantasy world in which the ordinary limitations we bring to such eroticizing are suspended. Can these remarks, then, be seen as justification of pornography as, after all, merely a harmless outlet for repressed sexual desires, with no actual consequences other than some possible self-injury to the pornography consumer as he wallows in his morally unwholesome pleasures? I do not believe so. Here the dialectic between symptom and cause propels us back to a consideration of the consequences of pornography's presence.

There is, I have argued, nothing harmless in the vicarious enjoyment of the representations of this eroticized domination. On the contrary, pornography escalates the dimensions of the problem by making it appear that violence is intrinsically erotic, rather than something that is eroticized. And as I and others have argued, it is libelous, since it portrays women as essentially masochistic, enjoying rape, and as being sexually fulfilled only when sufficiently humiliated and dominated. Beyond this, we must pay attention to the empirical data suggesting that pornography may weaken the censors that inhibit the sexualization of domination from pervading our sexual life in its most extreme forms. Men (particularly those with a low level of aggression anxiety) watching pornography are, at least momentarily, convinced that the brutality they see is not really brutality if it is a means to a felt sexual gratification.

Contrary to the claims of some of its apologists, pornography is not cathartic. Catharsis is a purging of unpleasant, undesirable emotions, particularly the emotions of pity and fear, by first exciting and then allaying them. Both the excitement and allaying of the emotions are accomplished by images accompanied by pain. In pornography the images that would excite and allay the sexual discharge are made to appear pleasurable. When murderous rage is portrayed in an appropriately cathartic work of tragedy, it is seen as leading to the most awful consequences. But sexual desire that must be satisfied by brutalizing a woman is portrayed in pornography as leading to the most ecstatic pleasures. To claim that the overflow of unhealthy sexual desires is "purged" in pornographic consumption is completely unsupported by psychological research into the effects of violence and pornography. Pornography, rather than purging sexual desires of a dangerous sort, exhibits horrid violence, sexually—that is, pleasurably—charged, as permissible, as well as possible.

The problem, in the end, is more than pornography. It is the eroticizing of the relation of power. Without this, pornography would simply revolt us all; it would not be stimulating to many. If the erotization of domination is so prevalent, is there perhaps something in the nature of eroticism that calls for the differentia of power relations? Plato spoke of Eros, as of necessity seeking what it lacked. Simone de Beauvoir says, "Eroticism is a movement toward the Other." The creation and maintenance of hierarchical relations between men and women is itself a guarantor of alterity. Yet, any reasonable reflection allows us to see what the defenders of patriarchy obscure by the motto "Vive la difference," namely, that among human beings, equality is not identity. Alterity and its consequent eroticism can be preserved in relations of equality. Indeed, the mutual and reciprocal giving and receiving of sexual pleasure, such that the other's desire and pleasure are constitutive of our own, would seem the very model for the interrelationship between equal persons.[8]

The eroticism of domination, rather than being demanded by the nature of eros, is an instrument for the maintenance of male prerogatives. Deirdre English writes, it is "a fantasy that is intended to make male supremacy more palatable to both sexes."[9] And given that what we have eroticized is so deeply embedded in our collective and individual psyches, be we sexist or feminist, pornography serves only to feed and rouse the lion within. It not only reflects but also contributes to the difficulties women face in their struggle for autonomy: difficulties in their own sexual identity, in establishing equality in intimate relations, and in their safety and freedom of movement as they try to Take Back the Night.

Notes

1. American Law Institute, Moral Penal Code § 251.4 (1), 1962.
2. Joel Feinberg, "The Idea of the Obscene," the Lindley Lecture given at the University of Kansas, 1979. Feinberg discusses the notion of an aptness word only in regard to "obscene," not in regard to "pornographic" or "erotic."
3. See Gayle Rubin, "The Traffic in Women: Notes on the Political Economy of Sex," in Reyna Reiter, ed. *Toward an Anthropology of Women* (New York: Monthly Review Press, 1975), 157–210, for an explication of the sex/gender system. Rubin does not discuss questions of legitimate versus illegitimate sexuality as such, but I believe that the notion is clearly part of the same complex of ideas that informs her formulation.
4. It may be more difficult to justify such a claim on utilitarian grounds or even on the basis of rights. Clearly, if one is abused or injured, there is some sense in which one has had some rights violated, even if the right be as general as the right to personal security and the right to the pursuit of happiness. In cases involving pornography, however, it may be very unclear precisely whose rights have been violated and what those rights are that have been violated. In many cases, a claim that rights have been violated would be less than obvious, and I am not certain that a strong claim could be made out in this manner. A justification on utilitarian grounds is still more problematic. It raises the dilemma

faced by utilitarians when a situation is presented in which a number of persons may obtain a great deal of pleasure cumulatively, whereas the harm to a single person is great but not as great as the cumulative pleasure of the benefactors of the victim's injury. To the extent that utility theory can handle the more general case, it can handle the more specific case.

5. Rosemarie Tong, "Feminism, Pornography and Censorship," *Social Theory and Practice* 8, no. 1 (Spring 1982): 4.
6. Tong, " Feminism, Pornography, and Censorship," 5.
7. In Zechariah Chafee, *Free Speech in the United States* (Cambridge: Harvard University Press), 506. Quoted in Tong "Feminism, Pornography, and Censorship," 11.
8. See Virginia Held, "Marx, Sex, and the Transformation of Society." *Philosophical Forum* 5 (1973–74): 168–84.
9. Deirdre English, "The Politics of Porn," *Mother Jones*, April 1980, 50.

SELECTION 45
FROM
Only Words

CATHARINE A. MACKINNON

IMAGINE THAT FOR HUNDREDS of years your most formative traumas, your daily suffering and pain, the abuse you live through, the terror you live with, are unspeakable—not the basis of literature. You grow up with your father holding you down and covering your mouth so another man can make a horrible searing pain between your legs. When you are older, your husband ties you to the bed and drips hot wax on your nipples and brings in other men to watch and makes you smile through it. Your doctor will not give you drugs he has addicted you to unless you suck his penis.[1]

You cannot tell anyone. When you try to speak of these things, you are told it did not happen, you imagined it, you wanted it, you enjoyed it. Books say this. No books say what happened to you. Law says this. No law imagines what happened to you, the way it happened. You live your whole life surrounded by this cultural echo of nothing where your screams and your words should be.

In this thousand years of silence, the camera is invented and pictures are made of you while these things are being done. You hear the camera clicking or whirring as you are being hurt, keeping time to the rhythm of your pain. You always know that the pictures are out there somewhere, sold or traded or shown around or just kept in a drawer. In them, what was done to you is immortal. He has them; someone, anyone, has seen you there, that way. This is unbearable. What he felt as he watched you as he used you is always being done again and lived again and felt again through the pictures—your violation his arousal, your torture his pleasure. Watching you was how he got off doing it; with the pictures he can watch you and get off any time.[2]

Slowly, then suddenly, it dawns on you: Maybe now I will be believed. You find a guarded way of bringing it up. Maybe the pictures are even evidence of rape.[3] You find that the pictures, far from making what happened undeniable, are sex, proof of your desire and your consent.[4] Those who use you through the pictures feel their own pleasure. They do not feel your pain as pain any more than those who watched as they hurt you to make the pictures felt it. The pictures, surrounded by a special halo of false secrecy and false taboo—false because they really are public and are not really against the rules—have become the authority on what happened to you, the literature of your experience, a sign for sex, sex itself. In a very real way, they have made sex *be* what it is to the people who use you and the pictures of you interchangeably. In this, the pictures are not so different from the words and drawings that came before, but your use for the camera gives the pictures a special credibility, a deep verisimilitude, an even stronger claim to truth, to being incontrovertibly about you, because they happened and there you are. And because you are needed for the pictures, the provider has yet another reason to use you over and over and over again.

Finally, somehow, you find other women. Their fathers, husbands, and doctors saw the pictures, liked them, and did the same things to them, things they had never done or said they wanted before. As these other women were held down, or tied up, or examined on the table, pictures like the pictures of you were talked about or pointed to: Do what she did, enjoy it the way she enjoyed it. The same acts that were forced on you are forced on them; the same smile you were forced to smile, they must smile. There is, you find, a whole industry in buying and selling captive smiling women to make such pictures, acting as if they like it.

When any one of them tries to tell what happened, she is told it did not happen, she imagined it, she wanted it. Her no meant yes. The pictures prove it. See, she smiles. Besides, why fixate on the pictures, the little artifact, at most a symptom? Even if something wrong was *done* to you, how metaphysically obtuse can you be? The pictures *themselves* do nothing. They are an expression of ideas, a discussion, a debate, a discourse. How repressed and repressive can you be? They are constitutionally protected speech.

Putting to one side what this progression from life to law does to one's sense of reality, personal security, and place in the community, not to mention faith in the legal system, consider what it does to one's relation to expression: to language, speech, the world of thought and communication. You learn that language does not belong to you, that you cannot use it to say what you know, that knowledge is not what you learn from your life, that information is not made out of your experience. You learn that thinking about what happened to you does not count as "thinking," but doing it apparently does. You learn that your reality subsists somewhere beneath the socially real—totally exposed but invisible, screaming yet inaudible, thought about incessantly yet unthinkable, "expression" yet inexpressible, beyond words. You learn that speech is not what you say but what your abusers do to you.

Your relation to speech is like shouting at a movie. Somebody stop that man, you scream. The audience acts as though nothing has been said, keeps watching fixedly or turns slightly, embarrassed for you. The action onscreen continues as if nothing has been said. As the echo of your voice dies in your ears, you begin to doubt that you said anything. Soon your own experience is not real to you anymore, like a movie you watch but cannot stop. This is women's version of life imitating art: your life as the pornographer's text. To survive, you learn shame and how to cover it with sexual bravado, inefficacy and how to make it seductive, secrecy and the habit of not telling what you know until you forget it. You learn how to leave your body and create someone else who takes over when you cannot stand it any more. You develop a self who is ingratiating and obsequious and imitative and aggressively passive and silent—you learn, in a word, femininity.

I am asking you to imagine that women's reality is real—something of a leap of faith in a society saturated with pornography, not to mention an academy saturated with deconstruction.[5] In the early 1980s women spoke of this reality, in Virginia Woolf's words of many years before, "against the male flood":[6] They spoke of being sexually abused. Thirty-eight percent of women are sexually molested as girls; 24 percent of us are raped in our marriages. Nearly half are victims of rape or attempted rape at least once in our lives, many more than once, especially women of color, many involving multiple attackers, mostly men we know. Eighty-five percent of women who work outside the home are sexually harassed at some point by employers.[7] We do not yet know how many women are sexually harassed by their doctors or how many are bought and sold as sex—the one thing men will seemingly always pay for, even in a depressed economy.

A long time before the women's movement made this information available, in the absence of the words of sexually abused women, in the vacuum of this knowledge, in the silence of this speech, the question of pornography was framed and debated—its trenches dug, its moves choreographed, its voices rehearsed. Before the invention of the camera, which requires the direct use of real women; before the rise of a mammoth profitmaking industry of pictures and words acting as pimp; before women spoke out about sexual abuse and were heard, the question of the legal regulation of pornography was framed as a question of the freedom of expression of the pornographers and their consumers. The government's interest in censoring the expression of ideas about sex was opposed to publishers' right to express them and readers' right to read and think about them.

Frozen in the classic form of prior debates over censorship of political and artistic speech, the pornography debate thus became one of governmental authority threatening to suppress genius and dissent. There was some basis in reality for this division of sides. Under the law of obscenity, governments did try to suppress art and literature because it was sexual in content. This was before the camera required live fodder and usually resulted in the books' becoming best-sellers.

Once abused women are heard and—this is the real hitch—become real, women's silence can no longer be the context in which pornography and speech are analyzed. Into the symbiotic dance between left and right, between the men who love to have each other, enters the captive woman, the terms of access to whom they have been fighting over.[8] Instead of the forces of darkness seeking to suppress what the forces of light are struggling to free, her captivity itself is made central and put in issue for the first time. This changes everything, or should. Before, each women who said she was abused looked incredible or exceptional; now, the abuse appears deadeningly commonplace. Before, what was done to her was sex; now, it is sexual abuse. Before, she was sex; now, she is a human being gendered female—if anyone can figure out what that is.

In this new context, the expressive issues raised by pornography also change—or should. Protecting pornography means protecting sexual abuse *as* speech, at the same time that both pornography and its protection have deprived women *of* speech, especially speech against sexual abuse. There is a connection between the silence enforced on women, in which we are seen to love and choose our chains because they have been sexualized, and the noise of pornography that surrounds us, passing for discourse (ours, even) and parading under constitutional protection. The operative definition of censorship accordingly shifts from government silencing what powerless people say, to powerful people violating powerless people into silence and hiding behind state power to do it.

In the United States, pornography is protected by the state.[9] Conceptually, this protection relies centrally on putting it back into the context of the silence of violated women: from real abuse back to an "idea" or "viewpoint" on women and sex. In this derealization of the subordination of women, this erasure of sexual abuse through which a technologically sophisticated traffic in women becomes a consumer choice of expressive content, abused women become a pornographer's "thought" or "emotion." This posture unites pornography's apologists from libertarian economist and judge Frank Easterbrook[10] to liberal philosopher-king Ronald Dworkin,[11] from conservative scholar and judge Richard Posner[12] to pornographers' lawyer Edward DeGrazia.[13]

In their approach, taken together, pornography falls presumptively into the legal category "speech" at the outset through being rendered in terms of "content," "message," "emotion," what it "says," its "viewpoint," its "ideas." Once the women abused in it and through it are elided this way, its artifact status as pictures and words gets it legal protection through a seemingly indelible categorical formalism that then must be negated for anything to be done.

In this approach, the approach of current law, pornography is essentially treated as defamation rather than as discrimination.[14] That is, it is conceived in terms of what it says, which is imagined more or less effective or harmful as someone then acts on it, rather than in terms of what it does. Fundamentally, in this view, a form of communication cannot, as such, *do* anything bad except offend. Offense is all in the head. Because the purveyor is protected in sending, and the consumer in receiving, the thought or feeling, the fact that an unintended bystander might have offended thoughts or unpleasant feelings is a mere externality, a cost we must pay for freedom. That the First Amendment protects this process of interchange—thought to thought, feeling to feeling—there is no doubt.

Within the confines of this approach, to say that pornography is an act against women is seen as metaphorical or magical, rhetorical or unreal, a literary hyperbole or propaganda device. On the assumption that words have only a referential relation to reality, pornography is defended as only words— even when it is pictures women had to be directly used to make, even when the means of writing are women's bodies, even when a woman is destroyed in order to say it or show it or because it was said or shown.

A theory of protected speech begins here: Words express, hence are *presumed* "speech" in the protected sense. Pictures partake of the same level of expressive protection. But social life is full of words that are legally treated as the acts they constitute without so much as a whimper from the First Amendment. What becomes interesting is when the First Amendment frame is invoked and when it is not. *Saying* "kill" to a trained attack dog is only words. Yet it is not seen as expressing the viewpoint "I want you dead"— which it usually does, in fact, express. It is seen as performing an act tantamount to someone's destruction, like saying "ready, aim, fire" to a firing squad. Under bribery statutes, saying the word "aye" in a legislative vote triggers a crime that can consist entirely of what people say. So does price-fixing under the antitrust laws. "Raise your goddamn fares twenty percent, I'll raise mine the next morning" is not protected speech; it is attempted joint monopolization, a "highly verbal crime." In this case, conviction nicely disproved the defendant's view, expressed in the same conversation, that "we can talk about any goddamn thing we want to talk about."[15]

Along with other mere words like "not guilty" and "I do," such words are uniformly treated as the institutions and practices they constitute, rather than as expressions of the ideas they embody or further. They are not seen as saying anything (although they do) but as doing something. No one confuses discussing them with doing them, for instance discussing a verdict of "guilty" with a jury's passing a verdict of "guilty." Nobody takes an appeal of a guilty verdict as censorship of the jury. Such words are not considered "speech" at all.

Social inequality is substantially created and enforced—that is, *done*—through words and images. Social hierarchy cannot and does not exist without being embodied in meanings and expressed in communications. A sign *saying* "White Only"[16] is only words, but it is not legally seen as expressing the viewpoint "we do not want black people in this store," or as dissenting from the policy view that both blacks and whites must be served, or even as hate speech, the restriction of which would need to be debated in First Amendment terms. It is seen as the act of segregation that it is, like "Juden nicht erwünscht!"[17] Segregation cannot happen without someone *saying* "get out" or "you don't belong here" at some point. Elevation and denigration are all accomplished through meaningful symbols and communicative acts in which saying it is doing it.

Words unproblematically treated as acts in the inequality context include "you're fired," help wanted—male," "sleep with me and I'll give you an A," "fuck me or you're fired," "walk more femininely, talk more femininely, dress more femininely, wear makeup, have your hair styled, and wear jewelry," and "it was essential that the understudy to my Administrative Assistant be a man."[18] These statements are discriminatory acts and are legally seen as such. Statements like them can also evidence discrimination or show that patterns of inequality are motivated by discriminatory animus. They can constitute actionable discriminatory acts in themselves or legally transform otherwise nonsuspect acts into bias-motivated ones. Whatever damage is done through such words is done not only through their context but through their content, in the sense that if they did not contain what they contain, and convey the meanings and feelings and thoughts they convey, they would not evidence or actualize the discrimination that they do.

Pornography, by contrast, has been legally framed as a vehicle for the expression of ideas. The Supreme Court of Minnesota recently observed of some pornography before it that "even the most liberal construction would be strained to find an 'idea' in it," limited as it was to "who wants what, where, when, how, how much, and how often."[19] Even this criticism dignifies the pornography. The *idea of* who wants what, where, and when sexually can be expressed without violating anyone and without getting anyone raped. There are many ways to say what pornography says, in the sense of its content. But nothing else does what pornography does. The question becomes, do the pornographers—saying they are only saying what it says—have a speech right to do what only it does?

What pornography does, it does in the real world, not only in the mind. As an initial matter, it should be observed that it is the pornography industry, not the ideas in the materials, that forces, threatens, blackmails, pressures, tricks, and cajoles women into sex for pictures. In pornography, women are gang raped so they can be filmed. They are not gang raped by the idea of a gang rape. It is for pornography, and not by the ideas in it, that women are hurt and penetrated, tied and gagged, undressed and genitally spread and sprayed with lacquer and water so sex pictures can be made. Only for pornography are women killed to make a sex movie, and it is not the idea of a sex killing that kills them. It is unnecessary to do any of these things to express, as ideas, the ideas pornography expresses. It *is* essential to do them to make pornography. Similarly, on the consumption end, it is not the ideas in pornography that assault women: Men do, men who are made, changed, and impelled by it. Pornography does not leap off the shelf and assault women. Women could, in theory, walk safely past whole warehouses full of it, quietly resting in its jackets. It is what it takes to make it and what happens through its use that are the problem. . . .

Sooner or later, in one way or another, the consumers want to live out the pornography further in three dimensions. Sooner or later, in one way or another, they do. *It* makes them want to; when they believe they can, when they feel they can get away with it, *they* do. Depending upon their chosen sphere of operation, they may use whatever power they have to keep the world a pornographic place so they can continue to get hard from everyday life. As pornography consumers, teachers may become epistemically incapable of seeing their women students as their potential equals and unconsciously teach about rape from the viewpoint of the accused. Doctors may molest anesthetized women, enjoy watching and inflicting pain during childbirth, and use pornography to teach sex education in medical school. Some consumers write on bathroom walls. Some undoubtedly write judicial opinions.[20] . . .

Pornography does not simply express or interpret experience; it substitutes for it. Beyond bringing a message from reality, it stands in for reality; it is existentially being there. This does not mean that there is no spin on the experience—far from it. To make visual pornography, and to live up to its imperatives, the world, namely women, must do what the pornographers want to "say." Pornography brings its conditions of production to the consumer: sexual dominance. As Creel Froman puts its, subordination is "doing someone else's language."[21] Pornography makes the world a pornographic place through its making and use, establishing what women are said to exist as, are seen as, are treated as, contructing the social reality of what a woman is and can be in terms of what can be done to her, and what a man is in terms of doing it.

As society becomes saturated with pornography, what makes for sexual arousal, and the nature of sex itself in terms of the place of speech in it, change. What was words and pictures becomes, through masturbation, sex itself. As the industry expands, this becomes more and more the generic experience of sex, the woman in pornography becoming more and more the lived archetype for women's sexuality in men's, hence women's, experience. In other words, as the human becomes thing and the mutual becomes one-sided and the given becomes stolen and sold, objectification comes to define femininity, and one-sidedness comes to define mutuality, and force comes to define consent as pictures and words become the forms of possession and use through which women are actually possessed and used. In pornography, pictures and words are sex. At the same time, in the world pornography creates, sex is pictures and words. As sex becomes speech, speech becomes sex.

The denial that pornography is a real force comes in the guise of many mediating constructions. At most, it is said, pornography reflects or depicts or describes or represents subordination that happens elsewhere. The most common denial is that pornography is "fantasy." Meaning it is unreal, or only an internal reality. For whom? The women in it may dissociate to survive, but it *is* happening to their bodies. The pornographer regularly uses the women personally and does not stop his business at fantasizing. The consumer masturbates to it, replays it in his head and onto the bodies of women he encounters or has sex with, lives it out on the women and children around him. Are the victims of snuff films fantasized to death?

Another common evasion is that pornography is "simulated." What can this mean? It always reminds me of calling rape with a bottle "artificial rape."[22] In pornography, the penis is shown ramming up into the woman over and over; this is because it actually was rammed up into the women over and over. In mainstream media, violence is done through special effects; in pornography, women shown being beaten and tortured report being beaten and tortured. Sometimes "simulated" seems to mean that the rapes are not really rapes but are part of the story, so the woman's refusal and resistance are acting. If it is acting, why does it matter what the actress is really feeling? We are told unendingly that the women in pornography are *really* enjoying themselves (but it's simulated?). Is the man's erection on screen "simulated" too? Is he "acting" too?

No pornography is "real" sex in the sense of shared intimacy; this may make it a lie, but it does not make it "simulated." Nor is it real in the sense that it happened as it appears. To look real to an observing camera, the sex acts have to be twisted open, stopped and restarted, positioned and repositioned, the come shot often executed by another actor entirely. The women regularly take drugs to get through it. This is not to say that none of this happens in sex that is not for pornography; rather that, as a defense of pornography, this sounds more like an indictment of sex.

One wonders why it is not said that the pleasure is simulated and the rape is real, rather than the other way around. The answer is that the consumer's pleasure requires that the scenario conform to the male rape fantasy, which requires him to abuse her and her to like it. Paying the woman to appear to resist and then surrender does not make the sex consensual; it makes pornography an arm of prostitution. The sex is not chosen for the sex. Money is the medium of force and provides the cover of consent.

The most elite denial of the harm is the one that holds that pornography is "representation," when a representation is a nonreality. Actual rape arranges reality; ritual torture frames and presents it. Does that make them "representations," and so not rape and torture? Is a rape a representation of a rape if someone is watching it? When is the rapist *not* watching it? Taking photographs is part of the ritual of some abusive sex, an act of taking, the possession involved. So is watching while doing it and watching the pictures later. The photos are trophies; looking at the photos is fetishism. Is nude dancing a "representation" of eroticism or is it eroticism, meaning a sex act? How is a live sex show different? In terms of what the men are doing sexually, an audience watching a gang rape in a movie is no different from an audience watching a gang rape that is reenacting a gang rape from a movie, or an audience watching any gang rape.

To say that pornography is categorically or functionally representation rather than sex simply creates a distanced world we can say is not the real world, a world that mixes reality with unreality, art and literature with everything else, as if life does not do the same thing. The effect is to license whatever is done there, creating a special aura of privilege and demarcating a sphere of protected freedom, no matter who is hurt. In this approach, there is no way to prohibit rape if pornography is protected. If, by contrast, representation *is* reality, as other theorists argue, then pornography is no less an act than the rape and torture it represents.[23]

At stake in constructing pornography as "speech" is gaining constitutional protection for doing what pornography *does*: subordinating women through sex. This is not content as such, nor is it wholly other than content. Segregation is not the content of "help wanted—male" employment advertisements, nor is the harm of the segregation done without regard to the content of the ad. It is its function. Law's proper concern here is not with what speech says, but with what it does.[24] The meaning *of* pornography in the sense of interpretation may be an interesting problem, but it is not this one. This problem is its meaning *for* women: what it does in and to our lives.

I am not saying that pornography is conduct and therefore not speech, or that it does things and therefore says nothing and is without meaning, or that all its harms are noncontent harms. In society, nothing is without meaning. Nothing has no content. Society is made of words, whose meanings the powerful control, or try to. At a certain point, when those who are hurt by them become real, some words are recognized as the acts that they are. Converging with this point from the action side, nothing that happens in society lacks ideas or says nothing, including rape and torture and sexual murder. This presumably does not make rape and murder protected expression, but, other than by simplistic categorization, speech theory never says why not. Similarly, every act of discrimination is done because of group membership, such as on the basis of sex or race or both, meaning done either with that conscious thought, perception, knowledge, or consequence. Indeed, discriminatory intent, a mental state, is required to prove discrimination under the Fourteenth Amendment.[25] Does this "thought" make all that discrimination "speech"?

It is not new to observe that while the doctrinal distinction between speech and action is on one level obvious, on another level it makes little sense. In social inequality, it makes almost none. Discrimination does not divide into acts on one side and speech on the other. Speech acts. It makes no sense from the action side either. Acts speak. In the context of social inequality, so-called speech can be an exercise of power which constructs the social reality in which people live, from objectification to genocide. The words and images are either direct incidents of such acts, such as making pornography or requiring Jews to wear yellow stars, or are connected to them, whether immediately, linearly, and directly, or in more complicated and extended ways.

Together with all its material supports, authoritatively *saying* someone is inferior is largely how structures of status and differential treatment are demarcated and actualized. Words and images are how people are placed in hierarchies, how social stratification is made to seem inevitable and right, how feelings of inferiority and superiority are engendered, and how indifference to violence against those on the bottom is rationalized and normalized.[26] Social supremacy is made, inside and between people, through making meanings. To unmake it, these meanings and their technologies have to be unmade. . . .

Law is only words. It has content, yet we do not analyze law as the mere expression of ideas. When we object to a law—say, one that restricts speech—we do not say we are offended by it. We are scared or threatened or endangered by it. We look to the consequences of the law's enforcement as an accomplished fact and to the utterance of legal words as tantamount to imposing their reality. This becomes too obvious to mention not only because the First Amendment does not protect government speech but because law is backed by power, so its words are seen as acts. But so is pornography: the power of men over women,[27] expressed through unequal sex, sanctioned both through and prior to state power. It makes no more sense to treat pornography as mere abstraction and representation than it does to treat law as simulation or fantasy. No one has suggested that our legal definition of pornography does what the pornography it describes in words does; nor that, if enacted in law, our ordinance would be only words.

As Andrea Dworkin has said, "pornography is the law for women."[28] Like law, pornography does what it says. That pornography is reality is what silenced women have not been permitted to *say* for hundreds of years. Failing to face this in its simplicity leaves one defending abstraction at the cost of principle, obscuring this emergency because it is not like other emergencies, defending an idea of an "idea" while a practice of sexual abuse becomes a constitutional right. Until we face this, we will be left where Andrea Dworkin recognizes we are left at the end of *Intercourse*:[29] with a violated child alone on the bed—this one wondering if she is lucky to be alive.

Notes

1. Some of these facts are taken from years of confidential consultations with women who have been used in pornography; some are adapted from *People v. Burnham*, 222 Cal. Rptr. 630 (Ct. App. 1986), rev. denied, May 22, 1986, and media reports on it; and *Norberg v. Wynrib* [1992] 2 S.C.R. 224 (Can.).

2. Women used in pornography have provided the basis for the statements in these paragraphs over many years of work by me and my colleagues, including especially Andrea Dworkin, Therese Stanton, Evelina Giobbe, Susan Hunter, Margaret Baldwin, and Annie McCombs. Treatments of some of this damage are provided by Linda "Lovelace" and Michael McGrady, *Ordeal* (1980) (her experience of being coerced to make *Deep Throat*), and, in fiction, by Kathryn Harrison, *Exposures* (1993) (experience of child model for sex pictures by her father). See also Collette Marie, "The Coercion of Nudist Children," *ICONoclast* 3 (Spring 1991): 1–6.

3. In the prosecution by Trish Crawford of South Carolina against her husband for marital rape, a thirty-minute videotape he took of the assault was shown. In it, Mr. Crawford has intercourse with her and penetrates her with objects while her hands and legs are tied with rope and her mouth is gagged and eyes blinded with duct tape. He was acquitted on a consent defense. "Acquittal of Husband Spurs Anger; Wife Accused of Raping Her," *Houston Chronicle*, April 18, 1992, sec. A, p. 3. The defendant testified he did not think his wife was serious when she said "no." Carolyn Pesce, "Marital Rape Case Acquittal Fuels Protest," *USA Today*, April 21, 1992, 3A. See also *State v. Jean*, 311 S.E. 2d 266, 272–73 (N.C. 1984) (cross-examination of defendant on viewing pornographic movie five days after crime of rape charged, when movie showed the same kinds of sex acts charged, if error, was harmless).

4. As the defense lawyer in *Crawford* put it to the jury, as the tape described in note 3 above was played, "Was that a cry of pain and torture? Or was that a cry of pleasure? "Marital Rape Acquittal Enrages Women's Groups," *Chicago Tribune*, April 18, 1992, 9C. This woman was clear she was being tortured. For the viewer who takes pleasure in her pain, however, the distinction between pain and pleasure does not exist. Her pain is his pleasure. This sexual sadism provides an incentive, even an epistemic basis, to impute pleasure to the victim as well. I believe this dynamic makes queries such as those by the defense lawyer successful in exonerating rapists.

5. In this setting, the only work regarded as part of the deconstruction school

that I have encountered that makes me hesitate even slightly in this characterization is Jean-François Lyotard, "The Differend, the Referent, and the Proper Name," *diacritics* 4 (Fall 1984). I read this work as an attack on the supposed difficulty of establishing that the Holocaust's gas chambers existed. It is, however, peculiar—and consistent with my critique here—that Lyotard does not mention that there are *Germans* who saw the gas chambers and survived to speak of their existence. His anatomy of silencing as a reality-disappearing device in its interconnection with the legal system in most useful, however. I am also unsure that this piece fits properly within deconstructicii as a theoretical approach.

6. Andrea Dworkin's brilliant article on pornography infused new meaning into Woolf's phrase. Andrea Dworkin, "Against the Male Flood: Censorship, Pornography, and Equality," 8 *Harvard Women's Law Journal* 1 (1985).

7. Diana E.H. Russell, *The Secret Trauma* (1986) and *Rape in Marriage* (1990); United States Merit Protection Board, *Sexual Harassment of Federal Workers: Is It a Problem?* (1981); *Sexual Harassment of Federal Workers: An Update* (1988); Majority Staff of U.S. Senate Judiciary Committee, *Violence against Women: A Week in the Life of America* (1992).

8. For further discussion, see Andrea Dworkin, "Woman-Hating Right and Left," in J. Raymond and D. Leidholdt, eds., *The Sexual Liberals and the Attack on Feminism* (1990).

9. As to the state's position on pornography, *American Booksellers Ass'n v. Hudnut*, 771 F.2d 323 (7th Cir. 1985), aff'd, 475 U.S. 1001 (1986), makes explicit the protection of pornography that years of posturing and neglect under obscenity law left to interpretation.

10. See his opinion in *Hudnut*, 771 F.2d at 323.

11. Ronald Dworkin, "Pornography, Feminism, and Liberty," *New York Review of Books*, Aug. 15, 1991.

12. Richard A. Posner, *Sex and Reason* (1992); *Miller v. City of South Bend*, 904 F.2d 1081, 1089–1104 (7th Cir. 1990) (Posner, J., concurring).

13. Edward DeGrazia, *Girls Lean Back Everywhere: The Law of Obscenity and the Assault on Genius* (1991).

14. I write about these issues in more detail in "Pornography as Defamation and Discrimination," 71 *Boston University Law Review* 793 (1991).

15. *United States v. American Airlines, Inc.*, 743 F.2d 1114 (5th Cir. 1984), cert. dismissed, 474 U.S. 1001 (1985) ("highly verbal crime," 1121; "Raise your goddamn . . ." and "We can talk about any . . ." are both on 1116).

16. *Palmer v. Thompson*, 403 U.S. 217 (1971) (holding that closure by city of Jackson, Mississippi, of public swimming pools formerly available to "whites only" did not violate equal protection clause of the Fourteenth Amendment because both blacks and whites were denied access); *Jones v. Alfred H. Mayer Co.*, 392 U.S. 409 (1968) (prohibiting discriminatory sale or rental of propery to "whites only"); *Blow v. North Carolina*, 379 U.S. 684 (1965) (holding that restaurant serving "whites only" violated Civil Rights Act of 1964); *Watson v. City of Memphis*, 373 U.S. 526 (1963) (holding that city's operation of large percentage of publicly owned recreational facilities for "whites only" due to delays in implementing desegregation violated the Fourteenth Amendment); see also *Hazelwood Sch. Dist. v. United States*, 433 U.S. 299, 304–5 n. 7 (1977) (stating that, in employment discrimination claim against school district, plaintiffs alleged that district's newspaper advertisement for teacher applicants specified "white only");

Pierson v. Ray, 386 U.S. 547, 558 (1967) (holding that black and white clergymen did not consent to their arrest by peacefully entering the "White Only" designated waiting area of bus terminal).

17. *The Yellow Spot: The Outlawing of Half a Million Human Beings* (1936) 176–77 (photos of "Jews not wanted" signs).

18. *Pittsburgh Press Co. v. Pittsburgh Comm'n on Human Relations*, 413 U.S. 376, 379 (1973) ("help wanted—male"); *Alexander v. Yale Univ.*, 459 F. Supp. 1, 3–4 (D. Conn. 1977), aff'd 631 F.2d 178 (2d Cir. 1984) (offer of "A" grade for sexual compliance); *Stockett v. Tolin*, 791 F. Supp. 1536, 1543 (S.D. Fla. 1992) ("F—me or you're fired"); *Hopkins v. Price Waterhouse*, 825 F.2d 458, 463 (D.C. Cir. 1987) ("walk more femininely . . ."); *Davis v. Passman*, 442 U.S. 228, 230 (1979) (". . .be a man").

19. *State v. Davidson*, 481 N.W.2d 51, 59 (Minn. 1992).

20. Documentation of the harm of pornography in real life is contained is Public Hearings on Ordinances to Add Pornography as Discrimination against Women, Minneapolis City Council, Government Operations Committee (Dec. 12 and 13, 1983); M. McManus, ed., *Final Report of the Attorney General's Commission on Pornography* (1986); *Pornography and Prostitution in Canada: Report of the Special Committees on Pornography and Prostitution* (1985). See also Diana E. H. Russell, "Pornography and Rape: A Causal Model," *Political Psychology* 9 (1988): 41; Gloria Cowan et al., "Dominance and Inequality in X-Rated Videocassettes," *Psychology of Women Quarterly* 12 (1988): 299, 306–7; Park E. Dietz and Alan E. Sears, "Pornography and Obscenity Sold in Adult Bookstores: A Survey of 5,132 Books, Magazines, and Films in Four American Cities," 21 *University of Michigan Journal of Law Reform* 7, 38–43 (1987–88) (documenting violence, bondage, sadomasochism, and gender differences in pornography); Neil M. Malamuth and Barry Spinner, "A Longitudinal Content Analysis of Sexual Violence in the Best-Selling Erotic Magazines," *Journal of Sexual Research* 16 (1980): 226–27 (documenting increases in violent sex in pornography).

21. Creel Froman, *Language and Power* (1992), 112.

22. *Olivia N. v. National Broadcasting Co.*, 141 Cal. Rptr. 511, 512 (1977), cert. denied sub nom. *Niemi v. National Broadcasting Co.*, 458 U.S. 1108 (1982) ("the complaint alleges that the assailants had seen the 'artificial rape' scene" on television).

23. This more sophisticated version is illustrated by Susanne Kappeler, *The Pornography of Representation* (1986).

24. "What matters for a legal system is what words *do*, not what they *say*. . . ." Edward J. Bloustein, "Holmes: His First Amendment Theory and His Pragmatist Bent," 40 *Rutgers Law Review* 283, 299 (1988).

25. *Personnel Administrator v. Feeney*, 442 U.S. 256 (1979); *Washington v. Davis*, 426 U.S. 229 (1976).

26. Postmodernism is premodern in the sense that it cannot grasp, or has forgotten, or its predicated on obscuring, this function of language in social hierarchy.

27. For an analysis of the place of pornography in male power, see Andrea Dworkin, *Pornography: Men Possessing Women* (1979), 13–47.

28. Andrea Dworkin has said this in many public speeches, including ones I attended in 1983 and 1984. The idea behind it was originally developed in her *Pornography: Men Possessing Women*, 48–100.

29. Andrea Dworkin, *Intercourse* (1987), 194.

SELECTION 46
FROM
Preventing Birth

JAMES W. KNIGHT AND
JOAN C. CALLAHAN

INTRODUCTION

OUR CENTRAL QUESTION IN this chapter is whether public policies permitting elective induced abortion and elective use of abortifacient birth control technologies are morally justifiable. . . .

PRENATAL MORAL STANDING: UNDERSTANDING
THE DEBATE

We supported Luker's (1984) suggestion that the contemporary abortion debate is so intractable because it involves a clash of complex worldviews. Embedded in these worldviews are opposing positions on the moral status of the prenatal human being.[1] Unhappily, the debate between those opposed to allowing elective abortion and those in favor all too often degenerates into mere assertion and the use of language which is "loaded" in a way that begs the question of the moral status of the prenatal human being. But it is not enough for those who oppose allowing elective abortion to call themselves "prolife" and to call conceptuses, embryos, and fetuses "babies" and take the matter to be settled. Nor is it enough for those who believe we must retain abortion as an option for women to call conceptuses, embryos, and fetuses "parasites" or to merely assert that women have a right to use their bodies as they see fit and take the matter to be settled. Trying to decide public policy responsibly must involve refusing to use language which implies that the opposition is against something any morally reasonable person would support or which simply begs the question. To call a prenatal human being a "baby" is already to assert that it has the moral standing and should therefore have the legal standing of a child. And to call a fetus a "parasite" is already to assert that it has no more moral standing and hence should have no more legal standing than a tumor. Such language on either side of the debate simply begs the question on the moral status of the prenatal human being and prevents rational discussion from proceeding.

Most opponents of elective abortion concede that women do have the important moral right to use their bodies as they see fit. But they argue that this right is limited when using one's body as one sees fit necessitates killing an innocent person. Thus, those who oppose permitting elective abortion hold that the argument based on this right to women also begs the question by simply assuming that prenatal human beings do not have the moral standing of persons. Most opponents of elective abortion insist that all human beings are persons from the moment of conception and that they must be treated as such from that moment.[2]

If prenatal human beings *are* persons, then moral consistency requires that we recognize that they have the same range of fundamental moral rights as persons generally, including the right not to be killed except for the most compelling moral reasons. Ordinarily, we believe that individual persons may not kill other persons except in cases of self-defense.[3] Thus, if prenatal human beings are persons, allowing elective abortion will not bear moral scrutiny. Further, our laws must be changed to preclude the elective use of induced abortion techniques, abortifacient birth control technologies, and contraceptives which might act as abortifacients, since only the moral reasons which justify killing persons generally will be sufficient to justify interfering with the establishment of even the earliest pregnancy. The crucial question, then, is whether we must accept that developing human beings are persons from conception onward and have the full range of fundamental moral rights possessed by all other persons.[4]

PRENATAL PERSONHOOD:
DECISION VERSUS DISCOVERY

Those who oppose elective abortion often say that "human life begins at conception." But it cannot be emphasized strongly enough that this is factually wrong. Life which is unquestionably human begins long before conception. Though not complete "human beings," human spermatozoa and ova are very much alive, and they are not bovine or feline or canine—they are living human gametes. To couch the question in terms of the beginning of life is really to muddle the issue, since this language makes the question of the morality of elective abortion seem like one that can be answered by a competent biologist. But the question is not when life begins. Life begins before conception, and the human conceptus, even at the very earliest stages, is unquestionably alive. What we want to know is whether the prenatal

human being should be recognized as a bearer of the same range of fundamental moral rights possessed by paradigmatic persons, among them the
right not to be killed without *very* good reason. The most able biologist in
the world cannot answer this for us, since the question is simply not a
biological one.

But it might be objected that although some who are opposed to elective
abortion and who have not thought carefully enough about the issue do
make the mistake of thinking that the question is when biological life begins, it is also true that not everyone who talks in terms of the beginning
of human life is making this mistake. For surely many who are opposed to
elective abortion mean to contend that the life of a *unique* human being, of
a distinct *person*, begins at conception and that it is because of this that
measures taken to prevent birth after conception are wrong.

The problem with this response, however, is that it is not a single claim.
For one can grant that the life of a unique human being *begins at* conception without granting that a distinct person *emerges at* conception, since
the two claims are not equivalent unless one begs the question in favor of
the personhood of the conceptus. That is, if one means by *human being* a
member of the biological species *Homo sapiens*, then it is uncontroversially
true that the life of a unique human being begins at conception. This is
merely a scientific claim, and it can be conclusively defended by scientists
as such. But the claim that a distinct person emerges at conception is not a
scientific one, for to call something a "person" is already to assert that it is
a bearer of moral rights. If in asserting that a human life begins at conception or that the life of a unique human being begins at conception the
opponent of elective abortion means to assert the biological claim, that can
be granted immediately. But if the opponent of elective abortion means to
assert that a person emerges at conception, this is an importantly different
claim. It is a moral claim and the very moral claim that is at issue in the
abortion debate. What the opponent of elective abortion needs to tell us is
why we must accept that the truth of the biological claim commits us to
accepting the moral claim.

But the opponent of elective abortion might assert that those who admit
that the life of a unique human being begins at conception are indeed committed to granting that, insofar as human conceptuses become distinct persons, the life of a distinct person begins here as well. For where did the life
of any adult person begin but at conception?

There are, however, at least two responses to this. The first is simply to
make the logical point that one can allow that the life of a person begins
at conception without allowing that the biologically human being present
at conception is yet a person. That is, just as one can allow that the first
tiny bud in an acorn is the beginning of the life of a future oak tree without

being committed to saying that the bud is already an oak tree, one can allow that conception marks the beginning of the life of a potential or future person without being committed to saying that the human conceptus is already a person.

This logical point leads to a second, more substantive response, namely, that we think the tiny bud in the acorn is quite clearly *not* an oak tree. And we think this because the bud does not yet have the characteristics of oak trees. Indeed, acorns with tiny buds are very unlike oak trees, even though every oak tree begins as a bud in an acorn. In just the same way, the new conceptus is very unlike beings who have the kinds of characteristics which compel us to recognize them as persons. What kinds of characteristics are these? We cannot offer a full account here. But perhaps it will be enough to point out that if we came across a being like E. T., a being that was not biologically human but that had certain characteristics we recognize paradigmatic persons as having (e.g., the capacity of suffer mental and physical pain, the ability to make plans, a sense of itself as an ongoing being), we would be compelled to hold that this being was a person and therefore must be treated in certain ways.[5] A human conceptus, however, has none of these characteristics. Indeed, like the mystery of the acorn and the oak, what is amazing is that such a radically *different* being will emerge from such a beginning.[6]

When, then, must we say of a developing human being that we must recognize it as a person? If we are talking about at what point in development we have a being with the kinds of characteristics that compel us to recognize it as a person, it seems that persons (at least human persons) are, like oak trees, emergent beings, and that deciding when to classify a developing human being as a person is like deciding when to classify a shoot as a tree. Very young trees lack many of the characteristics of grown trees (e.g., children cannot swing on them), but when a shoot begins to take on at least some of the characteristics of full-fledged trees, we think we are not confused in beginning to think of and speak of that shoot as a tree. Similarly, there is no clear distinction between where the Mississippi River ends and where the Gulf of Mexico begins. But we settle the issue by setting a *convention* that does not seem counterintuitive or unreasonable. We are faced with quite the same kind of question when it comes to the matter of human persons. Since prenatal human beings do not have the kinds of characteristics which compel us to recognize them as persons, we must, whether we like it or not, *decide* whether they are to be recognized (i.e., treated) as full-fledged persons as a matter of public policy even though they lack virtually all the morally relevant characteristics of paradigmatic persons.

THE CASE FOR PRENATAL PERSONHOOD:
THE LOGICAL WEDGE

One possible convention is to set the legal recognition of personhood at birth. Another is to set it at conception. Other conventions set the legal recognition of personhood at various stages of prenatality or at various points after birth. Those who oppose elective abortion generally insist that we *must* decide that personhood is to be recognized by the law from conception onward.

One common argument for this position is a theological one, resting on the doctrine of immediate animation, that is, the doctrine that a soul is infused by God at the moment of conception. This soul, it is held, is constitutive of personhood. This is the current dominant theory in Roman Catholicism. Interestingly, however, this has not always been the Roman Catholic view. Indeed, early, medieval, and premodern theologians (including St. Jerome [347–419], St. Augustine [354–430], Peter Lombard [1095–1160], St. Bonaventure [1221–1274], St. Thomas Aquinas [1227–1274], and the Council of Trent theologians [1566]) held that the human (or "rational") soul is not infused into the concepts until the conceptus takes on a characteristically human morphology, that is, a characteristically human shape with basic human organs (which occurs roughly by twelve weeks into gestation). This is the doctrine of mediate or delayed animation or hominization (see, e.g., Donceel 1970a, 1970b; Hurst 1983).

Reminiscent of the theological doctrine of delayed hominization is the secular doctrine of quickening utilized in British common law from the thirteenth century to 1803 and until the second half of the nineteenth century in American common law. Prior to the acceptance of Lord Ellenborough's Act by Parliament in 1803, abortion in England was not considered morally wrong, nor was it legally prohibited before the quickening of the fetus (i.e., the first perception of fetal movement by the pregnant women, usually around week sixteen of gestation). It was not until 1828, with the passage of New York's first statute dealing with abortion, that elective termination of pregnancy prior to quickening was proscribed by any American law. The legality of elective abortion prior to quickening was sustained at common law in a number of jurisdictions late into the nineteenth century (Quay 1960–61; Means 1968; Mohr 1978).

The secular ground for recognizing quickening as a significant point in gestation rested on the fetus's giving evidence of its capacity (ultimately) for independent survival, a reason, as we have seen, appealed to in slightly different form by the Court in *Roe*. But between 1860 and 1880, "regular" physicians stridently attacked the doctrine, arguing that gestation is a continuous process and that quickening is no more crucial to it than is any other point along the way to full development. Their moral campaign against elective abortion resulted in a burst of antiabortion legislation which left decisions regarding when a woman could procure a legal abortion in the hands of physicians (see, e.g., Mohr 1978).[7] The argument used against the moral relevance of quickening is one version of the central philosophical argument which is given today by opponents of elective abortion—an argument known as the *logical wedge*.

The logical wedge argument holds that if we are going to recognize adult human beings as persons with fundamental rights, including the right not to be killed, then logic compels us to recognize that, from the moment of conception, the human being must have those same rights. The argument proceeds by starting with beings everyone recognizes as having the rights in question and then by pointing out that a person at twenty-five, for example, is not radically different from one at twenty-four and a half, that a person at twenty-four and a half is not radically different from one at twenty-four, and so on. The argument presses us back from twenty-four to twenty-three to twenty-two and through adolescence and childhood to infancy. From infancy, it is a short step to late-term fetuses, because (the argument goes) change in location (from the womb to the wider world) does not constitute an essential change in the being itself. After all, you do not lose your right not to be killed simply by walking from one room to another. Similarly, it is argued, mere change of place is not philosophically important enough to justify a radical difference in treatment between infants and late-term fetuses.[8] The argument then presses us back to embryos and finally to conception, which is the only point in development where a clear line can be drawn between radically different kinds of beings. Logic and fairness, it is argued, force us to accept that even the zygote has the same fundamental right to life as the mature human being (e.g., Wertheimer 1971).

One objection to this argument is that conception itself is not clearly a discrete event. . . . it takes a bit of time for the conceptus to develop even into a two-celled being. Further, as we have also seen, until the blastocyst stage, the cells of the conceptus are not yet differentiated into the separate masses that will give rise to the placenta and embryo. . . . Thus, until the time of implantation, there is not even a very early embryo. But these biological facts are generally taken to be morally irrelevant by those who appeal to the wedge argument, since their reply is that it is still the case that after conception a being exists that is essentially and radically different in kind from the gametes which combined to issue in that new being. And this is why, it is held, conception is the only nonarbitrary point that can be used for marking the commencement of personhood and its attendant rights.

The significant objection to the wedge argument for prenatal personhood is that it turns on the assumption that we can never treat beings that are not radically different from one another in radically different ways. But if we accept this assumption, we shall be unable to justify all sorts of public policies which we believe are both necessary and fair. For example, this assumption entails that we cannot be justified in setting driving or voting ages, since withholding these privileges until a certain age unfairly discriminates against those who are close to that age (an eighteen-year-old is not radically different from a seventeen-year-old, and so on). Thus, the implication of the logical wedge argument is that setting ages for the commencement of certain important societal privileges cannot be morally justified: We must give the four-year-old the right to vote, the five-year-old the right to drink, the six-year-old the right to drive. But these implications, it is rightly argued, show that this kind of argument for prenatal rights is unsound (see, e.g., Glover 1977).

The response to this criticism of the argument, however, is that the granting of societal privileges is not fundamentally arbitrary even if there is some arbitrariness in selecting ages for the commencement of such privileges. Proper use of these rights, it may be argued, requires a certain degree of maturity— a sense of responsibility, background knowledge, experience, independence, and, in the case of driving, a certain degree of developed physical dexterity. Thus, it is because certain changes normally occur as a child matures into an adult that it is appropriate to set policies that acknowledge those changes. But this, it is further argued, is not the case when it comes to recognizing the right to life. That is, the proponent of this argument insists that after conception *no* changes occur that are relevant to recognizing the personhood, and thus the right to life, of a human being.

But this takes us back to the acorn and the oak. The bud and the tree simply are significantly different kinds of beings. And an adult human being simply is significantly different from a conceptus, which has none of the characteristics that compel us to recognize it as a being with the fundamental rights accruing to persons. Prenatal human beings do, of course, possess a full human genetic code. But this characteristic is neither necessary nor sufficient for personhood, since a genetically nonhuman being (recall E. T.) might possess the kinds of characteristics that compel recognition of it as a person, while any living human cell (e.g., a living skin cell) possesses a full human genetic code but is clearly not a person. It will not do, then, simply to assume that a human genetic code is sufficient to compel recognition of personhood. And it will not do simply to deny that there are significant, morally relevant changes between the time of conception and the time when we have a being which we unquestionably must recognize as a bearer of rights. Thus, we are once again confronted with the question of *deciding* where we shall set recognition of personhood and its attendant rights.

Notes

1. We shall use the term *prenatal* to refer to the full period of development from conception to birth. Calculating from conception, we shall use the term *conceptus* to refer to the developing human organism through the first two weeks of gestation, *embryo* to refer to the organism between weeks 2 and 6 of gestation, and *fetus* to refer to the organism from week 6 of gestation through birth. These stages are also commonly calculated from the first day of the last menstrual period, which adds roughly two weeks to their calculation (i.e., the conceptus stage is weeks 1–4, the embryonic stage is weeks 4–8, and the fetal stage is week 8 through birth).
2. Although in the clearest cases, persons are beings, which are understood to possess moral rights and have moral duties, it is customary in the abortion debate to discuss personhood exclusively in terms of prenatal rights and to put aside the question of duties. We follow this custom.
3. There may be other cases where killing is also justified, for example, in defense of one's country.
4. For an argument supporting allowing elective abortion which begins by assuming (for the sake of the debate) that prenatal human beings are persons, see Thomson (1971). Thomson suggests a thought experiment, which involves imagining that a violinist is unwelcomely hooked up to one's kidneys and will die unless he remains connected. Assume the connection is necessary for some months (i.e., comparable to bringing a fetus to term or viability). Thomson argues that even though the violinist is clearly a person with a strong right to life, and even though it would be "decent" of one to stay attached for the duration, disconnecting the violinist would not violate any of his moral rights. We mention this position only to set it aside, since many people have argued that the analogy between Thomson's example and pregnancy fails. For another discussion contending that the question of personhood is irrelevant to determining the morality of elective abortion, see Lomansky (1984).
5. Notice that films like *E. T.* turn on just this insight. In that film, the children recognize that E. T. is a person with the moral rights that attend personhood. The adults (particularly the bureaucrats) fail to see this. The audience, of course, identifies with the children.
6. For discussions of the kinds of characteristics which compel recognition of beings (including nonhuman beings) as persons, see, e.g., Warren (1973, 1985), English (1975), Fletcher (1979), Tooley (1972, 1983, 1984), and Feinberg (1980). For a somewhat different approach to the question of personhood, see Solomon (1983).
7. Regular physicians were generally the most highly educated and professionalized of nineteenth-century medical practitioners, who organized and took the political steps which led to the full professionalization of medicine as a licensed practice. See, e.g., Mohr (1978), Luker (1984), Petchesky (1984), and Hartmann (1987).
8. Much the same is said of the various physiological changes accompanying birth and closely following birth. That is, these changes are held not to transform the essential nature of the young human being and therefore not to be of moral import. Another way of arguing for the position we shall defend might include holding that such changes *are* of moral import, since once they occur, the young human being can be supported by persons other than its biological mother.

References

Callahan, Joan C. 1986a. "The Fetus and Fundamental Rights." *Commonweal* 11 (April): 203. Rev. and expanded in *Abortion and Catholicism: The American Debate*, ed. Thomas A. Shannon and Patricia B. Jung. New York: Crossroads.

———. 1986b. "The Silent Scream: A New, Conclusive Argument against Abortion?" Philosophy Research Archives 11 (1985): 181.

Donceel, Joseph F. 1970a. "Immediate Animation and Delayed Hominization." *Theological Studies* 31:76.

———. 1970b. "A Liberal Catholic's View." In *Abortion in a Changing World*, vol. 1, ed. Robert E. Hall. New York: Columbia University Press.

English, Jane. 1975. "Abortion and the Concept of a Person." *Canadian Journal of Philosophy* 5:233.

Feinberg, Joel. 1980. "Abortion." In *Matters of Life and Death*, ed. Tom Regan. New York: Random House.

Fletcher, Joseph. 1979. *Humanhood: Essays in Biomedical Ethics*. Buffalo, NY: Prometheus.

Glover, Jonathon. 1977. *Causing Death and Saving Lives* New York: Penguin.

Hartmann, Betsy. 1987. *Reproductive Rights and Wrongs: The Global Politics of Population Control and Contraceptive Choice*. New York: Harper and Row.

Hurst, Jane. 1983. *The History of Abortion in the Catholic Church*. Washington, DC: Catholics for a Free Choice.

Lomansky, Loren E. 1984. "Being a Person—Does It Matter?" In *The Problem of Abortion*, 2d ed., ed. Joel Feinberg. Belmont, CA: Wadsworth.

Luker, Kristen. 1984. *Abortion and the Politics of Motherhood*. Berkeley: University of California Press.

Means, Cyril C. 1968. "The Laws of New York Concerning Abortion and the Status of the Fetus, 1644–1968: A Case of Cessation of Constitutionality." *New York Law Forum* 14:419.

Mohr, James C. 1978. *Abortion in America: The Origins and Evolution of a National Policy, 1800–1900*. New York: Oxford University Press.

Petchesky, Rosalind Pollack. 1984. *Abortion and Women's Choice: The State, Sexuality, and Reproductive Freedom*. New York: Longman. Reissued, Northeastern Series in Feminist Theory, Boston: Northeastern University Press, 1985.

Quay, Eugene. 1960–61. "Justifiable Abortion: Medical and Legal Foundations," parts 1, 2. *Georgetown Law Journal* 49:173, 295.

Solomon, Robert C. 1983. "Reflections on the Meaning of (Fetal) Life." In *Abortion and the Status of the Fetus*, ed. William B. Bondeson, H. T. Engelhardt Jr., Stuart F. Spicker, and Daniel H. Winship. Boston: D. Reidel.

Thomson, Judith Jarvis. 1971. "A Defense of Abortion." *Philosophy and Public Affairs* 1:173.

Tooley, Michael. 1972. "Abortion and Infanticide." *Philosophy and Public Affairs* 2:37.

———. 1983. *Abortion and Infanticide*. New York: Oxford University Press.

———. 1984. "A Defense of Abortion and Infanticide." In *The Problem of Abortion*, ed. Joel Feinberg. Belmont, CA: Wadsworth.

Warren, Mary Anne. 1973. "On the Moral and Legal Status of Abortion." *Monist* 57:120.

———. 1985. *Gendercide: The Implications of Sex Selection*. Totowa, NJ: Rowman and Allanheld.

Wertheimer, Roger. 1971. "Understanding the Abortion Argument." *Philosophy and Public Affairs* 1:67.

SELECTION 47
FROM
Selling Babies and Selling Bodies

SARA ANN KETCHUM

THE "BABY M" CASE turned into something approaching a national soap opera, played out in newspapers and magazines. The drama surrounding the case tends to obscure the fact that the case raises some very abstract philosophical and moral issues. It forces us to examine questions about the nature and meaning of parenthood, of the limits of reproductive autonomy, of how the facts of pregnancy should affect our analysis of sexual equality,[1] and of what counts as selling people and of what forms (if any) of selling people we should honor in law and what forms we should restrict. It is this last set of questions whose relevance I will be discussing here. One objection to what is usually called "surrogate motherhood" and which I will call "contracted motherhood" (CM) or "baby contracts"[2] is that it commercializes reproduction and turns human beings (the mother and/or the baby) into objects of sale. If this is a compelling objection, there is a good argument for prohibiting (and/or not enforcing contracts for) commercial CM. Such a prohibition would be similar to laws on black market adoptions and would have two parts, at least: (1) a prohibition of commercial companies who make the arrangements and/or (2) a prohibition on the transfer of money to the birth mother for the transfer of custody (beyond expenses incurred) (Warnock 1985, 46–47). I will also argue that CM law should follow adoption law in making clear that prebirth agreements to relinquish parental rights are not binding and will not be enforced by the courts (the birth mother should not be forced to give up her child for adoption).[3]

CM AND AID: THE REAL DIFFERENCE PROBLEM

CM is usually presented as a new reproductive technology and, moreover, as the female equivalent of AID (artificial insemination by donor) and, therefore, as an extension of the right to privacy or the right to make medical decisions about one's own life. There are two problems with this description: (1) CM uses the same technology as AID—the biological arrangements are exactly the same—but intends an opposite assignment of custody. (2) No technology is necessary for CM, as is evidenced by the biblical story of Abraham and Sarah who used a "handmaid" as a birth mother. Since artificial insemination is virtually uncontroversial[4] it seems clear that what makes CM controversial is not the technology, but the social arrangements— that is, the custody assignment. CM has been defended on the ground that such arrangements enable fertile men who are married to infertile women to reproduce and, thus, are parallel to AID which enables fertile women whose husbands are infertile to have children. It is difficult not to regard these arguments as somewhat disingenuous. The role of the sperm donor and the role of the egg donor/mother are distinguished by pregnancy, and pregnancy is, if anything is, a "real difference" which would justify us in treating women and men differently. To treat donating sperm as equivalent to biological motherhood would be as unfair as treating the unwed father who has not contributed to his children's welfare the same as the father who has devoted his time to taking care of them. At most, donating sperm is comparable to donating ova; however, even that comparison fails because donating ova is a medically risky procedure, whereas donating sperm is not.

Therefore, the essential morally controversial features of CM have to do with its nature as a social and economic institution and its assignment of family relationships rather than with any technological features. Moreover, the institution of CM requires of contracting birth mothers much more time commitment, medical risk, and social disruption than AID does of sperm donors. It also requires substantial male control over women's bodies and time, while AID neither requires nor provides any female control over men's bodies. Christine Overall (1987, 181–85) notes that when a woman seeks AID, she not only does not usually have a choice of donor, but she also may be required to get her husband's consent if she is married. The position of the man seeking CM is the opposite; he chooses a birth mother and his wife does not have to consent to the procedure (although the mother's husband does).[5] The contract entered into by Mary Beth Whitehead and William Stern contains a number of provisions regulating her behavior, including: extensive medical examinations, an agreement about when she may or may not abort, an agreement to follow doctor's orders, and agreements not to take even prescription drugs without the doctor's permission.

Some of these social and contractual provisions are eliminable. But the fact that CM requires a contract and AID does not reflects the differences between pregnancy and ejaculation. If the sperm donor wants a healthy child (a good product), he needs to control the woman's behavior. In contrast, any damage the sperm donor's behavior will have on the child will be present in the sperm and could, in principle, be tested for before the women enters the AID procedure. There is no serious moral problem with discarding defective sperm; discarding defective children is a quite different matter.

COMMODIFICATION

There are three general categories of moral concern with commercializing either adoption (baby selling) or reproductive activities. The three kinds of argument are not always separated and they are not entirely separable:

(1) There is the Kantian argument, based on a version of the Second Formulation of the Categorical Imperative. On this argument, selling people is objectionable because it is treating them as means rather than as ends, as objects rather than as persons. People who can be bought and sold are being treated as being of less moral significance than are those who buy and sell. Allowing babies to be bought and sold adds an extra legal wedge between the status of children and that of adults, and allowing women's bodies to be bought and sold (or "rented" if you prefer) adds to the inequality between men and women. Moreover, making babies and women's bodies available for sale raises specters of the rich "harvesting" the babies of the poor. (2) Consequentialist objections are fueled by concern for what may happen to the children and women who are bought and sold, to their families, and to the society as a whole if we allow an area of this magnitude and traditional intimacy to become commercialized. (3) Connected to both 1 and 2 are concerns about protecting the birth mother and the mother-child relationship from the potential coerciveness of commercial transactions. These arguments apply slightly differently depending on whether we analyze the contracts as baby contracts (selling babies) or as mother contracts (as a sale of women's bodies), although many of the arguments will be very similar for both.

Selling Babies: The most straightforward argument for prohibiting baby selling is that it is selling a human being and that any selling of a human being should be prohibited because it devalues human life and human individuals. This argument gains moral force from its analogy with slavery. Defenders of baby contracts argue that baby selling is unlike selling slaves in that it is a transfer of parental rights rather than of ownership of the child—the adoptive parents cannot turn around and sell the baby to another couple for a profit (Landes and Posner 1978, 344). What the defenders of CM fail to do is provide an account of the wrongness of slavery such that baby selling (or baby contracts) do not fall under the argument. Landes and Posner, in particular, would, I think, have difficulty establishing an argument against slavery because they are relying on utilitarian arguments. Since one of the classic difficulties with utilitarianism is that it cannot yield an argument that slavery is wrong in principle, it is hardly surprising that utilitarians will find it difficult to discover within that theory an argument against selling babies. Moreover, their economic argument is not even utilitarian because it only counts people's interests to the extent that they can pay for their satisfaction.

Those who, unlike Landes and Posner, defend CM while supporting laws against baby selling distinguish CM from paid adoptions in that in CM the person to whom custody is being transferred is the biological (genetic) father. This suggests a parallel to custody disputes, which are not obviously any more appropriately ruled by money than is adoption. We could argue against the commercialization of either on the grounds that child-regarding concerns should decide child custody and that using market criteria or contract considerations would violate that principle by substituting another, unrelated, and possibly conflicting, one. In particular, both market and contract are about relations between the adults involved rather than about the children or about the relationship between the child and the adult.

Another disanalogy cited between preadoption contracts and CM is that in preadoption contracts the baby is already there (that is, the preadoption contract is offered to a woman who is already pregnant, and, presumably, planning to have the child), while the mother contract is a contract to create a child who does not yet exist, even as an embryo. If our concern is the commodification of children, this strikes me as an odd point for the *defenders* of CM to emphasize. Producing a child to order for money is a paradigm case of commodifying children. The fact that the child is not being put up for sale to the highest bidder, but is only for sale to the genetic father, may reduce some of the harmful effects of an open market in babies but does not quiet concerns about personhood.

Arguments for allowing CM are remarkably similar to the arguments for legalizing black-market adoptions in the way they both define the problem. CM, like a market for babies, is seen as increasing the satisfaction and freedom of infertile individuals or couples by increasing the quantity of the desired product (there will be more babies available for adoption) and the quality of the product (not only more white healthy babies, but white healthy babies who are genetically related to one of the purchasers). These arguments tend to be based on the interests of infertile couples and obscure the relevance of the interests of the birth mothers (who will be giving the children up for adoption) and their families, the children who are produced by the demands of the market, and (the most invisible and most troubling group) needy children who are without homes because they are not "high-quality" products and because we are not, as a society, investing the time and money needed to place the hard-to-adopt children. If we bring these hidden interests to the fore, they raise a host of issues about consequences— both utilitarian issues and issues about the distribution of harms and benefits.

Perhaps the strongest deontological argument against baby selling is an objection to the characterization of the mother-child relationship (and, more generally, of the adult-child relationship) that it presupposes. Not only does the baby become an object of commerce, but the custody relationship of the parent becomes a property relationship. If we see parental custody rights as correlates of parental responsibility or as a right to maintain a relationship, it will be less tempting to think of them as something one can sell. We have good reasons for allowing birth mothers to relinquish their children because otherwise we would be forcing children into the care of people who either do not want them or feel themselves unable to care for them. However, the fact that custody may be waived in this way does not entail that it may be sold or transferred. If children are not property, they cannot be gifts either. If a mother's right is a right to maintain a relationship (see Ketchum 1987), it is implausible to treat it as transferable; having the option of terminating a relationship with A does not entail having the option of deciding who A will relate to next—the right to a divorce does not entail the right to transfer one's connection to one's spouse to someone else. Indeed, normally, the termination of a relationship with A ends any right I have to make moral claims on A's relationships. Although in giving up responsibilities I may have a responsibility to see to it that someone will shoulder them when I go, I do not have a right to choose that person.

Selling Women's Bodies: Suppose we do regard mother contracts as contracts for the sale or rental of reproductive capacities. Is there good reason for including reproductive capacities among those things or activities that ought not to be bought and sold? We might distinguish between selling reproductive capacities and selling work on a number of grounds. A conservative might argue against commercializing reproduction on the grounds that it disturbs family relationships,[6] or on the grounds that there are some categories of human activities that should not be for sale. A Kantian might argue that there are some activities that are close to our personhood[7] and that a commercial traffic in these activities constitutes treating the person as less than an end (or less than a person).

One interpretation of the laws prohibiting baby selling is that they are an attempt to reduce or eliminate coercion in the adoption process, and are thus based on a concern for the birth mother rather than (or as well as) the child. All commercial transactions are at least potentially coercive in that the parties to them are likely to come from unequal bargaining positions and in that, whatever we have a market in, there will be some people who will be in a position such that they have to sell it in order to survive. Such concerns are important to arguments against an open market in human organs or in the sexual use of people's bodies as well as arguments against baby contracts of either kind.

As Margaret Radin suggests (1987, 1915–21), the weakness of arguments of this sort—that relationships or contracts are exploitative on the grounds that people are forced into them by poverty—is that the real problem is not in the possibility of commercial transactions, but in the situation that makes these arrangements attractive by comparison. We do not end the feminization of poverty by forbidding prostitution or CM. Indeed, if we are successful in eliminating these practices, we may be reducing the income of some women (by removing ways of making money) and, if we are unsuccessful, we are removing these people from state protection by making their activities illegal. Labor legislation which is comparably motivated by concern for unequal bargaining position (such as, for example, minimum wage and maximum hours laws, and health and safety regulations) regulates rather than prevents that activity and is thus less vulnerable to this charge. Radin's criticism shows that the argument from the coerciveness of poverty is insufficient as a support for laws rejecting commercial transactions in personal services. This does not show that the concern is irrelevant. The argument from coercion is still an appropriate response to simple voluntarist arguments—those that assume that these activities are purely and freely chosen by all those who participate in them. Given the coerciveness of the situation, we cannot assume that the presumed or formal voluntariness of the contract makes it nonexploitative.

If the relationship of CM is, by its nature, disrespectful of personhood, it can be exploitative despite short-term financial benefits to some women. The disrespect for women as persons that is fundamental to the relationship lies in the concept of the woman's body (and of the child and mother-child relationship) implicit in the contract. I have argued elsewhere (1984) that claiming a welfare right to another person's body is to treat that person as an object:

> An identity or intimate relation between persons and their bodies may or may not be essential to our metaphysical understanding of a person, but it is essential to a minimal moral conceptual scheme. Without a concession to persons' legitimate interests and concerns for their physical selves, most of our standard and paradigm moral rules would not make sense; murder might become the mere destruction of the body; assault, a mere interference with the body . . . and so on. We cannot make sense out of the concept of assault unless an assault on S's body is ipso facto an assault

on S. By the same token, treating another person's body as part of my domain—as among the things that I have a rightful claim to—is, if anything is, a denial that there is a person there. (1984, 34–35)

This argument is, in turn, built on the analysis of the wrongness of rape developed by Marilyn Frye and Carolyn Shafer in "Rape and Respect" (1977):

> The use of a person in the advancement of interests contrary to its own is a limiting case of disrespect. It reveals the perception of the person simply as an object which can serve some purpose, a tool or a bit of material, and one which furthermore is dispensable or replaceable and thus of little value even as an object with a function. (341)

We can extend this argument to the sale of persons. To make a person or a person's body an object of commerce is to treat the person as part of another person's domain, particularly if the sale of A to B gives B rights to A or to A's body. What is objectionable is a claim—whether based on welfare or on contract—to a right to another person such that that person is part of my domain. The assertion of such a right is morally objectionable even without the use of force. For example, a man who claims to have a *right* to sexual intercourse with his wife, on the grounds of the marriage relationship, betrays a conception of her body, and thus her person, as being properly within this domain, and thus a conception of her as an object rather than a person.

Susan Brownmiller in *Against Our Will* (1975) suggests that prostitution is connected to rape in that prostitution makes women's bodies into consumer goods that might—if not justifiably, at least understandably—be forcibly taken by those men who see themselves as unjustly deprived.

> When young men learn that females may be bought for a price, and that acts of sex command set prices, then how should they not also conclude that that which my be bought may also be taken without the civility of a monetary exchange? . . . Legalized prostitution institutionalizes the concept that it is a man's monetary right, if not his divine right, to gain access to the female body, and that sex is a female service that should not be denied the civilized male. (391, 392)

The same can be said for legalized sale of women's reproductive services. The more hegemonic this commodification of women's bodies is, the more the woman's lack of consent to sex or to having children can present itself as unfair to the man because it is arbitrary.

A market in women's bodies—whether sexual prostitution or reproductive prostitution—reveals a social ontology in which women are among the things in the world that can be appropriately commodified—bought and sold and, by extension, stolen. The purported freedom that such institutions would give women to enter into the market by selling their bodies is paradoxical. Sexual or reproductive prostitutes enter the market not so much as *agents* or subjects, but as commodities or objects. This is evidenced by the fact that the pimps and their counterparts, the arrangers of baby contracts, make the bulk of the profits. Moreover, once there is a market for women's bodies, all women's bodies will have a price, and the woman who does not sell her body becomes a hoarder of something that is useful to other people and is financially valuable. The market is a hegemonic institution; it determines the meanings of actions of people who choose not to participate as well as of those who choose to participate.

Contract: The immediate objection to treating the Baby M case as a contract dispute is that the practical problem facing the court is a child custody problem and to treat it as a contract case is to deal with it on grounds other than the best interests of the child. That the "best interests of the child" count need not entail that contract does not count, although it helps explain one of the reasons we should be suspicious of this particular contract. There is still the question of whether the best interests of the child will trump contract considerations (making the contract nonbinding) or merely enter into a balancing argument in which contract is one of the issues to be balanced. However, allowing contract to count at all raises some of the same Kantian objections as the commodification problem. As a legal issue, the contract problem is more acute because the state action (enforcing the contract) is more explicit.

Any binding mother contract will put the state in the position of enforcing the rights of a man to a women's body or to his genetic offspring. But this is to treat the child or the mother's body as objects of the sperm donor's rights, which, I argued above, is inconsistent with treating them as persons. This will be clearest if the courts enforce specific performance[8] and require the mother to go through with the pregnancy (or to abort) if she chooses not to or requires the transfer of custody to the contracting sperm donor on grounds other than the best interests of the child. In those cases, I find it hard to avoid the description that what is being awarded is a person and what it being affirmed is a right to a person. I think the Kantian argument still applies if the court refuses specific performance but awards damages. Damages compensate for the loss of something to which one has a right. A judge who awards damages to the contracting sperm donor for having been deprived of use of the contracting woman's reproductive capacities or for being deprived of custody of the child gives legal weight to the idea that the contracting sperm donor had a legally enforceable *right* to them (or, to put it more bluntly, to those commodities or goods).

The free contract argument assumes that Mary Beth Whitehead's claims to her daughter are rights (rather than, for example, obligations or a more complex relationship), and, moreover, that they are alienable, as are property rights. If the baby is not something she has an alienable right to, then custody of the baby is not something she can transfer by contract. In cases where the state is taking children away from their biological parents and in custody disputes, we do want to appeal to some rights of the parents. However, I think it would be unfortunate to regard these rights as rights to the child, because that would be to treat the child as the object of the parents' rights and violate the principles that persons and persons' bodies cannot be the objects of other people's rights. The parents' rights in these cases should be to consideration, to nonarbitrariness, and to respect for the relationship between the parent and the child.

CONCLUDING REMARKS

The Kantian, person-respecting arguments I have been offering do not provide an account of all of the moral issues surrounding CM. However, I think that they can serve as a counterbalance to arguments (also Kantian) for CM as an expression of personal autonomy.[9] They might also add some weight to the empirical arguments against CM that are accumulating. There is increasing concern that women cannot predict in advance whether or not they and their family[10] will form an attachment to the child they will bear nor can they promise not to develop such feelings (as some of the contracts ask them to do). There is also increasing concern for the birth family and for the children produced by the arrangement (particularly where there is a custody dispute). A utilitarian might respond that the problems are outweighed by the joys of the adopting/sperm donor families, but, if so, we must ask: Are we simply shifting the misery from wealthy (or wealthier) infertile couples to poorer fertile families and to the "imperfect" children waiting for adoption?

These considerations provide good reason for prohibiting commercialization of CM. In order to do that we could adopt new laws prohibiting the transfer of money in such arrangements or simply extend existing adoption laws, making the contracts nonbinding as are prebirth adoption contracts (Cohen 1984, 280–84) and limiting the money that can be transferred. There are some conceptual problems remaining about what would count as prohibiting commodification. I find the English approach very attractive. This approach has the following elements: (1) It strictly prohibits third parties from arranging mother contracts; (2) if people arrange them privately, they are allowed; (3) the contracts are not binding. If the birth mother decides to keep the baby, her decision is final[11] (and the father may be required to pay child support; that may be too much for Americans); (4) although, in theory, CM is covered by limitations on money for adoption, courts have approved payments for contracted motherhood, and there is never a criminal penalty on the parents for money payments.[12]

Notes

1. In "Is There a Right to Procreate?" (1987b), I argue that there is an asymmetry between the right not to reproduce (as in the right to access to abortion and contraception) and the right to reproduce in that a decision to reproduce (unlike a decision not to reproduce) involves two other persons—the person who is to be produced and the person who is the other biological parent. Thus, the claim of a privacy right to reproduce is a claim to a right to make decisions about other people's lives, and those people's rights and interests must be weighed in the balance. Furthermore, I will argue (and this paper is part of that argument) that issues of reproductive privacy cannot be entirely separated from issues of sexual equality.

2. Terms such as "surrogate mother" and "renting a womb" are distortions—the surrogate mother *is* the mother, and she is giving up her child for adoption just as is the birth mother who gives up her child for adoption by an unrelated person. This language allows the defenders of paternal rights to argue for the importance of biological (genetic) connection when it comes to the *father's* rights, but bury the greater physical connection between the mother and the child in talk that suggests that mothers are mere receptacles (shades of Aristotle's biology) or that the mother has a more artificial relationship to the child than does the father or the potential adoptive mother. But, at the time of birth, the natural relationship is between the mother and child. (I discuss this issue further in "New Reproductive Technologies and the Definition of Parenthood: A Feminist Perspective" [1987a].) A relationship created by contract is the paradigm of artificiality, of a socially created relationship, and the most plausible candidate for a natural social relationship is the mother-child bond. I will be using "contracted motherhood" and "baby contracts" (a term offered by Elizabeth Bartholet) rather than "surrogate motherhood" and "surrogacy." I will use "baby contracts" as the more general term, covering paid adoption contracts as well as so-called surrogate mother arrangements. I have not yet found a term that is either neutral between or inclusive of the motherhood aspects and the baby-regarding aspects.

3. She may still lose a custody fight, since the male of the adopting couple is the genetic father of the child, but in that case, she would still be the legal mother of the child and have a right to maintain a relationship.

4. I do not mean to suggest that there are no moral problems with AID. See Krimmel (1983) for an approach that presents arguments against both.

5. Indeed, there is a technical reason for her not to sign the contract. The wife of the sperm donor in CM intends to adopt the resulting child. If she is a party to the contract, it would be more difficult to avoid the conclusion that the arrangement exchanges money for adoption and is thus contrary to baby-selling laws.

6. Robert C. Black (1981) argues, in response to an argument of this sort, that "in any realistic view of the situation, the only 'family' whose future is at stake is the one the child is predestined to enter—that of the childless married couple—not the *nominal, intentionally temporary 'family'* represented by the surrogate mother" (382, emphasis added). Surely, this is a disingenuous response. Mary Beth Whitehead's family is just as much a family as the Sterns' (and it is larger); even if we are to ignore her, we must consider the interests of her children (what effect does it have on them that their half-sister is being sold to another family?) and her husband and the integrity of the family unit. Some

surrogates report problems their children have with the arrangement in "Baby M: Surrogate Mothers Vent Feelings," by Iver Peterson (1987).

7. This is the position that Margaret Radin (1987) develops and relies on in "Market-Inalienability." "Market-inalienability ultimately rests on our best conception of human flourishing . . ." (1937). Radin's article provides a very thorough discussion of and argument for prohibiting commodification of personal services.

8. M. Louise Graham (1982) argues that traditional contract doctrine and precedent would prohibit requiring specific performance against the birth mother:

> The rule that a contract for distinctly personal, nondelegable services will not be enforced by specific performance is nearly universal. The reasons given for the refusal to enforce are the difficulty of gauging the quality of any performance rendered, prejudice against a species of involuntary servitude, and a reluctance to force a continued relationship between antagonistic parties. (301)

9. See, for example, Joan Hollinger (1985, 865–932) for a well-developed analysis of new reproductive technology issues as pure (or almost pure) autonomy issues.

10. One former surrogate reports that her daughter (eleven at the time of the birth and now seventeen) is still having problems: "Nobody told me that a child could bond with a baby while you're still pregnant. I didn't realize then that all the times she listened to his heartbeat and felt his legs kick that she was becoming attached to him." Another quotes her son as having asked, "You're not going to give them me, are you?" (Peterson 1987, B1).

11. This presupposes a presumption in favor of the birth mother as custodial or deciding parent. I have argued for that position on the grounds that, at the time of birth, the gestational mother has a concrete relationship to the child that the genetic father (and the genetic mother, if she is not the gestational mother) does not have (Ketchum 1987a). Without that presumption and without a presumption of sale or contract, each case would be subject to long custody disputes.

12. This, I think, helps us get around Radin's double-bind problem (1987, 1915–21).

References

Black, Robert. 1981. "Legal Problems of Surrogate Motherhood." *New England Law Review* 16 (3): 380–92.

Brownmiller, Susan. 1975. *Against Our Will: Men, Women, and Rape*. New York: Simon and Schuster.

Cohen, Barbara. 1984. "Surrogate Mothers: Whose Baby Is It?" *American Journal of Law and Medicine* 10:243–85.

Frye, Marilyn, and Carolyn Shafer. 1977. "Rape and Respect." In *Feminism and Philosophy*. Mary Vetterling-Braggin, Frederick A. Elliston, and Jane English, eds. Totowa, NJ: Littlefield, Adams.

Graham, M. Louise. 1982. "Surrogate Gestation and the Protection of Choice." *Santa Clara Law Review* 22:291–323.

Hollinger, Joan Heifetz. 1985. "From Coitus to Commerce: Legal and Social Consequences of Noncoital Reproduction." *Michigan Journal of Law Reform* 18:865–932.

Ketchum, Sara Ann. 1984. "The Moral Status of the Bodies of Persons." *Social Theory and Practice* 10:25–38.

————. 1987a. "New Reproductive Technologies and the Definition of Parenthood: A Feminist Perspective." Presented at Feminism and Legal Theory: Women and Intimacy, a conference sponsored by the Institute for Legal Studies at the University of Wisconsin–Madison.

————. 1987b. "Is There a Right to Procreate?" Presented at the Pacific Division Meetings of the American Philosophical Association.

Krimmel, Herbert. 1983. "The Case against Surrogate Parenting. *Hastings Center Report* 13 (5): 35–39.

Landes, Elizabeth A., and Richard M. Posner. 1978. "The Economics of the Baby Shortage." *Journal of Legal Studies* 7:323–48.

Overall, Christine. 1987. Ethics and Human Reproduction. Boston: Allen and Unwin.

Peterson, Iver. 1987. "Baby M: Surrogate Mothers Vent Feelings." *New York Times*, March 2, 1987, B1, B4.

Radin, Margaret. 1987. "Market-Inalienability." *Harvard Law Review* 100:1849–937.

Warnock, Mary. 1985. *A Question of Life: The Warnock Report on Human Fertilization and Embryology.* Oxford: Basil Blackwell.

SELECTION 48

Commodification or Compensation: A Reply to Ketchum

H. M. MALM

THE PRACTICE OF SURROGATE motherhood raises at least three sorts of moral questions.[1] First, there are questions about the nature of surrogate motherhood itself. Is there something inherently wrong, for example, with intentionally becoming pregnant when one does not intend to raise the child? Second, there are questions about the status of the arrangements when they involve a transfer of money. Is it morally wrong for one person to offer, and another person to accept, payment for being a surrogate mother? What is being purchased? Third, there are questions about the legal status of the arrangements. Should they be regarded as binding contracts?

Sara Ketchum (1988) addresses questions of the second sort in "Selling Babies and Selling Bodies." She argues for a ban on paid surrogacy arrangements by arguing that persons are not the sort of thing that may be bought, sold, or rented. In one sense Ketchum's arguments are successful. She has shown us, or perhaps reminded us of *why* it is wrong to treat persons as objects of sale. In another sense they are unsuccessful. For while she intends her arguments to provide grounds for prohibiting paid surrogacy arrangements, she has not argued that these arrangements *do in fact* treat persons as objects of sale. That is, while she has defended premise 1 in the following argument, she has not defended premise 2.

1. It is morally wrong to treat persons, including babies, as objects of sale.
2. Paid surrogate motherhood arrangements treat persons as objects of sale.
3. Therefore, paid surrogacy arrangements are morally objectionable.

The failure to defend premise 2 is not simply a failure to defend the obvious. Though it is possible that the payments made in paid surrogacy

468

arrangements are payments for the baby, or for the use of the woman's body, it is also possible that they are not.. They may be payments for the woman's services—compensation, that is, for the efforts and risks of bearing a child, e.g., not drinking coffee or alcohol for nine months, not engaging in enjoyable but potentially dangerous activities, for the risks involved in giving birth, and for the effort it may take to return her body to the condition it was in prior to pregnancy.

In this essay I develop the distinction between compensating a woman for her services, and paying a woman for the use of her body, and then evaluate some of Ketchum's arguments in its light. I argue that since this distinction allows us to reject premise 2, we cannot prohibit paid surrogacy arrangements on the grounds that they treat persons as objects of sale. I then discuss some of Ketchum's arguments that can be offered against the compensation-view of the payments. I argue that they too provide inadequate grounds for prohibiting the arrrangements.[2]

I

Ketchum's acceptance of premise 2 can be seen in the structure of her paper and in some of its particular passages. After introducing the topic of paid surrogacy arrangements, she distinguishes three sorts of arguments that may be raised against the commodification of persons.

> 1) There is the Kantian argument . . . [that] selling people is objectionable because it is treating them as means rather than ends, as objects rather than persons. . . . 2) Consequentialist objections are fueled by concern for what may happen to the *children and women who are bought and sold.* . . . 3) Connected to both 1 and 2, there are concerns about protecting the birth mother and the mother-child relationship from the potential coerciveness of commercial transactions. These arguments apply slightly differently *depending on whether we analyze the contracts as baby contracts (selling babies) or as mother contracts (as the sale of women's bodies)* although many of the arguments will apply to both. (emphasis added) (Ketchum 1989, 118)

She then offers a number of particular arguments explaining why it is wrong to treat persons as objects of sale, and concludes by claiming "these considerations provide good reason for prohibiting commercialization of [surrogate] motherhood" (Ketchum 1989, 124). But absent from Ketchum's discussion is an argument that *connects* paid surrogacy arrangements *with* the commodification of persons. Without this argument, even the most forceful arguments about the wrongness of selling people cannot do the work she wants them to do.

The question before us may be stated as follows: Are we committed to viewing the payments made in paid surrogacy arrangements as payments for either the baby itself or for the use of the woman's body? To see that we are not, it will be helpful if we first grant, as Ketchum does, that the payments made are not necessarily for the baby itself, and then examine what Ketchum finds wrong with paying a woman for the use of her body. In the section titled "Selling Bodies," Ketchum writes:

> The disrespect for women as persons that is fundamental to the [surrogacy] relationship lies in the concept of the woman's body implicit in the contract. I have argued elsewhere, in the context of abortion laws, that claiming a welfare right to another person's body is to treat that person as an object.... [T]reating another person's body as a part of my domain—as among the things that I have a rightful claim to—is, if anything is, a denial that there is a person there.... We can extend this argument to the sale of persons. To make a person or a person's body an object of commerce is to treat the person as part of another person's domain, particularly if the sale of A to B gives B rights to A or to A's body.... (Ketchum 1989, 121–22)

Ketchum seems to be assuming that if I pay you to bear a child for me, then I acquire a right to your body, treat you as an object of my domain, and (or) deny that you are a person. But this assumption is flawed. It fails to take into account the difference between (a) my paying you for *me* to use your body in a way that benefits me, and (b) my paying you for *you* to use your body in a way that benefits me. The difference between these two is important because it determines whether my payments to you give me a right to your body, and thus whether they treat your body as an object of commerce and you as less than a person. To illustrate it, suppose that you own a lawnmower. (I do not mean to suggest that women's bodies are on a par with machines.) If I need to have my lawn mowed then I may (a) pay you for *me* to use your lawnmower to mow my lawn, in which case I *rent* your lawnmower from you, or (b) pay you for *you* to use your lawnmower to mow my lawn, in which case I pay you for your *services*. In the former case I acquire a right to your lawnmower—the right to use it for a limited period of time. In the latter case I do not. Any right I have here is at most a right to insist that you do with your lawnmower what you said you would. But that is not a right to your lawnmower.

When we apply this distinction to the issue of surrogate motherhood we see that there is no need to view the payments to the woman as payments for the use (i.e., rental) of her body—the customer does not acquire a space over which he (or she)[3] then has control. He may not paint it blue, keep a coin in it, or do whatever else he wishes provided that he does not cause permanent damage. Instead, the woman is being paid for *her* to use her body in a way that benefits him—she is being compensated for her services.[4] But this does not treat her body as an object of commerce, or her as less than a person, any more than does my paying a surgeon to perform an operation, a cabby to drive a car, or a model to pose for a statue. My payments to the surgeon do not give me a right to her arm, make her an object of my domain, nor deny that she is a person. Indeed, recognizing that persons can enter into agreements to use their own bodies in ways that benefit others *reaffirms* their status as persons—as agents—rather than denies it. Given this, we cannot prohibit paid surrogacy arrangements on the grounds that they involve the buying and selling or renting of babies and women's bodies.

II

Though Ketchum does not address the compensation-view of the payments, some of her arguments against paid surrogacy arrangements may seem to stand even given that view. In the section titled "Selling Babies" she writes:

> Perhaps the strongest argument against baby selling is an objection to the characterization of the mother-child relationship that it presupposes. Not only does the baby become an object of commerce, but the custodial relationship of the parent becomes a property relationship. If we see parental custodial rights as correlates of parental responsibility or as a right to maintain a relationship, it will be less tempting to think of them as something one can sell. We have good reasons for allowing birth-mothers to relinquish their children because otherwise we would be forcing children into the care of people who either do not want them or feel themselves unable to care for them. However, that custody is waivable in this way does not entail that it is saleable or even transferrable. If children are not property they cannot be gifts either. (Ketchum 1989, 119–20)

As this passage suggests, one may object to paid surrogacy arrangements on the grounds that (a) since they require that custody of the child be *transferred* (by sale or gift) from one person to another, then (b) they require that we view the parent-child relationship as a property relationship. And that is morally objectionable.

Let us grant that the parent-child relationship is not a property relationship, as well as adopt Ketchum's suggestion that parental custodial rights be viewed as rights to maintain a relationship. The problem with the above argument is that there is nothing in the nature of surrogate motherhood arrangements that requires that custody be transferred rather than waived. In order for one parent to gain sole custody of a child, he or she need not acquire the other parent's parental custodial rights, such that he or she would then have two parental custodial rights—two rights to maintain a relationship—when before he or she had only one. Instead, one parent may obtain sole custody of a child merely by the other parent's *waiving* his or her custodial right. The one would then have sole custody because he or she is then the only one *with* custody. But his or her right to maintain a relationship has not, somehow, doubled in size. (This is supported by the fact that a judge is not required to find a parent with sole custody *twice* as unfit as a parent who shares custody, before she would be justified in removing a child from that parent's care. Indeed, we may think it should be just the reverse.)

Another way to object to paid surrogacy arrangements, given the compensation-view of the payments, is to argue that there is an important moral difference between compensating a woman for the efforts and risks of bearing a child, and compensating a woman for the efforts and risks of, say, mowing a lawn, posing for a drawing, or performing an operation. But making this argument requires that we can explain what that difference is, and the differences suggested by Ketchum seem to me to be inadequate. She writes:

> We might distinguish between selling reproductive capacities and selling work on a number of grounds. A conservative might argue against commercializing reproduction on the grounds that it disturbs family relationships, or on the grounds that there are some categories of human activities that should not be for sale. A Kantian might argue that there are some activities that are close to our personhood and that a commercial traffic in these activities constitutes treating the person as less than an end (or as less than a person). (Ketchum 1989, 20)

Ketchum's first suggestion, that paid surrogacy arrangements disturb family relationships (while typical forms of work do not?), won't draw an appropriate line because many forms of work run that risk. Laura Purdy (1989) points out that women risk their lives and health by building bridges, working on farms, and even for the postal service. Yet few of us would regard the disruption of the family that would be occasioned by the woman's death or serious illness as legitimate grounds for prohibiting women (or mothers) from these jobs. Further, divorce, remarrriage, and adoption all risk disruption of the family, yet we would not want to deny a woman these options simply because she is a mother.

The second suggestion, that "some categories of human activities should not be for sale," is also inadequate. In order to make use of it, we would have to know what these categories are or at least how to distinguish them from others. But Ketchum does not tell us. Her comment that "some activities are close to our personhood . . . " is likewise of little help. (It is not clear whether this is offered as a third suggestion or as a way to clarify the second.) If, on the one hand, it refers to those activities that distinguish persons from other beings, then reproduction is certainly not one of them. On the other hand, if it refers to those activities that we identify with—

those by which we conceive of ourselves—then it is a mistake to think that all women (or all women in their childbearing years) conceive of themselves as essentially childbearers. What we do with some parts of our lives need not define who we are; a woman who is paid to bear a child for another need not conceive of herself as essentially a childbearer any more than a woman who is paid to teach a college course need conceive of herself as essentially a teacher.

Perhaps there are ways to mark an important moral difference between compensating a woman for the efforts and risks of bearing a child, and compensating her the efforts and risks of typical (and unobjectionable) ways that she uses her body to benefit others. But Ketchum has not told us what they are. And without that information we cannot use the difference in a case against surrogate motherhood.

The last objection I will address focuses on coercion and exploitation. Ketchum writes:

> All commercial transactions are at least potentially coercive in that the parties to them are likely to come from unequal bargaining positions and in that, whatever we have a market in, there will be some people who will be in a position such that they have to sell that in order to survive. Such concerns are important to arguments . . . against baby selling and surrogate contracts. (Ketchum 1989, 20)

It is true that offers to enter into paid surrogacy arrangements are *potentially* coercive. It is also true that by permitting these offers we increase the risk that poor women will be exploited. The question, however, is whether these risks provide adequate grounds for prohibiting paid surrogacy arrangements. The following four points should help to show that they do not.[5]

First, as John Robertson (1983, 28) discusses, offers to be paid to bear a child for another are not "unjustly" coercive. They do not leave the recipient worse off than before the offer was made. (For contrast, consider the gunman's "Your money or your life" offer which does leave the recipient worse off.) Second, there is evidence that the opportunity to be paid for one's services in bearing a child has not been widely exploitive of poor women. Statistics indicate that the "average surrogate mother is white, attended two years of college, married young, and has all the children she and her husband want."[6] These are not the characteristics of the group we envision when we express concerns about protecting the poor from exploitation.

Third, though it is possible that the opportunity to be paid for one's services in bearing a child *will become* widely exploitive of poor women (as the arrangements increase in popularity), the same may be true of any opportunity to be paid for one's services. Yet we would not serve the interests of poor women in general if, in the efforts to protect them from exploitation, we prohibited them the means of escaping poverty. (Ketchum recognizes this point and cites Radin [1988, 1915] in its defense.)

Finally, the concern about exploitation and coercion seems to presuppose that the act of bearing a child for another is so detestable, so degrading, that few women would enter into the arrangements were they not forced to do so out of economic necessity. But the statistics mentioned above suggest that this is not the case. Further, some women enjoy being pregnant and may view their act as altruistic.[7] They are doing for another what that other cannot do for him or herself, and thereby allowing that other to know the joys (and pains) of raising an offspring. And if our aim is to protect those women who *do* view bearing a child for another as degrading, but nonetheless feel forced to do so out of economic necessity, then we can protect those women by putting restrictions on who can *enter into* paid surrogacy arrangements—we do not need to prohibit the arrangements entirely. One may object that such restrictions would be *unfair* because they would prohibit poor women from doing something that other women were allowed to do. But that seems to presuppose that the restrictions would be denying poor women a good, rather than protecting them from a harm, which, if true, would suggest that our initial concerns about coecion and exploitation were misguided.

Notes

1. Though I will continue to use the lay term "surrogate motherhood," it is a misleading name for the practice it identifies. In typical cases (i.e., those not involving embryo transfer) the woman bearing the child is both the genetic mother of the child and the birth mother. The only "mother" role she does not (intend to) fulfill is the social one. Were this enough to render her a surrogate mother then we should have to refer to women who relinquish their children for adoption, and to men who donate sperm to sperm banks, as "surrogate mothers" and "surrogate fathers." The term seems to be rooted in the oppressive notion that a women's proper role in life is to be a childbearer for a mate. Were that the case, then the woman being paid to bear a child could be viewed as a surrogate for another woman.

2. Some of the arguments I discuss are also discussed (and some in more detail) in my "Paid Surrogacy: Arguments and Responses" (1989). Also, it is worth noting that my arguments defend only the permissibility of the arrangements. Their legal enforcement is a separate issue.

3. Though I use the masculine pronoun when referring to a customer of surrogate motherhood arrangements, the customer need not be male. A woman with ova but no uterus may wish to have one of her ova fertilized, in vitro, with sperm from a sperm bank and then pay another woman to carry the conceptus to term. The possibility that a woman may be a customer of surrogate mother arrangements counsels against our objecting to these arrangements on the grounds that they treat women as "fungible baby-makers for men whose seed must be carried

on" (Radin 1988, 1935). (Radin makes this objection within the context of our current gender ideologies.)

4. Laura Purdy (1989) raises the possibility that "lurking behind objections to surrogacy is some feeling that it is wrong to earn money by letting your body work, without active effort on your part. But this would rule out sperm selling as well as using women's beauty to sell products and services." Notice that on the compensation-view of the payments the woman is not being paid for something her body does. She is being compensated for the efforts she must make, and the risks she incurs, in the nine-month process of bearing a child.

5. Purdy (1989) offers some different, and in many ways more detailed, responses to the argument from exploitation.

6. The statistics are from "Surrogate Motherhood: A Practice That's Still Undergoing Birth Pangs," *Los Angeles Times*, March 22, 1987. Radin (1988) cites them as well.

7. Radin rejects this point on the grounds that "even if surrogate mothering is subjectively experienced as altruism, the surrogate's self-conception as nurturer, caretaker, and service-giver might be viewed as a kind of gender-role oppression" (Radin 1988, 1930). I respond to this claim in "Paid Surrogacy: Arguments and Responses."

References

Ketchum, Sara. 1984. "The Moral Status of the Bodies of Persons." *Social Theory and Practice* 10:25–38.

———. 1989. "Selling Babies and Selling Bodies: Surrogate Motherhood and the Problem of Commodification." *Hypatia* 4 (3): 116–27.

Malm, H. M. forthcoming. "Paid Surrogacy: Arguments and Responses." *Public Affairs Quarterly* 3 (2): 57–66.

Purdy, Laura. 1989. "Surrogate Mothering: Exploitation or Empowerment?" *Bioethics* 3 (1): 18–34.

Radin, Margaret. 1988. "Market Inalienability." *Harvard Law Review* 100 (8): 1849–1937.

Robertson, John. 1983. "Surrogate Mothers: Not So Novel after All." *Hastings Center Report* 13:28–34.

INDEX